A FAMILY BIOGRAPHY

1662 to 1908

DRAWN CHIEFLY FROM OLD LETTERS

BY

ISABELLA & CATHERINE SCOTT

Printed for Private Circulation.

(75 Copies)

"*'Tis opportune to look back upon the past and contemplate our forefathers.*"—SIR THOMAS BROWNE.

"*We generally have a great love for our grandfathers.*"
—BURKE.

London
JAMES NISBET & CO., LIMITED
22 BERNERS STREET, W.
1908

This scarce antiquarian book is included in our special *Legacy Reprint Series*. In the interest of creating a more extensive selection of rare historical book reprints, we have chosen to reproduce this title even though it may possibly have occasional imperfections such as missing and blurred pages, missing text, poor pictures, markings, dark backgrounds and other reproduction issues beyond our control. Because this work is culturally important, we have made it available as a part of our commitment to protecting, preserving and promoting the world's literature.

CONTENTS

CHAPTER I

Introduction

CHAPTER II

1681–1746

CHAPTER III

1688–1778

CHAPTER IV

1721–1787

CHAPTER V

1751–1793

CHAPTER VI

1782–1808

CHAPTER VII

1803–1812

CHAPTER VIII

1812–1817

CHAPTER IX

1817–1820

CHAPTER X

1820–1824

CHAPTER XI

1824-1829

CHAPTER XII

1829-1831

CHAPTER XIII

1831-1832

CHAPTER XIV

1832-1835

CHAPTER XV

1836-1841

CHAPTER XVI

1842-1845

CHAPTER XVII

1846-1853

CHAPTER XVIII

1851-1875

CHAPTER XIX

1853-1854

CHAPTER XX

1855-1863

CHAPTER XXI

1863-1875

CHAPTER XXII

1875–1894

CHAPTER XXIII

CHAPTER XXIV

APPENDIX

I

II

III

IV

V

VI

VII

ILLUSTRATIONS

Reproduced from the original paintings and photographs by Frederick Hollyer

A FAMILY BIOGRAPHY

CHAPTER I

INTRODUCTION

In the following pages my sister Catherine and I give for the benefit of our nephews and nieces, and of their children, such particulars as we have been able to collect relative to the history of our family. It appeared to us that there were many facts known to us, and others that might be learned from my father and mother, and from other sources, which if not soon gathered together and written down, would be lost to the coming generation. This would certainly have been regretted.

It was not till a year or two before my father's death that I began to make any systematic inquiry on the subject. He was then the only one surviving of his generation, and except as to his father's life, his own, and those of the relatives he had known, he could tell me extremely little. It has been surprising, therefore, to find how much of the history of the family it has been possible to recover. The following have been the chief sources of information:—

1. *Letters.*—My father was in possession of a large number from various members of the family beginning with the year [illegible]. These [illegible]

belonged to Mr. J. E. Taylor and his first wife, my father's sister, and which Mr. Taylor, shortly before his death, gave to my father.

There were also letters preserved by Mrs. Robert Scott of Bath, which I was able to see at the death of her daughter, Mrs. Elliott. These were afterwards in the hands of my cousin, John Edward Taylor, the second of that name, and at his death they were destroyed.

2. *Notes* made by my mother of information given her bv Mrs. Robert Scott of Bath, my father's first cousin. These notes gave the names of members of the family from John Scott of Salisbury to Mrs. R. Scott's own generation, and a few particulars of some of them. As she was connected with the family by birth as well as by marriage, she was very familiar with its history, and no doubt much more could have been learnt from her if she had been further questioned. Names being furnished in this way, it was not difficult to ascertain the dates of birth and death of each individual.

3. *Two lists* giving the date of the birth or death of many members of the family. One of these is in the handwriting of my father's cousin, Anna Selina Scott of Sherborne, and the other in that of her eldest sister, Mrs. Petty. The years mentioned lie between 1754 and 1871.

4. *Parish registers* at Ilton and Milborne Port in Somersetshire, and (for the Sprint family) at Thornbury in Gloucestershire, and Newbury in Berkshire. Also the register at Dr. Williams' Library, London.

5. *Tombstones* in the churchyards at Milborne Port and Curry Mallet.

6. *Deeds* which relate chiefly to property that has long since passed out of the family; also some wills and marriage settlements.

7. *Inscriptions* in two Bibles.

8. *Mourning rings* (in memory of seventeen different persons), most of them given to my mother by our cousin, Anna Selina Scott. These all have the date of death inscribed.

9. *A printed memoir* of J. E. Taylor, sen.

10. *A Family Pedigree of Prestwich of Hulme* in the *History of the County Palatine and Duchy of Lancaster;* by Edward Baines; edited by James Croston, F.S.A.—1888. This relates to my mother's family.

I may mention here that the register at Milborne Port Parish Church contains no entry of the baptism of any member of the family, except the following: "John, son of Mr. Robert Scott, was baptized at a separate congregation, Jan. 11, 1721." The reason of this is that this Robert Scott and his descendants were Nonconformists, and their children were not baptized in the Parish Churches. Marriages and burials are recorded—marriages in a Dissenting Chapel, or other place not belonging to the Church of England, being illegal previous to the year 1836.

As soon as I began to collect information I felt it necessary to go into Somersetshire, to make a search in the parish registers there, and in May 1879 I arranged with my cousin, Mrs. Elliott of Bath, that we should go together. She was pleased to come with me, though she felt little or no interest in the family history. It was enough, she used to say, if one knew the history of one's father, and she was greatly amused at our travelling about on such an errand. We went first to Ilminster, near which are Ilford, Ilton, and Ashford, where John Scott (the first Scott of whom we know anything) and some of his descendants lived. (See map.) Ilford is in the parish of Ilton, and in the parish registers at Ilton we found a number of entries, which are the earliest I have discovered, of baptisms, marriages, and deaths, in the Scott family. Sherborne and Milborne Port were also visited.

On the north side of the Milborne Port Church is the family tomb of the Scotts of that town and of Sherborne. It is of the kind known as a "table tomb," and is in good condition. It was my father's wish that we should keep it in repair. The inscriptions on its four sides give the dates of birth and death of Robert and Hannah Scott; of their son, John Scott, and Mary, his wife; and lastly, of Samuel and Grace Scott, and their children. A window in this church has been put up by Mrs. Elliott in memory of these four generations of the family. It is by Clayton & Bell, and represents physical and spiritual blindness. Mrs. Elliott told me that she chose this subject in allusion to the blindness of her aunt, Grace Downing Scott, to whom she was much attached.

On our return to Bath, Mrs. Elliott gave me a good many old deeds which had been preserved in the family, and which I have found useful in fixing names and dates.

In 1892 I went again to Milborne Port and the neighbourhood. This was soon after Mrs. Elliott's death, and when my brother Russell had inherited from her the cottages called "Russell Place." He wished to see this property and his tenants, and asked me to come with him. We took with us his youngest daughter, Grace, then thirteen years old. On this occasion we went into the house at Milborne Port formerly belonging to Robert Scott, my great-great-grandfather, and were kindly shown over the lower rooms and garden. Later, when my brother had returned to town, Grace and I went to Ilminster, and drove round Ilford, Ilton, Curry Mallet, and Ashford, all within a very few miles of Ilminster. What I have to say about these places appears further on. I examined the register at Curry Mallet, but found no entries referring to the family. The clergyman there, however, told me that there was a tomb with Scott names upon it in the churchyard. I found it—also a table-tomb—and very similar to that at Milborne Port, with inscriptions on panels round.

Many little facts concerning the family were gleaned on these visits to Somersetshire.

The letters of my grandfather and grandmother Scott are almost all in shorthand, as well as a few written by other people. My grandfather habitually wrote to his near relatives in an early and simple form of shorthand. Happily the learning to decipher it was not difficult, as amongst his papers I found a key to the characters. In the case of the earlier letters no envelopes were used, as double postage was charged if a letter consisted of more than a single sheet. The address and the postmark, giving the date, therefore remain on them. Punctuation has been frequently supplied, and occasionally a writer's spelling has been corrected. In the headings of the letters, "Russell Scott" standing alone always means my father. My grandfather is distinguished by the addition of "Rev."

Large extracts have been made in the following pages from the letters which have come down to us. By means of them we have endeavoured as far as possible to let each individual tell his or her story, with only such interruption from the compilers as was necessary in order to supply details not given in the letters.

Read separately, few of these letters are of any special interest. Many of them were written by persons of no superiority of mind or literary skill, and only every-day events and feelings are recorded. Yet taken together they give much insight into the lives and characters of the writers. This it is that must give interest to our book, if it is to have any.

The work of reading and choosing the letters was done chiefly at Broomfield, South Reddish, near Stockport, during the last years of my mother's life, when she had a reader who could give help by copying whatever was wanted. As will be seen by the title-page, this book has been compiled jointly by my sister Catherine and myself. My share in it has consisted chiefly in collecting the materials, hers in filling in what was required to complete the story—by much the most difficult and troublesome part of what had to be done. It will be noticed that we have written throughout in the first person singular. This arose from my having begun the work; and the use of the first person was continued as a matter of convenience. It must not be supposed, however, that my sister's share in the book has been less than my own.

ISABELLA SCOTT.

BOGNOR, *January* 1908.

CHAPTER II

THE DESCENT OF THE FAMILY FROM JOHN SCOTT OF SALISBURY—THE ELDER BRANCH

1681–1746

It was a matter of common knowledge in the family, as reported by my father and by his cousin, Mrs. Robert Scott of Bath, that the earliest ancestor of the name of Scott of whom anything was known, was John Scott; that he came from Salisbury and settled at Ilford, a hamlet in the parish of Ilton, near Ilminster. He was always spoken of in the family as "John Scott of Salisbury."

No attempt has been made by me to find any trace of him in the parish registers at Salisbury, as there is no clue to the Christian names of his parents. In the register at Ilton his name first appears, with that of his wife, Mary, in the entry of the baptism of their eldest child, Mary, born in 1681. The baptisms of all their other children follow in due course. Later on, in 1715, there is the entry of the burial of his wife, but his own death must have taken place away from home, as there is no mention of it. He was a yeoman, as appears from the indenture of apprenticeship of his son Robert—that is to say, he farmed his own freehold. The district in which he lived was a purely agricultural one. An old rate-book of the parish of Ilton, in the possession of Mr. John Baker, Solicitor, of Ilminster, was shown to me by Mr. Baker in 1879, from which it appears that John Scott was Overseer of the Poor in 1700, a circumstance which Mr. Baker held to be proof that he was a man of substance. In the year 1686 his signature is amongst those which vouch for the correctness of the rate, and for several succeeding years he signed the book in this way before he was himself rated. Afterwards he was rated for a place called "Bakers." His death took place not long before 1719, as we find from a deed in my possession. This deed is the marriage settlement of his daughter Jane. It is dated 1719, and mentions her father as "lately deceased." The amount of her marriage portion was £200. A meadow of ten acres called "Lilsden," in the parish of Isle Abbotts, Somerset, and one of four acres called "Fishpools," in the parish of Ilton, were settled on her by her husband. When I visited Ilford in the summer of 1892, with my niece, Grace Mary Scott, I was unable to discover either "Bakers" or "Fishpools."

The houses in Ilford are quite old, and are substantially built of stone with thatched roofs. No tradition remains as to which house John Scott occupied. The two that we entered had stone floors, uncarpeted, whitewashed walls, and large heavy oak tables and wooden chairs. They were extremely bare, neat, and clean. The rooms were large and low, and the fire-places the old-fashioned ones without grates, meant for burning fuel on the hearth. Altogether there was such an old-world look about the place that one could almost fancy it had been preserved for us exactly as it was in John Scott's time.

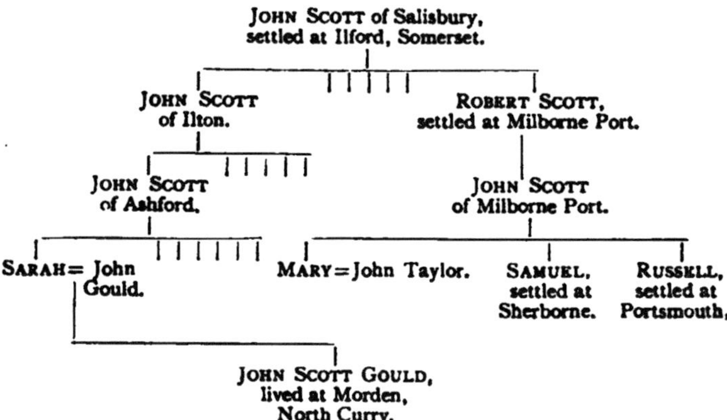

The above sketch will help to make clear what follows. A more complete genealogy will be found in the Appendix.

Of the children of John Scott of Salisbury only the eldest son John, and the second son Robert, left descendants. The remainder of this chapter must be given to the history of the "Elder Branch," the descendants of John. Not much is now known concerning them, and as that branch of the family has been extinct for over sixty years, our relationship to them has become very remote. I fear, therefore, that the few facts I have to mention can have but little interest for any one.

John, the eldest son of John Scott of Salisbury, has been called "of Ilton" to distinguish him from his father. He, like his father, was a yeoman. Beyond that fact, and that he married and had six children, nothing is known of his life. He died in 1748, and was buried at Ilton. He and all his descendants were members of the Church of England.

The wife of this second John Scott and some of his daughters lived after his death at Curry Mallet. Their tomb is in the churchyard there, and has the following inscriptions on it:—

> "Erected in memory of Thomas Tommas who died Feb. ye 4th 1723 aged 80 years.
>
> "Also Mary Scott wife of John Scott of Ilton and daughter of the above-named Thomas Tommas died Feb. ye 19th 1783 aged 88 years.
>
> "In memory of Phœbe Scott daughter of John and Mary Scott who died May ye 16th 1804 aged 76.
>
> "In memory of Edward Barrington who died Jan. ye 13th 1798 aged 52 years. Also Hannah Barrington widow and relict of Edward Barrington and daughter of John and Mary Scott died July ye 4th 1807 aged 72 years."

From the fact that the monument, which is a "table tomb," is a handsome one, and that there are rings with inscriptions in memory of some of the family, it may be presumed that they were in easy circumstances. I have had the tomb repaired and the lettering repainted. We were told by Mrs. Robert Scott of Bath that Miss Phœbe Scott knew all the history of the family. What a pity it did not occur to her to write a Family Biography!

The third John Scott was "of Ashford," the house in which he lived. He was the eldest son of the second John, and the only one of that family who left children. Like his father and grandfather, he farmed his own land. Ashford is near Ilminster. I visited it in 1879. It is a good, substantial farmhouse, with thatched roof and lattice windows, as the photograph shows, and has certainly not been altered externally since it was built. The farmer, Charles Goodland, who occupied it, knew the name of the Scott family quite well; his grandparents had been servants in the house. I saw his mother, but she could tell me very little. The Scotts, she said, were "nice people but plain"; more than once she repeated "plain people but wealthy." She had often heard of them from her father and mother, and of Miss Avice riding on a pillion. The photograph shows the horse-block in front of the house from which Avice must have mounted. An old labourer whom I saw at the same time said that his father had worked for Mr. Scott of Ashford. His father used to speak of seeing old Mr. Scott sitting in the chimney corner, cutting thatching-pegs ("spars" the old man called them) and sipping gin. His reputation in the family was that of a stern, repressive man. He is said to have been very careful and saving, and to have left at his death £40,000. The yeomen of those days were no doubt far more prosperous than their successors, the tenant farmers of the present time. I possess two small brooches containing the white hair of this John Scott and his wife.

Five of their children lived to grow up. Of their daughters, Mary, Catherine, Sarah, and Avice (pronounced Av-iss), only Sarah married. There are a good many letters from Mary to Mrs. Robert Scott of Bath, one specimen of which will be given later. Catherine was drowned in 1777 in a pond in the garden at Morden, at the age of twenty. It was believed that she had thrown herself in, but why or how this happened I have not been able to discover. Avice was a great invalid, completely crippled with rheumatism. Robert Hooper Scott was the only son. He did not marry. Mrs. R. Scott of Bath reported that he was a studious, literary man, much interested in astronomy, concerning which he left many manuscripts. She said he was named after an uncle, Robert Hooper, and from him inherited considerable property, including Morden (at North Curry, Somerset), the house in which he lived. His sister Mary lived with him at Morden, and kept his house. He died in 1829 without leaving a will, and his property went to his two sisters, Mary and Sarah (Mrs. Gould), and to his nephew, John Scott Gould. This Mrs. Gould is the last of the children of John Scott of Ashford of whom anything remains to be said. Her husband, John Gould, was in the woollen trade; he died early from an accident, and left one son only, John Scott Gould. The widow with her son lived for many years with her father at Ashford, where the child was brought up. He was nervous and peculiar, and his grandfather is said to have treated him harshly. His mother, Mrs. Gould, was described to me as a very kindly, gentle old lady, very simple and quiet in her habits, and strongly disapproving of finery in dress and of much gadding about. When I visited Ashford in 1892 I was allowed to go over the house, and was shown the initials of John Scott Gould on a pump in the back-kitchen, and a hole in a shutter through which it is said that his mother watched on Sundays to see that her gooseberries were not stolen. After inheriting Morden House, Mrs. Gould, with her son and her sister Mary Scott, removed there. There is frequent mention of J. S. Gould in the letters, and I possess his miniature. He was a shy, retiring man, and is said to have been much respected. His wife was a Miss Barrett. It was reported in the family that his mother selected his wife for him, and chose Miss Barrett because she had shown herself to be thrifty by wearing a gown she had turned three times! He died in 1846, and his property went to his wife, who left it to her relations. Her nephew, Major Barrett, still lives at Morden House.

This concludes what I have to say of the elder branch of the family, the descendants of John Scott of Ilton, of whom John Scott Gould was the last.

CHAPTER III

ROBERT SCOTT OF MILBORNE PORT—THE SPRINT FAMILY

1688–1778

WE now take up the history of Robert, the second son of John Scott of Salisbury. About him I have a little more information than of his father. He was my great-great-grandfather. He was born at Ilford, in the parish of Ilton, Somerset, in 1688. At the age of fifteen he was bound apprentice to a Mr. Robert Everett, a linen-weaver of Milborne Wake, Somerset, as appears from the indenture of his apprenticeship, a copy of which is given in the Appendix. He spent the greater part of his life in Milborne Port, Somerset, where, according to Mrs. Robert Scott of Bath, who was his great-grand-daughter, he carried on the business of a linen-weaver. He had a small mill, making tick and dowlas, the staple of the district. Mrs. Robert Scott also said of him that he was a "jocular" man. From his grand-daughter's letter, given further on, it is clear that he was both grasping and violent in temper.

His house at Milborne Port is still standing, and a photograph of it is reproduced here. It has a pretty garden, and stands just below the Wesleyan Chapel, between the chapel and the stream. The stream flows through what was his garden, the two parts of which are connected by a very small old bridge. The part of

Milborne Port in which it stands was called "Kingsbury."

Curiously enough an old bill has survived which shows that this Robert Scott was, at any rate in his doctor's opinion, a man of comparative wealth.

Mr. Scott's Bill of Kingsbury

For Several Journeys
for Internal & External Medicines } £42 0 0
& curing Your Son's Face

The bill is not receipted; from which we may infer that he disputed it. I found it inside the cover of an old Bible.

His wife was Hannah, daughter of the Rev. John Sprint, and widow of John Francis. This Hannah was the grand-daughter of the Rev. Samuel Sprint, one of the two thousand ministers ejected from their livings by the Act of Uniformity in 1662.

Robert was the first Nonconformist of the family, having become so after his marriage, his wife being daughter and grand-daughter to Nonconformist ministers. Down to my own generation all his descendants have remained Dissenters. He had an only child, John, who died before him in 1774. He himself died in 1778, leaving the whole of his property without exception to his eldest grandson, Samuel. This consisted of his house, and of land in Milborne Port, most of which was sold later. One field, the last remains of the family property in Milborne Port, and situated about half a mile outside the town, was inherited by my cousin, Mrs. Elliott, from her aunts. She built upon it ten cottages in pairs, with good gardens, which she called "Russell Place," and bequeathed the property to my brother Russell, who still has it. She once said (and this should not be forgotten) that she hoped this property would always remain in the family.

Milborne Port is a large village, very quiet and old-fashioned. Probably as many as half the houses are two hundred years old or more. It is neat and well-paved, and looked very pretty, as I saw it in 1879, in the sunshine of a most beautiful May day. It is a very old borough, and before the passing of the Reform Bill, sent two members to Parliament. It is mentioned in Domesday Book as possessing "three mills." The "bourne" running through it is a mere rivulet, but is the principal source of the river Yeo. "Port" means gate or entrance. The Anglo-Saxon form "porte" was borrowed directly from the Latin "porta" (Skeat's Etym. Dict.).

Before relating anything of Robert Scott's descendants it will be well to give the remainder of this chapter to our Sprint ancestry. To the younger members of our family their name is probably hardly known, but for several generations much pride was felt in the fact of our descent from them, as being men who in critical times made great sacrifices to principle. They were amongst those who refused to comply with the requirements of the Act of Uniformity, an Act which came into force on St. Bartholomew's Day (August 24), 1662, by which two thousand Ministers, Lecturers, Masters and Fellows of Colleges, and Schoolmasters, were ejected from their posts and silenced. For a large number of these men this meant the loss of all means of support for themselves and their children, in addition to the loss of the work to which their lives were devoted.

The Act obliged all who would keep their livings or lectureships, to make a declaration in public before the 24th August in that year, of their unfeigned assent and consent to all and everything contained in the Book of Common Prayer, as at that time altered and amended. The great majority of the clergy could not even see the book before the date fixed, as it was published only a few days before August 24th. When it was obtained and examined it was found to be such that a fifth of the clergy, on one ground or another, were unable to assent to it as "*containing nothing contrary to the Word of God*"—nor could they submit to make some other declarations imposed on them by the Act, amongst which were declarations against "*endeavouring any change in Church or State,*" and "*that it is not lawful upon any pretence whatsoever to take arms against the King.*" This they declined for fear of contributing to the betraying the liberties of their country.[1]

Some further account of the chief reasons which made two thousand, out of the nine thousand ministers of the Church of England, refuse compliance, and of the sufferings which they incurred in consequence, will be found in the Appendix, together with a brief summary of the "Act of Uniformity," and extracts from Calamy, and from the historian, R. H. Green. These will make clear some of the causes of the rise of Nonconformity, a movement in which the Sprints and their descendants

[1] See Calamy's "Life of Baxter," chap. x.

shared. If my readers will look to what is said there, they will understand something of the theological position of these ancestors, and will appreciate the zeal and earnestness with which they held their opinions. The fact that they, and their descendants after them, were Nonconformists has had a most important influence on the history of the family; which has been led to hold Liberal opinions both in politics and religion, in all branches of it, down to the present time.

Our connection with the Sprints, through the marriage of Hannah Sprint (widow of John Francis) with Robert Scott, is shown in the table on next page.

For the following particulars as to the Sprints who lived in the sixteenth and seventeenth centuries we are indebted to the "Dictionary of National Biography," as well as for additional information as to the John Sprint who wrote "Cassander Anglicanus." Of him it relates that

"Having been ordained, he attached himself to the Puritan party, and took occasion, when preaching at the University Church, to inveigh strongly against the ceremonies and discipline of the English Church. On being called to account by John Howson, the Vice-Chancellor, he defied his authority and was sent to prison. This occasioned a great ferment among the Puritans, and the matter was referred to the Queen and Council. A commission was appointed, and Sprint compelled to read his submission in Convocation. In 1610 Sprint was appointed Vicar of Thornbury in Gloucestershire, where he continued for some time to hold views adverse to the Anglican ritual; but he was finally induced to conform by the persuasion of Samuel Burton, Archdeacon of Gloucestershire. He afterwards published a book called 'Cassander Anglicanus, Shewing the necessitie of Conformitie to the prescribed ceremonies of our Church in

JOHN SPRINT (A).
Apothecary in Gloucestershire.

JOHN SPRINT, D.D. (A).
Admitted to Corpus Christi College, Oxford . 1560.
Appointed Dean of Bristol . . . . . 1571.
" Treasurer of Salisbury Cathedral . 1584.
Died . . . . 1590.

JOHN SPRINT, M.A. (A).
Elected student of Christ Church College . 1592.
Became Vicar of Thornbury, Gloucestershire . 1610.
Published "Cassander Anglicanus" . . 1618.
Died . . . . 1623.

JOHN SPRINT, M.A.
Became Vicar of Hampstead, London . . . . . 1633 (C).
Ejected . . . . . . 1662 (C).
Died . . . . . . 1692 (A).

SAMUEL SPRINT.
Baptized . . . . Jan. 1622 (B).
Student of Trinity College, Camb. . . (C).
Ejected from South Tidworth. . . . 1662 (C).
Died . . . . about 1695 (C).

Children of Samuel Sprint:

HANNAH, bap. July 6, 1651 (N).

SAMUEL, bap. Oct. 18, 1652 (N).

MARTHA, bap. Sept. 24, 1654 (N).

JOHN SPRINT, Minister at Milborne Port, *d.* 1718 (D).

Children of John Sprint:

John Francis = HANNAH = Robert Scott.
John Francis: *m.* July 22, 1706 (F); bur. June 8, 1710 (F).
Hannah: *b.* Oct. 3, 1681 (K); *d.* June 27, 1767 (L).
See Table II.

JOHN, *d.* unmarried.

MARY FENWICK = Rev. Henry Rutter.
m. at Milborne Port, Mar. 6, 1715 (E). Still living in 1772 (D). No children.

Child of John Francis and Hannah:

MARY = Joseph Brett.

SAMUEL SPRINT BRETT (H).

Two daughters.

(A) "Dictionary of National Biography."
(B) Parish Register, Thornbury.
(C) Calamy's "Account of Ejected and Silenced Ministers."
(D) Josiah Thompson's "History of Dissenting Congregations."
(E) Marriage Sermon of Mary Sprint (Mrs. Rutter).
(F) Parish Register, Milborne Port.
(H) Letters.
(K) Old Bible of Hannah Sprint's.
(L) Scott Monument, Milborne Port.
(N) Parish Register, Newbury, Berks.

Case of Deprivation,' which had considerable effect on beneficed Clergy of Puritan tendencies. . . . In his defence of Conformity Sprint does not attempt to justify the Anglican position, but rather argues that the rites are non-essential, and that no minister of the Gospel is justified in abandoning his ministry because they are enjoined upon him."

A copy of this book is in Dr. Williams' Library at University Hall, Gordon Square, London.

John Sprint was the author of several other works, including a "Letter sent to a man grievously afflicted in conscience and fearfully troubled in mind." (For a list of them, see the "Dictionary of National Biography.") He died in 1623, and was buried in St. Anne's, Blackfriars, leaving two sons, half brothers, John and Samuel. Both took Holy Orders, and were among the ejected ministers of 1662.

Samuel Sprint, the younger brother, was born at Thornbury in Gloucestershire, where his father was Vicar. All we know of him beyond this is to be found in Calamy's "Account of the Ministers Ejected or Silenced by or before the Act of Uniformity," and in his "Life and Times." The following is extracted from these books, copies of which we possess. Our copy of Calamy's "Account" belonged to John Scott of Milborne Port (Hannah Sprint's son), and bears his name in his own handwriting. It is the Second Edition, 1713. See p. 340 for the following:—

"Mr. *Samuel Sprint*. His living, *South Tidworth*, was worth at least £120 per An. He was Son to the famous Author of '*Cassander Anglicanus*,' & much of his Judgment as to our Ecclesiastical Controversies. He was born at *Thornbury* in *Gloucestershire* about 1624; & bred in *Trinity-College* in

Cambridge, where he had for his Chamber-fellow Dr. *Isaac Barrow*. They study'd in Consort and went both together to Mr. *Abraham Wheelock*, to discourse with him about the *Arabick* Language, which they were desirous to learn: But upon hearing how great Difficulties they were to encounter, & how few Books were in that Language, and the little Advantage that could be got by it, they laid aside their Design. Upon Mr. *Sprint's* leaving the University, he was chosen Master of the Free School at *Newbury* in *Berks*, where he continu'd several Years till he was called to *Tidworth*. He was an intimate Friend of Mr. *Woodbridge's*, and of the same pacifick, healing, Catholick Spirit. A compleat Scholar, a very useful Preacher, and one of strict Piety. Of wonderful Modesty and Humility, and therefore contented to live in an obscure corner, tho' he had large Offers elsewhere. His Conversation was equally Pleasant and Profitable. His Preaching was very Instructive, but his Way of Delivery not so Popular as that of some others. His Carriage was such, as recommended him to the good Esteem of all the sober Gentry in those Parts. One of them (and he a Justice of Peace of Note) inviting him to his House, and desiring his Acquaintance, told him, That he thought him a Man of the most universally good Character of any in the County; for he never heard any one speak ill of him; But they who most freely loaded other Nonconformists with Reproaches, spoke very well of him. And yet he was not secure from the Ill-will of some of the neighbouring Clergy, who were so severe and violent in Prosecuting him, that he was to be Excommunicated, for not receiving the Sacrament in his Parish-Church at *Christmas*, notwithstanding, that his Wife lay upon her Death-bed at that very Time. To prevent it, he rode to *Farnham*, to Bishop *Morley*, and told him his Case: And his Lordship was pleased to tell him, That his Chancellor should not treat him so severely as he imagin'd & expected: And accordingly the Prosecution was stopp'd. The Bishop made him stay and dine with him, and discours'd with him about his Nonconformity. Mr. *Sprint* telling him, that the *declaring unfeigned Assent and Consent* was what he could not be satisfy'd to yield to, the Bishop told him, He must not Philosophize upon the Words '*Assent and Consent*'; nor suppose, that the Parliament did by *Assent* mean an Act of the Understanding, and by *Consent* an Act of the Will: For no more was intended, than that the Person so declaring, intended to read the Book: And therefore, if he would make the Declaration in the Words prescrib'd in the Act, and then say, that thereby he meant no more than that he would read the *Common-Prayer*, he would admit him into a Living. Mr. *Sprint* thank'd his Lordship, but could not think that Expedient warrantable. Afterwards Mr. *Sprint* mention'd the Cross in Baptism, as what he could not comply with. To which the Bishop reply'd, This was honest Mr. *Dod's* Scruple: But gave no other Answer than this: *That the Cross was only a visible Profession of our believing in a Crucify'd Saviour, in Conformity to the Practice of the Primitive Christians, who cross'd themselves: By this Action as by Words, owning their being Christians:* But it did not thence appear to Mr. *Sprint*, that it might lawfully or safely be a *Term of Communion.*[1] He was very Temperate and Abstemious: Which being once taken notice of, at a Gentleman's Table, one then present, who had liv'd in Bishop *Hinchman's* Family when he was Bishop of *London*, told him, That if he was a Conformist, he must expect no great Preferment: For he once heard Bishop *Hinchman* recommend a Person to Archbishop *Sheldon*, as one very fit for some Ecclesiastical Promotion; of whom the Archbishop said, I believe your Lordship is mistaken in the Man; I doubt he is too Puritanical: Whereto the Bishop reply'd, I assure your Grace he is not; for he will drink a Glass of Wine freely.

"He took great Notice, and frequently made mention, of the Care that Divine Providence took of him, and his numerous Family, he having Six Sons and Two Daughters, when he was cast out of his Living. And it was very remarkable, that when he put the Lives of Three of his Children into the little Estate that he took at *Clatford* near *Andover*, he was directed to pitch

[1] *i.e.* a condition for admission into the Church or of continuance in it.

upon those Two sons, who only out-lived him, of all his Eight Children, to be of the three that were put into the Lease. So that after he remov'd from *Tidworth*, which was about the Year 1665, he spent the remaining part of his Life, which was about Thirty Years, in that obscure Village; preaching as Opportunity offer'd, at *Andover*, (which was a mile from the Place of his abode) and also at Winchester. On his Death-bed he declar'd his full Satisfaction in the Cause of Nonconformity. He had but a very inconsiderable Allowance from his People, whom he preach'd amongst: But was us'd to say; If the Bottle and Satchel held but out to the Journey's End, it was sufficient. He was exercis'd with a very lingering Sickness, which carry'd him off, and thro' the whole of it he discover'd great Longings to be at rest.

"Having mention'd above, the Book call'd '*Cassander Anglicanus*,' of which this Mr. *Sprint's* Father was the Author, I think it not improper to communicate to the World a Paper concerning it, which was written by this son of his, with his own Hand; a Copy of which was sent me by the Grandson of the Author, with Assurance, that it was drawn up by his Father, this Mr. *Sprint* of *Tidworth*. The Paper was verbatim thus:

"1. This Book meddles not with *Subscription*, but disclaims it. P. 237.

"2. In all the arguments, it supposeth, that the Ceremonies impos'd are Inconveniences, and the Churches Burthens.

"3. By the Quotations p. 194, 196, and elsewhere, it adviseth us to bear witness against them, and to express our *Dissent* from them, and then Conform: Which is not to *Assent;* and much less to declare our *unfeigned Assent*, as well as *Consent* to them.

"4. Bishop *Laud* said, It had been no great Matter, if this Book and the Author had been burnt together.

"5. This Book is not fully comprehensive of the Author's Judgment: For besides what is extant of his in Print (viz. his *Bellum Ceremoniale* printed by another,) and what he hath left in Manuscript, this Book, as he hath acknowledg'd to his Acquaintance, hath suffer'd much by the Hands of the Bishop's Chaplain, that was appointed the Reviser of Books to be printed."

A glimpse of Samuel Sprint in his old age is afforded us by an interesting passage in Calamy's "Historical Account of my own Life" (see p. 303 of vol. i. of the edition published in 1829).

When about twenty years of age, in 1691, Edmund Calamy went to Andover for a few days and preached there one evening. He says :—

"I found there were two several parties among the Dissenters at Andover, and two several congregations, though they at that time had but one place of worship. One party were called Presbyterians, and old Mr. Sprint, (ejected in 1662 from South Tidworth,) was their pastor. He preached in that town every other Lord's day; and on the Lord's day when not employed there, he went to Winchester and preached. The other party were pretty warmly congregational and Dr. Isaac Chauncy had been their pastor, though he had for some time left them (for what reasons I cannot say) and they were destitute.

Calamy further relates that being asked, much to his surprise, to settle amongst these people as their minister, he replied that he was pursuing his studies closely and was not for engaging in any pastoral work as yet, and then said :—

"'I understand that there is an old gentleman in your neighbourhood, an eminent divine (whose books I am not worthy to carry after him) who preaches to you in this town every other Lord's day. Fix him wholly amongst you, and ease him of the trouble of going at his advanced age to Winchester once a fortnight; and as you will this way pay but a decent respect to one of his great worth, so I should think you would take a step that would much promote the interest of piety and charity.' The old woman" [she had been previously mentioned as a grave old woman in a high-crowned hat] "seemed perfectly astonished at my proposal, and cried out 'What, Mr. Sprint! old Mr. Sprint! Alas! he is a Baxterian! He is a middle way man! He is an occasional conformist! he is neither fish nor flesh nor good red herring!' Upon this I could not forbear smiling and said 'Mother, mother, he is a good man and great! He is moving apace towards Heaven himself and helping others thither too; and he is well fitted to it. You do not to me discover your wisdom in reflecting on a man of his worth and eminence. However, said I, (who was willing to be a little plain before parting, and to leave something with her in her own vulgar language that might stick and abide by her,) such carriage to him would never, while the world stands, induce me to listen to such a motion as yours. For the very same names as you give to him now, would you in a little time give to me, and, perhaps, yet worse; crying that you had got out of the frying pan into the fire.' With this our discourse broke off, and she only said farther, 'Nay, sir, if it be so, then I wish you a good night,' and she dropped me a courtesy and went off. The rest soon followed her and left me alone and gave me no farther disturbance. The next morning I waited on Mr. Sprint at Clatford, where he lived, and gave him an account of what had passed the night before. I found him a very venerable old gentleman, and very frank and pleasant in conversation. He was much diverted with my relation, and gave me an account what difficulties he had met with among that people, but without any heat or passion. I returned the same evening to Whitchurch."

On Mr. Sprint's reasons for his occasional conformity, to which the old woman objected, some light is thrown by the following passage from Calamy's "Life of Baxter," vol. i. p. 309:—

"After this (1664) the *Nonconformists* were not a little divided among themselves, as to the Lawfulness and Expediency of Worshipping God in the Public Churches, over and above their Private Meetings still kept up with great Secresie. Mr. *Baxter* and Dr. *Bates*, and several others with them, were for frequenting the Public Churches, when better Helps were not to be had; and for resorting to them now and then, tho' they had their Choice, to show their Charity. They were for having their most usual Communion with those Assemblies, which they tho't were manag'd most agreeably to the Rule and End of Worship; and yet for having Occasional Communion with others, as Members of the Catholic Church, to show their Catholic Communion with all the Body of Christ. But others were vehement for an entire Separation."

Samuel Sprint died about the year 1695, leaving a son, John, of whom an account may be seen in a manuscript book in Dr. Williams' Library, entitled "A Collection of Papers by Josiah Thompson, relating to the formation of early protestant dissenting Congregations." The Collection was begun in 1772, and in vol. iv., under the heading "Milborne Port," will be found the following:—

"About the year 1700, & some imagine it may be 2 or 3 years later, Mr. John Sprint settled here: and was the first Minister at Milburn Port. His Father was ejected from Tewxbury[1] in Gloucestersh^r & afterwards settled at Andover, Hants, & was Pastor to a dissenting Congregation there till his Death. Mr. Sprint Junr had lived several years in Sr Henry Ashurst's Family at Clapham as Tutor to his Sons. He married while in that Station & was greatly respected by the Family, but loseing his Health He was advised by his Friends to return into the Country; when He embraced his first Invitation to ye pastoral Care at Winburn Dorsetsh^r. From that Place He soon removed to Stalbridge in ye same County & where He had ye Care of a very respectable Body of People. But as He was a Gentleman of too liberal Principles for some pious tho rigid nonconformists of ye antimonian stamp, this Situation also, became very disagreeable to Him; & He left it, & came &

[1] This is a mistake. South Tidworth, Hants, was the place.

lived at Milburne Port, about ye above mentioned Period.—Such was the spirit of his Neighbourhood at Stalbridge, that the Justices removed Him & His Family by a Special Order to *Sturminster*. But a Gentleman of Fortune was so kind as to procure Him a legal Settlement, by giving Him a Lease of a Small Estate, and His Friends prevailed with Him to return, & to fill up the Duties of their Pastor a little longer at Stalbridge. . . .

"Immediately on Mr. Sprint's coming to Milbourn Port, He licensed a Room, belonging to his Dwelling House, and by ye assistance of his Friends it was soon fitted up in a decent Manner for a Place of Public Worship.—As it was gradually carried on, so it is said the Desk was raised & fixed before ye Pulpit could be finished & He allways made it his constant Practice at Milbourne Port to read & pray in ye Desk; and never ascended into the Pulpit except to preach. With Regard to Dress He was also particular, as He allways wore a Cassock & a Rose[1] in his Hat.

"Altho He had no Invitation to ye Place, nor any Prospect of Supporting Himself & Family by preaching: yet He soon met with great Incouragement, both from the Inhabitants & adjacent Villages. His Piety & learning & his happy manner of address soon procured for Him attention, & Respect from all Quarters. For sometime He only preached once a Day, to his Friends here, & the other half of ye day He preached at Temple Combe. This was his stated course for several years; till there was such an encrease of Numbers, at both Places, as ennabled each of them, to give a decent Support to a Minister, & then He confined His ministerial Labours wholly to Milbourn Port.—On his first coming to Milbourne Port He likewise opened a Grammar & Boarding School,[2] which was soon filled up, by

[1] No doubt a rosette.

[2] This must have been at Little Venn, a house still existing near Great Venn, the house of the Medlycott family, the principal landowners of the place. From Miss Anna Scott and Mrs. Robert Scott we learnt that John Sprint built Little Venn, and lived there. When seen in 1879 it had been altered and probably enlarged.

young Gentlemen of Rank & Fortune from Dorsets[r] as well as Somerset[r], and altho He had great Difficulties to struggle with, from y[e] Spirit of the Times & that Violence of Party which was so high in his Neighbourhood especially in y[e] close of Queen Ann's and the beginning of King Geor: Reigns yet from ye happy Manner in which He asserted and that easy tho' bold & consistent Manner in which He vindicated y[e] Principles of Liberty which he espoused, He met with y[e] most respectful Usage from all Ranks even when their Contests were y[e] warmest.—At last the Death of his good Friend Mr. Hoskins (a Gentleman of considerable Fortune at *Purse-Caundle* & the principal Support of the dissenting Interest here) it is said sat so heavy upon Him, as to overset Him and so bring on his Death soon after. He died in 1718 deeply & justly lamented, not only by His own People, but by a very numerous and extensive acquaintance. . . . His son was educated for the Ministry, & preached occasionally when his Health would admit of it, but never took the Charge of any People. . . . Mr. Sprint published several single Sermons, which He had preach'd on public Occasions: and they all bear strong marks of the Fervour of his Piety & the Warmth of his Benevolence and public Spirit. But a Wedding Sermon of his (as was y[e] Custom of those Days with some dissenting Ministers) made y[e] greatest Noise of any of his Publications. In this Discourse He is said to have assumed too much authority & Power on y[e] side of y[e] Husband: which was very warmly resented by y[e] other sex. Lady Chudleigh & Miss Singer (afterwards Mrs. Rowe) who were both his acquaintance, took up their Pens, & vindicated what they apprehended to be their greatly injured Rights, and that in so spirited & superior a manner as did great Honour to them. There is also a short anecdote which is kept fresh in the Memory of the People here by being so often repeated, as to that rough Usage it brought upon Him from some of his best Friends: viz. that being unexpectedly overtaken by a heavy Storm of Raine at a few Miles distant from Home, He very opportunely (as He imagined) recollected that He was but a little Way from a Friend's House where He would be sure to meet with a kind & hospitable Reception, as it had been their constant & usual Way of treating Him. But He was sadly mistaken & disappointed. For unluckily ye Master of ye House was abroad, and the Mistress so soon as she saw it was Mr. Sprint, assumed all at once a very cold & forbidding air: she only returned his Compliments to her with a Curtsey, & said *My Husband is not at Home sir* & then turned Her Back upon Him.[1] . . .

"After Mr. Sprint's Death this Society was greatly dispirited, as they could only procure occasional supplies. Mr. Sprint's generous spirit in not insisting on a fixed subscription from those who were well able to contribute towards the support of a Minister, was now Found to be a very sensible disadvantage to them. He was satisfied with what they gave Him in ye way of a Complement or Benevolence, and as He had a flourishing School his Circumstances were allways easy, and he Found no Difficulty in affording his children a liberal Education."

He left two daughters. The younger, Mary, married the Rev. Henry Rutter, minister at South Petherton, and lived to an old age. Of Hannah, the elder, I have already mentioned that she was married in the first place (at Milborne Port) to John Francis, and secondly to Robert Scott.

My sister and I possess two little relics of her which have been kept in the family, and were given to us by our cousin, Mrs. Elliott—a white muslin apron which she embroidered, and which has her initials, H. S., and the date 1698; and her Bible, in which is the inscription, "My grand-daughter hannah Sprintt was bourne in october 3rd 81." In another hand are the words "Hannah Sprint 1702"; and the following words in a handwriting that Mrs. Robert Scott said was her

[1] The story, as it came down in the family, was that Mr. Sprint had rebuked women in his sermons for receiving their husbands' friends in their husbands' absence, and that the tables were turned on him as related above.

father's, "Hannah Sprint was first married to — Francis and then to Rob[t]. Scott, by whom she had an only son, John Scott, Father to Mary Scott. Hannah Sprint gave this to her Grand-daughter Mary Scott from whom it descends to her daughter Mary Ann." Finally Mary Ann has written her name beneath—" Mary Ann Taylor."

A copy of the Wedding Sermon by John Sprint, mentioned in Thompson's "Collection of Papers," is in my possession, and is a most amusing production. Besides this sermon we have one preached by him on the accession of George I., full of hopefulness and joy in having a Protestant king. Extracts from both will be found in the Appendix.

CHAPTER IV

JOHN SCOTT OF MILBORNE PORT—THE RUSSELL FAMILY

1721–1787

Of John Scott, our great-grandfather, who lived at Milborne Port, no more is known than of his father Robert. Some particulars as to their property have been gathered from Wills and Marriage Settlements, and these may as well be given. He was born in 1721, and grew up an only child. Like his father, he was a linen-weaver—that is to say, he had a small linen-factory at Milborne Port, and probably they were in partnership. At the age of twenty-nine he married Mary, only child of John Russell of Bradford Abbas, near Sherborne, Dorset. She received £1200 as her marriage portion from her mother, Mary Russell, widow. John Scott's father, Robert Scott, gave on his side a house called "Toogood's Tenement," with land on the east of it called "Barley Close," and on the west of it called the "Paddock," in Kingsbury Regis, which is a part of Milborne Port.

In a memoir of his grandson, John Edward Taylor, which appeared in the *Christian Reformer* of March 1844, it is stated that this John Scott "displayed no ordinary zeal in the cause of Protestant Dissent and Civil and Religious Liberty." His own house was for a time licensed for public worship, pending the building of a new Meeting-house in Milborne Port. The licence has been preserved, and I now have it. He died at the age of fifty-three, in 1774, leaving three children, Mary, Samuel (so named after his great-great-grandfather, Samuel Sprint), and Russell.

One of the letters of his daughter Mary states that her father died without making a will, as he said the law would divide his property just as he would wish. His wife survived him thirteen years. She owned several fields and cottages in Bradford Abbas, and in a codicil to her will, dated May 22, 1780, she directed that if her daughter Mary should marry, £1600, part of her estate and effects, should be placed in trust for her. Her grand-daughter, Mrs. Robert Scott of Bath, said that she was a handsome, stern woman, and that she always used the Russell arms.[1] She continued to live at Milborne Port after her husband's death, and was an important member of the little congregation of "Protestant Dissenters" in that place.

[1] There was a tradition amongst the descendants of this Mrs. John Scott, no doubt received from her, that the Russells of Bradford Abbas were members of the family from which the Dukes of Bedford arose. Very probably it was so. In an essay of J. A. Froude's, "Cheneys and the House of Russell," to be found in his "Short Studies on Great Subjects," it is said that "the Russells, or Rozels, are on the Battle Roll as having come from Normandy with the Conqueror. They played their part under the Plantagenets, not without distinction, and towards the end of the fifteenth century were a substantial family settled at Barwick in Dorsetshire."

Froude then proceeds to relate the history of a certain John Russell, who, having been taken into favour by Henry VII., rose rapidly in the service of the court. He was employed by Henry VIII. and Wolsey in difficult and dangerous undertakings, and for fifty years took an active part in the eventful public life of his time. His services were splendidly rewarded. He was created Earl of Bedford, and Woburn Abbey was granted to him as well as Covent Garden and "the seven acres." "So commenced," says Froude, "the new birth of the Russell house."

The chapel still exists, and the people now call themselves Congregationalists.

When at Milborne Port in 1879 I was shown an old chapel-book in the possession of Mr. Parsons, a surgeon. It began with the "Covenant of the Church" (signed by its members), of which I give a copy in the Appendix. The rest of the book consisted chiefly of lists of subscriptions of the congregation. Mrs. Scott's was by much the largest. She paid £1, 6s. 3d. quarterly, I think. And at the end of the book was a copy of a codicil to her will, by which she bequeathed £60 in trust for the use of the minister of the chapel, on condition that her descendants should be left in undisturbed possession of the pew on the left hand side of the pulpit. The "Covenant" was dated April 22, 1744, and was signed by thirty-two church members.

Then followed the names of twenty-seven who were admitted later. The last three of these were—

Mrs. Scott,	admitted	member of the	Church	Sept. 3, 1769
Miss Scott,	"	"	"	Nov. 5, 1769
Mr. Russell Scott,	"	"	"	Sept. 5, 1779

The chapel has since been rebuilt. As it was Mrs. John Scott who brought the name "Russell" into the family, which has since been used as a Christian name through several generations, it is worth while to mention what little has been learnt of the Russell family from Mrs. Robert Scott of Bath, and from inquiries at Bradford Abbas.

John Russell, the son of John and Zipporah, was born in 1688, and lived at Bradford Abbas, a small village near Sherborne. He was in the linen-trade.

He lived in his own house, and had a little land. He was buried in Bradford churchyard, between the belfry and the south door, but his tomb is indistinguishable. He was churchwarden for many years, though a Nonconformist. A half brother of his, named Martin Russell, lived at Sherborne, and left property to Christ's Hospital, London, stipulating that presentations should be given preferably to lads from Sherborne bearing the name of "Russell." The town has the power of presenting, and there are always one or two such lads in the school.

From a deed in my possession, dated 1723, I find that Mary, wife of John Russell, was the daughter of Edward and Agnes Richmond of Bradford Abbas.

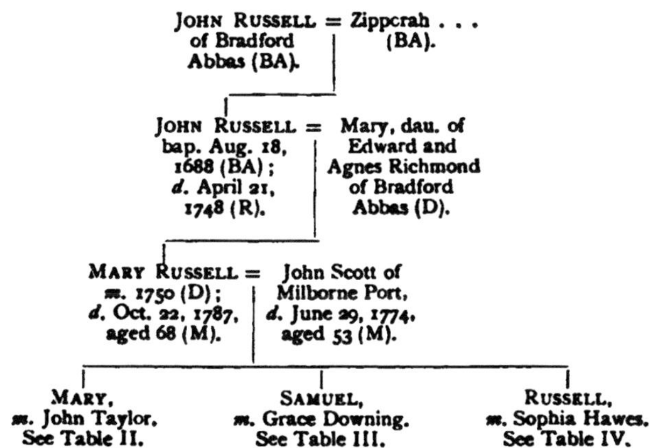

The statement that John Russell was a churchwarden is confirmed by the fact that when in 1879 I visited Bradford Abbas, I found inside the cover of one of the registers the following words: "This book was bought for the sum of nine shillings by John Russell in 1727."

(BA) Bradford Abbas register. (R) Mourning ring. (D) Deed.
(M) Scott Monument at Milborne Port.

CHAPTER V

MARY SCOTT OF MILBORNE PORT AND JOHN TAYLOR

1751–1793

THE children of John Scott of Milborne Port were Mary, Samuel, and Russell. With them the letters begin.

Mary was born in 1751. She had considerable ability and a literary turn of mind. Small books of verses by her remain, but none of these are worth giving here. Her printed works were "The Messiah" and the "Female Advocate," copies of which I possess. The latter is a defence in verse of some of the women writers of her time, most of whom are now wholly forgotten. In 1776 Mary took her brother Russell to Daventry (pronounced Daintry) to instal him as a pupil in the dissenting Academy there. She here met the Rev. John Taylor, who held the post of classical tutor, and soon afterwards they were engaged to be married. Her mother, Mrs. John Scott, was constantly suffering in health, and Mary refused to leave her; their marriage was therefore postponed for eleven years, until after Mrs. Scott's death.

The following letters are the earliest that have come down to us. They give us a little insight into the life of the family at Milborne Port after the father's death. Our first letter is from Mary's brother Russell to Mr.

Taylor, written from home at the age of sixteen, apparently after having been for one term at the Academy.

RUSSELL SCOTT *to* Rev. JOHN TAYLOR.

MILBORNE PORT, *July* 29, 1776.

REV^{D} DEAR & HON^{D} S^{R},—You desir'd me to write soon, I have done it; If I mistake not when I had the pleasure of seeing [you] last I desir'd you to write to me soon & you promis'd me you would, did you fulfill your promise, yes, but was it soon, no, what was your excuse then for omitting to write before; you say travelling from one place to another; A poor excuse indeed; what, not spare one hour to write to a friend, surely, you was not engag'd every hour in the Day successively for a Month; I have great reason to imagine an *Inclination* was wanting; had I promised to write to a friend & my Engagements had been so great, that I could not have spar'd the time whilst it was day, I would have depriv'd myself of sleep rather than disappoint a friend, especially you who are my dearest unrelated friend on Earth; Do not think my Dear S^{r} you have not been thought nor talk'd of by me, but let me tell you, there has not been a Day nor even an hour, but you have occur'd to my mind & was the topick of my Conversation when I had an Opportunity of mentioning your name. I cannot help giving you an account how many times I have been disappointed. Post after post I expected a Letter from my Dear Friend & could not imagine the reason of his silence & I had now given over all hopes of hearing from him. On Thursday as I was going by the post office, I stept in for the news paper, where to my great surprize, I found a Letter directed to me & another to my sister, upon examining the post mark I concluded they came both from you. On opening $\frac{t}{y}$ directed to me I found my Dear Mr. Taylor to be the Author; I conjectur'd $\frac{t}{y}$ directed to my sister came from him also, altho' there was Art used, as I suppos'd to deceive me. If you remember S[r] the Directions were wrote with a Different hand & it was seal'd with a Different seal. I suppose you thought I should not take any Notice of these things, but this is not all I know by, as my sister was opening the Letter I look'd over her shoulder to satisfy my curiosity & saw the date, but more of this hereafter. I know you my dear Mr. Taylor to be a Man of honor, deny this if you can. I fancy you are ready to say within yourself I cannot deny it, my conscience will not let me, there, I will tell him when I see him that he is not so easy to be deceiv'd as I thought he was, give me leave to add a Word or two more on this subject. I may say it is well for you, you wrote when you did or else you [would] have been condemn'd for violating your promise. I begun to think how well you had illustrated that doctrine of yours; perhaps you know not what I mean. I will tell you. I beleive S[r] there was a time when you said that Men were more steady in *friendship* than *Women. I deny it.* Not you nor 10,000 of my own sex shall persuade me to beleive it, for I know otherwise. I say *friendship* is most steady amongst the *fair Sex*, these are the real Sentiments of my heart; & it would give me joy to hear you had imbib'd them, but I hope your heart is not so much harden'd as to persist in your obstinate & stubborn way as too many of our sex do. But to whom am I speaking, to my friend & I hope my sincere friend, therefore I trust he will forgive my making so free with him, for I cannot help it.

I have not had the pleasure of seeing Mr. Toller, I am not certain whether he is in the country or not. But expect to hear tomorrow as there are a great number of Ministers expected to meet here; your old fellow student Mr. Fawcett has been ordain'd since I came home; his confession of Faith & his answers to the Questions propos'd to him, are very much approv'd of; there were two or three very orthodox Ministers present, they would not intermeddle with it. My Sister desires her Compliments to you & she is greatly indebted to you for your kind enquiry after her health; she has been very poorly these two or three days past. I hope to be at Daventry tuesday fortnight—but I suppose to your great sorrow, as well as to mine, my sister will not return with me. I return you thanks for your kind Admonition & also for desiring to know how I have improv'd my time since I have been at home. I must confess I have not look'd in any Latin Book, so as to reap any Benefit from it since I had the pleasure of seeing you last.

My sister has a friend that has lately open'd a Boarding-School, who desir'd her to draw up a Little plan on Education for her use, which she has done; her Health being in so indifferent a state that she could not write without great pain, she desir'd me to transcribe it for her, which I have accordingly done, & since that time I have been jaunting about amongst my friends. Adieu.—I am, my dear Friend, your sincere & affectionate Friend, RUSSELL SCOTT.

P.S.—Please to excuse bad writing for I am in very great haste & have not time to mend my pen.

The above letter was addressed: "Rev. John Taylor, Stand, n^r^ Manchester."

Mr. Taylor's father came from Yorkshire and settled as a farmer at Stand, near Manchester. Some of his descendants are still there. They are still farmers, and are the principal members of the little Unitarian congregation there. The five letters from Mary Scott to John Taylor which follow are addressed: "The Revd John Taylor, at the Academy, Daventry, Northamptonshire." Mr. Taylor was at this time twenty-four years of age. He had received his early education at the Grammar School of Stand. When he decided to enter the ministry he went to the Academy at Daventry to prepare himself for it, and was for a time classical tutor there before taking charge of a congregation.

MARY SCOTT *to* REV. JOHN TAYLOR.

Nov. 30, 1776.

SIR,—The reluctance with which I sit down to answer your letter is perhaps equal to the pleasure which according to your own account you felt in writing it. I must confess it has vex'd & mortify'd me exceedingly: little did I think from the very trifling encouragement I gave you, you would think yourself secure of me. I repeatedly assur'd you that I could not think of marrying without *horror*, & that if it were possible my aversion to the married state could be surmounted, it must be by very slow degrees, & when you importun'd me to tell you (the morn^g^ y^t^ I left Daventry) if I felt no particular attachment to you, I told you, & most truly did I tell you, that I felt no other sentiments for you than those of esteem; I added indeed that I did not feel that extreme aversion to you which I once did, & that I could not tell whether time would produce any further alteration in the nature of my regard for you, but that if it should not, I never could think of marrying you; this declaration was extorted from me, by your assuring me of y^r^ resolution to persevere, in opposition to every argument I could suggest to induce you to decline your pursuit. I wished you, as you was determined on persevering, to consider the affair as very dubious, that y^r^ disappointment, if I could not see things in a different light from w^t^ I then did, (& do still view them) might be less painful to y^o^, than it otherwise would be. As I did not entertain a thought in regard to you, which, if necessitated to have done so, I should have blush'd to have avow'd to the whole world, I treated y^o^ wth the utmost frankness. Little did I think how much that frankness would be misconstrued; but your Sex are so presuming & encroaching in those affairs, that no Woman can tell how to treat you who is not as artful & designing as yourselves.

Thus much just resentment has dictated, & now let us attend to reason. And Reason tells me that the connection you propose would not only be an imprudent, but even a sinful one, if it were to take place at present. I have communicated the affair to my Mother; I promised I would do you justice & that engagement has been most strictly discharg'd. I plac'd your virtues in the fairest point of View, nor blended with them one alloy of imperfection. She burst into Tears & in an agony of grief entreated me not to leave her without a friend, opprest with *disappointment, sorrow & pain.* Had she claim'd y[e] prerogative of dictating which Parents in general do on those occasions, my Heart would have revolted from an authority which I think no Parent has a right to exert over a Child arriv'd at Years of Discretion. But as she did not, Duty, Gratitude, affection conspir'd to oblige me to assure her I would not leave her. I never expected happyness but in the Discharge of Duty, & am persuaded I shall find higher felicity from attending her & endeavouring to soften those Afflictions which her other Children have envolv'd her in, than I could derive from the affection of the tenderest of Husbands; the consciousness of having violated the first of moral Duties would embitter every pleasure & render me the miserable victim of the most poignant self-reflection. You must remember, Sir, that I have frequently told you I never would marry except I thought my Mother's happiness would be promoted by seeing me settled in Life, & I hardly thought it possible it should, as her Ideas of Men and Marriage are if possible more tremendous than her Daughter's. I assur'd you I would give you up at once if she suggested the least objection, & if you attempt to persuade her to acquiesce in your wishes, I do most seriously assure you that you will not only degrade yourself in my esteem, but that my heart will revolt from you more strongly than it has ever yet done; for I am firmly persuaded that the Man who wishes me to act contrary to my Duty in *any* instance is both unworthy my regard in any degree & incapable of feeling a pure & disinterested affection for me. My Mother has no objection to your Character, but if she could reconcile herself to the prospect of parting with me, she would deem it presumption in me to marry, in that very precarious state of Health I have suffer'd for several years past; this it seems is no objection with you, but you must allow me to say, it ought to be a very strong one with me. Your Sympathy tho' it might afford a proof of y[r] Affection for me, could not avert, could not mitigate disease, or capacitate me to discharge the peculiar duties of my situation in Life. I need not tell you that every new relation brings with it new duties & new cares. I cannot discharge those that are already incumbent on me in such a manner as I wish to do, & to enter into a State that must necessarily enlarge those duties & those cares, whilst my incapacity to acquit myself according to my Ideas of propriety continues, would in my opinion be tempting providence. I must insist on your not attempting to stagger my resolution; inclination should submit to Duty, & you surely would be criminal in a very high degree, if after this representation which I have given you of my situation, you should endeavour to persuade me to take a step incompatible with gratitude & filial affection; for I have not a doubt but my Mother's Days would be shorten'd by my leaving her. She told me last night she did not think she could survive a separation. Your good sense, I doubt not, will lead you to discern the propriety of dropping all intercourse between us; it will convince you that my objections are insurmountable; but if your judgment should still be so much biass'd by inclination as not to perceive their force, consult Mr. Robins, who is an impartial person, & I am persuaded a sincere friend to both. You may if you please communicate my Letter to him, my confidence in his candor is such, that delicate as the subject is, I can have no objection to his seeing it; I have not a doubt but he will view things in the same light in which I do & that his Arguments will lead you to acquiesce in my determination.

I presume it is now unnecessary for me to desire you not to think of visiting Somersetshire at Christmas, & if you should chuse to have your Letters return'd, I will find some way or other of conveying them to you. . . .

I intended to have requested the favour of Mr. Belsham, not to mention the worst part of my poor Brother's conduct to Mr. Palmer, if when they have an interview he should enquire about him, for without doubt he will hear of his having quitted Dav^ty, & as he at present appears to be penetrated with a lively sense of his past guilt & folly, I would if possible keep that a secret. Will you do me the favour to make that request for me, but I am afraid his extravagance will be known in this part of the World by means of Mr. Toller. Dear unhappy youth, I can only think of him with fear & trembling; he desires his respects to Messrs. Jacomb, Bealy & French, & if they will be so kind as to fulfill their promise of writing to him, they may address their letters to him at the Rev^d Mr. Thomas's Grammar School at French Hay, near Bristol, ye will I flatter myself deliver this message for him. We left our friends in Hampshire on Thursday, and yesterday morn^g I parted from him; our sensations on both sides were too exquisite to admit of Description; he was much dejected the whole time we were at Broughton;[1] my Health would not suffer me to attend him to French Hay, as I intended, so I sent him from Salisbury in the Bath Coach, & suppose that he arriv'd at the place of his destination early this afternoon.

And now Sir I must bid you farewel, be assur'd that whilst you deserve it I shall always think, always speak of you with esteem, always be interested in your happyness, always rejoice to hear of your welfare. For altho neither Duty nor prudence will suffer me to form that intimate connection with you which you propos'd, yet I am y^r very Sincere friend, M. S.

This letter is endorsed in shorthand by John Taylor: "Very angry at my forwardness after her visit."

Mary had evidently been staying a second time at Daventry. She no doubt went there in order to remove

[1] Near Salisbury, the home of her friend, Miss M. Steele.

her brother. Nothing is known of Russell's misconduct beyond the allusions to it in these letters. He was only sixteen years old at the time, and was very differently spoken of a few years later by the Rev. T. Lindsey. How long he remained at Frenchay is not known. The wife of the Mr. Thomas, mentioned above, was a cousin, one of the Russells of Bradford Abbas.

MARY SCOTT *to* REV. JOHN TAYLOR.

March 10, 1777.

SIR,—W^n I wrote to y^o last, I wrote under ye influence of ye liveliest sympathy y^t ever Man feign'd, or Woman felt; but as ye emotions of the Mind must necessarily vary wth ye variation of those circumstances wch excited them, I acknowledge surprize and resentment are at present ye predominant passions of my Soul. Y^r Letter of ye 17th of Feby reached me this Day fortnight, & it really afforded me extreme pleasure to find ye was likely to be "restor'd to yourself & friends again." The ties of our common Xtianity oblige me to wish y^r welfare & usefulness. I wrote to y^o ye Day before y^o last wrote to me, so y^t our letters cross'd each other, but I must confess I thought ye Style in wch my Letter was written entituled it to an answer e'er now, especially as I condescended earnestly to request y^t ye w^d write to me very speedily. I did n^t think then y^t my conduct in y^t respect w^s an instance of condescension, but y^o h^v afforded my Mind a most painful conviction y^t a Woman does *greatly condescend* w^n she expresses any particular esteem for a Man. Had I not desir'd y^o to write soon, I sh^d h^v infer'd from ye circumstance of our Letters crossing each other y^t y^o expected to hear fr^m me e'er y^o wrote again, but surely y^t cannot be ye case as I w^s even importunate with y^o to write soon. A most *egregious blunder* I now see I committed in thus acting, but as it is ye first fault of ye kind I ever did commit, I hope it may be deem'd a *venial error*. The motives fr^m wch it flow'd were laudable, but in a World like this, I find (with ye utmost grief) it is possible to carry even some virtues to an excess. Perhaps you may suppose y^t as y^o h^d wrote to me before y^o Rec^d my last, y^t Letter w^d supersede ye Necessity of writing to me a second time; but is not such a supposition, if y^o h^v indulg'd it, utterly inconsistent wth y^t Affection y^o still profess to feel for me? I must say Sir y^t I cannot but suspect y^r heart to be incapable of feeling ye refin'd tendernesses of Love. No Man who truly Loves w^d suffer ye Woman he lov'd to ask in vain; except by a compliance wth her request his peace of Mind w^d be violated, or his honor or Virtue render'd liable to impeachment. He w^d even find pleasure in anticipating her Wishes. W^t then must I think of y^o, either y^t y^o h^v designedly impos'd on me, or y^t ye imposition practis'd on me is ye consequence of a *prior self-deception.* These two inferences seem ye most natural ones y^t I can possibly draw from y^r present conduct, and as y^e last is y^e most candid, I think it incumbent on me to indulge y^t supposition.

The pleasure y^r last Letter afforded me w^s so great, y^t I began a long Letter to y^o almost immediately and answered y^t part of y^r Letter y^t related to $Relig^n$ & even y^e question y^o ask'd me in regard to y^e light in wch I then consider'd y^o but laid it by unfinished, because I thought I sh^d soon hear fr^m you again. Prudence now forbids me to send it. I w^d transcribe as much of it as has a relation to y^r religious scruples if I was able, but I am not, & it might not be of any use to y^o, if I w^s & so it is of no consequence. However Sir I beg y^o to assure yourself y^t y^o need not be under any apprehension of my misconstruing those scruples. Such a doubt w^d n^t h^v arisen in y^r Mind if y^o had known me thoroughly. In y^r last letter y^o say y^t y^r only wish is to render me satisfy'd & easy; y^r conduct speaks a very different Language, y^t seems to indicate y^t y^r *only aim* is to perplex & render me unhappy. My Mind is at present in a state of great irresolution, for 2 days past I h^v been strongly inclin'd to put an immediate end to ye connection between us; but as the style in wch my last Letter was written must induce y^{o} to think my Sentiments for y^{o} were then different from what they once were, y^{t} I may not give y^{o} ye least reason to charge me wth levity, nor give my fr^{ds} room to accuse me of precipitation, I once more give y^{o} an opportunity of vindicating y^{r} conduct if y^{o} h^{v} any solicitude to do so. If y^{o} do not give me an assurance y^{t} y^{r} *future* conduct will be very different from y^{r} late conduct, I will drop all intercourse wth y^{o}. I can be happy without any connection wth y^{o}, but I cannot be happy whilst we are in ye unsettled way we h^{v} been in for ye last 4 months. Strange & unaccountable as w^{s} y^{r} behaviour in consequence of ye Letters y^{o} Rec^{d} fr^{m} me whilst at Birmingham I w^{d} h^{v} overlooked y^{t} as y^{r} Mind was in so painful a Situat^{n}. But y^{o} are going on again in y^{e} *same track*, & I have too much spirit patiently to submit to be y^{r} *Dupe*. W^{n} I wrote to y^{o} last, I was almost forgetful of myself, to soothe, to comfort y^{r} Mind, & if possible to contribute to ye restoration of y^{r} peace, w^{s} all my care; I felt for y^{o} sensations too agonizing to admit of description, I theref^{r} requested y^{o} w^{d} n^{t} fail letting me hear fr^{m} y^{o} every week whilst y^{r} uneasiness continued; as y^{o} had written a second time before y^{t} Letter reach'd y^{o}, & as I had desir'd y^{o} to devote y^{t} Week to study, I sh^{d} n^{t} h^{v} been displeas'd if y^{o} had omitted to write to me; at ye same time I confess, y^{t} if y^{o} had only wrote *Six lines*, I sh^{d} h^{v} esteem'd such an instance of y^{r} attention to my peace, as a stronger demonstration of ye Sincerity of y^{r} Affection, than all ye high flown declarations y^{o} h^{v} repeatedly made of it. But y^{t} y^{o} sh^{d} omit to write to me last Week, as well as ye preceeding Week, is quite astonishing. Do y^{o} think Sir y^{t} y^{o} are to treat a Woman to w^{m} y^{o} profess an attachment wth as little attention as y^{o} w^{d} a fr^{d} of y^{r} own Sex? If y^{o} do y^{o} greatly deceive yourself, for there is not a Woman on Earth, y^{t} has one Grain of *Sense*, *Spirit* or *delicacy*, y^{t} will endure such treatment from y^{o}. For my own part I declare I w^{d} not submit to be trifled with by ye greatest Peer in ye Realm, I do not want y^{o} to pay any servile submissions to me Sir, nor have I any caprices with wch I wish your compliance, but as I never trifled with y^{r} peace of mind, never kept you a moment longer in suspense than ye return of ye post oblig'd me to, I therefore thought I had reason to expect y^o w^d pay some attention to my peace. . . .

Altho 4 months have elaps'd since we parted (& y^o must h^v heard me say w^n at Dav^{ty} that I was almost constantly confin'd ye 3 Winter Months) notwithstanding y^o h^v written 5 Letters, y^o have never once mentioned my Health, if y^o had indeed regarded me wth affection y^o must h^v felt some concern on y^t acc^t. What prospect of happyness Sir, c^d I have in a Union for Life wth a Man, so little dispos'd to sympathize with me in Affliction? Is it n^t reasonable to think if such an event were ever to take place, y^t instead of endeavouring to soften ye trials providence might see fit to exercise me wth, y^o w^d aggravate them, if not by premeditated insult, at least by neglect? It w^d grieve me to indulge any suspicions concerning y^o injurious to y^r Sincerity or honor. I w^d n^t wrong my greatest enemy even in thought if I knew it, if I sh^d in any respect wrong y^o, y^o must not blame me but y^r own *unaccountable behaviour.* Lest y^o sh^d h^v vouch'd safe to return a reply to my last Letter, e'er this reaches y^o, to prevent ye perplexity which such a circumstance might mutually involve us in I take ye freedom to acquaint y^o Sir, y^t if y^t sh^d be ye case I shall nevertheless *expect* a *particular* answer to ye *Surmises* exprest in this Letter, before I write to y^o again, if I ever sh^d write to y^o again; more than that, I expect y^r answer will be *speedy*, for I repeat it again I will not be y^r *Dupe*; if y^o still give me reason to suspect y^o of an intention of trifling wth me I will terminate ye connection between us. If y^o suffer more than one post to intervene between ye Receipt of this and the expected answer to it, I w^d not h^v y^o be surpriz'd if y^o find I take other measures than I h^v yet taken to convince y^o I mean to break wth y^o *for ever.* M. Scott.

Endorsed by John Taylor: "Vexed at my silence. Will not be my Dupe."

MARY SCOTT *to* REV. JOHN TAYLOR.

TUESD. EVE., *April* 16, 1777.

You will I daresay be surpriz'd to hear from me so soon, as I wrote to y° by ye last post. But my present situation is so very painful y^{t} I cannot suffer my pen to lie silent, since y° and y° alone can alleviate my uneasyness. There is surely a singular severity in my fate y^{t} obliges me to render those who are most dear to me wretched, whilst I am actuated by ye strictest principles of Duty. Y^{r} Curiosity is by this time I doubt not awaken'd; without farther preface therefore I will acquaint you with ye cause of my present distress. I rode out this morn^{g} for an airing, & after my return seem'd considerably refresh'd by the ride, & sat down to Dinner wth a tolerable Appetite; whilst we were sitting at Table I happen'd to look on my mother, & was astonish'd to see ye distress painted on her countenance, & beg'd to know what was ye matter, she made me no reply till my importunity oblig'd her to speak; she then said she almost wish'd she might take ye Smallpox. I ask'd her why she w^{d} indulge such a wish, she reply'd y^{t} then she w^{d} be in *nobody's Way*. Judge how much such a reply shock'd me. In an agony of Grief I assur'd her she was not, & entreated to know w^{t} cause I had ever given her to entertain such a Supposition. She readily acknowledg'd that I never had, y^{t} she did not think she was in my way, but she fear'd she was in somebody else's way. Too well did I guess to whom she alluded. My very Soul was pierc'd wth anguish (for tho' I did wth concern, I now confess it, entertain an *Apprehension rather* than a *belief* of y^{t} Nat^{r} myself, I c^{d} not, c^{d} not bear that another person sh^{d} indulge it). I rose from table in an unutterable Agony. I believe I suffer'd a momentary fit of Phrenzy. I doubt I said things wch I ought n^{t} to h^{v} said. I cannot recollect my expressions. But only y^{t} I told her I sh^{d} be distracted if she indulg'd such unworthy Apprehensions of y°. Y^{e} perturbation of my Mind w^{s} too much for my frail frame, I w^{s} affected I cannot tell how. I was oblig'd to go to Bed. I got ab^{t} half an hours sleep wch a little refresh'd me, but I feel myself so much exhausted y^t^ I can write no longer. Good-night, may y^o^ h^v^ sweeter repose than I expect to enjoy.

Wednesd. morn^g^.—After having past a Night even more painful & restless than I fear'd it w^d^ be, I am sat down to finish my Letter, I intended when I began it to have requested you to write to my Mother, but I think she w^d^ be displeas'd wth me if she were to know I had mentioned to y^o^ what passed between us yesterday. Besides I took a step last night wch I think entirely supersedes ye Necessity of y^r^ writing, for I read to her that paragraph in your Letter in answer to my *unkind surmise;* she seem'd quite satisfied with it, & assur'd me y^t^ she w^d^ not only guard against speaking, but against *cherishing* any unworthy thoughts of y^o^, so y^t^ my Mind is considerably more at ease than w^n^ I began to write to y^o^. Y^o^ see I am no Stoic where y^o^ are concern'd. Let not this little incident prejudice y^o^ against my Mother. Remember she does not *know* y^o^ (I wish she did) but she knows *y^r^ Sex.* She knows, she well knows, how artful, how selfish, how deceiving Men (& Men professing Piety) are, & therefore it is not to be wonder d at if for a few transient moments she suspected y^o^. I am sure I never heard her express herself in such high terms in any Man's favor in my Life as she has in yours. But y^o^ have forgotten y^r^ promise, or acted inconsistent with it, for in ye Letter y^o^ wrote me before y^o^ went to Birmingham, y^o^ desir'd me to assure her y^t^ y^o^ never w^d^ give her a moment's uneasiness, y^t^ y^o^ w^d^ despise, detest yourself if y^o^ were capable, but for a moment, of interrupting ye comfort of ye infirm and distress'd. Y^o^ told me also y^t^ I need n^t^ h^v^ laid y^o^ under such solemn restrictions to desist from y^r^ pursuit, for since it was so extremely contrary to what I judg'd to be my duty, it w^d^ argue ye greatest insensibility & cruelty in y^o^, to wish me guilty of an action y^t^ w^d^ occasion me such severe self-reflections. That y^o^ had too great a veneration for ye obligations of Conscience, too great a regard for my peace, to wish it; & added "never, never, shall y^t^ heart wch I w^d^ do all in my power to soothe & comfort, never shall it feel one pang on my acc^{t} whilst I can possibly help it." Judge now, whether I c^{d} be otherwise than pain'd by y^{r} violating in a few months so generous a declaration. Surely it may convince y^{o} y^{t} I am not y^{t} capricious being y^{r} last Letter insinuated me to be. Had I deceiv'd y^{o} by ever giving you reason to expect a speedy union wth me, y^{o} w^{d} h^{v} had much reason to complain, but surely y^{o} must remember y^{t} I frequently told y^{o} when at Daventry last y^{t} I c^{d} n^{t} marry yet a great while, & urg'd y^{t} impossibility, as an insuperable objection against y^{r} perseverance. As often as I urg'd it, so often did y^{o} declare y^{r} resolution to wait for me any length of time, provided I w^{d} give y^{o} an assur'd hope of being united to me at last; and tho' I have never given y^{o} y^{t} assurance in positive terms, yet I w^{d} have done so in my last Letter if yours had not been written in so unusual a Style. Nay, I will yet give it y^{o}, (since nothing can shake ye constancy of y^{r} Attachment to me) if it will render y^{o} more happy than y^{o} at present are. Indeed y^{r} last Letter hurt me exceedingly, but unkind as some expressions in it were, there was so much tenderness blended with y^{t} unkindness, & y^{r} Affection for me was display'd in such lively colors, y^{t} I c^{d} not be angry wth you. Oh, if y^{o} have any regard for my peace, if you wish me to live, endeavor to be happy, assure me y^{t} y^{o} will be so. Nature cannot much longer, I believe, endure those violent emotions of Mind I have suffer'd with very short intermissions for near 6 months past, for it is nearly so long since I first heard of Poor R's misconduct. He was so closely twin'd about my Heart y^{t} neither tongue nor pen c^{d} express ye extreme anguish I felt for him; scarcely had the anguish of my Mind subsided into that calm & settled anxiety I now feel, e'er it was doom'd to feel on y^{r} acc^{t} sensations no less exquisite in their degree tho' of a Different Nature. Violent & long continued grief will ruin ye strongest constitution, and such are ye Effects it has produc'd on mine y^{t} I have scarce a hope left of recovering them, even tho' I sh'd live a few years longer, wch I believe will be impossible without a great & speedy alteration in ye State of my Health. You can do more to forward its recovery than any other person; ye knowledge y^{t} y^{o} were endeavoring to be happy w^{d} operate on me like a Charm. For "my peace all hangs upon thy faithful Breast" & if y^{o} will not endeavor to be comfortable & easy I cannot even wish to live. I cannot indeed pretend to give you any hope of a speedy union, yet mutually assur'd of ye ardor and constancy of each other's affection, if we are not unaccountably perverse we may be great sources of comfort to each other. If y^{o} will study to be happy I will do all I can to recover my Health; if you will not, then must I bid farewel to every hope of peace on Earth. . . .

Endorsed by John Taylor: "Distress on account of her mother wishing to take the smallpox because she thought she was in somebody's way. Very tender and affectionate."

MARY SCOTT *to* REV. JOHN TAYLOR.

May 7, 1777.

Your two Letters reach'd me this morning just as I was sitting down to a solitary Breakfast; the pleasure they afforded me render'd me insensible to the low gratifications of animal nature, & my Tea was as cold as Water just fetch'd from the pump e'er I recollected any thing about it. So that I may say I breakfasted on Love this Morning. If I knew how to be angry wth y^{o} I w^{d} chide y^{o} severely for ye apology y^{o} make in y^{r} Second Letter about ye postage; I am indeed hurt by ye insinuation it seems to contain. Have I ever given y^{o} reason to suppose me of a mercenary temper? Still more is my Heart pain'd by an interrogation in y^{r} 1st Letter "Can I promise y^{t} I will not be asham'd of y^{o}, y^{t} I have no thoughts of deceiving y^{o}"? So far, so very far, am I from being *asham'd* of y^{o}, y^{t} I do not hesitate to acknowledge my regard (my Affection let me say) for y^{o} to any of my friends. I feel no sentiments for y^{o} wch I could not cherish wth pleasure in ye last moments of my Life, & therefore I know not why I sh^{d} be asham'd of y^{o}. And as to deceiving y^{o}, I thought my past conduct w^{d} h^{v} exculpated me fr^{m} every suspicion of y^{t} Nature.

Why was I so backward to avow my tenderness for y°, but fr^m^ an apprehension y^t^ there was a possibility of mistaking ye emotions of Gratitude for those of Love, & from a fear of deceiving y° thro' inadvertance? Had not y^t^ *apprehension* restrain'd my pen I sh^d^ have acknowledg'd my affection for you long before I did. I was determin'd to be convinced y^t^ I lov'd y°, before I told y° so; but had y° not been unhappy I believe it w^d^ have been long before I sh^d^ have obtain'd y^t^ absolute certainty of it I now have. I cannot think it possible I ever sh^d^ become indifferent to y°, except a total revolution were to take place either in y^r^ Character or my own—events wch I hope never will happen. Assure yourself y^t^ "my Soul acquiesces in y°, y^t^ y° are ye Man of my *voluntary choice*," y^t^ I do at present, & hope I ever shall, value y^r^ merit ab^v^ all worldly price; that I hope no length of time, or distance of place, will ever disunite my Heart from yours, at least whilst y° continue as firmly attach'd to me as I believe y° are at present. Your present conduct greatly endears y° to my Heart. The generality of Men, even Men of merit, w^d^ I fear have acted a very different part, & w^d^ have endeavor'd to have importun'd my Mother into a Compliance wth their wishes; y° have acted more nobly & shown yourself capable of reducing to practise all those fair Ideas of excellence wch in speculation have long charm'd my Soul. Indeed I now find myself compel'd to think Providence formed us for each other, & can very easily believe y^t^ we may not only be *better* & *happier* in this state of existence for our mutual attachment, but even *thro' Eternity*. Accept then my dearest Love the Heart wch you have so long solicited, a Heart as fond, as faithful, (& I believe I must add) as *proud*, as ever animated a female bosom, a Heart wch tho' formed for Love, never felt (& I trust never will feel) for another Man those sentiments it feels for you. . . .

And now I will give y° an account of my own painful situation. Some years before my Father's Death he plac'd a Sum of Money in ye Funds; not having quite as much by him as he wanted he desir'd my Grandfather to supply him with two Hundred Pounds, which he readily did, without receiving or desiring any Security for it, (as my Father was his only surviving Child), but afterwards whenever any part of my Father's conduct displeas'd him, he used to upbraid him about this Money, & threaten that he would have it again. This irritated my Father, & he told him he would sell out & pay him; then he would absolutely refuse to be paid, & has often declared that he never meant to have it. Thus matters remained till my Father's Death. He made no will, for it was his desire that his Children should share alike, & as his Estate was chiefly personal, he said the law would divide it as he wished; my Mother's Jointure, in case of her dying intestate, being to devolve equally amongst all her children. My Eldest Brother thought fit to be offended when he found he was on the same footing as Russell & myself; and my Grandfather (instigated I presume by my Brother) demanded y[e] 200 pounds of my Mother. She ask'd him what security he had to show that it was ever borrowed; he acknowledged he had none; she then refus'd to pay it, for he acknowledg'd that it was not a Legal debt, & that he never sh[d] have had it if my Father had lived. I cannot give y[o] any Idea of his Rage; every aspersion that malice could suggest did he throw on my Mother's Character; my Brother too represented her as the worst of Mothers. I had forgot to tell y[o] that my Grandfather demanded a Hundred pounds for y[e] interest of the two Hundred; his whole demand was three Hundred & some odd pounds. Our Family affairs were a subject of conversation for y[e] whole Town. However my Mother at length promis'd to give him Two Hundred pounds, (I cannot say pay, for he confesses it was never borrow'd) & took up two Hundred pounds which she had out on a mortgage; & last Saturday was a Week sent a receipt in full, to know if he chose to sign it; if he did, his Servant was to come to our house & receive a Bank Note for that Sum. Two Hundred pounds he said was better than nothing, & therefore he agreed to sign it. We pleas'd ourselves with y[e] assurance as we then thought it, of having no more trouble about that affair, but greatly were we disappointed. On Monday when my Brother was acquainted with my Grandfather's having given a receipt in full, he was much displeas'd, & to such a height has his anger grown that he never intends to come near his Mother more, & not only so, but he has left ye Meeting on account of it. I have been long appriz'd of ye treatment I must expect to receive from him if I should ever survive my Mother, but I hop'd we should have been on civil terms as long as she lived. All Family harmony is I fear at an end. I see by his present conduct what I must expect hereafter. Surely he might content himself with ye certainty of possessing all his Grandfather's Fortune (except an Estate of 30 or 40 pounds a year wch devolves to one of his Nephews at his Death) without wishing to impoverish Russell & myself. I am indeed grieved to ye Soul to see him discover so selfish a disposition, & betray such a want of Duty & Affection to his Mother, & of Respect to our excellent friend Mr. Newton, ye Worthy Dissenting Minister in this Town. I thought he would thankfully have accepted ye 200 pounds, (for it was on his account alone that my Grandfather wanted it) & not have insisted on a Hundred & 20 pounds for Interest. His undutiful conduct greatly disturbs my poor Mother, yo will easily believe, & my own Heart is greatly pained by losing in this manner a Brother whom I sincerely loved, tho' I have too much reason to believe he never had much friendship for me. What will ye World say when ye Affair comes to be known? when it is seen, as it soon must be, that all intercourse is dropt between us? How painful Family differences are to a Mind that superadds to religious considerations, a thousand fair Ideas of Moral Beauty! Whether I shall ever have comfort in either of my Brothers seems at present a dubious matter. . . .

Afflicted as I am, I am comparatively happy now yr Health & peace are restor'd. I earnestly pray yr religious peace may never more know interruption, & yt no misunderstanding may ever again arise between us. In ye World we must have tribulation, but in ye enjoyment of each other's Affection I hope we shall have peace.

My poor Brother, how I long to see him! & perhaps I never shall see him again under any Character but yt of an enrag'd enemy. My Heart aches for my Grandfather, for I hear he is likewise a subject of his displeasure, & is not treated by him as he ought to be treated by one so much obliged. May God forgive him as freely as I hope I do. An improper education[1] has ruin'd his temper; gratify'd in every wish of his Heart, whether proper or not, he soon learnt to think all with whom he was connected ought to be subservient to him. As long as I could hope for ye least influence over him, I strove to bring him to a better temper, but he never would be free with me. At ye same time never w^{d} express those Illiberal sentiments in my presence wch he was ready enough to avow to other people; his behaviour before me was generally specious, but I have been frequently pain'd by hearing of his imperious treatment of his dependents. Yet he is what ye World calls a very Virtuous Young Fellow, for he is neither a Swearer, a Drunkard, nor a Libertine, & has more worldly Wisdom than any man of his age I ever knew, tho' in ye present case he does not discover it; for his conduct to my Mother is very impolitic, as well as undutiful, as she can dispose of her Jointure amongst her Children in what proportion she sees fit. Whatever Animosity he might have cherished in his heart, I thought he would have suppressed it, from motives of self-interest as long as she lived. . . .

The only reason I had for wishing y^{o} to settle in or near London, was because I thought we could then see & hear from each other more frequently. Dissenters in London are indeed what y^{o} say of y^{m}; but are those in ye Country better principled, or more humble? I cannot think they are; sure I am y^{t} they are not as far as my acquaintance amongst y^{m} extends. I know not but very few Dissenting Congregations in which there is not, or has not lately been, disturbances. There has within ye last fortnight been a very great falling out between a Dissenting Minister in ye next Town [Sherborne] & his people, & he is about to leave them. . . .

I am afraid from some expressions in y^{r} last Letter, y^{t} y^{o} are as fond of forming New Schemes & Systems of Religion

[1] He was brought up by his grandfather Scott.

as ever, & greatly fear yt propensity of yours will be a Source of Inconvenience & discomfort to us both in future Life. In matters of Religion, I fear our Sentiments become wider & wider; there seems no probability that we should ever think alike. Now I cannot help fearing yt this difference, if ever we should be united by ye marriage tye, may produce a shyness between us, if it does not occasion open contention. And this apprehension gives me very great pain. It is to me a surprizing circumstance, that Persons whose sentiments are so similar on every other subject of Importance, should differ so widely in matters of Religion as I doubt we do. . . .

I have been reviewing my Letter with sentiments of amazement at ye fond Epithets yt have fallen from my pen, & I feel my Mind in a most awkward situation on that account. Never before did I write such a Letter as this; yet think not that I mean to retract what I have written. No, the fondest, tenderest Sentiments my Heart is capable of feeling are no more than what your generous affection, your strong & steady Attachment to me, entitle you to.

I expect very shortly to have ye pleasure of seeing my dear Miss Steele, my more than Sister. She talks of visiting her Estate in Somersetshire. Oh, if you love me as much as yo tell me yo do, yo will always feel a fraternal affection for her. How I long to introduce yo to ye acquaintance of each other! I assure you she thinks very highly of yo; she told me in her last Letter yt your Character rose in her esteem every time she heard from me, & that she never in her Life so much admir'd any Man whom she had never seen. As her Estate lies but a few miles from hence, I hope to pass a Week or 10 Days with her when she comes in ye Country. I shall not feel that uneasyness on leaving my Mother that I do when I take a long journey; for if she should be worse than usual, I can be with her in an hour. I have some faint hopes that change of air, tho' but for a short time, may be of a little service to my Health which still continues considerably impair'd. I have discontinued riding on Horseback for more than a fortnight past, a circumstance which I believe contributes to retard ye progress of my Recovery; but I find it difficult to procure a double Horse[1] in this Town, & still more so to find a proper person to ride with me, & I am not able to walk far enough to obtain any benefit from walking. Indeed I have little expectation of enjoying for any length of time such a degree of Health as would render Life comfortable; but if my *dearer self* be blest with ease & strength I can smile in pain. . . .

This Letter I presume will not reach Daventry till Sunday, when it is probable y^o will be abroad, so that I know not when I must expect an answer to it, & I do not much like, when I consider ye Sentiments it contains, that it should lie two or three Days in a Servant's Hands; tho' I seal my Letters so securely that there is scarcely a possibility of looking into them. I thought to have finished it last post Day, but was not able to.

Poor R. is to come home for a Month at Midsummer. He told me some time ago, he was ready to wish it were possible that time might never come, for he knew not how he should bear to see his Mother. I am apt to think his situation must be rather dull, for there are none but small lads there, except they have had any fresh ones since he has been there. However I prevailed on my Mother to consent to his being a parlor boarder whilst he continues there, that he might be preserved as much as possible from ye danger of forming improper connections a second time, & as ye Gentleman's Wife whom he is with, is a near relation of my Mother's, I doubt not but they are very kind to him.—Adieu—

You see I cannot leave off writing whilst one blank space remains. I wish I had a larger one at present. My Mind is much distressed; the more I ruminate on y^o difference of our Religious Sentiments ye more strongly do my former apprehensions of Misery from our connection recur to my Mind; I would not pain ye Heart I love, but 'tis necessary in cases of this nature to avoid ye least reserve. My doubts & un-

[1] Evidently she rode on a pillion.

happyness on this account are proportioned to ye Strength of my Affection, and misery seems almost inevitable. If we should not see each other in London, or somewhere or other that we may talk over this & some other matters this Summer, I know not how I shall support ye uneasyness of my Mind. I know not what to think, how to act, or what to wish; & forgive me if I add, am almost ready to regret that I love you lest it should be ye means of rendering us both wretched. I am much afraid what I have said in this P.S. will give pain to that Heart in which, were it possible to avoid it, I would never excite any emotions but pleasurable ones. But my peace of mind is fled, I am ready to fear for ever, & my domestic afflictions tho' great are absorbed in a distress of a more poignant & tender nature. Farewell, may you be ever blest.

I believe I have omitted to thank you for your second letter, but be assured my Heart has a grateful sense of your attention to everything that concerns my peace. This is a very inconsistent Letter. I hope you are much happier than I, else your situation must be very painful. . . .

Endorsed by John Taylor: "Spoiled her breakfast, a charming letter. Account of her unhappy situation with her grandfather and brother. Alarmed at some wild expression in my letter in regard to religion. Greatly alarmed."

Rev. John Taylor *to* Mary Scott.

Daventry, *Saturday, May* 24, 1777.

I suspect my dearest Miss Scott will *not* be greatly surprised when she receives another Letter from me, for I am persuaded she *must* be considerably surprised at my not mentioning some things of gr^{t} importance in my last. One is in regard to my coming down into Somersetshire at the Vacation, wch I hope she will give me leave to consider as certain, provided Providence spare the life & health of us both. 'Tis at Milborne Port I presume that I may hope to enjoy this pleasure, but w^{n} she w^{d} choose that I should come, I am at present ignorant, and wish to be informed as soon as she can with convenience. Our Vacation commences this Day 3 weeks (Saturday). And great as my pleasure has hitherto ever been, to set my face tow^{ds} my Dear Friends in Lancashire, 'tis a pleasure I cannot think of enjoying, till my Dearest Creature, w^{m} I hope always to consider as my dearest & nearest Relation, has blest me with her company in Somersetshire. Say then, my Love, have you any objection to my setting out directly for Somersetshire on Monday the 26th of June? after wch I may hope to arrive at Milborne P. some Day in the same week, which will depend entirely upon the mode of travelling, wch I am as yet uncertain about & sh^{d} be greatly obliged to you to tell me which you would have me take.

I dont know that I ever told you what a great walker I am. I hope you dont start with disgust, I will not walk except you should give me leave. And yet I must tell you that it is with me by far the most pleasant way of travelling—that it is infinitely less fatiguing & painful to me than riding on Horse back—that I should prefer it even to a chaise, because I am perfectly free & easy—can go on or stop—can choose my Road, go out of my way if there be anything particularly curious to see, wch I have been hitherto particularly fond of, but now I suppose the object at the End of my Journey will in a great measure prevent my curiosity by the way. I can also travel wth m^{ch}, nay inconceivably less care, & almost as much expedition as if I had a horse to attend to. But you will be ashamed to think of my undertaking such a Journey on foot, and the appearance it will have in the Eyes of the world, for it w^{d} be neither possible to keep it a secret, nor worth the while to attempt it. And tho' I could rather wish that consideration might not influence my beloved, yet if that must be the Consequence I will come by London in the stage coaches, w^{ch}

after all may perhaps be the best way of travelling; tho' *hardly in Midsummer.* My great peculiarity in y[e] mode of travelling will hardly warrant the saying so much about it—But I hope this is the only article that needs settling.

You see, my dearest, I treat you as a *friend.* But you may perhaps think my freedom does not *over well* become me, till I have cleared up some doubts & surmises w[ch] subsist between us. I was greatly alarmed & vexed at what you mentioned in your last Letter, that I had not been sufficiently upon my guard in talking of my attachment to you, or that you should hear of it again. I am also very much surprised. But I beg you will be easy on this head, for I have not said any thing to any body that I think *can* sink you in the least in their esteem. I thought I had been always aware of the Danger of letting the exultations of my own heart be manifest to any of my friends; however I have often checked myself in speaking of you, but tho' it is I acknowledge very difficult to conceal the pleasing emotions & inward joys of the Soul, yet it is more difficult for those who are witnesses of them, or only suspect them, to withstand the Temptation w[ch] such discoveries lay them under to scandalize & misrepresent the character & conduct of those in question—and that merely from a principle of Envy—because they enjoy not, or are not capable of enjoying, the same pleasures themselves; both, & especially the Latter, mortifying considerations, sufficient to set both wit & curiosity at work to find out or invent what they may turn into a laugh. So that on these accounts it's scarce to be expected that any two persons should have a strong and ardent attachment to each other without feeling, or rather beholding, a few random shots of Envy; a little inconvenience, & that rather intended than real. 'Tis w[t] I should submit to wth the greatest cheerfulness for the pleasure & satisfaction which I experience from a knowledge of your affection. But [I] am so fully aware how different the Case must be [with] the Woman, especially one of your delicacy, that I promise you to be more upon my guard—tho' I cannot tell any particular Instance wherein I have been imprudently communicative. But as those whom one least suspects may sometimes betray our secrets, I will endeavour to lay them under no temptation.

I have no great expectation that any material change in y[r] circumstances with your friends is likely to take place soon, & yet I am very unhappy in the thought of your living so very miserable a Life long. I suppose it were quite in vain to offer my Interposition, as being more likely to exasperate than produce any good effect. However I should be happy to know if there is anything that I could do, or any particular mode of behaviour w[n] at Milborne that will in any measure tend to the peace & comfort of my Dearer self. I should be very desirous y[t] y[r] poor grandfather might discover a better Temper, so near as he must be to an Eternal world. The world and violent passions sh[d] not have such an ascendant in *young* persons, but it is shocking in those who are just going to leave all behind; soon there will be far other employment than Lawsuits, Contracts for gain, persecution & cruelty. But indeed the absolute tyrany w[ch] passions, dispositions & habits contracted in youth, exert in old age, ought to make young persons particularly on their guard against them at first. Be so good as to comply with the Request I here make.

Assure yourself, my dearest, that there was nothing of Jealousy in my assigning you the young women as your particular province in y[e] random sketch I gave you. I had two other stronger & more just reasons. They were these—First, I feared if I assigned you a part in my Instructions of the Men, however well you may be qualified for the Task, or useful it may be, yet y[e] oddity of the thing w[d] surprise & disgust you—And then I am aware how difficult it is for Ministers to adopt any schemes of Improvement for the young women without incurring some little stain on one of their characters, especially at first—On this account, & a consequent habit of inattention to it, the young women in most societies are I think shamefully neglected—On w[ch] account I was from the first extremely happy in having found one who can serve them, & more especially that she will consent to do it. Pray tell me how long time I may hope to stay with you —dont forget—Yours, J. T.

Address: "Miss Scott, Milborne Port, Somersetshire."

The following letter was written before Mary received the one from John Taylor which has just been given. Both letters bear the same date, "May 26"—the one at Daventry, the other at Yeovil. Mary had gone to Yeovil to visit her friend, Miss M. Steele, whose "little estate in Somersetshire" has been before mentioned.

MARY SCOTT *to* REV. JOHN TAYLOR.

Postmark "YEOVIL," 26 *May* [1777].

I happened some time ago to travel with a Gentleman who asserted he never did anything of which he repented; very different from his I am sure is my Fate, for I am daily doing or saying something or other y[t] supplies me with subjects for regret. I have been vexed with myself ever since I wrote to y[o] on Saturday on account of one Paragraph in that Letter, which I fear will give y[o] pain. I mean that in which I mentioned my conjectures of your having been very communicative of your attachment to me. There was a threat in it which I think might as well have been spared, for surely my desire would have been sufficient to have induc'd my Taylor to alter any part of his conduct respecting myself which gave me pain. I will be more explicit than I could be then. I do assure you I am no longer solicitous y[t] our connection should be kept secret. I care not who knows it, care not who knows that I am engaged to you, but if y[o] speak of me in that light, take care y[t] y[r] confidence y[o] express in me be placed in my *honor*, not in my *Love*. Y[o] will perhaps deem this a strange request, but it is a necessary one. Decorum prescribes a Thousand absurd modes of conduct to our Sex, from which you are happily exempted; one of these is that a Woman ought not to acknowledge her affection for a Man, whatever his merit or attachment to her may be, till she is married to him; till that time she is to behave to him with reserve (nay to endeavor to persuade him y^t she is indifferent to him) & to speak of him to others with Coldness. According to this rule in ye course of my acquaintance I should have told you a Thousand falsehoods, & endeavor'd to inspire ye World with a belief of my thinking lightly of y^o; whereas I have never intentionally told y^o one untruth, & even when I thought it impossible y^t I ever should return y^r Affection, spoke of y^o in ye highest terms of approbation to others. For I ever thought ye claims of honor, truth & humanity, infinitely superior to ye rules of *Decorum*. These principles therefore always actuated my conduct in regard to y^o. Men in general, whatever degree of affection they may appear to feel for a Woman, or how solicitous soever they may seem to obtain hers, do commonly make her on finding they have succeeded ye subject of their ridicule, or at least grow insolent, assuming, or negligent, in their conduct to her. Was it possible for me to avoid despising beings so lost to gratitude or honor? Was it possible for me not to shudder at ye Idea of an intimate connection with any of them? Yet I knew some men were capable of forming nobler sentiments, & determined if it should ever be my Fate to be addrest by such a one, I would treat him with ye utmost ingenuousness; I would tell him all my Soul. For I was ever persuaded that there were some few Men so superior to ye rest of their Sex, that a Woman might not only indulge an Affection for them consistent with Virtue, but that it might be *even a Virtue* to Love them. However y^o must know as well as I that ye World is incapable of making those nice discriminations, which is a sufficient reason why neither y^o nor I, should in our present circumstances be ostentatious of my Affection for y^o. Another favour I must request of you, which is that if any of your Acquaintance should be curious to know why our Union is defer'd, you will tell them that there are peculiarities in my situation y^t will not admit of my entering into such an engagement at present. This y^o know will be ye truth, & yet will convey no information of ye motives which have chiefly influenced my Conduct in this affair, which I confess I should be glad to have kept as secret as possible. My Mind is exceedingly pain'd by ye Idea of its being known, lest ye World should suppose me, & you also, to be impatiently expecting an event, which tho' according to ye course of Nature we may expect to survive, is yet I hope at a remote period.

Now let me proceed to touch a little on ye subject of your last Letter which I had not leisure to do on Saturday. I told you then I thought there seemed not to be so great a difference in our religious sentiments as I had formerly feared, & I am inclin'd to think ye difference would appear still less, if we thoroughly understood each other. You concur with me in thinking establishments have been, & are still, not only expedient but necessary, & does not that afford a strong presumption that they always will be so, whilst mankind continue ye same frail, capricious & inconstant beings they at present are? To say ye truth I look upon ye Church of England to be, under Providence, ye chief Bulwark of rational Christianity in our Nation. Dissenters appear to me to dissent as much from Xtianity as from ye Church of England; some disgracing their understandings & their religious profession by all ye extravagances of Fanaticism, others setting up reason as ye ultimate judge of all articles of Faith, and sapping ye very foundation of Christianity. I speak of Dissenters considered as Societies, doubtless there are numberless individuals whose conduct renders them ornaments to religion & human nature. But altho' you allow ye expediency of establishments in ye present condition of Mankind, you seem to think them of bad tendency; if that could be proved I could not grant that they were expedient. I readily acknowledge establishments are liable to abuse, but are not the modes of a Sect equally so? And y^o will not surely argue ye uselessness or pernicious nature of a thing merely from its abuse? . . . . . .

And tho' I think ye Labourer worthy of his Hire I would have ye hireling always obliged to labor. Some Provision must be made for ye Preachers of ye Gospel, for how spiritual-minded soever they may be, they are not all Spirit. If they are not in a great measure independent on their hearers their Persons & their ministry will sink into contempt; it therefore seems to me expedient that temporalities should be annexed to Spiritual Cures. Yet I would not wish the teachers of the Gospel to be rich, except in Faith & Good Works. The middle rank of Life seems most eligible for them. The extremes of Riches or Poverty are great trials to a Man's graces. Agur's prayer,[1] will always be the Prayer of every ***Wise Man***. It seems to me that ye provision made for Ministers should be such as to afford them a competent enjoyment of ye necessaries & even conveniences of Life, yet not so liberal as to administer to ye gratification of their Vanity. You do not I think seem to approve of any stated provision for them. On your Scheme I cannot conceive how they are to subsist. Indeed my Love I think y^o refine too much; when Mankind are Angels your plan may be carried into execution, but it seems not probable to me that it should before. You suppose & consider ye World as extending to a much longer date than I do. What motive induces you to entertain this supposition? . . . You are of opinion that a time will come when Mankind will be in a much better situation in regard to Morals than they now are, when Xtianity shall be purified from all ye corruptions that have been accumulated on it. There may be such a time; some passages in ye Apocalypse seem to favor that Notion; yet I confess I know not how to reconcile it with other passages of Sacred writ, that appear less liable to misconstruction, particularly with ye account which our Lord gives of his Second Appearance in ye 24th Chapter of St. Matthew. He seems to represent Mankind as at that time remarkably thoughtless of futurity & immersed in sensual gratifications. And that ye Dissolution of ye World should take place at a time when moral depravity is at an

[1] "Give me neither poverty nor riches" (Prov. xxx. 8).

alarming height, seems to me to be analogous to all the past *singular* interpositions of Providence—as ye Deluge, ye destruction of Sodom, & even ye advent of the Messiah. Now that we have both explained our Sentiments in some degree, I think we do not differ quite so much as I have hitherto apprehended.

Yeovil.—I am just retired from a Large circle of Company to indulge myself in ye pleasure of conversing with you. Visits of Ceremony are things I hate. Miss Steele came to our house last Tuesday, & Wednesday Evening I accompanied her hither. Her society has afforded me much pleasure. . . .

I am in a painful Dilemma in regard to y^{r} coming into Somersetshire; sometimes I think it will be best for y^{o} to come; at other times am in great anxiety least my Mother should be rendered more unhappy. I have consulted Miss Steele, & two or three friends besides, & they are unanimously of opinion that y^{o} ought to come. I know not what to say, y^{o} must do as y^{o} will. If y^{o} do come y^{o} may come more conveniently than y^{o} could have done in ye Winter; there is a Coach or Diligence, or both, goes from Oxford to Bath 3 times a Week in one Day; & there is likewise a Diligence goes 3 times a Week from Bath to Weymouth, & that comes within 3 miles of our House; so that you may be with us by 11 o'clock in ye morning. . . .

Miss Steele desired me to present some very polite message to y^{o} when I came up Stairs, but I have entirely forgot what it was. But she has always been your very good friend. Supper waits for me, I can add no more than that I am Sincerely yours, M. S.

Endorsed by John Taylor: "Not to mention confidence in love, but honour, nor tell cause why not married. Says must do as I will about coming."

The following letter is the last written by Mary Scott that has come down to us. It is of later date by ten years than the earlier letters, and is written in shorthand. John Taylor has endorsed it: "Last letter before marriage." Mary's mother had died in the previous October.

It will be noticed that Mary calls him "Edward." It was a name she had given him. In those more formal times it was not usual for married people to call each other by their Christian names, and still less so for people who were merely engaged.

MARY SCOTT *to* REV. JOHN TAYLOR.

[*April* 30, 1788.]

I received your letter, my dear Edward, yesterday afternoon. I do not know whether you forgot to tell Mr. Owen the time you wished him to meet us, or whether I forgot to tell you, but I cannot get out by 11 o'clock, I must interline that. The wind has been so cold for some days past that I have not been able to go out yet, & I fear it will not become more mild till we have rain. Whether I shall be able to meet you at Church at the time proposed is uncertain; but you must come at a venture for aught I know.

Twice have I desired you, my dear Edward, to present your Mother in my name with a copy of the "Messiah," but whether you have given orders to the Bolton bookseller, as I desired you, I cannot tell. I am glad your sale produced you so much. I hope you will not have occasion to borrow much money. Pray do not forget the license, as Mr. Petty did when he went to be married. You do not tell me whether you design to come through Bristol or not. If you do, you will get there on Saturday evening I suppose, & you need not leave it till Tuesday morning early; then you will have time to call upon your acquaintance. I wish you to see poor Mrs. Barrett. And I think there would be nothing amiss in your calling on Mr. Loyde & settling with him for such extra copies of the "Messiah" as he has sold.

You will remember, only such as he has sold, my dear Edward, as he has had a quarter of a hundred for which he is to be accountable to me. The reason you may assign for my desiring you to call is that you will not be in Bristol again for a twelvemonth, & my brother perhaps not for a much longer time. Mr. Loyde is to give 1s. 6d. per copy. I should also be glad if you would call at Mr. Martin's, silk dyer in Wine Street, & enquire when the body that I sent him to be dyed will be sent to me. I must bid you adieu, my dear Edward. Mary Hebditch is come to carry my letter to Sherborne; I do not choose to send this letter to the Councillor's; the direction might occasion some speculation.

I hope it will please God to alter the weather soon. I am afraid it will be bad weather on Sunday & Wednesday sennight. What I shall do then I do not know. Indeed, indeed, I am in a very unfit state to be married. People begin to enquire when you come I find, though I have not yet been seen out of doors. You did not tell me whether you had got a supply from Daventry, though I was very anxious to hear.

And now I close a correspondence of eleven years, in the hope that you will be a more agreeable companion than you have been a correspondent. Were it not for that hope I should be wretched indeed. Pray remember me kindly to your Father, Mother, & all your family.

Thursday morning.

You will send me a few lines to inform me which way you come & when I am to expect you.

Addressed: "The Rev. J. Taylor. To be left till called for at the Post Office, Manchester, Lancashire."

John Taylor and Mary Scott were married on May 7, 1788, at the Parish Church of Milborne Port. For her portrait see p. 206.

The following extract from a printed Memoir of

their son, John Edward Taylor, relates to his father's life at this period:—

"On his marriage in 1788, Mr. Taylor removed to Milborne Port, where he resided but a short time, for we find him a settled minister at Ilminster in the same year. At this place he was associated with the Rev. John Noon. . . . This union in holy things was not, however, of long continuance. The leaven of a new era was now actively at work in society, and nowhere probably was it more strongly felt than in the unfettered, reflecting, and benevolent minds which filled the pulpits of the English Presbyterian Church. The result in regard to the ministers at Ilminster was very diverse; they both threw off the clerical costume indeed, but Mr. Noon substituted a green coat, while Mr. Taylor put on a drab one. The first had become a Jacobin, the second a Quaker; both doubtless being equally sincere, and both impelled by influences which they could not control and were scarcely able to define."

From Ilminster Mr. Taylor removed with his wife to Bristol, where he opened a school. They lived at No. 1 St. James's Square, and there Mrs. Taylor died, on June 4, 1793, after a married life of only five years. Their children were a daughter, Mary Ann, born February 25, 1789, in the house that had been her grandfather's at Milborne Port, and a son, John Edward, born at Ilminster on September 11, 1791.

REV. RUSSELL SCOTT *to* JOHN TAYLOR.

PORTSMOUTH, *June 6th*, 1793.

DEAR BROTHER TAYLOR,—Your letter this morning found me unprepared for the melancholy intelligence it contained. . . . Amidst the regret & grief I feel at her loss it is a consolation to reflect that the exchange of worlds is to her the completion of all her best desires & hopes. I feel a satisfaction too that her last moments were composed & placid. Had it been the divine will, I should have wished once more to have seen her in this life. . . .

How are the children? I bless God that they are left to the care of a Father who knows his duty to his children, & who will to the utmost faithfully endeavour to discharge it. I much wish to see them & I much wish to see you. I cannot now fix the exact time, but I hope nothing will occur to prevent my being with you soon. Let me hear from you as soon as convenient, & give me every particular respecting my late much loved sister & her dear children. My wife is but poorly. She sympathizes most sincerely with you & with me, & desires to be remembered. Farewell. Your sincere friend and brother,

RUSSELL SCOTT.

Addressed: "John Taylor, No. 1 St. James Sq., Bristol."

As the following two letters refer to Mrs. Taylor, they are inserted here, though of rather later date than some that succeed them.

Miss MARY STEELE *to* Rev. RUSSELL SCOTT.

BROUGHTON, *March* 13, 1795.

SIR,—I must have appeared very negligent & unfriendly in not noticing the Message you sent me by Mrs. Howe concerning your much loved Sister's Drawings. When Mr. Taylor first mentioned it to me I told him I should be greatly obliged for any single piece, but that I by no means wished to monopolize them all, as there were other Friends of my Dr Mrs. T.'s to whom they would be equally valuable. He sent them however all. . . . I wish I knew which you would prefer; if you recollect any you particularly wish to select, will you be so kind as to inform me? If not, as their chief value to us both arises from the Consciousness of the Dear Hand that formed them, I will divide them as equally as I can between us, & send them to your direction. . . . Oh Sir, how inexplicable are the dispensations of Providence!—What a fate was Our Ever Beloved, ever Lamented Friend's! How was her Genius depressed, her Virtues hidden, the generous, the exquisite sensibilities of her heart tortured! But why all this to you,—pardon me—it seems to soothe a heart, big with a thousand fond recollections, to be addressing one to whom she was equally dear. Oh, may my spirit be permitted to recognize her in that World of Bliss she now inhabits, whose Memory will be cherished & revered till the summons to follow her arrives.

I was very sorry that I was so unfortunate as to miss seeing you in Somersetshire, but I hope you & Mrs. Scott will favor me with a Visit at my solitary Abode. It would give me sincere pleasure to see you here; Summer has rendered it a little pleasanter. I hope Mr. T. will bring the D[r] Children to see me. I cannot help flattering myself that Mary Ann at least will not inherit his Rigidity, though she should be bred a Quaker, yet I fear Mr. T.'s System must be peculiarly baneful to such a Mind as hers seemed to promise to be even at so early a period. Perhaps she may one Day thank us for preserving every little memorial of her Dear Mother.

I beg my respectful Compts to Mrs. Scott, & sincerely wishing you every personal & domestic felicity, am, Sir, Your Obliged Humble Servant, M. STEELE.

Miss MARY STEELE *to* Rev. RUSSELL SCOTT.

Nov[r] 20th, 1795.

D[R] SIR,—I must have appeared very negligent & unfriendly, I doubt, in so long deferring to send the Drawings. . . . I have divided them as equally as I could between us, as Mr. Taylor told me he did not wish that any of them should be sent to Sherborne. I shall send 2 boxes of them according to your direction by Rook's Waggon from Romsey on Tuesday next. I thought it best to write by Post to inform you of it. I sincerely thank you for your very kind Letter. I read it with feelings congenial to your own. To the latest hour of life your beloved Sister's Memory will be dear to me, & it was a soothing, sad indulgence to weep over the Effusion of a Brother's Sorrow for her. Nothing but the full Conviction of her Earthly Comfort being for ever destroyed could have reconciled my Mind even in the degree it is to our separation—tho indeed there is one thought that above all others should check the rising murmur, that it is the Will of God.

You know, I presume, that I was favoured with a Visit from the Dear Children—& you will imagine what I felt, when folding the Dear Girl in my Arms, I could scarcely help fancying her Blessed Mother was looking down upon us from the Regions of felicity. Notwithstanding the restraints of Education I could trace many resembling traits in her Infant Mind. They both of them appear to me to possess Capacities much above the common. Ah! how much is it to be regretted that their opening faculties should be cramped by that cold & rigid System their Father has adopted. A Love of Truth & Benevolence, however, he will assiduously endeavour to instil.—I find he is not removed from Bristol, & mean soon to enquire for their welfare, which my Absence has prevented for some time. I earnestly wished to know the fate of the Papers, but could not take the liberty of speaking to Mr. T. on the Subject when I saw him.

I should be happy to have an interview with you either Here or at Yeovil. . . . I hope we may one day mutually augment the little treasure so dear to Affection; my Stock, alas, is but small, tho to me invaluable. . . . I beg my Compts to Mrs. Scott, and am, D[r] Sir, with the sincerest good wishes, y[r] Obliged &c. M. Steele.

Addressed: "Rev. Russell Scott, Portsmouth, Hants."

Very little is now known concerning Mrs. Taylor's married life; that it was far from happy is evident from the two preceding letters; but how this came to be so is a most puzzling question. Her husband was to the end devotedly attached to her—this we learnt from their daughter—and he continued to be attached to her memory, as his son said many years later, "perhaps more than any person ever was who had been so long a widower." Yet Miss Steele, and apparently my grandfather also, believed that it was he who was responsible for the unhappiness of the marriage. This is curious, as the impression given by Mrs. Taylor's letters, written before her marriage, is that she had great faults of temper, and showed a want of forbearance towards him such as might go far to ruin the peace of their home.

On the other hand Mr. Taylor certainly felt that he had been in fault, for we find him in a letter, written long after to his daughter, mourning over what he called his "duplicity of conduct and carelessness of his wife's peace."

No doubt great trouble arose from the fact that they were not in sympathy in their religious opinions. We have seen how greatly she had dreaded any such difference of opinion. She had said (p. 58) that as a consequence of it "misery seemed almost inevitable." And her worst fears were to be realised. Mr. Taylor continued as before to make "new schemes and systems of religion," and two years after their marriage he became a Quaker. Perhaps it was chiefly by this "cold and rigid system" that, as Miss Steele believed, her friend's "earthly comfort was forever destroyed."

Quite late in life Mr. Taylor is said to have become a Swedenborgian.

The letters to his daughter, of which a good many follow, show how tender Mr. Taylor was as a father, and it is certain that the children's early home was a happy one. The following verses, written by his daughter many years later, show what was her feeling towards him:—

A Fragment

Mancunium! where my childish days
  Were spent in sweet serene content;
Where knowledge pour'd its early rays,
  And hope its bright illusions lent;

Where many a sweet and social bliss
  'Twas mine to taste, 'twas mine to feel,
And friendships form'd in days of peace,
  Whose fervour yet has known no chill;

Where on my head paternal love,
  With fond peculiar tenderness,
Would call down blessings from above,
  And be itself the chief to bless;

Where now his dear remains repose,
  In the cold bosom of the earth;
While still in many a bosom glows
  The loved remembrance of his worth;

Oh! all unlovely as thou art,
  Mancunium, I must love thee well;
These memories bind thee to my heart
  With an indissoluble spell.

CHAPTER VI

SAMUEL SCOTT OF SHERBORNE—REV. RUSSELL SCOTT AND HIS WIFE

1782–1808

In the preceding chapter I have mentioned all that is known of the daughter of John Scott of Milborne Port. Of the two sons, Samuel was the elder. He was a woolstapler in Sherborne (from which town Milborne Port is about two miles distant), and had a woollen factory there. He married Grace Downing, one of seven sisters, daughters of Mrs. Betty Downing, of whom it is remembered that they all married in order of age, before they were twenty-five. He had twelve children, of whom four died in infancy.

No pleasant remembrance of him remains. My father had a vivid recollection of his surliness at home, especially to his wife and his son Russell. The eldest son, Samuel, went to America to escape the evils of home, and lived there, unmarried, to the end of his life. Russell, the second son, was mentally deficient, and to him the father was very harsh. His third son, Robert, became a chemist at Bath. His wife was a most amiable woman. "How very few much younger women possess her sweetness and liveliness of disposition," once wrote her daughter-in-law. Yet my father used to say that he had rarely heard his uncle speak otherwise than roughly to her. For a view of him in early life, see the letter from his sister Mary, dated May 7, 1777. Later we find his niece Sophia writing of him: "The love of money is the rock on which Uncle's good qualities have suffered woeful shipwreck."

His daughters were known to us in our early life when we visited them at Sherborne. Those who did not marry lived till their death in the house in Long Street, which their father had built.

The second son of John Scott of Milborne Port was my grandfather, the first Russell Scott. The following account of his life was given to me by my father. I wrote down a good deal of it in his own words, sitting beside him in the garden at the Manor House, Eastbourne, and have gathered a few other particulars from letters and other sources.

My grandfather was born at Milborne Port, Somerset, on April 26, 1760. He was fourteen years old when his father died. Little is known of his education, except that he went at about sixteen to the Dissenting Academy at Daventry, and later to the Academy at Homerton. This was an orthodox Dissenting Academy; here my grandfather's opinions changed in the direction of Arianism. As to the doctrinal position of his parents and of himself in early youth, we have little information, but in the Appendix will be seen the "Church Covenant" of the "Congregation of Protestant Dissenters" at Milborne Port, which my grandfather signed at the age of nineteen. He left Homerton in consequence of his change of views, and completed his divinity studies at Hoxton Academy, under Dr. Kippis.

Since 1662, when the Act of Uniformity was passed, the Nonconformists had been shut out from the national Universities, but had been determined to secure for their young men, as far as possible, an education equal to that of which they were deprived. Hence arose a remarkable succession of Academies, conducted at first by individual men. Later, in 1757, Warrington Academy was founded, from which Manchester College (now at Oxford) has sprung. It was the principle of this Academy that instruction should be given in all the subjects pursued at the Universities, and no obligation whatever was laid on the students, or on their teachers, in regard to their theological opinions.

My sister remembers that Dr. Martineau more than once spoke of the very great success of these Academies in imparting a liberal education, especially to those who were being trained for the ministry. He said the Dissenters at that time were determined, as far as possible, to have a learned ministry.

In 1782 and 1783 we find my grandfather in London. He was then studying medicine in the hospitals, wishing to acquire a little medical experience in case he should settle as a minister in some country district, where there might be no doctor within reach of the poor.

In London it was, no doubt, that my grandfather made the acquaintance of the Rev. Theophilus Lindsey, one of the most valued of his early friends.

Mr. Lindsey had been for many years the greatly beloved Vicar of Catterick in Yorkshire, but had resigned his living in 1773, having become convinced that the doctrine of the Trinity was unscriptural. This sacrifice was made when by doing so he gave up that on which he depended for a maintenance, and incurred the disapprobation of nearly all his friends. A most interesting account of him and of his wife, and of the mental trials involved in this decision, is given in Mrs. Cappe's "Memoirs." He founded Essex Street Chapel, London, now Essex Hall, and was minister there for many years.

It is pleasant to read in the following letters Mr. Lindsey's account of my grandfather as he was at this time—a very different account from that which his sister had to give of him in her letter of November 30, 1776.

Rev. T. Lindsey *to* Miss Scott.

London, *July* 2, 1782.

. . . Any little civilities that it has been in my way to show to your brother he is well entitled to from the seriousness of his disposition and that honest ingenuous mind and love of truth which appears to be, and I trust will remain and grow, in him. In the part, however, which he has taken, he will have difficulties to encounter with, which you also have experienced, and which every one must expect who is constrained to go contrary to the religious sentiments of others, especially on points which those others, unfortunately and mistakenly, think to be essential to salvation, whereas no opinions whatsoever are absolutely necessary to recommend us to the favour of God, but only sincerity in seeking his truth, and in following it in our lives when we have found it.

I am in good hope that one most near & dear to you may some time or other see in this light the sentiments which you and your brother have been led to embrace from searching the Scriptures of truth for yourselves.[1] But should it be otherwise,

[1] This probably alludes to their having given up belief in the doctrine of the Trinity.

you will make all due allowances for long associations of ideas and narrow habits of thinking, which many persons, otherwise of great improved abilities and learning, can never break through, even when the strongest and most glaring evidence is placed before them. We are to love Christ more than father and mother; but then it is a part of our christian duty always to honour and repay that affection to parents which is due to them.

I write now in expectation of your brother calling upon me, and am interrupted so that I can add no more, but my hopes that his health may be confirmed in the country, and that you may be a mutual comfort and support to each other. I remain with sincere esteem, Madam, your friend and servant,

T. LINDSEY.

Addressed: "For Miss Scott, Milborne Port, Somerset."

The same to the same.

LONDON, *Nov^r* 4, 1783.

D^a MADAM,— . . . I hope it will please God in his kind providence to restore you to the enjoyment of perfect health: but should the fatherly discipline be longer continued, you know the hand from which it comes, and how to improve it.

Your good brother is most intent upon his medical pursuits, so that they leave him no vacant moments at all. I hope the application will not be prejudicial to him, and was glad to see him look so well the other day in the midst of it when he called upon us. I am sorry to be constrained to be short at this time, your brother being to be here tomorrow morning for this letter for you, and I not having found leisure to write it till a few minutes ago, since he told me of the opportunity of sending it to you. I hope and have no doubt but your happiness will continually increase in the friendship of such a brother, so seriously disposed, and bent upon the best things, and so diligent and industrious.

At all times any little services of mine are at your command; for I am with a sincere esteem, very sincerely yours

T. LINDSEY.

My grandfather had, when studying medicine, become intimate with the family of Dr. William Hawes, of 8 Spital Square, Bishopsgate Street, and in 1783 was engaged to Dr. Hawes' eldest daughter, Sophia. He was twenty-three years old, and she a year younger. The engagement lasted seven years.

On the fly-leaf of an old commonplace book I found the following, written in my grandfather's shorthand—

"'Two friends here met in unity of heart,
Here met indeed—but only met to part.'

Taken from the window at Hornsey Wood. July 25th 1785. These lines only struck me amongst many others as I was walking up and down the room; I instantly showed them to my much beloved Sophia, and then wrote them down, and have placed them here that I may not forget them."

From the lines having been scratched on a window, it was probably at an inn that my grandfather found them. His Sophia must have been in the room with him, for he instantly showed them to her. This one little incident is all that has come down to us of the history of the seven years' engagement. No letters of that time remain, and my father could tell me nothing of it.

It was in 1788 that my grandfather was settled as minister of the High Street Chapel, Portsmouth, his first charge having been at Wrington, near Bristol. His predecessor in the ministry at Portsmouth was

Dr. Wren, of whom my father remembered hearing that he had received the thanks of the United States Congress for the aid he had given to American prisoners in making their escape.

Sophia Hawes, my grandmother, lived for five years before her marriage with her great-uncle, Benjamin Hawes, in the parish of St. Mary, Islington. The old man had lost his wife, and for some years she took the place of a daughter to him; probably it was on his account that for two years after my grandfather was settled at Portsmouth the marriage was still postponed. When the uncle died, they were married, 4th May 1790. She was a devoted wife and mother, and my father always held her memory in the highest veneration. When I asked him for further particulars about her, his lips trembled as he answered, "She was one of the very best of women." This was his only reply.

My grandparents lived in the High Street, Portsmouth. From the year 1804 till their death they occupied a house which after some years my grandfather purchased, and which he bequeathed to his son. My father gave it to my brother Russell, and it has since been sold. It is on the same side of the High Street as the chapel, and is the second or third house from the chapel to the left as you face it. The number of the house is now 125. It contains two rooms only on each floor (six in all), with also a kitchen and servant's room built out at the back. It is a well-built little house, and has not been altered since my grandfather lived there.

The family life was of course exceedingly simple.

My father said of his father: "Never was there a more studiously careful and economical man." His salary, my father said, never exceeded £130 a year, and at one time was considerably less, and though both he and his wife had a little private property, about £3000 between them, his income was considerably under £300 a year.

It was no doubt owing to his care in the management of this small income that he always had, as I believe was the case, some part of it to spare for others. He was generous both from temperament and from principle, and taught his son to feel that to spend a part of what he earned on others was a duty. The family too were most hospitable, and we find in the letters very frequent mention of the friends who were staying with them.

One of the very few indulgences that my grandfather allowed himself was the buying of books. He was a great reader, and loved his books. In course of time they covered the walls of his small library in double rows, and filled many shelves in other rooms, and on the landings of the staircase. He left, I believe, * about six thousand volumes. Books at that time were not easily obtainable in country towns; there was, however, a "Reading Society" in connection with my grandfather's congregation, of which he was secretary; and the monthly meetings were held at his house. Books were obtained from London, passed round amongst the members, and after being read, were sold by auction among them. Theology was excluded. Many of the books in his library were bought on these occasions.

My grandfather was a man of strong political views,

* This is a mistake. The number of these volumes [illegible]

a decided partisan of reform in Parliament, at a time when it had few supporters, and opposed to the then existing penal laws and to many abuses which have since been removed.

Dr. Priestley, shortly before he left for America in April 1794, knowing my grandfather's opinions, said to him that he (Dr. Priestley) would soon see him there; but my grandfather never felt that things had come to such a pass as to make that step necessary. He watched, however, with anxiety the trial for treason (in the same year) of Horne Tooke, Hardy, and Thelwall, considering that an adverse verdict would be such a blow to freedom of speech in England as to make him think seriously of settling in America. His sister-in-law, Miss Sarah Hawes, remained with Mrs. Thelwall in the Old Bailey, awaiting the verdict of the jury. The accused were acquitted.

Political feeling ran higher at that time than the present generation can easily imagine, and there was a great amount of espionage. My grandfather and Sir John Carter had reason to believe that even the number of calls they exchanged in one particular week was reported to the Government. Sir John Carter was a leading Whig in the town, a great friend of my grandfather's, and a member of his congregation.

My grandfather was a burgess of Portsmouth, one of the old close boroughs. The burgesses were appointed for life, and their number seldom exceeded twenty, and these, with the Mayor and Aldermen, about thirty-five men in all, elected the two representatives of Portsmouth in Parliament. The Corporation was a very exceptional one; its representatives in Parliament during a long series of years, when Tory principles were in the ascendant, being in the Opposition. My father was made a burgess on coming of age, a strong testimony to the confidence felt by the Aldermen—in whose hands the appointment lay —in the stability of the liberal principles instilled into him by my grandfather. How little freedom of speech there was in England at this time is clearly shown in the following extract from Belsham's "Life of Theophilus Lindsey" (p. 352):—

"Mr. Lindsey sympathized deeply with those political characters who, whatever indiscretions some of them might be chargeable with, suffered from that which, in his estimation, was the overstrained rigour of the law both in Scotland and England, penalties far beyond the demerit of any crime which could be proved against them. Among these sufferers, the person on whose behalf Mr. Lindsey was in the highest degree interested was the Rev. Thos. Fyshe Palmer . . . a Fellow of Queen's College, Cambridge . . . a man of excellent understanding, unimpeachable morals, and of great simplicity of character . . . a zealous friend to liberty. . . . He was concerned in the republication of an Address to the People of Scotland concerning the Reform of Parliament; for which, in the autumn of 1793, he was tried by the Circuit Court of Justiciary; & being convicted, a sentence was passed upon him . . . of transportation for seven years to Botany Bay." . . . Mr. Lindsey writes in a letter dated Dec. 14, 1793: "Mr. Muir and Mr. Palmer are on board the hulks with the felons, and many of my friends have been to see them. I also hear from Mr.

Palmer & have sent him some books. . . . The situation is upon the whole horrible. Mr. Palmer, however, is most cheerful in the midst of it, and Mr. Muir not otherwise . . . both of them supported by their integrity and future hopes."

They were detained for a time off Portsmouth, where my grandfather, Mr. Lindsey says, "was indefatigable in offices of kindness to these persecuted reformers, while the ship which conveyed them remained at Spithead." They sailed on May 3, 1794—never to return.

Rev. THEOPHILUS LINDSEY *to* Rev. RUSSELL SCOTT.

LONDON, *March* 26th, 1793.

DEAR SIR,—. . . Both my wife & I are greatly concerned at the very infirm state of your health, owing to that radical gouty indisposition, which seems to have been born with you. And we really think that you would do well to look out, if there be anything which you can do in the way of business, or in which Mrs. Scott may be able to bear a part, and to embrace it. Any thing of this kind, mercantile or any other, I am very far from thinking incompatible with the duty of a teacher of the gospel, or to disqualify for it. And with regard to Sermons, I think you should not be nice about giving your own compositions, but transcribe with little alteration, unless perhaps of the text, from Jortin, Secker, Pyle, Duchall, etc. etc. with now and then some little addition, and not much, which would be particularly applicable to your congregation, and make it sufficiently your own.

With respect to Dissenting ministers I do not think that matters are likely to mend in this country but the contrary. Through fears of the world, or of being singular, or now to recommend themselves to the reigning powers, their rich members will desert them, as they have begun to do in some places already, through the influence of the court and the fear of losing their places under it. And they will be more and more scouted and ill-treated by Churchmen. On the Sunday before last, the 17th, at Chowbent, Mr. H. Toulmin tells me, that in the midst of service, a recruiting party, (who with their attendants had been parading at 11 and 12 o'clock on the Saturday night, with torches, and huzzaing and knocking at the houses of Dissenters) passed by the Chapel with drums and fifes, and shoutings when opposite to it, crying "down with the rump," so as to hinder him from going on till they had done; and after service, a party of the rabble waited to lay hold on him to put a cockade in his hat, as they had forced many of the congregation, but being apprized of their design, he escaped out by another door. And Mr. Chandler of Gloucester told me on Sunday that he had heard thence from Mr. Tremlett that there was an information lodged against Mr. H. Toulmin, for something said in conversation. Such are the times we seem dropt into, within a year, but which unfortunately seem as if they would last. . . . We rejoice that Mrs. Scott & your little boy are quite well & yourself better. Accept our kind regards to yourselves and best wishes for him. . . .

The "little boy" was my grandfather's first child, Russell, born 1791. His second child, whose birth is mentioned in the following letter, was Sophia Russell.

Rev. RUSSELL SCOTT *to his Sister-in-law.*

PORTSMOUTH, *Sep.* 13, 1793.

MY DEAR SARAH,—You will find by my letter to your Father that I stand engaged to write to you by this day's post, and I am happy to communicate a continuance of the same favourable appearances which I mentioned yesterday. Mr. Taswell says we shall finish our campaign with much greater credit than the army is likely to do before Dunkirk. . . . Though this said damsel did not come into the world with that commanding appearance which attended her brother's entrance into life, yet she is a large fine fat child, much in the common run of new-born infants. . . .

The same to the same, a week later.

You deserve a letter & therefore I sit down to write you a line or two. . . . Yesterday morning a box came from Gosport, directed to me. On opening it I discovered its contents were for my two Sophias; I instantly carried all upstairs. My wife desires me to say she likes the bonnet in reality very much and that she thinks the caps very pretty ones. She says she must write you a lecture on the subject, and to tell you my opinion on the subject there is great occasion for one. . . . Your next letter from hence will I hope be written by your sister herself, and if in the fervour of her displeasure she should omit to send my acknowledgements for this mark of your affectionate attention to her and her babe, I beg you to accept them now.

Russell is very well, and becomes daily more and more engaging. He was at Meeting this afternoon and behaved very well while they were singing & during 17 minutes of my sermon; being then tired of holding his tongue he gave the signal for going out. . . . You will remember us affectionately to your father and brothers. . . .

Addressed: "Miss Sarah Hawes, Spital Square, London."

Rev. T. LINDSEY *to* Rev. RUSSELL SCOTT.

LONDON, *May 6th*, 1794.

DEAR SIR,—I should not have written to-day, as I have so little time left for it, if I had not got a bit of a frank for you, which however will suit the dimensions of my letter.

There are a few characters, who by their benevolent dispositions, and upright, manly, generous conduct, compel one's affectionate regards and esteem the more you see and know them, and these have always been mine and my wife's feelings towards yourself, so that you are not to wonder that we are at any time desirous of expressing our regards. . . .

My wife has just come back from the Exhibition, but the crowd and stifling were so great that without much difficulty she could not move along. Dr. Priestley's picture by Morland she does not like at all. It seems that by Opie is not in the Exhibition. . . .

The same to the same.

June 30, 1794.

Dear Sir,—We are relieved by having some little account of you at last; though it is not so good as we could have wished; but we hope that the proposed expedition to the west will recruit both father and daughter, and rejoice that the good mother needs it not immediately, though the change of air must be of benefit. . . . No direct accounts, nor indeed any accounts here have been received, nor it is said, could yet be received of Dr. Priestley's arrival in America. In about ten days, or a fortnight, it may be looked for.

You will hear, if you have not already heard, of many migrations out of the west among Dissenters—some who have already suffered or are threatened, and others willing to get out of the storm which they think to be coming. . . . I suppose you will procure as long a furlow as you can. *Our* kind regards and every good wish attend the travellers, and I remain always, Dear Sir, affectionately yours, T. Lindsey.

My grandfather's brothers-in-law, Thomas and Benjamin Hawes, were soapmakers, but probably not at this time, as in the following remarkable letter mention is made of a purchase of starch. My grandparents assisted them, by placing the whole of their small capital, £3000, in their hands.

BENJAMIN HAWES *to* REV. RUSSELL SCOTT.

LONDON, *January* 6, 1796.

FRIEND SCOTT,—The early trial of your friendship induces me to request a Letter of attorney for the remainder of your reduced [annuities]. It may perhaps appear extraordinary to apply so early. If you consider the enormous prices of starch—& that we have this day made a purchase of 2600 lbs., which quantity I have often bought for £820; that in consequence of the manufacture of starch being stopped we purchase all we can procure, your surprise may cease.—This, my Dear Friend, is a part of (forgive me) the present damnable & ruinous politics pursued by our Heaven-Born minister [Pitt] (another time let us prefer a Hell-Born). The astonishing prices of goods transforms the great traders & speculators into sharks who live by swallowing up the small fish, who, if they live now, is owing to good fortune or clemency. We class ourselves (with vanity) among the higher orders of tradesman, & he certainly is enabling us to procure very great profits; but if we had had £10,000 unemployed in business, we could have made that in one week, with ease & certainty, £20,000. Can you then wonder at the monied interest, at the large & extensive commercial interest, who owing to the distress, the ruin, and confined capitals of others, are making money in this city almost by cartloads, supporting this wicked, this accursed, and I hope ever to be execrated minister? No, my dear friend. No wonder that commerce by enlightened men is severely judged; it harrows the soul, it habitually, by constantly reflecting on what I can get, sees scarcely thro' any medium but interest. We do not expect to want your friendship further, but having made very extensive engagements we wish to have some certain supplies in case our usual resources fail us. Excuse me for not saying more than necessary, having at present too much on my head & hand, & writing this at 12 o'clk on Tuesday night, as I shall not have time to-morrow. I am, with best affections to all, Yours,

BENJAMIN HAWES.

BENJAMIN HAWES *to* REV. RUSSELL SCOTT.

Jan. 19th, 1796.

MY DEAR FRIEND,—I received your kind attention to my request in course, & believe words between us are quite unnecessary. I hope we shall be able to do without it, but I fear we must stretch every resource, though we mean to keep a corps of reserve, fearing unexpected calls. The magnitude of my purchases alarms me, & makes me reflect on the old saying "few have [been] injured from doing too little, but many too much." However at present we see our way clear. I have recovered my health, & tho' I have miscarried in two important events[1] of my life, & am amidst greater exertions & a much larger portion of care, I feel a lightness of heart, a pleasure arising from social pursuits, which my situation before prevented. I perceive that our opinions of mankind are formed from our heart. I have received instances & many *proofs* of sincere well-wishing, which tho' my heart is guarded against the deceptions of the artful knave, yet am I certain there is genuine friendship. If unfortunately our affairs should take an unsuccessful turn, which to all probable appearances is very unlikely, rest assured you shall have a hint, & be careful you take it.

I hope you have taken advantage of this fine weather; do—if you think not your health of sufficient importance to yourself—do, for the sake of those you love, embrace every opportunity of exercise; encourage it in your son; set him the example of activity; remember that health & strength gives vigor to the mind, fortifies us in the hour of temptation, & frequently prevents us falling victims to vices that result from ill health & weakness.—Remember swimming & running is better than dancing

[1] One of these events was no doubt his marriage, which was a most unfortunate one. The story of it, as I heard it, was that he was engaged to be married, when a mutual acquaintance made mischief between him and his intended wife. His engagement was broken off, and six weeks after he married the second lady, and repented almost as soon as it was done. She made his home most uncomfortable, and in later life gave way to intemperance.

& Latin, that arithmetic & writing is better than the Classics. As I suppose you mean your son for Trade, cultivate & improve every opportunity to instruct in writing & arithmetic, in health, caution & prudence.

Excuse this hasty & crude address, & remember me affectionately to all. . . .

The following letter to his sister was dictated by Russell, the eldest child of my grandfather, at the age of four years and four months. Sophia was staying at her grandfather's, Dr. Wm. Hawes, 8 Spital Square, London.

PORTSMOUTH, *Feby* 24, 1796.

MY DEAR SISTER,—I beg of you to thank my Aunt Maria & Aunt Sarah for the letters they have taken the trouble to write to me. I hope you are well, my dear Sister, & I beg my Aunt Maria & Aunt Sarah will *date* my letters. The great dog dont live [at] the next house. My Papa sends you a thousand kisses & wishes to see you very much. He had so bad a cough that he could hardly preach last Sunday & his head was bad, but he is much better to day. I learn Grammar at school & I can tell you what it is. Grammar is the art of using any words according to certain established rules, & I can tell you, sister, what is the difference between General Grammar & Universal Grammar, & English Grammar. Grammar in general & Universal Grammar explains the principles which are common to all languages. I could say more but Mamma thinks I had better not. All my schoolfellows said on Monday the French were *landed* at Spithead & one of them was afraid. Eleven of us were to fight for my Governess & she said we were stout fellows, & John Pike & Edward Pike & Russell Scott & a great many more of them. We have got a bad pen, sister, but we will try to fill the paper with all the words I can put in. The letters I write at school are—R—V—N—M—I—L—D—s. The last letter I wrote you was not [written] by Mr. Savery but by Miss Wilkinson (Hannah's sister). Beg of my Aunts to write me some letters, for I like them very much, & you, sister, answer me my letters. George Porter *did* send you some kisses by my Uncle & I *wonder* he did not give them to ye. Amen. Your affec^ate^ Brother, RUSSELL SCOTT.

P.S.—I am just going to bed, & I beg you will excuse me for not saying any more. O, dear Sister I forgot to tell you I am reading such a pretty book. I am reading it to my Mamma, Hannah, & to Miss Wilkinson. It is entitled the "History of the four Robins." [1] It gives an account of boys who take birds' nests & throw the young cats from the house, drown puppies in their mother's sight, & pull legs off flies, set cocks fighting, blind them, pull the feathers from chickens & a great many other things; but there is one girl & boy that know better than this naughty boy, Master Jenkins is his name. Now I must go to bed, really I must, my dear Sister.

Fifteen months after this letter was written the little boy died, to the very great grief of his parents, of water on the brain. He was a child of great promise. He was buried in the graveyard of the Chapel in the High Street, always called the Meeting-house yard, and his name is still to be seen on the tombstone erected to the memory of his father and mother, on the left hand side of the entrance door. My grandfather's old friend, the Rev. Theophilus Lindsey, wrote:—

LONDON, *July* 1, 1797.

DEAR SIR,—We were most truly affected on hearing from worthy Mr. Porter of your late loss of a most beloved and promising son, but have felt inexpressibly more for you on reading your own most moving narrative of your tender anxieties whilst there was any hope of life and endeavours to preserve it; and in seeing the humble and kindly submission of the parents to

[1] By Mrs. Trimmer.

POST CARD

THE ADDRESS TO BE WRITTEN ON THIS SIDE

POSTCODE

A person who makes blue pigment, paint-
dye etc especially one who makes laundry blue

orchall + Indigo Blue Maker

such an awful and afflictive providence, when the delight of their eyes, and for whose increasing virtue and future usefulness they had formed the most well-grounded hopes, was taken away from them. . . . I cannot tell you how much I was interested in a child of such hopes, and so amiable, from the incidental mention you had sometimes made of him. . . .

The following letter was written by the Rev. Rochemont Barbauld, the husband of Mrs. Barbauld, the authoress. The beautiful dirge written by her after his death, "Pure Spirit! O where art thou now?" may be remembered.

The young ladies mentioned in the letter were, the one a sister of Mrs. Scott's, and the other a niece of my grandfather's, the second daughter of Samuel Scott of Sherborne, who were then both paying a long visit to Portsmouth.

Rev. ROCHEMONT BARBAULD *to* Rev. RUSSELL SCOTT.

HAMPSTEAD, *December* 22[d], 1800.

DEAR SIR,—The opinion which I trust you have formed of me & the candour which is one of the characteristic features of your mind have, it is my hope, prevented your being led by unfavourable appearances to suspect me of either not having felt, or else having forgotten, the kindness with which you received the stranger & treated him as a brother. You have, I do not doubt it, done me the justice to suppose what is really the case, that ever since my return hither I have longed to express my thanks to you, Sir, & to Mrs. Scott, but have been hindered by occupations and engagements accumulated by my absence from home. I can assure you with truth, that you & your amiable family have been almost daily present to my thoughts. My heart delights in recollecting that under your roof I have enjoyed the satisfaction of becoming acquainted with persons whom to know is to love & to esteem; the pleasures of unreserved, rational, instructive, interesting & cheerful conversation, & the joy of acquiring that truly valuable treasure, a new friend, in whom are found all that cordial sympathy & active zeal, which we expect only from an old friend; & besides, that agreement of opinion and feeling in all important points, & that similarity of mind as to the mode of thinking & viewing objects, which form one of the strongest cements that can unite souls together. My being obliged to go to Portsmouth, which at the time appeared to me an irksome task, full of trouble & vexation, has turned out one of those events, which my mind dwells upon with gratitude & pleasure; for it has proved the occasion of my lighting upon what I have not frequently met with, a man after my own heart. . . .

And now, dear Sir, I hope you will allow me to beg your acceptance of a few books, which I have happened to mention to you, & the perusal of which will, if I mistake not, afford you entertainment, & even no small satisfaction on some interesting points; at least they have done so to me. Permit me next to entreat you to prevail on Mrs. Scott to wear for my sake the Norwich shawl which accompanies these books, & will prove comfortable perhaps during the wintry season. . . . Desirous also as I am of contributing to little Sophia's amusement & improvement, I have presumed to complete her set of "Evenings at Home," & to add to it the new edition of "The Parent's Assistant." If I have by this provided for some years to come rather than for the present, I trust to her candour and *wisdom* that *Sophia* will take it in good part. Miss Scott expressed a wish of seeing a new French grammar, which, I told her, was very well spoken of by proper judges; & this has induced me to venture upon getting a copy which, in the hope of its answering her purpose, I assume the freedom of sending, convinced, that she too well deserves her name [Grace] and is too *gracious* not to accept in a kind manner what is offered out of sincere regard. As I have much at heart not to be forgotten by Miss Hawes, I should think *that* a very fortunate circumstance which should lead her to associate her remembrance of me with her contemplation of the stars; & therefore I would beg of you to obtain of her to accept from me as a keepsake the Astrarium, which must have reached Portsmouth, I imagine, a fortnight ago & upwards. Mr. Johnson at my request consulted respecting it Mr. Bonnycastle, who is of opinion, that it is not ill adapted to answer the purpose you have in view, & who gave the preference to the one that was sent. If this lady, & dear Mrs. Scott & Miss Grace and my young friend & you, dear Sir, will do me the kindness not to reject these trifles, but to consider them as small tokens of affectionate remembrance, meant to express my wish of being sometimes in the thoughts of those whom I shall never forget, I shall deem it an additional proof of the friendly regard you five have been pleased to testify towards me. . . . I am, dear Sir, Cordially Yours, ROCHEMONT BARBAULD.

The under written charade, turned into verse at my request by my wife, I have just been hatching in the hope that it may serve as a Christmas entertainment:—

My first of a two legged bear is the name;
If I give you an inch, you the second will claim;
For the third my heart glows with affection's pure flame.

I expect an answer in verse to this charade. . . . The parcel in which this letter is to be enclosed ought to contain, besides the shawl, the following books:—

Guthrie's Geography 4to & Maps to ditto folio
Brooke's Gazetteer
Collection of Hymns
Campbell's Lectures, 2 vols
Thoughts on the Divine Goodness
Modest Apology
Aiken on the Cow-Pox
Parent's Assistant, 6 vols bound in 4
Evenings at Home, vols 4th 5th 6th
Lévizac's French Grammar

On February 3, 1801, my father was born. His sister was seven years old, and his birth was a source of great thankfulness and rejoicing. He was named Russell, like his brother. At five months old he was taken to his grandfather's house in Spital Square, to be baptized by the Rev. T. Lindsey, who had also baptized the elder boy.

Miss M. A. HAWES *to* GRACE DOWNING SCOTT.

[PORTSMOUTH, *Spring* 1801.]

MY DEAR MISS SCOTT,—You see by the length of my paper & the size of my writing that I am in a fair way of performing my promise, which if I fulfill to the extent of my present intention I shall give you credit for a considerable share of patience, if you are not tired of it. You are a strange girl, you say in one of your *little notes* "I feel myself not a little indebted to you"; now do tell me what for & *I* shall feel obliged. You have had several opportunities of writing, neither of which you have availed yourself of as you ought, but follow my example & write me a long letter very soon, for I embrace the very first I have had. My intention was to write by your astrarium, & I have often asked Mr. Scott when he was going to send it. He will I believe send it now, with what he received from your father a few days ago. I am quite glad of it, for I am sure the time you have been without it must have appeared long. Thank you for the pincushion. I "will not indeed refuse it," but accept with pleasure as coming from you. I am afraid you were very much disappointed if you placed much confidence in the appearance of the candle, for no parcel arrived at Sherborne for you from Portsmouth. How unlucky it was, the Astrarium coming just the morning you left us! As I suppose your Uncle told [you] it was entirely owing to the delay of the persons at the shop it was bought at, & my brothers were surprised to hear it was not in time, as they thought they had taken every necessary step for its being forwarded in proper time.

I think it proper, situated as your heart unfortunately is, to say, painful as the news must be to you, that we have not heard anything of Mr. De B. Do not fret & lose the good looks you got at Portsmouth about it, but remember the old adage "that while there is life there is hope." I am obliged to you for sending me that Winter piece of Campbell's. He is indeed a favourite of mine, as I think he would be of yours if you read his "Pleasures of Hope." Mr. Scott has had it down & it is now in circulation.

You must expect by this time an account of the little boy; he is indeed a fine fellow, & of his age a great boy, he is good humoured & to us a very pleasing child, quite a little fatty, but as lively as any little thin child need to be. . . . We go on much the same as while you were here, except the rogue of a boy puts us out of the way a little sometimes, but so pleasing an intruder of our usual occupations cannot prove an unwelcome one. I wish you were here to see him. You would make an excellent nurse with your strength. . . .

You will be told the truth, you say, respecting my health. You are very good in thus wishing to hear of me. I am really I think better. What delightful weather we have! I am delighted at the approach of spring, but to you it must be doubly pleasant, for you are in the country & can see all its rich variety. I wish I could borrow a cap of some fairy (but these unfortunately are not fairy days) that would transport me to you for a pleasant walk or two. Oh! the country has attractions to me which London with all its splendour & gaiety never can have.—But Portsmouth is exceedingly pleasant in comparison with the Metropolis.—I have neither gone on "briskly" with shorthand or astronomy, for we have really been more engaged than you can suppose, from one thing to another, but now the days get longer we are to do better. For a week past I have staid an hour with Mr. S., which has been devoted to the globes, & I am to read to him on astronomy after dinner till tea.[1] If we keep to this plan

[1] My father said with reference to this, that dinner was at 3 o'clock and tea at 5.

we shall do very well. I am writing out the glossary from Bonnycastle, which you did, & intend getting up & doing some of it before breakfast of a morning. . . .

I have some intention of purchasing a pair of globes on my return to London (where I shall be very glad to see you) to do some problems on them. We have been quite unlucky at our star-gazing, for we have scarcely had to say one star-light night, for we have not caught a glimpse of the milky way. I must now leave off writing. I have thrown open the blinds & yet cannot see. Was I in the habit of making apologies I should for this letter, but I have written quite in haste. Present my compliments to your mother & tell her I am very glad to hear she is so well; & assure her of my sincere wishes for the continuance of her health. Adieu. Yours very affectionately,

MARY A. HAWES.

The use of vaccination had been at this time very recently discovered. Jenner's first experiments were made in 1796. No doctor in Portsmouth would use the new method, and my grandfather himself vaccinated his child.

Mrs. SCOTT *to her Sister*, SARAH HAWES.

PORTSMOUTH, *Decr 29th*, 1802.

MY DEAR SARAH,—As I have just said, in a line or two on Harriet's paper, I have intended to write to you most days since you left us, as every hour appeared to turn up something to relate, few things being uninteresting when we have been in the habit of taking a part in all that passed. If I had related all I felt the propensity to do of dear boy, it would of itself more than filled my sheet.

Friday morning.—I only got on thus far with my good intentions on Wednesday night. Fanny made a stay & I was obliged to get Sophia & dear boy's supper, which, with getting them to bed, fully engaged me till nine.—Poor Sophia passed a bad night & was worse yesterday; to-day she appears better though in considerable pain; it is chiefly in her head and neck, which draws her aside in a most uncomfortable way; I trust we shall get rid of it soon; my spirits are very much inclined to be depressed with this return of it. . . . Dear boy is in full chat with his sister, who is putting the map of England together, and just saying "that is Hertfordshire, Sister." He is now as full of the Counties as he was of his grammar[1]—Sophia has accomplished putting it together since you went, & can call for each county. She desires me to give her love & she is very sorry she cannot write, that she has a great deal to write about her Brother. . . . He is, as you know my dear Sarah, as little trouble as a child can be.—He has not forgot Aunt Sarah. Sometimes he says you will come home, though, when asked, he says Aunt Sarah's gone home London to see Grandpapa & Grandmamma, & that his "Guvness" is gone to Salisbury. I have wished for you very often to see & hear him. On Xmas-day when I had helped him to pudding, having neither fork or spoon laid him, he said so prettily "With my fingers, Mamma?" He gets now to manage his dinner very tolerable. . . .

Xmas has appeared so very, very, little like it that I cannot tell how to persuade myself it is this present season of the year, & I had not a little difficulty to believe it Xmas-day, and that you were all assembled together. We dined at two, as planned, had an early tea and Mr. S. was upstairs soon after five. I set very close to work the evening. Mr. S. came down, he said, to see how I was, I appeared so left to myself. How fortunate you were my dear Sarah in your day for travelling. We took a walk before dinner. . . . We have only taken this walk since you left us, but I really do mean to walk, as well on my own account as Mr. S.'s. I have thought of you in some of your dirty walks since you left us. To-day we are going to dine at Mrs. Crosby's. I have but little inclination to leave Sophia, but Fanny's business is done, and I shall be home to see her to bed. . . . I remain as ever most affectionately your sister,

S. S.

[1] He was under two years old.

My father used to say that he believed he was sent to school at the age of eighteen months, and this probably was so, as it will be noticed that in the preceding letter, written when he was a year and eleven months old, his "governess" is mentioned. The governess was a Miss Wishaw, an early friend of my grandmother's. No doubt this was the school mentioned in the letter of the elder boy. My father was taught there till he was eight or nine years old; after that his father taught him.

The following letter gives the only other glimpse we have of my father in his early childhood. It was written by his mother (when he was six years old) from Spital Square, where she was paying a visit to her father and mother. It was found in my father's desk after his death in 1880.

Mrs. Scott *to her Son.*

[1807.]

Mamma is quite pleased with her dear Russell's letter & glad to find he remembers so much of what he reads about the Kings. Dear Grandmamma and Aunts were all pleased with my dear Russell's letter, & thought he was a very good boy to take so much pleasure in writing & reading. Do you do any sums, my dear, or do you forget them now you read & write so much? How good, my dear, Pappa was to write the copy of your letter for you to save your time when you wanted to write by Mr. Borrel. Your letter, my dear, to your aunt Harriet came to me in bed, & I sent it by your Grandpapa to your Aunt Harriet, who thought you deserved a hat for liking writing so much, & her letter she thought a very good one for such a little boy, & she desires you will send her the remainder of it. Then you must begin again to write to Mamma who likes very much to hear from you. I hope, my

love, you are a very good boy & have almost eaten up all the plums I sent you. I shall soon I hope send you something else for being good. Are you still top in your class? I am my dear boy's very affectionate Mamma,

SOPHIA SCOTT.

The year after this letter was written Dr. Hawes died, and the home at Spital Square was before long broken up. A house at Lavender Hill, Wandsworth, was taken by his son Thomas on a long lease, and to this the family removed.

Dr. Hawes was a man of considerable repute, a friend of Goldsmith's (whom he strongly though vainly urged not to go on taking the famous James' powders which finally caused Goldsmith's death), and was the founder in 1774 of the Royal Humane Society.

In connection with this Society there are two interesting engravings of "A Young Man Restored from Drowning," which came to us from our grandfather's house at Portsmouth. One of them gives a portrait of Dr. Hawes; he is sitting on the bed beside the young man; the other figure is that of Dr. John Lettsom, his friend and fellow physician. The following amusing lines written by Dr. Lettsom are still remembered:—

"When any sick to me apply,
I physics, bleeds and sweats 'em;
If after that they chance to die,
What's that to me? *I. Lettsom.*"

He was the principal founder of the Royal Sea-bathing Infirmary at Margate.

The Royal Humane Society placed to Dr. Hawes' memory a tablet (which still exists) in St. Mary's Church, Islington, with the following quaint inscription :—

To perpetuate,
while this frail marble shall endure,
the meritorious exertions of an individual,
and to excite the emulation of others,
the Governors of
the Royal Humane Society
have caused this tablet
to be inscribed with the name of
WILLIAM HAWES, M.D.
by whose personal and indefatigable labours
an institution honorable to the nation,
and highly beneficial to the world at large,
was founded, fostered, and matured,
and long, very long, may it flourish,
the ornament and the pride of Britain.
This excellent, unassuming,
persevering philanthropist
was born in Islington, Nov. 28, 1736;
died in Spital Square, Dec. 5, 1808;
and was buried on the 13th near these walls.
Go, reader, and imitate those virtuous actions,
which the latest posterity
will applaud and venerate;
and which the recording angel
has registered in Heaven.
Well done, good and faithful servant,
Enter thou into the joy of thy Lord!

His wife died in 1815 at the Lavender Hill house, which continued for many years to be the family home.

We have oil portraits (reproduced on p. 101) both of Dr. Hawes and of his wife Sarah, whose maiden name was Fox, and of their eldest son. We have also a small volume of "Tracts" on political subjects by her brother, William Fox. These tracts probably do not represent the views of any political party, but are interesting as expressing the opinions of an advanced reformer at the time that the French Revolution was in progress. W. Fox was a Quaker.

A genealogical table in the Appendix gives the names of Dr. Hawes's descendants to my father's generation. In early life my father was on terms of great intimacy with these cousins, and their names will frequently appear in the following pages. For many years past, however, we have seen very little of the Haweses, Gurneys, and Donkins, and some of my younger nephews and nieces may even not be aware that they have cousins of those names.

CHAPTER VII

LETTERS OF JOHN TAYLOR TO HIS DAUGHTER

1803–1812

We now come again to letters of John Taylor; they are addressed to his daughter. Ten years had passed since the death of his wife, and Mary Ann, when the following letter was written, was fourteen years of age, and at school. He was living at Hulme (now part of Manchester), where he kept a school in connection with the Society of Friends.

John Taylor *to his Daughter.*

Hulme, 11th 10th 1803.

My Dear Child,—After I had left Liverpool, I was sorry I had not requested thee to write to me, especially if thou shouldst feel thyself *at all* unwell.—It will be a Satisfaction to me to hear this from thee at least by the monthly meeting; and write to me before if there should be any Occasion.

On seventh Day I had drinking Tea with me a young Man & his wife from Macclesfield, who seem inclined to come among Friends from the Methodists. Thou mayst tell Sarah Spurr that they were of that Sort called Revivalists. And I believe it is from having tried Revivalism to the utmost they find that there is not that Satisfaction in anything that the Creature can do, which may sometimes be found by quietly and patiently waiting upon God. His wife seems a very quiet, humble, heavenly-minded woman, & I have met with another woman lately, come to live [illegible] from the same sort of Methodists, and is I think very much of the same disposition; indeed I had great pleasure in conversing with her. Her Husband also I think rather better of than my Macclesfield Friend. May they hold on; and if they meet with Difficulties and Discouragements, still press forward to the mark for themselves. . . .

I seem begun chattering by letter with thee as I used to do with thy mother—Send me a familiar, not a formal Letter in return.—Perhaps thou mayst not soon find me in the Humour to write thus again, if thou do not repay me in kind.

The People are well at Snapehill[1] &c., but I have not yet heard from thy Uncle at Sherborne, though I wrote to him, I believe, before thou came Home. I believe I have nothing interesting that I *can* say farther, unless it be that I am thy affectionate Father, JOHN TAYLOR.

Address: "Care of Sarah Spurr, Liverpool."

JOHN TAYLOR *to his Daughter*.

4 day 8mo 22^{d} 1804.

DEAR DAUGHTER,—I seem as if I could not well omit the opportunity of writing by some one going to the Monthly Meeting, if it be only to request that thou wouldst desire thy mistress to let thee write a few lines in Return. It would have given me pleasure to have seen thee, either at Hardsham or at Liverpool; but as I have been a good deal from Home of late & shall have to come to Liverpool so soon, at the time of the Monthly and Quarterly Meeting there, I have thought it best to stay at Home. I hope thou art diligent, particularly in thy French; & that thou wilt endeavour to acquire, as much as possible, the true pronunciation, now thou art taught by a native of France. If thou take care to secure this Talent in a good Degree, thou wilt never lose it.

[1] Snape Hill was a farm at Stand, near Manchester—the family home. At this time it belonged to a brother of Mr. Taylor's, Samuel Taylor, who had a family of thirteen children.

I understand there are some Uneasinesses among you; I hope thou wilt always take the Side of Duty & Seriousness; if so thou wilt always have Reason to be satisfied with that Conduct. I hope thou dost not let any Person see my letters; though my only objection is the indifferent writing, and I should wish there to be always an open Communication of Sentiments between us, which cannot be if our Letters are not confined to ourselves. But perhaps thy Governess may require to see what Letters thou receivest; if so, I submit. . . .

Address: "At S. Spurr's, Cazneau Street, Liverpool."

JOHN TAYLOR *to his Daughter.*

[*Postmark, Oct.* 9, 1804.]

DEAR DAUGHTER,— . . . I cannot be sufficiently thankful for that Goodness which has lately, I hope for good, visited me in my low Estate. I gave thee a Hint how it had been with me in Meetings & among Friends while at Liverpool; and how that has often been the case with me before time in that place. As it now appears to me very great & surprising; O may it be permanent! And may a Blessing rest on my Children; that the Sins of the Father may not be visited upon them. . . . Last Evening I entered Edward as a Scholar with John Dalton. He is to attend in Falkner Street twice a week & John [Dalton] once at Hulme. The object is for him to learn the Mathematics. . . .

JOHN TAYLOR *to his Daughter.*

[*Postmark, June* 4, 1808.]

MY DEAR DAUGHTER,—Many a time do I endeavour to be thankful & really feel so, to the Almighty, that he has given me a Daughter, who with very little exception, has been, & I hope will always continue to be, a source of comfort to me. If anything can be the means of settling thy poor wandering father, & establishing him in the way of true peace, it must be the filial affection of his Children, of which he has already so good a specimen in his Daughter. Continue thy Love & Confidence to me, my dear girl, & thou mayst be assured I will never stand in the way of thy Happiness whenever thou art disposed to settle in Life, even if it be with a poor man, who is industrious & well disposed; though I should think it a great pity that thou, who canst so well improve Leisure & Competence, shouldst be deprived of them. I say this now, that we may always be on open & liberal terms with each other in a matter of the greatest importance to young people, a want of which between parent & Child has given what I may call a darker colour to the fate both of thy Mother & me. Which I should not now have mentioned but to encourage thee to be without reserve to me. . . .

JOHN TAYLOR *to his Daughter*.

. . . Thou speaks of a plentiful re-inforcement of Argent; but I hope thou wilt not need it, for I assure thee it is a very scarce article. However I shall put myself to inconvenience to get thee home again—for, as Edward says, when we sit down to supper, even a well furnished table is unsatisfactory without a woman at it. . . . Farewell, my dear maid. I have the full idea of thy Mother while I am writing to her daughter and that of the beloved but unworthy, J. T.

Address: "Hannah Kilham, Western Bank, Sheffield."

In 1811 we find M. A. Taylor paying a round of visits among her friends in the South of England. Her first visit was to the house of her uncle, Samuel Scott of Sherborne. Her cousins there were about her own age. There were then living at home, Grace Downing, Eliza, Sarah, and Anna Selina.

Mary Ann seems to have been absent from home nine months, and the next few letters were written to her during that time.

JOHN TAYLOR *to his Daughter.*

[*Postmark, Oct.* 28, 1811.]

DR M. A.,—After long expectation, we rec^d^ with great pleasure thy letter last first day morning, as I was going to Meeting. We thought it a long time, but thou wast as I supposed with thy Cousins at Melbury.[1] I am pleased thou hast had a jaunt to Weymouth, a place so much talked of, and also with the Enquiries of some of my old friends thou meetest with here & there, of whom we may talk more when we have thee at home. And when dost thou think of setting thy face towards it? . . .

I am pleased with the arrangement thou hast made for going to Broughton[2] & Portsmouth, only I expect it will not be in thy power to accomplish it. Thou cannot go to Broughton till our friends are at home to receive thee.

. . . Since I wrote the above I have waited about a fortnight in hopes of hearing from thee, and now have received thy letter. Awful indeed is the Intelligence it contains; but I may say, in consequence of what Mary Dunscombe had told me, I was not very much surprized at it. Thos. Dunscombe had such an attack before, as had for more than a week affected his faculties a good deal and almost deprived him of Memory, that I was convinced he would never again be like himself. But indeed the Change is awfully sudden, tho' the mind might not have been wholly unprepared to expect it. Tell Mary D. of my tender sympathy with her in her present affliction. And indeed, little as I have known of the circumstances of her fate since I left the West of England, I cannot help thinking, that she as well as her friend thy Mother, from the circumstance of both their Husbands having relinquished the profession in which they were accepted as future Husbands[3]

[1] A village near Ilminster where Mr. and Mrs. Petty lived.

[2] The home of her mother's old friend, Miss Steele, since married to Mr. Dunscombe.

[3] Thomas Dunscombe, like John Taylor, had been a Nonconformist minister.

and other matters, they must have experienced considerable course of trial, but I am sensible the path of my Wife must have been incomparably more trying. The history both of Thos. Dunscombe and myself has often furnished, & I believe ever will furnish to me while I have memory, matter of serious & of deep Reflection.

I think thy reasons are good for making some longer stay at Broughton, if, when thou hast been there awhile, Mary Dunscombe desires it. But she has a wide circle not only of Acquaintances but Relations, so that unless thou finds a longer Visit in some degree necessary for her consolation in her Affliction, I should think a fortnight long enough. Indeed I do not know that she ever expected thee to stay a longer time.

We go on as comfortably as we can without thy company, and Fanny is quite determined to do her best till her Mistress comes home. Affairs about Snapehill are very bad among the families. Farewell my dear love; always keep a Conscience void of offence both towards God & man; O that I had done so! J. T.

JOHN TAYLOR *to his Daughter.*

12 mo. 8, 1811.

. . . I wrote pretty soon after thy arrival at Broughton, in answer to thy letter informing us of it. Since then I have been in such a State of Mind, & had so much writing to do, & of such a particular kind, that my Mary Ann must excuse me when I tell her I could hardly make up my mind to write to her. The fact is, we have been engaged in a very violent war about the Lancasterian School. This began very soon after my Return from the West of England, & was continued till the Anniversary. To enter into all the particulars would be tedious.

. . . But I could not write to thee sooner, for while this School business was undetermined I could do nothing else.

I could not rest night or day and have often on account of trouble of mind for the School & myself (but principally on account of myself) had very bad nights, getting up sometimes at midnight to write to O. Wood 3 long letters, besides other pieces of writing on this subject. . . .

We want thee sadly to come home, or rather we want thee at home, for I would not wish thee to come till thou art filled, as Paul says, with thy friend's company. I must tell thee that my friends say I have been too violent & personal in my opposition to Ottiwell Wood, & to have acted imprudently gives me great pain, for I feel condemnation of myself.

I am glad thou hast, as thou says, been introduced to thy Mother's acquaintance. O, mayst thou be like her, only more happy! I wish thou hadst time to transcribe the little poems thou so much admires; the prose pieces will I hope be thy own, when thy kind friend has enjoyed them as long as her friends can wish in this world & is prepared for the blissful Society of her many highly valued Friends & the nobler employments of a better. My recollections concerning her are very painful to myself, very painful indeed—He only who knows my guilt & misery can remove it. O that I may be washed in that precious blood, that cleanseth from all sin! Tis true I never saw any comparable in my eyes to thy Mother, but my duplicity of conduct & carelessness of her peace wrings my Heart. I wish (together with my Son) to be affectionately remembered to thy Mother's Friend.

When thou gettest to Portsmouth give my dear love to thy Uncle, Aunt, & their dear children, & write immediately, and I will write thee again without delay, I hope. Farewell, my dear love. . . .

Address: "At M. Dunscombe's, Broughton, near Stockbridge, Hants."

Rev. Russell Scott *to* Mary Ann Taylor.

Portsmouth, *Dec.* 13, 1811.

Thanks, my dear Mary Ann, for your most interesting letter received yesterday morning. It has long been my wish for you to visit the most tenderly & most deservedly beloved friend of your dear Mother, knowing it was from her & her alone you could become thoroughly acquainted with your Mother's character, & receive just impressions of her virtues & talents. Your visit at Broughton has I hope had a tendency to soothe the mind of Mrs. Dunscombe, under the severe loss she has sustained. The retrospective view which she would naturally take with you of her early friendship with your dear Mother & my much loved sister, would awaken recollections in unison with her present feelings under the loss of Mr. D. I felt a wish on that occasion to write to Mrs. D. & to sympathize with her under her affliction, but as so little communication had of late years subsisted between us I feared it might have the appearance of obtruding myself on her attention. . . .

Remember, my dear, that you take the Portsmouth coach & not go to Gosport. Desire to be set down at No. 124 High Street. Come when you will my dear Mary Ann, you will be most tenderly welcome to the heart of your affectionate uncle. . . .

John Taylor *to his Daughter.*

[*Postmark. Feb.* 5. 1812.]

My Dear Daughter,—I don't know that I have written to thee in answer to thy letter & thy Uncle's informing us of thy arrival at Portsmouth. Though I did not feel freedom in my mind at all to break in upon Mary Dunscombe in the midst of her troubles, my Heart sympathized with her and I am pleased but not surprized, at thy saying it is not unlikely the remainder of her course thro' this Vale of tears may be more smooth and tranquil in pensive widowhood than in the married state. She has such a numerous group of beloved friends to look upon in Faith and memory, to all of whom she has been kind and greatly endeared, that though there must be intermingled feelings of sorrow, even bitter sorrow, yet upon the whole the current of her thoughts and existence will I doubt not be comfortable; living very much upon the past and sweetly anticipating the rejunction with those she has loved and the Society of innumerable other congenial minds. . . .

And thou hast given us according to thy wonted manner a most delightful description of thy friends and the country ab[t] Southampton. This was an unexpectedly novel & interesting Scene; but indeed thou hast met with many of them in the course of thy long peregrination. And now my dear love dost thou not think it is time to begin setting thy face towards home?—thou hast been at Portsmouth six weeks this day, receiving & giving pleasure to thy kind friends there, who I have no doubt do every thing in their power to make thy stay among them comfortable and agreeable, but by this time I think thou must so far be filled with their company & kindness, as to feel a little longing after that *dearer spot thy home.* Suppose thou have pretty soon a little conference with thy Uncle (to whom I wrote a few days ago giving a hint on the subject) upon the time and manner of thy intended return to thy father's house. And I cannot write those words without expressing a Wish, a trembling wish & hope, that thou mayst return with the same heart and dispositions (affections I mean) to Father, Brother, honour, love and goodness, with which thou left it. I have confidence in thee my dear, that thou wilt be as thou always hast been, a comfort and delight both to thy Father & thy Brother, as well as to all thy friends, of whom thou hast found so many, in yonder new part of the world. Troubles of many sorts, very heavy troubles come upon me; so that in my Children I hope I may be favoured to have, as I always have had, great comfort and pleasure—What these troubles are it is not necessary, nor possible for me to explain particularly—Troubles with respect to my Brothers, all my brothers and their families, with respect to B. Oakden and my Son. The former, having got so much money since last year at this time, when he was afraid of not being able to meet his demands, that I was obliged to borrow for him in two different places, & also at his earnest request to go with him to the Bank, to shore up his credit by the Declaration that I was a partner and going at the end of the year to add a thousand pounds to their capital—yet now, as soon as Edward's time is expired, he talks of nothing but retiring from business, and giving it up to Edward entirely—And his mind is all afloat looking East, West, North, and South, for a country Retreat, the farther from Manchester the more agreeable.

The troubles relating to the Lancasterian School have hurt my mind very much, and at present there is a secession, for aught we know a permanent secession, of all the Socinian Members, from the Committee—The particulars it is impossible to enter into. But above all, the troubles of my own mind allow me no rest, no sound rest and quiet, either by night or day—The troubles of my heart are indeed enlarged, as with respect to myself, indeed they ought to be—But with these things, my dear Girl, it is not necessary while thou art at this distance to trouble thee, but on these and many other accounts I want the comfort of thy company; & so does Edward. We had last Evening B. Oakden to drink tea with us, & his wife & niece, which last came near an hour before the others, and I could not help admiring how comfortable it seemed to have a female about the House. . . . But the troubles of myself & family, or rather my Father's family, lie nearest my Heart—Wm. Hulme, the kind friend as well as brother of my Brother Jonathan, has lingered with an unknown complaint, inclining him very much to drowsiness, and after going out into the Garden he sat down in his Chair & died—It will be an irreparable loss to Jonathan's large but helpless family. . . .

This waft of a whim of Benjamin Oakden, this turning my son adrift when he is loose of his Apprenticeship, at the time when he unexpectedly, as well as without solicitation, proposed to take him into Partnership and form a connexion with him at least for several years, while Edward is young—to have that prospect removed is very painful to my mind. If B. O. still pursues his intention of removing into the Country, I hope he will at least let his Capital remain in the firm, & become a sleeping partner—For I tell him I shall not consent that my whole property, & my Daughter's also, shall be intrusted to the young man by himself. Edward sees clearly the impropriety of entrusting the whole of mine & his Sister's property merely to his good conduct, and good success too, which may not always follow the best conduct—I tell Benjamin it was with him & him alone that I trusted my own & thy property with a view to a permanent partnership that was to have begun now. But I want thee to hasten home that we may consider these & other things together more freely. And therefore having waited with patience hitherto I am now anxious to have thee at home. And may the God of all consolation give us a happy meeting and comfort us together.

Give my love to Brother & Sister for all their kindness to thee; and to the dear Children—And tell me what plan you have fixed on for thy Return—I suppose thou wilt go to his mother-in-Law's, the Widow Hawes—as also how long thou meanst to stay in London & thy plan for coming home. Edward or myself would like to meet thee at London; I may say myself; for Edward has no Idea of the possibility of his leaving home, for the weight of the business lies upon him at present. . . .

Just while I think of it, Ellen Oakden seems to think we want thee for that our Linen is not quite so clean as it used to be. So that thou seest we want thee, but chiefly for the sake of thy company, which I hope will give, as it always has given, pleasure to thy affectionate Father. . . .

Shortly after writing the above letter Mr. Taylor had a stroke of paralysis, and his daughter returned hurriedly from Portsmouth to nurse him.

She preserved the foregoing letters carefully, and during her years of nearly complete blindness, towards the end of her life, they were occasionally read to her by her maid.

MRS. DUNSCOMBE (MISS STEELE) *to* MARY ANN TAYLOR.

BEVIS HILL, *Feb.* 12, 1812.

Never, my dear Miss Taylor, did I wish so much to be young again as when conversing with you—but alas such wishes are vain. . . . Oh my dear Mary Ann I could not tell you *then*, nor can I *now*, how much your beloved Mother lived again in you—Your Letter was *anxiously expected*, but it made amends for its delay when it did arrive. I will not deny that I wish to be loved by you. . . . To have appeared not wholly unworthy of having been your Mother's Friend is enough to satisfy my Ambition; & that I have been permitted once to [see] the Child of her Affection & the Inheritor of her Talents & her Virtues will ever be reflected upon with soothing satisfaction while Memory holds her Seat, though Providence in its "Mysterious Wisdom" chose so awful a Moment for the fulfilment of my Wishes.

. . . I have passed many languid, melancholy hours since you ceased "to steal me from myself away," but am rather better than I have been. Tell Mr. Scott that I have often regretted that the paths of Life have so divided us, & that though my Home is now rendered desolate it would give me much pleasure to see him there. . . . Farewell my dear Miss Taylor. My heart forms many a fond Wish for your future happiness & to hear of their fulfilment will ever afford sincere pleasure to Your Affectionate, M. DUNSCOMBE.

REV. RUSSELL SCOTT *to* JOHN EDWARD TAYLOR.

April 25, 1812.

. . . I have heard that my nephew Edward Taylor is become a snuff-taker. Will you permit me to transcribe for your inspection an account of different ingredients which a snuff manufacturer purchases of a druggist who is an acquaintance of mine, & on whose veracity I can place the greatest reliance. I put it on paper when I heard it that I might make no mistake. 10 cwt. of ivory black (at least) annually, 5 cwt. of ochre, do., 5 cwt. of red venetian do., a *large quantity* of verdigris & of pearl ash, a *considerable quantity* too of grains of paradise & of the *hottest* long pepper. These quantities he could not recollect without reference to his book, & therefore would not speak at random. All these ingredients, the snuff manufacturer allows to be used in his snuff. Verbum sat.—Very truly & affectionately yours R. SCOTT.

John Pounds.

No mention has been made in this book of the most remarkable member of the congregation of which the Rev. Russell Scott was minister. John Pounds was a poor crippled cobbler who rescued from the streets many of the poorest and most neglected children in Portsmouth whom he taught and trained. He found friends in the minister and congregation of the High St. chapel, and regularly attended the services there with his boys and girls. He died in 1839 aged 72, and was buried in the small graveyard belonging to the chapel, where later a monument was erected to his memory by public subscription. Inspired by this example Ragged Schools were soon opened far and wide in Great Britain.

For further particulars see "The Story of John Pounds" by R. Everett Jayne. Epworth Press 1925.

CHAPTER VIII

LIFE AT PORTSMOUTH

1812–1817

FOR ten or eleven years, from 1808 onwards, my grandparents had in their house some nephews to educate. Hampden, Russell, and Sidney Gurney, and Benjamin, Thomas, and William Hawes, all in turn spent some years at Portsmouth. These Gurneys were children of my grandmother's sister, Maria, who had married John Gurney (a barrister), and he being a good Liberal, had named his boys after John Hampden, William Lord Russell, and Algernon Sidney. Russell Gurney lived from the age of three to ten under the care of his uncle and aunt. Benjamin Hawes, who was four years older than my father, afterwards became Sir Benjamin Hawes, and was M.P. for Lambeth and Deputy Secretary for War. He always attached the greatest importance to the two years he had spent in Portsmouth.

Education in those days was almost exclusively classical, but my grandfather endeavoured to make it something wider. My father once said that he had a faculty for developing thoughtfulness.

MR. JOHN GURNEY *to* REV. RUSSELL SCOTT.

Aug. 13, 1812.

DEAR BROTHER SCOTT,—I intended to have sent you a longer letter than I have now time to write. . . . I cannot express the sense which Maria & I have of your and Sister Scott's kindness to our dear Boys. If they fulfil our hopes hereafter, to you both will it be principally to be ascribed. Thus far our hopes have been surpassed. I do not think that any boy of ten years of age can be sent to School with more prospect of improvement and less ground of apprehension of injury than Hampden, & we have been delighted by hearing that he has already impressed Mr. & Mrs. Cogan much in his favor. Dr. Cogan was there on Saturday. Mr. C. praised his understanding & application; Mrs. C. the contented manner in which he received all that was done for him, & said she thought they should have nothing but pleasure with him. . . . Our Russell is very happy at the thought of rejoining you, and Sydney seems so at accompanying him.—I am, dear B^r S. very truly yours, J. G.

The above-mentioned Hampden became a clergyman of the Church of England, and was for many years Rector of St. Mary's, Bryanston Square, and greatly looked up to. Russell Gurney became Recorder of London and M.P. for Southampton. Their father subsequently became a Baron of the Exchequer. We always heard of him as Baron Gurney.

Boys who were destined for business were in those days taken early from school. Of the three Hawes cousins who were placed under my grandfather's care, Benjamin was withdrawn at the age of sixteen, Thomas and William at thirteen, when they were sent into their father's counting-house, his theory being that boys should enter business not later than fourteen.

In the year 1812, and for some years afterwards, a very frequent visitor at my grandfather's house was Mr. William Johnstone Fox. He was from 1812 to 1815 the Unitarian minister at Chichester, having lately left the Independents and joined the Unitarian body.

From his daughter, Mrs. F. Bridell Fox, I have received some extracts from his private journal, in which my grandfather and his family are mentioned. The following are all that seem worth inserting here:—

"*Nov.* 9, 1812.—The last has not been a very busy fortnight. I have preached at Fareham, and again experienced at Portsmouth the kindness of my dearly beloved Scotts. Amiable & charming family! from the bottom of my soul I love ye. I record my affection for my own gratification, for never, unless a sudden & premature death throw them into your hands, will ye see these declarations of esteem. O richly may the blessings of heaven descend upon ye!

"*April* 12, 1813.—Spent Wednesday to Saturday at Portsmouth—days of calm & sweet enjoyment.

"*June* 13.— . . . What is far more deeply interesting is that Mr. Scott, my dear, useful, good friend is very ill. Dr. S. was summoned & I went with him yesterday. Dr. S. says he hopes he will get through, but the illness will be lingering. Preserve him, O God! for his family, his friends, society. Spare for the sake of pure religion one to whom we may boldly appeal for an example of piety & goodness. One whose acquaintance will refute a thousand such books as Andrew Fullar's.

"*June* 18.—Heard twice from Portsmouth. A joint letter which, O my Sophia, I shall preserve with feelings little suspected by thee—my friend is not worse. Dr. S. thinks he will be before he recovers. This he does not expect in less than a month. What will that dear family feel! How willingly would I, if possible, alleviate their uneasiness by my own suffering.

"*Sept.* 5.—Went on Thursday to Portsmouth. Mr. S. much recovered, but not quite well. Mrs. S. from home. Stayed, felicitously, till Saturday afternoon."

From the letters of this time it is clear that on the side of my grandfather and his family the feelings of friendship and regard were equally warm.

Many friends besides Mr. Fox visited the house, and many were the talks at the supper table on Sunday evenings to which my father listened. Modern Biblical criticism was at that time in its infancy, and my father remembered that on one occasion Dr. Pye Smith, who was present at supper, said to my grandfather in a voice full of gravity and emotion, and with tears in his eyes, that he had come to the conclusion that the *Song of Songs* could not be received as inspired scripture. The break with the old ideas as to the inspiration of the Bible was a painful one.

MARY ANN HAWES *to* RUSSELL SCOTT
(*at the age of eleven*).

LAVENDER HILL, *July* 4, 1812.

Thank you, my very dear Russell, for your letter & note. Never apologize to me about your writing. I conclude of course you either can now or soon will write a good hand, & I much prefer having a full sheet to any specimen of your penmanship. Sit down when you have a quarter of an hour to spare & write as if you were talking to me & never forget, dear boy, that whatever interests you will be interesting to me—Was it not rather paradoxical to say three times in your letter you were in want of time?—It certainly did not tend to lessen the evil of which you thus repeatedly complained. The way in which I wrote "prince" was quite accidental, but as a token of my disapprobation of his conduct I will in writing to you avoid a capital. Have you heard that he frequently cries, a silly habit enough for a man of fifty, & one which you I am sure have long since got the better of?

When he saw the letters which were in the Gazette he burst into tears & exclaimed "he was sure he never hurt anyone or did any harm—he did not know why he should have such a letter sent him"—a great baby was he not, Russell? As a public man what can we expect but acts of folly from a mind so weak and imbecile. Thank you for the winders. Should you ever be a rich man & make me a handsome present, believe me I shall not value it as much as this trifle from your boyish purse. When I sit winding my cotton &c. on them I think of many things I have heard you say. I have heard too that you gave your sister a pound note & was pleased with the disposition it manifested. You indeed deserve a garden when you take so much trouble in procuring the mould for it. I am glad Mrs. Pussy & family cannot now frequent it.—I wish (but what is the use of wishing!) you were near enough to work in & enjoy our garden.—I was much pleased with seeing Mrs. Siddons—Her address was most interesting, & the sweet tones of her voice in her last address to the public no one can imagine, so low & soft & yet loud enough to be heard in so large a house. . . .—Adieu Russell. Remember me very kindly to your circle & believe me aff[ly] yours. . . .

GRACE DOWNING SCOTT *to* MARY ANN TAYLOR.

Aug. 18, 1812.

Shall I tell you, my very dear Cousin, that I returned about a week since from a visit to my sister at Melbury. How often in a peculiar manner were you then present to my imagination; busy memory depicted the pleasant rural walks we had so often enjoyed together. It is true I paced over the same ground, but it was in a kind of mental solitude, for the friend of my heart, to whose conversation I had listened with delight, was no longer my companion. Never my dear cousin can I think but with pleasure of the time we passed in each other's society; it is often a theme on which my fancy delights to ruminate. Do not therefore, however dark appearances may be, ever suspect me of culpable neglect or ingratitude. You know my dear Cousin, I am mistress of nothing now, no, not even of my time, to employ it as I would wish; otherwise a greater share of it should be devoted in writing to you. . . . We have very lately seen a letter from Mr. Pilcher in America who speaks of my Brother to this effect "Cousin Samuel is quite well & well settled, nor does he or myself feel the least wish to revisit England, excepting for the pleasure of seeing friends & acquaintance." In another part of his letter he mentions, "the question in this Country is, 'what can he do' when speaking of any particular person; manual labour is held in high estimation & it is customary in these Northern States to see Generals, Captains etc. driving teams &c. &c. Mr. Scott tells me he is more respected by the people when working in the factory, with his jacket spotted with cotton, than when riding in Marland's Chaise with his best." . . .

Grace Downing Scott was blind. She had lost her sight in 1806, at the age of twenty-four, from an attack of what was called "Gutta Serena." Another trouble had previously fallen on her in the death of a young man to whom she was much attached. Her interest in him has been already alluded to, in what seems a rather unfeeling manner, in the letter from M. A. Hawes to her, written in the spring of 1801.

Mrs. Scott *to* Mary Ann Taylor.

Portsmouth, *Oct.* 1, 1812.

. . . Some long months have elapsed since our separation, but we cannot cease to lament how unfortunate we were to lose you so soon, and under such an afflictive dispensation. On few occasions, my dear Mary Ann, in the course of not a short life, have I so much lamented a separation from any one as I did on your mournful departure. Indeed there was but one feeling in our family. You may not have heard Russell was so much affected that he could neither eat or drink. I thought him ill, till after lying on the bed he recovered. *You* might be surprized if you knew how high you stand in his and Benjamin's estimation. There is a general anticipation of the arrival of your letters many days before they reach us. You know Benjamin's quick step—when your letters arrive, wherever Sophia is, he bounds through the house "M. A. T.—M. A. T." Your reading the *Lady of the Lake* is often the subject of conversation.

We have not heard of your Father's going to the sea-side, we hoped he would. Remember me very affectionately to him with my most anxious wishes for a more perfect recovery than he has yet experienced. Sophia has had a bad attack of pain on her chest a week or two ago, and a slight return of it last week; she is now nearly as well as usual. Could we procure her a little more strength of constitution it would be a great comfort to us. . . . Adieu my dear Mary Ann, with regards to your brother and best wishes to you and him, I am most tenderly and affectionately your aunt, SOPHIA SCOTT.

BENJAMIN HAWES, Junior (*age sixteen*) *to* RUSSELL SCOTT (*age twelve*).

Feb. 15, 1813.

MY DEAR RUSSELL,—I am greatly indebted to you for your very kind & excellent letter which gave me great pleasure—a sure attendant on your letters. I could fill a sheet, yes & more too, with my various feelings on our separation, but it is a subject on which I do not like to dwell & on which I could not fully express myself. I am very much pleased to hear your good account of my Brothers. If I judge by your letter, they are happy, contented & good boys, which if so, includes all my wishes. Pray how do Thomas [Hawes] & Russell Gurney agree together? I want a full account; do they answer your expectations? . . . I was sorry to find we both shared a like fate, with regard to the eclipse. However, you saw the clouds, but I had a difficulty even in discovering them. Therefore you who saw beyond them ought certainly to be contented. . . . It is the largest we shall have for many years to come, according to Capel Lofft, which much increases my disappointment. . . . Pray what do you think of [Leigh] Hunt's sentence? Uncle Gurney thinks it severe; that is not I believe the general opinion. Sending them to distant jails was on the tapis, but surely the separation of two brothers was nearly equivalent to it. Two years imprisonment to men, however, who generally lead a sedentary life, is not so trying as to those who find activity their chief enjoyment. They are in the two best jails, I believe, & they can have their books & friends which will greatly ameliorate their sentence. But still they "can't get out," they "can't get out" as the Starling says, which must be a great bar to enjoyment, and the clanking of felon's chains a doleful music to the ear. Mrs. Siddons read on the 10th, *Macbeth*, for the benefit of Widow Cherry. Tickets half a guinea each!! & no money to be taken at the doors. Did you not think Mr. Rowe's speech a very able one? I was much delighted with it, but I am afraid his petition will make but poor progress when it is started. The opposition is too strong & powerful to contend against. However it shows his firmness & resolution & is an opportunity to the friends of Religious liberty to avow themselves. Even that will do good.

The Anti-catholic petitions gain ground considerably all over the country. I see few able to make any stand against bigotry & intolerance. But whatever be the result of the present apparent evil we know it will terminate in the production of some greater good. Were you not pleased with Lord Thanet? It did him great honour. What an admirable & masterly performance is the Princess's letter! It clearly vindicated herself & bespeaks her to be, that is to say if it be her own composition, a woman of very superior understanding.—I am yours very sincerely & truly, BENJAMIN HAWES, J[r].

J. E. TAYLOR *to his Sister.*

LONDON, *Sept.* 5, 1813.

MY DEAR SISTER,— . . . I beg to request your acceptance of the 2 books you will receive herewith, being the two last productions of Lord Byron. Although my friend Dr. Hardie assured me, almost the last word I spoke to him, that he would not forget to obtain the *Giaour* for you, I shall not be sorry if, by your receiving this before you get his Copy, I forestall him. . . .

This morning Dr. Davis & I spent in a visit to Mr. Leigh Hunt, the Editor of the Examiner, at the Jail in Horsemonger Lane. He is a very interesting & agreeable young man, & all things considered quite as comfortable as can be expected in prison. I think of leaving London on Tuesday morning. Covent Garden Theatre opens tomorrow & I stay over the night to be there. I expect on getting to Portsmouth to find a letter there telling me all the news of Manchester since I left you. As this letter is quite a work of supererogation & I had in the beginning of it no other object than to request you would oblige me by accepting the poems, I mean to make it a short one & shall conclude by hoping my Father is in good health (and what is perhaps of more consequence) good humour, & by begging you will remember me affectionately to him. . . .

Addressed: "Islington St., Salford."

JOHN TAYLOR *to* J. E. TAYLOR.

9mo 15th, 1813.

MY DR EDWARD,—Last week I sent a letter to my Brother Scott, with a Receipt for two year's allowance from thy Trustees for thy board, which Rec^t^ had been forgotten in the hurry &c. of thy departure. I was necessitated to write from this circumstance. I was desirous to see what Mary Ann had said in her letter, on *this particular subject alone* & the sale of the House at Milborne,[1] & had got her letter in my hand for this purpose, saying I must see it, but, she not having confidence in me, (which I never violated in any case with Respect to her) she snatched the letter & put it into the fire, which obliged me to write. I was greatly hurt by the want of confidence, & especially by the mean suspicion which could rise in her heart toward her Father —& was carried to too great Resentment of it, for which I am truly sorry. And I must further add that I am very sorry, & hope ever shall be sorry, that I have given you any trouble about myself; as my peace with God through Xt's Spirit & Righteousness is of infinitely more importance. And I am truly sorry that any thing (how irritating soever it may appear to be for the Moment) should for a moment divert my attention from that point. Let not this self-condemnation which words express, be considered by you as justifying what I see wrong in my Children. I cannot help both seeing & feeling at such times & on such occasions—& sometimes may speak, to deliver my own soul; lest silence be considered as approbation. . . . For as I have often said, when I have given my Advice, I wish you to follow your judgment.—I do not think a parent can in the sight of God possibly be exonerated from the duty of tenderly advising. If thou can read this I am glad, & can only add that I am thy loving sorrowing Father, JOHN TAYLOR.

Addressed: "At Russell Scott's, Dissenting Minister, High St., Portsmouth, Hampshire."

My father was from an early age greatly interested in politics. He remembered seeing "No Popery" chalked on the walls at Portsmouth in 1807, when he was six years old, and also the death of Mr. Wyndham, which happened in 1810. When he was about twelve years old the trial of Lord Cochrane took place and

[1] The house which had belonged to Robert Scott, and of which an illustration has been given.

interested him extremely. He remembered that his father allowed him one evening to sit up till midnight while they read the verbatim report of the trial. The Peninsular War was going on all through his boyhood. He used often in later life to speak of the wonderful changes for the better that he had seen in the national life of England, and would say that whatever changes his children might live to see they could not equal those that he had lived through.

His early interest in politics is alluded to in the following letter:—

Rev. Russell Scott *to* J. E. Taylor.

Portsmouth, *Jan.* 7, 1814.

. . . We were very pleasantly surprised on Wednesday in the last week, on opening a parcel brought by one of the London coaches, to find it came from our highly esteemed friend Edward. Its contents gave general satisfaction to all parties. Sophia's countenance expressed great pleasure on receiving the part destined for her acceptance, & she accepted it very willingly I assure you. She left us on Monday morning. . . . A letter on Wednesday informed us she arrived safely at Lavender Hill at half past 6, which was as soon as we expected, after a tolerably good journey for the season of the year; that she found herself engaged with her Aunt Mary Ann to a dance &c. on Twelfth Night at the celebrated Mr. Thelwall's. . . . Talking of my dear girl I have forgotten your parcel. I hope you will excuse me. The viand you so kindly intended for Russell almost intoxicated him for a time. Roscoe's pamphlet was continually in his hand & he could talk of nothing for some days but Roscoe & Canning. He intends thanking you himself for it. . . . The reading of the *Bride of Abydos* was a source of great gratification to us all. When it arrived Sophia had been poorly for some days with a cold in her eyes & was unable to read it either to herself or us;

this was a sore mortification to her & a disappointment to us, as she was desirous of reading it to us. On Friday evening she accomplished it, by taking a part in the old & finishing it in the new year. It is our practice to take a grateful leave of the past, & to welcome in the approaching year. . . .

Mrs. Scott *to* Mary Ann Taylor.

Portsmouth, *Jan.* 12, 1814.

It is scarcely necessary, my loved Mary Ann, that I intrude myself into so much good company as that of my Husband, Sophia and Russell. From their letters you will receive such general information that nothing can remain for me to acquaint you with, but to assure you and our Cousin Edward with the utmost truth, that I rank you both in the number of our most sincere friends, and only lament that distance so divides us as to render personal intercourse almost impracticable, except a few times in the course of each of our lives. . . . I am happy in the tenderness subsisting between you & our Child. I am a strong advocate for family attachment. She is most happy in this respect; few I believe experience more kindness or stronger affection from her family connexions than falls to her lot, and of which she has a just sense. We are parted, my dear Mary Ann, from her for a long, very long time; it is for her pleasure, and enjoyment, as much as friends can bestow on her, and it is right we should submit to the privation of her society which is become very naturally a great increase to our happiness. . . .

Russell Scott (*age nearly thirteen*) *to* J. E. Taylor.

Portsmouth, *Jan.* 12, 1814.

I was too much obliged to you, my dear Cousin Edward, for the very kind present you sent me to confine the expression of my thanks to a message. It afforded, I assure you, an ample "viand to my political appetite" & the more so as coming from you. I had from the time of your departure wished for something to remind me of one who during his short stay with us had left so indelible an impression on my mind. It is for this reason that your kind present is the more valued by your very affectionate Cousin, RUSSELL SCOTT.

Be so kind as to remember me affectionately to Uncle & Cousin Mary Ann.

BENJAMIN HAWES, Junior, *to* RUSSELL SCOTT.

February 7, 1814.

MY DEAR RUSSELL,—I have much to say & but little time, as I was not informed of Mrs. Caney's departure till late this evening, & as I know your affection for me (which I assure you is mutual) always renders a letter acceptable, I endeavour never to let an opportunity pass unnoticed. . . .

You, I dare say, have heard of the Thames being so completely blocked as to become passable. It was not fairly frozen, but the large masses of ice were so completely jambed between Black Friars Bridge & London [Bridge] that by means of planks to cover the disjointed fragments, & aided by a few harum scarum watermen to answer their own purpose of making money, thousands & thousands of the most "thinking nation" were tempted to cross the River, amongst the rest were b. h.[1] & who think you? Uncle Thomas! It was a most dangerous piece of Ice for if one of the fragments had given way most probably the whole would have given way—which indeed it did on Saturday night,—carrying everything before it & doing the most incalculable injury on this side of Black Friars Bridge. It was certainly the most providential circumstance that it happened in the night tide, for had it happened one tide later, or on Sunday, for one was as probable as the other, lives without number would have been lost. . . . The sight on Sunday afternoon from our wharf was most grand to see; apparently the whole river moving as it

[1] Himself.

were, carrying all before it, crushing barges, fairly lifting them up & throwing them across each other. But Saturday night was by far the worst, as by Sunday afternoon we were in a great measure prepared to receive the shock. On Sunday morning everybody was alive that had any property on the water; it was more like the middle of the week than the Sabbath, & indeed the busiest times could not equal it; all preparing for the return of the Ice (which had moved up the river) by the afternoon's tide. Black Friars Bridge appeared (if I may hyperbolize) ready to sink beneath its weight—the concourse of people was so great. Three barges were crushed just before our Wharf.

The elegant edition of the History of the Bible, I beg Uncle's acceptance of, to be placed on the right hand side of the library next to Horæ Biblicæ.—Believe me your ever Sincere friend,

B. Hawes.

Benjamin Hawes, Junior, *to* Russell Scott.

Old Barge House, { *January 12th*, 1811 / *January 12th*, 1815!! }

Do you remember, my dear Russell, between 6 & 7 in the evening, *four years ago*, your putting your head into the coach door saying "Is there a person of the name of Hawes inside?" I answered you immediately by saying "Pray is your name Russell Scott?" my returning home with you; Sophia's welcoming me at the door; Aunt's having the Tea ready, sitting on the right-hand side of the fireplace, telling me I had no appetite, because I ate only one piece of toast; your going to tell Uncle I was come (& what I whispered to him); the cold Fowl for supper; Mary Martin coming for the shoes! &c &c. Really I begin to think I am there, it appears but yesterday, & yet 4 years has elapsed; so short the time appears that before I could convince myself it was 4 years I was obliged to reckon on a piece of paper. I can only say how happy I should be to spend the time over again. 'Twas the first two years I truly enjoyed, & which taught me to enjoy what are to come. Tell

Uncle—to him I owe all—I would say more but I cannot. To Aunt say—I do not forget her kindness, her affection—to Sophia, her's too—I cannot say more. I have shed tears on a subject which perhaps I ought to regard with cheerfulness, but I cannot help thinking of the night we parted. . . . My kind love to Brothers and Sydney. . . .

BENJAMIN HAWES, Junior, *to* RUSSELL SCOTT.

March 16, 1815.

MY DEAR RUSSELL,— . . . The return of Buonaparte is indeed extraordinary. I wait for the evening Papers before I close my letter to give you the latest information. The Spanish war is not relinquished. No doubt but that we shall have Mexico.

Thursday Evening News.—Buonaparte entered Paris on 14th; Bourbons all flown to the Netherlands; 500 English came over in the last Packets; numbers still waiting at Calais; can get no conveyance or passport; Hemp rose 3 to 4 £ p. Ton; Tallow on arrival 2 or 3 £ p. Ton better, & mending on the spot.[1] Soult has been in constant correspondence with Emperor Napoleon, & has been tried by Louis 18 by a Military Commission, which no doubt hastened the event. . . .
Your ever affectionate Cousin, B. HAWES, Junr.

SOPHIA RUSSELL SCOTT *to* MARY ANN TAYLOR.

. . . You of course know Mrs. Petty is with us; you will see her very much altered; instead of robust health she is quite incapable of exertion, and her character is altogether as much changed, and to my mind improved . . . Mr. Petty is just as he ever was, all cheerfulness and good temper. One evening at Mr. Crosby's he *danced* the first time in his life, till between one and two o'clock, and was the life of the party; indeed from all we hear it was quite a loss not being present.

[1] Tallow was needed for his father's business.

The same to the same.

Oct. 2, 1815.

. . . Wednesday last we had fixed for leaving our beloved cottage [at Staplers, Isle of Wight], but Neptune assumed a terrific form & detained us till Thursday morning, when we had a very fine though not a very calm passage. Portsmouth is disagreeable indeed, but here we are & here we must be contented, & rather seek to discover its advantages than to enumerate its much more obvious deficiences. A finer three months than we had it were impossible to select, not one wet day, two or three times a refreshing shower for a few hours, & over—Papa continues quite well; should he but continue so, what happiness! Russell I daresay you would not recognise; scarcely any of his friends have done so at first sight; he is health itself & has grown an inch & three quarters since we left home. . . .

From the time I last wrote to you, till the last ten days of our stay in the Island, we were not alone. Aunt and Uncle Gurney with their two eldest girls came to us, & immediately after them, Benjamin; he is not the B. H. you knew him, he has lost that life & vivacity we used so much to enjoy. . . . I must now leave off for we are every minute expecting Aunt Sarah, who has been at Worthing some time, to return to us, & I must run up to my dear Mamma who I am afraid thinks her girl has been too long from her. . . .

Holidays were chiefly spent in the Isle of Wight, at a cottage at Staplers, near Newport. My grandfather considered the island half spoiled when turnpike roads were introduced.

Mr. Taylor had partially recovered from his illness of 1812, but his health was broken, and he had recently suffered from another paralytic attack. His daughter had much to bear at this time from her father's extreme irritability, until his death eighteen months later.

SOPHIA RUSSELL SCOTT *to* MARY ANN TAYLOR.

Jan. 24, 1816.

It were needless, my dear Mary Ann, to tell you how much pain your letter gave me; it contained a decided avowal of what has before been but too evident. Ah, Mary Ann! you perhaps little think how often my thoughts stroll to Manchester, & how ardently imagination desires there to paint you all happiness, but I am compelled to hesitate & fear it an illusion; but its cause I feel sacred; one on which I can say nothing; the conviction that it is not *himself* but his *disease* is the only one which could disarm it of its poignancy. It is under such trials that religion shows its superiority to everything earthly, & teaches us to bear with composure and serenity what without it would be overwhelming; but I foresee you will again tell me it is easy to reason; it is so, would to Heaven I could do more!

We lost Aunt Sarah only last Saturday; the wonderful improvement in her health & spirits makes us reflect on her visit with peculiar pleasure; indeed she says she has recovered a larger share of both than she thinks she ever should otherwise. My loved Grandmamma is to her an irreparable loss.

. . . I fear I foresee an obstacle to my visiting you, in my Mamma, who, every time I talk of it, which is not very seldom, becomes more and more inclined to recall her consent. I believe it is the repeated accidents with the coaches that is the chief cause. As we sat up to watch in the New Year she said, "You have my best wishes, my love, but I am very glad you are not going to Manchester this year." I hope I am beginning to think of my Russell's leaving us with more composure; he is becoming reconciled to it. I think if a sister may judge, he improves rapidly; he is now a delightful companion; he opens his whole mind to me, which gives me the opportunity of endeavouring to lead him, to check, or encourage. . . .

I do not think I have told you anything about our Lancasterian School this long time; it flourishes beyond my most sanguine expectations. I have not indeed a wish ungratified; if ever I feel a glow of pride warm my cheek it is when I enter that school; it is when I see my welcome in all their countenances. I could scarcely have supposed so great & evident an improvement in children taken from the worst society in so short a time. In addition to habits of neatness, order, &c. I am very anxious to instil care & economy. I have it in my head & at my heart, to establish something of a Savings Bank, which I think would possess the advantage of inducing them to lay by their little earnings, & would give us an opportunity of assisting and advising them in spending it. Next Committee day I must do something in it. . . .

Sophia Russell Scott *to* Mary Ann Taylor.

Jan. 15, 1817.

. . . Heaven grant the too sufficient cause you have had for depression may be lessened, if not removed! You have said but little on its cause; I have made but little direct reply; both probably from the same cause, the delicacy & feeling due to a parent, but believe me your Sophia has not the less keenly sympathized with you. How thankful do I feel for this comparatively happy change in my dear Uncle! Dear, indeed, he must be to me, & you know not how painfully I anticipate the change from the affection he used to express to, perhaps, indifference; but your severe, your greatest trial is, I trust, over. . . . I have not told you we have parted from our Cousins.[1] They left us on Tuesday last to our regret. Most completely have we enjoyed the four months they have spent with us. This visit of our Cousins has made me painfully interested for Sarah, whose health is I fear more serious than I at first imagined, and whom the more I know, the more I love. Her character wants time to unfold before it can be justly appreciated. . . .

[1] Some of the Sherborne family.

CHAPTER IX

RUSSELL SCOTT'S FIRST YEARS IN LONDON

1817–1820

THE time had now come when it was necessary for my father to leave home to prepare for business. His uncles in London were consulted, and a little later they gave him important assistance. His Uncle Thomas was especially kind.

THOMAS HAWES *to* REV. RUSSELL SCOTT.

LONDON, *December* 23, 1816.

MY DEAR SCOTT,—I have read Mr. Adams' letter very attentively & given the Contents of his & yours considerable reflection, & the result is earnestly to recommend the acceptance of his offer. . . . What I am most anxious for in Russell's 1st entering into Business is for him to attain a general knowledge of & Habits of Business . . . that will make him equal to any more desirable situation that may offer, & be the means of *establishing him respectably in Life*. If he attains Habits & knowledge of Business I don't think at a suitable Age he will want Friends or Means to accomplish it. . . . To see him in the Prospect of being respectably fixed in Life will indeed be to me a source of real pleasure. Though not in the habit of making professions, on this occasion I must say that you & yours have a very strong hold on my affections, arising from real Worth in those whose Avocations do not furnish the same Means of providing for their Family as are in the Power of other Branches of our Family. . . . Remember me affectionately to all around you & believe me,—Sincerely Y^{rs}.

THOMAS HAWES.

SOPHIA RUSSELL SCOTT *to* MARY ANN TAYLOR.

[*Jan. or Feb.* 1817.

. . . I am much happier about my Russell since his situation is fixed. It is we hope most eligible, with Mr. Adams, a celebrated accountant; he is not accustomed to take youths, but makes Russell an exception to oblige Uncles. Russell delights in figures, besides which he will have an insight into general business. He is I believe to be at Uncle Gurney's, where my wishes have long placed him. It is an anxious time, is it not? Sometimes I can scarcely help repining that just as he is become a friend & companion I must relinquish him almost for ever; for what is the intercourse of an hour or two in the day for a few weeks in the year at most, compared with what we have always enjoyed. . . .

It was finally arranged that my father should live with his Uncle Thomas and Aunt Sarah at Lavender Hill, Wandsworth Road, while he worked in Mr. Adams' office. His delight in figures was a marked trait throughout his life.

SOPHIA RUSSELL SCOTT *to* MARY ANN TAYLOR.

April 10, 1817.

. . . I have deferred writing to you till Mr. Carter's last day & now I must write, though perhaps I have seldom felt so much disinclination to address *you*, but you will I know forgive me when I tell you *this* is my brother's last day; to-morrow morning he quits us; wherever I may strive to send my thoughts, to this they will revert, to this alone are they fixed. Pity me, feel for me, my Mary Ann. I dare not permit myself to say more or I shall say nothing else. Oh! that I could sleep away *to-morrow morning!* Few, very few, have been my trials, but this is indeed one; yet every circumstance is as we wish, and I hope I am grateful. . . .

RUSSELL SCOTT *to his Sister.*

LAVENDER HILL, *April* 14, 1817.

At length, my dear sister, the time is arrived which has placed between you & me a distance of nearly 70 miles. It would be useless to describe to you my feelings of regret on this occasion, because you are already acquainted with them. But you will not be sorry that the dread which you know I entertained of my commencement of my London career is in a great measure worn off, & that I have hitherto enjoyed myself much more than I expected. You shall now have some of our proceedings during the age which appears to have elapsed since we left. . . . For the remainder of the journey we had our own good company[1] to which you may guess we had no objection. I observed the time several miles & found the average pace to be rather more than 9 miles an hour. . . . We found our prog very acceptable, & as I could not eat much breakfast I should not have been sorry had it been a whole loaf instead of half of one. We thought of you between dinner & tea time, & agreed that Papa was sitting with you by the fireside. We arrived here about 10 minutes before six, & as we did not leave the Blacksmith's Arms till past 9 we were but $8\frac{3}{4}$ hours. . . .

Lavender Hill, where the above letter was written, and where my father was to live for the next few months, was the name given to a few houses on rising ground on the Wandsworth Road. As before mentioned, Uncle Thomas Hawes took a house there (in 1810 on a long lease), soon after Dr. Hawes' death, to make a home for himself, his mother, and his sisters.

As the Wandsworth Road was part of the high road from Portsmouth to London, passengers by coach were able to alight conveniently at the garden gate, or

[1] His mother went with him.

parcels were left there by the coachmen. Wandsworth was in the year 1817 a delightful country village. The old houses, detached or semi-detached, had each its large garden, and there were fine trees shading the road. For half a century from this time Lavender Hill continued to be a most familiar spot to all connected with the family.

Rev. RUSSELL SCOTT *to his Son.*

PORTSMOUTH, *April* 16, 1817.

Your absence, My dear Russell, occasions a vacuum in my mind, which nothing but yourself can fill. When you left me I felt as if I had parted with you for ever, & so indeed I have, compared with the enjoyment I have derived from having you constantly with me. . . . It is however no small consolation to my mind that you are fully aware your success & respectability in life must depend on your own exertions, your prudence, sagacity, & good conduct. . . . We have my dearest child, the fullest confidence in your principles, & trust that God will preserve them to you. . . . Farewell.

SOPHIA RUSSELL SCOTT *to her Brother.*

PORTSMOUTH, *April* 16, 1817.

. . . The boys have been very busy taking possession of your room, and making various alterations, rather more than I sanction. William and Sydney are its present occupiers; they are very jealous of Tom's entering.

How rejoiced I am we did not know when you were to commence your equestrian lessons, and as much so that the worst is over, and so *well* too. Can it be, my dear Russell, that you are *quite, quite* gone! Oh that I could persuade myself otherwise! . . .

A few days after writing the above letter Sophia left home for a visit to her cousins in Manchester.

SOPHIA RUSSELL SCOTT *to her Brother.*

MANCHESTER, *May* 7, 1817.

. . . Here indeed I am, my loved Russell, though I can scarcely persuade myself of the fact, that I am so many, very many miles away from Papa, Mamma & yourself. . . . I found Mary Ann looking remarkably well, poor dear Uncle sadly altered, though more in mind than body. He appears to have very little recollection, & is obliged to be treated at times like a child, but he is affectionate & M. A.'s manner to him very much so. . . . I am most agreeably disappointed in Manchester; the town itself certainly appears smoky, but this part is quite clean, airy, & very pleasant, & the country around superior to my expectations. . . . Most fondly your Sister,

S. R. SCOTT.

MRS. SCOTT *to her Son.*

May 7, 1817.

Your Papa, my dear boy, has written to you as well as he could with the boys around him, yet am I desirous of throwing in my mite of a few lines to express to you the warm & lively interest I feel in everything that relates to you, my dearest boy, & how many painful feelings I have experienced in parting from you. It will be a work of time to get accustomed to our home without our children. Your sister after not a short 4 months will return to us, but you we can never look to again, but as our visitor. Happy as we are, & beyond our expectation happy in your prospects, it is a painful thought thus to have lost you, but your happiness is our comfort; this we trust is insured to you, feeling as we do the utmost confidence your conduct will be right and good. I have the fullest persuasion, my dear boy, you possess the highest principles of good conduct & integrity; from these I trust, I pray, no temptation will ever withdraw you. Be always open to us, my dear boy, tell us your thoughts, your every action; this will be your security, your happiness in all situations.

Your few lines on Saturday morning were a great pleasure to

us, as every word & every line will be, you are fully persuaded. Situated as you are we know we must not expect much, but all you can give us, not to deprive yourself of pleasure or rest, we know you have the desire to give us. We are now longing to know exactly how the week has passed with you—I hope no return of poorliness such as you felt on Saturday, but be sure you tell us if you are at all indifferent in any way, & if you are disposed to write never make postage an object. We even like to hear the names of your debtors' & creditors' accounts. We are much pleased that Mr. Adams appears to be so pleasant; such persons as his clerks appear, are not the persons to form favourable [views] of those that employ them.

Your few words after seeing sister off, on Monday, were most acceptable to us. We are wishing the time away till Friday morning, to hear of her. I trust it will be to your satisfaction & ours. I can scarcely bring my mind really to think of her at such a great, very great distance, but so it is. How I should like to take a peep at her just now, & how much I should enjoy taking a seat by your side between hours 2 & 3! Tell us how you go on, & whether you feel yourself quite comfortable in this & every other respect. You will, my dear boy, I suppose, read this on Friday evening, between the hours of 9 & 10, & I ought to spare you, tired & sleepy as you are likely to be. Tell me if you read my letter easily or not.

Give my love to your Aunt Harriet and assure yourself, my dearest boy, of the most lively interest and tender affection of your Mother, S. S.

This letter was written in shorthand, as were all letters addressed to my father by his father and mother. His sister and he, in writing to each other, did not use shorthand.

RUSSELL SCOTT *to his Sister.*

LAVENDER HILL, *May* 11, 1817.

MY DEAR SISTER,—You must excuse me if my letter be not so long as I could wish, as I have just finished writing a long sheet full to Papa & Mamma, & as I do not write shorthand very fast, this has occupied me some time. Your letter on Friday gave me great pleasure, & I was philosophical enough to make a calculation of the quantity of enjoyment I should derive from reading it out of my dinner hour, when the other clerks were absent; & having done this with as much mathematical accuracy as if I had been taking a solar observation . . . I convinced myself of your safe arrival at Manchester by observing your handwriting & the postmark & put it into my pocket-book, though not without a considerable inclination to violate my resolution. In a short time however, this became no longer necessary; for Mr. Adams being gone to the Isle of Ely, three of those diligent and praiseworthy young men, his clerks, granted themselves leave of absence, and went to see the Exhibition; a fourth seated himself by the fire and began reading; the fifth was busily occupied in examining the very intricate affairs of a nobleman, who, like many others, spent his money faster than he got it; all this occasioned the most perfect silence in the office, & I thought it a fit opportunity to peruse my letter, which I did as comfortably as I could wish, nor did I repent not having read it before.

On Monday evening you will not be surprised to hear that I enjoyed myself at Mr. Addington's. He was out the greater part of the evening. Mrs. A. asked me if I played chess; I said, "A little," & thought that was being as modest as needful. She replied "If you play a little, I play a very little," but when we came to the contest she was decidedly the superior player. Mr. A. stood by the latter part of the last game, & although he is I believe very little disposed to allow an observation to be made by a spectator when he himself plays, he was frequently interrupting Mrs. A. with "Bad, decidedly bad," etc., which I believe only made her do worse. They were both so kind as to wish me to come frequently. . . .

I went to hear Mr. Fox to-day, Aunt Sarah accompanied me. We had a sermon well worth going 6 miles to hear from the words, "Who made thee to differ from another?" He is very well; I went to speak to him in the vestry, while Aunt Sarah went to Mr. Addington's. . . . When I followed Aunt to Mr. Addington's Mrs. A. gave me a general invitation to dine there any Sunday. Of this I shall frequently avail myself, as it will give me an opportunity of attending Dr. Lindsey of an afternoon. I had indeed determined not to attend public worship twice a day, not being able to think of any way in which I could accomplish it; but this will enable me to do it & is indeed the only way in which it could be done. It will be very pleasant also to spend the evening there so frequently as I am likely to do, & I wish the inhabitants of Serjeants' Inn & Barge House,[1] but more particularly the former, would follow the example.

I walk constantly 11 miles a day, & should 2½ more, were it not for Aunt Sarah's kindness.[2] . . . I hear nothing of riding on horseback though I believe Uncle Thomas' horse is standing idle in the stable. I do not know how to account for this, nor am I the only one to whom it is a matter of surprise. Aunt Sarah mentioned it last night at supper & said she had supposed that during Uncle's absence I should have the use of his horse. I would not wish always to ride, but it takes from the pleasure of a walk to know that you must do it, whether agreeable or otherwise, every night. However it has its advantages; it gives me time for contemplation & reflection; I meditate as I go along on something said in the letters I have received, or on what I intend saying in my own. I consider the advantages of the situation in which I am placed, of the kindness of my friends, & wish for some one to whom I could communicate all my thoughts & feelings, but find no one in whom some requisite is not wanting. These are the usual channels of my thoughts from ½ past 8 when I get out of the bustle of London & its neighbourhood, till ¼ past 9

[1] The houses of his uncle Gurney and uncle Benjamin.

[2] She sent him as far as the first turnpike in the chaise. There were no omnibuses in those days, nor (my father said) till thirteen years later.

when I approach Lavender Hill, & begin to think of the end of my walk. At this time you may think of me musing in this way, & should I occupy a place in your thoughts for 5 minutes, it is more than probable I may then be thinking of you.

Friday was a great day with me. I heard from you in the morning, & from Papa & Mamma in the evening by waggon; but what was my surprise, when the post arrived the next day (yesterday) at Mr. Adams', to find a letter for me from Papa. I was somewhat alarmed; but though this subsided on my opening it, my surprise did not, for I found he had written to desire me to request Aunts would allow me to have a loaf & butter with milk & water set before me of a morning, instead of breakfasting at Barge House, saying it would give me more of the country air, of Aunts' company, & of time to write home. I have written to say that I do not think it will have any of these advantages, as I shall be as long breakfasting here as at Barge House, & the only difference it will make is, that whereas I now set off at ¼ past 7 I must then begin breakfast at 20 minutes past & set off as soon as I have done. Its disadvantages will be breakfasting an hour earlier, having no rest on the road, & almost renouncing all intercourse with Uncle & Benjamin. Aunts are perfectly willing that I should breakfast here, but think the present plan preferable on my own account, as indeed Mamma thought when in London, & was pleased at it. . . .

It is now ¼ past 8 & I have been writing all day except at meals & while I was gone to Mr. Fox's. Let me hear from you about the middle of next week. I have a shocking pen as you may see. My affectionate remembrances to Cousins M. A. & Edward. Farewell my dear sister.—Your very affectionate brother, RUSSELL SCOTT.

Addressed: "Miss Scott, Mr. Taylor, Islington St., Salford, Manchester."

Mrs. Scott *to her Son.*

Portsmouth, *May* 12, 1817.

. . . Respecting, my dear boy, your breakfasting as we proposed, you will for a time at least oblige us by complying with it as proposed in your Papa's letter of Friday, contrary as we believe it will ever be to us not to yield to every reasonable wish of yours. We were much pleased that you gave your opinion upon it so properly & freely, this we shall always wish you to do, to have you free and open on every thing. I feel anxious about your walk; do, we beg, sometimes at least get up on the Clapham Stage, & relieve yourself by riding & keep a separate account with your Papa & me for all this *extra expense.* We conclude you received the £5, 5s. of your uncle before he went. Be sure you make a good dinner at the eating house; if you want another slice, order it manfully, & if you feel empty after your walk, have a plain biscuit or two in your pocket.—Most affectionately your Mother, S. S.

Rev. Russell Scott *to his Son.*

Portsmouth, *May* 29, 1817.

. . . We were very glad to find that you had determined on standing up to dance; we wish you had acquitted yourself more to your own satisfaction, though we are inclined to believe that it was not quite so bad as your account of it represents it to have been. It was however very comfortable for you to have had your cousin Harriet for a partner, who, though an excellent dancer, would be disposed to make every favourable allowance for your deficiences. What think you, my dear boy, of taking a few lessons in dancing before the next winter? It will enable you to acquit yourself with propriety, if not with high excellence, & what is of considerable consequence with you, it will tend to give you confidence in your own ability to dance as well as is necessary for you, or as you may wish. . . .

RUSSELL SCOTT *to his Sister.*

June 8, 1817.

. . . Cousin Edward expresses his surprise that Benjamin should hold the political sentiments he does. But I think in another part he assigns a reason which will nearly account for it. He says "How many are there who are Churchmen in religion & Aristocrats in politics merely because it is fashionable & customary so to do, or because it requires less investigation of the subject to hold these sentiments!" Now this I consider to be pretty much Benjamin's case. He professes to dislike political discussion, & I do not think that he has much relish for it, & he therefore determines to be satisfied with things as they are. But this is not the only reason to be given; his intimacy with Dr. Stoddart is another; a little bit of fear, too, is a third. He has frequently said "Suppose the mob on the 2nd of December had come to our manufactory; what a situation should we have been in!" Another thing too which has lessened my surprise respecting this is, that not only in this case but in many others he has manifested a disposition to justify what is considerably wrong, because it may chance to be prudent, or advisable, or expedient, or politic, or convenient. Thus he will surrender the rights & liberties of the whole nation because of the crimes of a few individuals. On this principle too he justifies duelling, tho' he acknowledges it to be merely wrong, & inconsistent with the profession of Christianity. On this principle he goes to church almost every Sunday, rather than not go to Twickenham so early, while he considers himself as a Dissenter. Indeed I have been sorry to observe in him a complete disregard of the maxim of doing no evil that good may come. I have already said too much on this subject; more than enough, I suppose, to remove your surprise if you felt any at what Benjamin has said to cousin E. I should say however that it must be taken with considerable allowance, for in a conversation I had with him a little while ago, he said that he thought Parliament ought to be triennial, & the right of suffrage coextensive with taxation. . . .—Your very affectionate brother,

RUSSELL SCOTT.

Rev. RUSSELL SCOTT *to his Son.*

PORTSMOUTH, *June* 18, 1817.

. . . We wish you, my dear boy, to give William the half crown from yourself, and to give it to him yourself. The next time he drives you to the turnpike, when you get out of the chaise, you can just say to him, "William, you have a little additional trouble on my account, be so good as to accept this"; giving him the half crown. There is nothing in doing this, my dear boy. You must endeavour to accustom yourself to do things of this kind, in this sort of way, as you will occasionally find it necessary to give a gratuity of this kind, to the servants of others for the additional trouble we may occasion them. It will induce them to do anything for us more readily & cheerfully. . . .

Mr. James Carter called to say that his son James would leave school on Saturday morning next, with the Gurneys, for London, & that as they were going to Wandsworth Common, he should take the Wandsworth stage & proceed to Lavender Hill, where you will of course find him Saturday night on your return home. He will not I dare say be disposed to walk to London on Sunday to hear Mr. Fox or Mr. Anybody else; it will therefore be a great attention to his Father for you to remain at Lavender Hill on Sunday & devote yourself to him. . . .

SOPHIA RUSSELL SCOTT *to her Brother.*

ISLINGTON ST., SALFORD, *June* 22, 1817.

. . . How grieved & how surprised I am at your account of B. Hawes. I had no idea the change was to the extent you mention. I had hoped the principles instilled at Portsmouth would have had more influence. Your principles, my beloved Russell, I firmly believe are too excellent, too deeply rooted to be changed by interest, fashion or those with whom you may associate, & most grateful do I feel for the conviction. Your sister scarcely knew how much she loved you till she was so completely separated from you; it is one of my greatest pleasures to picture Papa, Mamma & yourself at your different occupations. . . . You have probably heard from home that Uncle Taylor has had another attack, which has weakened him very much, & has almost annihilated the gleam of intellect which remained when I came hither. He is very feeble indeed & alters almost daily. . . .

Do you see much of Mr. Fox? Many of Cousins' friends are Unitarians, one most zealously so, a Mr. Coe, who heard Mr. Fox [deliver] five or six of his lectures last Autumn. I quite enjoy a bit of Unitarian chat with him now & then. He is I think one of the trustees of Mr. Goodier's Chapel at Oldham. I very much miss not seeing the "Repository" & "Reformer." In other books & monthly publications I am very well off, for Edward belongs to a very excellent & extensive library. Most fondly, my dear brother, your friend & sister, S. R. Scott.

Mrs. Scott *to her Son.*

June, 1817.

. . . The evening of Thursday was I hope in every respect pleasant & gratifying to you. I was I assure you quite delighted at your seeing Kemble & Mrs. Siddons; it would have been one of the highest treats I could enjoy, & so thinks your Papa. I have a great pleasure in thinking I have seen him so lately in "The Stranger." You did not, my dear boy, I hope fail to thank your Aunt Gurney for her kindness in taking you. In a line or two I had from your Aunt Sarah she tells me she set out with you on Saturday morning, & that you would have written a few lines had you known there was a parcel.

We were quite pleased at having your different stages & to know your hours & minutes exactly. The difference of clocks[1]

[1] Greenwich time was not kept beyond London until after the introduction of railways.

will not make us many minutes out. I shall never fail, my dear boy, if I can help it, looking at Billetts coach in the evening & thinking you saw it in the morning; it appears, my dear boy, as if we were nearer to each other than we really are. We shall however soon meet, though it will be a week longer than you expect. . . . I cannot describe how much I dreaded the first few weeks from you, but these have I hope passed over very tolerable. We were much pleased to hear your distance in walking appeared less to you; if you continue to walk I feel persuaded you will endeavour to make the best of it, as I hope & trust you will anything that may arise not so pleasant to your feelings. Continue, my dear boy, to think aloud to us, & you will I think find that our views & wishes tend to promote pleasant & happy feelings in your mind. As you associate in life you must learn to form a true estimate of character; to say all we know, all we think, will not do in our general intercourse in life; & what I have always felt important, not to repeat to a person what others may have said of them in any way that may not be agreeable to their feelings; in a word to promote general liking & good opinion in our connections as much as we possibly can.

I believe, my dear Russell, your Papa told you how much pleased we were with the account you sent us of your expenses; but do not make your grand object to save all you can; you have a sum which we hope will enable you to expend wherever & whenever it is right & proper for you to do it. In looking over your accounts I did not see coach hire the Sunday you were coming from town with your sister, neither did I see ½ a crown to W^m^ which I requested you to give to him; & has not your hair wanted cutting? I merely name these things as hints for the future. In your sister's letter yesterday she is very anxious to hear from you, which she probably may before this time. She is quite well after her excursion, but I am very sorry to say much alarm is apprehended for Mr. Taylor, who had again last Friday a slight attack; we feel for him. Fondly & most affectionately your Mother, S. S.

From an old account book, it appears that my father's monthly allowance at this time was five guineas, and that his expenses were chiefly in clothes, dinners on week days, and postage.

SOPHIA R. SCOTT *to her Father and Mother.*

MANCHESTER, *June* 28, 1817.

. . . In the afternoon we drank tea at Mrs. Hunter's. On our return we found Uncle just taken very ill; apparently he had been in a fit. . . . That night Mary Ann & a woman sat up with him and a most distressing night he had; and to describe to you the day we passed on Thursday would, my Papa and Mamma, be scarcely possible. The state of restlessness he was then & still is in exceeds what I could have imagined. He is just now a little more composed & asleep, & I have taken that opportunity of writing. Mary Ann has just said, "Do not write a long letter;" she does not like me away. She says she should not know what to do without me. I am very thankful to be of any use or comfort to her, but it is a severe trial. Indeed, my Mamma & Papa, ill as he is, restless as he is, I feel to love him more & more. There is such an indescribable innocence about his every word "Yes, if you please" & "I should be thankful" is his general reply. He is perfectly unconscious of everything that passes, but when we ask him a question his reply proves he knows what we say. I do not think he suffers any pain; he had a blister on, on Wednesday night on the top of his head, which relieved him from the dreadful state he was in. . . . Dr. J. thinks he will go off composedly. Heaven grant he may! Dear Mary Ann is very, very much distressed, & more so to-day from thinking him very much better yesterday, more so than I could. . . .

Your letter yesterday was an increased cordial to me. Uncle seemed to notice it, and took it in his hands. When I asked him if I should send his love, he answered in his sweet way

'Yes.' . . . Oh, my Papa & Mamma you will sympathize in our feeling. I am only afraid of your feeling too keenly. May Heaven bless you, my Papa & Mamma. Yours tenderly,

S. R. S.

Mr. Taylor died July 3, 1817.

From some stanzas written by his son, "On viewing the dead body of my Father," we may quote the following:—

And I would right willingly learn
  That high independence of soul,
Which taught thee so promptly to spurn
  Self-interest or passion's controul.

Which shaped every thought of thy mind;
  From which every act took its course;
In sorrow which made thee resigned;
  Which gave every purpose its force.

And though by the power of disease
  The strength of thy mind was o'erthrown,
In its ruin the relics of these,
  Its distinguishing features, were shown.

Thy life was so virtuous and pure,
  So tranquil and calm was its close,
That our trust is most steadfast and sure
  Thy spirit in Bliss shall repose.

Shortly after Mr. Taylor's death Sophia returned to Portsmouth. While in Manchester she and her cousin, John Edward Taylor, had become attached to each other. A little later they were engaged, but seven years elapsed before Mr. J. E. Taylor was able to make an income sufficient to enable them to marry.

Of the letters from Sophia to her future husband

only those written in 1818 and 1819 remain; they were given to my father after her death.

Rev. RUSSELL SCOTT *to* J. E. TAYLOR.

PORTSMOUTH, *Nov.* 11, 1817.

Really, Edward, there have been such frequent and ample communications of late between you and Sophia that I have not been able to edge in one quarter of a sheet. Now however that a box is going, & she has written so lately to you by post, I am going to try if I cannot find a snug corner for two or three lines between the cracknels. In your letter of the 20th of September, which came to me by frank, you mention the mode you proposed of arranging your late father's effects between you & your sister, and which appears to me to be the best that could be adopted for your mutual advantage. . . . In this letter, my dear Edward, you refer to the state of your feelings respecting Sophia, & say she is a daughter of whom her parents may be proud. . . . When we first became acquainted with your attachment to Sophia I must candidly confess to you I was sorry for it, because the near relationship that subsists between brothers' and sisters' children has in all cases appeared to me to be an objection to such a connexion. Had my Sister's son been different from what I believe him to be it might have proved a considerable obstacle in my mind to the union, though even in that case I should have stated my objections, offered my opinion, and given my advice, & then left my child to consult her own welfare & happiness. There is one circumstance it is necessary for me to mention, Edward, & it is no trivial one; it is your duty well to consider it. I have no dowry to give my daughter. My income as you must know is small, & the one half of that depends not on my life merely, but on my health & my ability to discharge the duties of my profession.[1] To a man of business a wife without

[1] His salary at no time exceeded £130 a year.

money cannot be desirable, at least not so desirable as one with money. I am sorry for her sake that this must be the case. "Oh," you will say, "she possesses qualities which money cannot purchase"—very true, & she may possess those qualities which are necessary to your happiness in the marriage state, in a greater degree than some women who have a great deal of money that you may be acquainted with. But still, Edward, a little money is desirable after all & I wish I had it for her. But what we have not we cannot give. . . . I have dealt sincerely with you, Edward, and you may also assure yourself that I am—Your affectionate friend, R. SCOTT.

The two following letters refer to arrangements that were being made for my father's going into the business in which later he became a partner.

Mrs. SCOTT *to her Son.*

[*November*, 1817.]

. . . Your not having been asked to dinner at Mr. Cory's I hope was only on account of their house being in an unsettled state—I should hope not any objection on the part of Mrs. Cory.[1] Ladies, my Russell, have sometimes credit for what they do not really deserve, but there are things which arrangements on their part make it necessary for them to decide. I shall be glad to hear you are going there again soon. It would be a pleasant feeling to me for you to take your dinner in a family, but where we have so much to be grateful for we must not think of little things which we should prefer being otherwise. You are I dare say always quite respectful & attentive to Mrs. Cory. . . .

I shall be very much pleased if you have two comfortable rooms near the wharf. What I most liked in Bennett Street was thinking Mrs. Reynolds disposed to be kind and attentive to you. It is of particular consequence for you to fix with desirable persons in this respect. Let us know without loss of

[1] Wife of his future partner.

time if any thing be fixed on for you. It appears particularly kind of your uncle Benjamin to be thinking about you, engaged as he is . . .

Mrs. Scott *to her Son.*

PORTSMOUTH, 1817.

. . . Speaking or rather writing on the subject of your hat, your father wished to have added, respecting money, that you need not be in the least anxious, as what you now receive will be continued till the first payment of your earnings. Therefore my dear boy, only we beg, think of spending what you have to your own satisfaction & credit, & in that way that will make you appear to advantage to others. Your Papa and I have two or three times said to each other "we hope Russell continues his account of what he expends, & will continue to let us see it"; but one motive have we for wishing it, to suggest anything that may be an advantage to you, for we feel the fullest confidence you have no disposition to expend in any way but what will be fully approved by us both. I often think, my dearest boy, how thankful we have reason to be in your prospects. Before you are 17 years of age all is arranged in the kindest possible manner to make you in easy circumstances, in all human probability, for life; which nothing we have reason to believe will counteract but misconduct on your part, which we have the firmest confidence in you, will never occur. Most highly were we gratified at the full approbation expressed by your uncle [Thomas] of your conduct, in a letter we lately received from him, & the confidence we feel of the continuance of it makes us beyond expression happy. . . . I am, my dear boy, with most sincere and tender affection YOUR MOTHER.

With regard to this letter, my mother remarked, "What his mother says about making a good appearance was a very necessary hint to him. He was very unobservant about clothes and would make do with anything he had."

In January 1818, my father's two uncles, Thomas

and Benjamin Hawes, joined Mr. Cory as sleeping partners in a coal business—a business that has since become one of the largest in the coal trade—with the view that my father should on coming of age take a part of his uncles' share, and be made a partner. At the same time my father, having left Mr. Adams's, came into Mr. Cory's counting-house in order to learn the business.

Twenty years previously, when these uncles were young, my grandfather and grandmother had materially assisted them by putting the whole of their property (about £3000), no doubt at some risk to themselves, into the hands of the brothers, interest at 5 per cent. being paid. It was therefore felt that my father had a strong claim on his uncles, and the arrangement with Mr. Cory was made chiefly for his benefit.

New Barge House Wharf, Mr. Cory's place of business, immediately adjoined the Old Barge House, where my father's uncle Benjamin lived, and where the Messrs. Hawes had their soap manufactory. It was on the south side of the river, exactly opposite Temple Gardens. At this time all coal was brought to London by sea, there being no railways, and the business was necessarily carried on at the river-side.

In recent years great changes have been made on the spot so well known to my father; most of the old buildings have been removed, and large warehouses and factories have taken their place. When I was there quite lately, I was told that the coal wharf had very recently been built over.

My father's hours on first going into Mr. Cory's office were from 6 A.M. to 8 P.M. His uncle Benjamin used sometimes to call at the counting-house as early as 6.30 A.M., and if he found my father not yet at his work, would, by way of a hint, leave his compliments, or such a note as the following, which I found after my father's death amongst his papers:—

MY DEAR RUSSELL,—Was I you I would be first, certainly not last. I have been up since ½ past 4, been to Newgate Market, done my business there, & home ½ past 6. I hold it as a maxim, no business can be well conducted without the Eye of a principal from beginning to end.—Yours affly

B. H.

At this time it became necessary for my father to live near the Wharf, hours of work being too long to allow of his returning at night to Lavender Hill. Lodgings were taken for him at 19 Bennett Street, a little street leading from Stamford Street to Christ Church. He had two very small rooms, for which he paid 11s. 6d. a week, his salary being at that time £100 a year. These long hours continued for seven or eight years.

Amidst all the changes that have taken place in that neighbourhood, Bennett Street still remains, and No. 19 is evidently just as it was in my father's time.

Mrs. SCOTT *to her Son.*

PORTSMOUTH, *Jan.* 3, 1818.

. . . Our anxiety about you, my dear boy, has been very great since you left us,[1] though you have been very good in letting us hear frequently. Your letter this morning, few as the lines were, was a great comfort to us. At present it is painful, & very painful, to think of you returning after the business of the day to a solitary room. At first I know you must feel it,

[1] He had been at home for Christmas.

much as you are disposed to meet it as you ought, & with us to think it is necessary. We are rejoiced that you feel your lodging "as comfortable as you can expect, after being accustomed to live with friends." You must form your habits to be engaged as soon as you enter them, as much as you can, to avoid feeling the want of society. What would your Papa, sister & I not give sometimes to pass an hour or two with you! We are feeling now the desire of seeing you again as strong as before you were with us. The new scenes you are entering upon we long to talk over with you. Do, we beg, as much as possible let us know in what way your hours pass, from the time of your rising till you go to rest. We hinted to you a journal; you can do it concisely in your letters to us & it will not take up much time. Tuesday or Wednesday morning let us hear again. We wish to be informed as minutely as you can how you manage in every respect. We hope from what you say Mrs. Reynolds will be attentive to your comfort; perhaps her talking may proceed a little from this disposition. *Does she provide your breakfast & tea or do you?* We understand from your letter you do not dine at your lodgings. Where do you take your dinners & about what time? . . . We think, my dearest boy, it will be better for you in general to receive any invitation expressly from your aunt or uncle Benjamin, & if Benjamin urges it, to say you had rather not unless asked by them. Mr. Cory being on the spot will make any invitation from him pleasant. Did you see Mrs. Cory or any of the family? Let us know all you can of him & them. We want to know where to think of you tomorrow. You must be very particular not to appear at all to neglect Lavender Hill. I wish you could sometimes get there of a Saturday night, or you could sometimes in the week. Let us hear every thing you can, we shall then be better able to judge. You did not, I conclude, mention to Benjamin any plans we thought of for next summer, that led him to tell you Mr. Cory would not leave London, nor must you. If you cannot come to us you are sure, my dearest boy, of our coming to you. I do not feel at present that I can hold out till summer without seeing how you are & all your goings on. You say, my dear Russell, you are far from being satisfied with yourself the first & second day of your entering upon your business. Do not be uneasy or dissatisfied; your desire to do well will be sure to accomplish it; we have no fears for you, & to make you easy respecting your uncle Benjamin, we send you a copy of his letter by the monthly parcel—"My dear friends, I have only time to say from the little I have seen of Russell, there is every prospect of his activity & attention. He seems cheerful. He has now the most unpleasant time to go through; dark and cold at the waterside, is not the most agreeable. It will soon pass away; it will be cheerful & wholesome. His disposition seems excellent. As I must attend to it [the business] at first I shall see a good deal of him. The more I see of Cory the more I like him. No pride, his disposition appears good, active & persevering. I wish you were here for a few days." Sending you the copy of this letter is between ourselves . . . Our loves to all—Tenderly YOUR MOTHER.

Addressed: "Messrs. J. & B. Hawes, Old Barge House, London."

SOPHIA RUSSELL SCOTT *to her Brother.*

January 6, 1818.

. . . This parcel will, we please ourselves, meet you as you enter your lodgings for the evening, cheer your solitude a little, & not make your closet or sideboard look *less* comfortable. We shall have great pleasure, my Russell, in replenishing it, & to add in any degree to your comfort, now so far & so unwillingly separated from you, will increase our enjoyment. We have thought of you much, very much, but we had not pictured you *alone* & "out of spirits" last week, or we should indeed have thought of you painfully, but the worst is, I trust, over. You now most probably have your books etc. around you; tell us everything you can, for we are interested in every trifle. *Does Mrs. Reynolds provide well for you? do you sup, or take tea & supper together?* So kind an invitation to Serjeants' Inn is a very pleasant prospect for you. I have no doubt you will soon feel your consequence & usefulness in the business; at present it must be an uncomfortable feeling, but do not be dissatisfied with yourself; I am sure you have no reason. . . .

We thought of you my Russell & drank our love to you as the year was closing upon us, & we thought of you as you were, *asleep*. . . . We hope you will enjoy a bit of the Sherborne turkey & a slice of ham for breakfast & supper; the cakes etc. we hope you will not wish to return to us. . . .—Your affectionate Sister, S. R. Scott.

Rev. R. Scott *to his Son.*

Portsmouth, *January* 7, 1818.

. . . We hope you will make a point of hearing the Doctor [Rees] while he lives. Mr. Fox you will of course hear in the evening when you can conveniently; but you will have opportunity of hearing him when the Doctor's impressive exhortations can be heard no more. I know no preacher under whom I could be a hearer with so much pleasure & satisfaction, as the Doctor, for a continuance. . . .

It was very kind in your Uncle [Thomas] to propose your having the better room upstairs at your lodgings. I rather hope you have taken this room, it being larger & more airy, & perhaps it will be more retired & private than that below stairs. Independently of your Uncle's great kindness in proposing to defray the expense for the present, I should like you to have this room. Pray, my dear boy, in what state are your finances? You have extra expenses, have you a sufficiency to meet & discharge them? Tell me when you write, that, if you stand in need of any additional supply, you may have it without delay. I hope by this time you begin to feel a little comfortable in your lodgings. Have you any of your books with you yet, to amuse you & render your solitude a pleasure?

What a sad beginning for you! To be induced to stay at Barge House, & then to be deserted, was not the most friendly act under your then circumstances; & still worse to be suffered the next morning to go & whistle for a breakfast. . . . It was kind & polite of Mr. Cory to invite you to partake with him. I hope, my dear boy, you will not on any consideration be prevailed upon to go to Barge House without the express invitation of your Uncle Benjamin or your Aunt Hawes. But I think your Mamma has written to you on this subject; I was sorry not to have time on Sunday to see what she wrote, that I might avoid writing on the same things. I should have written to you on Sunday, but three services & the Lord's Supper were quite as much as I could accomplish. . . .

You need not, my dear boy, be apprehensive of going too much to Serjeants' Inn; from what your Aunt Gurney says you will always find a welcome there, go as often as you may. And in her, under any existing difficulty, you will find a friendly counsellor & a judicious adviser; that is, I mean, if any thing should arise about which you might be desirous of consulting a friend when there may not be time for writing to us. Farewell, my dearest boy. May Heaven's best blessings always attend you, prays your faithful friend and affectionate Father,

RUSSELL SCOTT.

Mrs. SCOTT *to her Son.*

[1818.]

. . . Glad are we, my dear Russell, always to hear from you, & the oftener you write, strange as it may appear, the more I am persuaded you will find to say to us.

I think with you, my dear Russell, that your sister's not coming to London at this time is for the best; I hope she will be quite strong & well enough to return with you, if all circumstances suit at that time. You will not I hope exceed 5 weeks from this time. I reckon weeks with no small anxiety,

I give you my word. I so long to have you again chatting with us.

Your feelings, my dearest Russell, respecting receiving from us, are highly to your credit, but we certainly feel the desire of contributing to your comfort & enjoyment in any way we can; & spending that sum in the way your Papa proposed we thought might be a pleasure to you. You are therefore not to consider it a loan. If, my dear Russell, you are placed in a situation to provide for yourself, or nearly so, we have great reason to be thankful. Our most earnest prayer is you may deserve it by the strictest integrity, diligent & upright conduct, with a strong sense of obligation to those you derive it from. But, my Russell, you are not to think that you have been a [burthen] to us for 17 years; it was your right as our child, & never have you been any expense to us but what we must approve. That you have felt inclined to decline the trifle your Papa sent was, we are fully persuaded, from the best motives possible. We are therefore still more desirous of your accepting it. I shall be very glad for you to find that you have a little surplus at the end of each quarter, but we do not by any means wish you to be confined in your expenses, but to expend if any occasion makes it necessary, as far as is prudent & right. . . . How does your alarum answer or are you now able to rise without it? . . . I must wish you good night as your Papa is putting out the fire. . . .

Mrs. Scott *to her Son.*

PORTSMOUTH, *Feb.* 17, 1818.

. . . You ask us respecting Serjeants' Inn; this perhaps you are most interested in our replying to. We should be very sorry of a shadow of displeasure on the countenance of either your aunt or uncle Gurney. If it were so, I think it most likely arose from your Uncle thinking you appeared a little too much out of your business by staying there, and of an evening getting rather later home than they might think best for you. I would therefore guard against it, & now as I suppose you will be two evenings in the week at the lecture, you had we think better not regularly stay, and certainly sometimes avoid it however agreeable it may be, when your aunt and Maria are not at home. I should rather prefer your not having dinner up for you after dinner is over in the family; sometimes it is of no consequence, I dare say. When it happens that dinner is over in their family, cannot you, as a chance thing, return & enjoy your cold tongue at your lodgings? You are now the man of business & you will I doubt not more & more feel the necessity of devoting yourself to it. . . .—Most tenderly YOUR MOTHER.

RUSSELL SCOTT *to his Sister.*

LAVENDER HILL, *Feb.* 22, 1818.

MY DEAR SISTER,— . . . Last Sunday I heard Dr. Cogan's funeral sermon; Mr. Aspland delivered a very excellent discourse from the words "The good man shall be satisfied with himself." Aunt Gurney thought there was a want of feeling in it, & at the time she made the observation I was inclined to agree with her, but have since thought that it was merely a determination to command his feelings. . . . I returned to my lodgings for a short time, & then went to Barge House to dinner; they did not wait until I arrived, although I was not a moment after time. Uncle & Aunt Benjamin only were present. About 9 o'clock Aunt talked of going to bed, & thinking this a broad hint, I very soon wished them Good night. . . . You *of course* understand that this visit was by invitation. . . .

MRS. SCOTT *to her Son.*

April 14, 1818.

. . . Your Papa will tell you we are quite glad you applied to us for money. We only wished you to have done it sooner. Our only wish is to relieve under every circumstance your every want, your every anxiety. Farewell till we meet & can converse over much together. . . .

SOPHIA RUSSELL SCOTT *to* J. E. TAYLOR.

PORTSMOUTH, *January* 5, 1818.

. . . It was a great trial parting with my brother again, & many are the anxious feelings we still have about him. It is painful to think of him after his day's fag going to his solitary room, & at 6 o'clock these cold dismal mornings by the water-side. He is resolved to make the best of it, & to exert himself to the utmost; he makes not the slightest complaint & the only dissatisfaction he expresses is with himself. Uncles speak of him in the highest terms. I do not think there is the slightest danger of his resorting to company for relaxation; he is quite desirous of reading, & improving all his leisure, & he has a home at Serjeants' Inn and Lavender Hill. Mr. Cory appears to be everything we can wish. Russell says his manner to him is very gratifying. . . . Russell is attending Mr. Hazlitt's lectures upon Poetry at the Surrey Institution—a treat I do indeed envy him. . . .

The same to the same.

PORTSMOUTH, *March* 2, 1818.

. . . My Papa, Mamma & Mr. Holland are gone out to drink tea, and to attend a fortnightly lecture preached this evening by Mr H. My boys & I, perhaps not the least happy of the family, have been discussing the affairs of our own & many of the countries of Europe, over the cordial of our tea-pot, & I thought as I led and encouraged their observations that you would have been pleased could you have overheard them, but their principles too, I fear are destined to be subverted by that detestable 'New Times.' . . . I am going to see Kean. It is scarcely prudent perhaps, but it is irresistible; he performs three nights. This evening in "Richard"; tomorrow "Sir Giles Overreach"; Wednesday, "Othello." Papa and Mamma wish me to see him each night, & I am very willing, provided I do not feel the worse, for I would not, I assure you, risk a repetition of the last two months. It is a long time since

I have had so much indisposition as this winter & I trust it will be as long ere it returns. Had I not this hope I should *very seriously* wish you to relinquish all idea of ever transplanting so "tender a plant," for I would never marry with the prospect of ill health. . . .

Mrs. Scott *to her Son.*

June, 1818.

. . . In planning our journey, my dear Russell, to Sherborne, it was not without the hope you would be able to join us there. The desire of seeing you is ever strong, & in very many respects it is very desirable, if you can be spared, that you should give us the meeting there. Spending two or three weeks quite in the country is very desirable for your health, & you will there enjoy as much of your father, mother and sister's company as you could possibly here, with the additional pleasure of seeing such very near connections as your father's brother's family, all of whom are disposed to be attached to you. I hope, my dear Russell, you will have no reluctance to join us there; it will indeed be a great disappointment to us if you have. . . .

Russell Scott *to his Sister.*

Lavender Hill, *Sunday, June* 21, 1818.

My dear Sister,—Since you with so much patience supposed I should write to you "one of these days" I have taken advantage of James Carter going to Portsmouth this morning to send you a few lines. Uncle Thomas was kind enough to provide me with the requisites—a comfortable desk, pen, ink, paper etc., when he left the regions of the sleepers soon after 5 o'clock. . . .

I assure you I do not feel comfortable in disappointing you all, as I fear I shall by this letter. I should enjoy myself much more alone with you at Portsmouth, and although being in the country is desirable, it is not so much so to me as to most Londoners, who are confined within doors and have not the enjoyment of the more pure air of the Thames, nor of coming into the country as I have. Mr. Cory has not left town for a single day since we began. This is another reason why I should not like to go any where besides to Portsmouth. If he should suddenly leave town, I should wish to be able to return at a few hours' notice; indeed there is nothing but the entire enjoyment of your company, which I should have at Portsmouth, & the pleasure of visiting my native town, which would reconcile me to leaving business. On the whole, pleasant as is the idea of seeing you all in a short time, I hope you will consent to postpone it until you return to Portsmouth.

I will give you a brief account of my evenings since I wrote. On Thursday I was engaged with my parcel and letters; on Friday I was just going to bed at about half past 9 when a summons came from Barge House. I found it proceeded from Uncle Benjamin, B. H. & Arthur Steele. They said the manufacturer, philosopher & astronomer had failed in resolving a question in the rule of three, & that they had therefore sent for the mathematician, by which appellation they had the politeness to designate me. . . . After a little consideration, I was fortunate to resolve it to the satisfaction of them all. I stayed with them until about half past 10, & then returned home to bed. Last evening I arrived here a little before 9, & walked with Uncle for some time in the garden. To-day I am going to Dr. Rees' as usual. The rest will depend on circumstances. Next Sunday morning I shall endeavour to arrange with Hampden to take a ride with him before breakfast. . . .

Several letters passed on the subject of the proposed visit to Sherborne. They show how greatly Mrs. Scott was distressed to find that her son had no wish to join the party there. Finally, he seems to have been driven to write something that was considered satisfactory. His letters, however, have not been preserved.

Mrs. SCOTT *to her Son.*

SHERBORNE, *July* 8, 1818.

. . . Disappointed as we must feel in not seeing you here, when we thought it so certain, yet we think it perfectly right your not coming under the circumstances you state. . . . I most anxiously wish you ever to have a strong feeling of the tender tie of family connection, a character devoid of this loses so much of what is really excellent that it almost ceases to be estimable. Your friends here have all kind & affectionate feelings towards you, & that you should have anything like indifference towards them mortified us, I assure you, more than you can suppose. . . . However, my dear Russell, you are now to consider us satisfied. Indeed, not to give way willingly to what is right in business, we should think very wrong on our parts, & would very ill become us after what has been done for you. . . .

Your sister is enjoying your cousins quite. We are much pleased with Anna; she very, very much pleases & interests us. She says she quite wants to know her cousin Russell. Your uncle said on Sunday, without our dropping a word upon the subject, that he quite hoped you would have been able to have met us here. I was very glad to be able from your letter, which I received at noon, to say, that circumstances obliged you to give up the pleasure of seeing them. . . . We hear of your cousin Robert here & think how much better you are off than him. He is obliged to be at business close, from 7 in the morning till ten & eleven at night, has not drunk a cup of tea out of his own house but once since he was in business, & says he must do it if he gets a living. . . . Ever most tenderly your mother, S. S.

SOPHIA R. SCOTT *to her Brother.*

Novr. 6, 1818.

. . . What a shock is the death of Sir S. Romilly! Where shall we now look for [such] a champion of virtue & humanity? where find such a head & heart as he possessed? . . .

From RUSSELL SCOTT. (*In shorthand.*)

Letter from myself at 18 years of age to the same worthy personage at some future period.

BENNETT STREET, *Jany.* 29, 1819.

Being very shortly about to enter on my nineteenth year, I have determined to put in execution a plan which I have had for some time of committing to writing my thoughts on various subjects, thinking that it may hereafter be at least curious, if not useful, to observe what changes may have been produced in them by the lapse of time. And to begin with the most important—I hope I am fully convinced of the value of religion. I consider its external observance of great importance, particularly to those of my age, to fortify the mind against the temptations which assail us. I regret that principally owing to the circumstances in which I am placed that I seldom attend public worship more than once a day [on Sundays]. This, however I regularly do, nor have I more than once or twice at most, for the last two years, suffered anything to prevent it. I attend Dr. Rees nearly every Sunday—for various reasons—partly I am afraid, because it is respectably attended, and because I am not dependent on the pew opener for a seat, but principally because of the sound practical discourses delivered by Dr. Rees. The pleasure and perhaps also the improvement which I derive from hence is in some degree diminished by the difficulty I find in preserving the connection between the sentences. I am convinced however that I derive more benefit from attending Dr Rees than I did from hearing Mr. Fox. I make a point of being at the Old Jewry when the Lord's Supper is administered, conceiving it to be a duty clearly enjoined by our Lord on all his followers. With regard to baptism I consider it (contrary to the principles in which I was brought up) as merely intended for proselytes, and not intended as a perpetual ordinance. It was I think practised by the Apostles as being the customary symbol of conversion from one religion to another in that age and country, but not instituted either by our Lord or by them as a Christian ordinance. As to the great subjects of controversy in the Xtian world, I have very little leisure to attend to them, nor do I consider them of so great importance as I once did; for I find that however great these may be in theory, in practise there is no very material difference between the orthodox and the heterodox. I am however most fully persuaded, and derive considerable satisfaction from the belief of the strict unity of the Deity, an opinion which I have no doubt will gradually become general. On the subject of the atonement I feel considerable difficulty. The Calvinistic account of it appears to me as derogatory to the character of God, as it is horrible in itself and repugnant to reason, while that of the Unitarians seems not sufficiently to explain many parts of Scripture, or in what sense Christ is said to have died for men. Whether this last observation be just or not however I feel by no means certain, and hope at some future period to be able to pay some attention to the subject. I feel no hesitation as to the doctrine of original sin, never having, I believe, doubted its fallacy. The duration of future punishments has I think been designedly left by our Lord in some degree of obscurity. I am strongly inclined however to a belief in the final salvation of all men.

To proceed however to a subject of greater importance to me as an individual, as it is to regulate my future conduct, viz., the course to be pursued in the coal trade. First in regard to supplying housekeepers with best coals. As the law in my opinion very unnecessarily obliges the name of the coal [some word or words omitted] and as it would be totally impossible to carry on the trade if the exact number of sacks of that sort were mentioned, I think the custom practised by every coal-merchant without exception of calling them "Walls-end" perfectly justifiable, for as the party receiving them understands no more by this term than that he has the best, he is not deceived. Nor do I think the case altered, if within certain limits seconds are mixed with them, since this is sometimes an improvement. But with respect to manufacturers the case is different. If a coal of a different quality be delivered to that ordered, it is generally a fraud & always a deception. I would therefore be extremely cautious in this respect, and avoid it at least in every case whenever it is attended with prejudice to the consumer. Substitution to a dealer or retailer, as it cannot be accomplished without direct falsehood, I consider wholly unjustifiable. [words illegible] are neither more nor less in my opinion than actual fraud. The practise of them is a disgrace to the trade and will I hope, hereafter be abandoned by a larger proportion of it than it now is. Were I about to enter into a partnership in a house I would make their abolition, if practised, a *sine quâ non*, and would rather have a hundred pounds placed annually to my debit than consent to them. T. W. & J. H.[1] have set a most meritorious example in this respect. If I should be at any future time of a different opinion, let me on reading this remember that it was written after twelve months acquaintance with the trade, and after mature deliberation, so that I cannot consider it to be formed without sufficient opportunity of judging. Let me in that case take shame to myself for having suffered the love of wealth to overcome that love of honesty which I now possess.

With respect to politics, they occupy very little of my attention. I attach however less importance to them than I formerly did, as well as to controverted opinions in divinity. Although far from approving the conduct of the present ministers,

[1] My mother said that these initials stand for Thomas, William & James Horne—Quakers.

I do not think them quite so bad as their opponents would represent. Reform in Parliament is, I think, highly desirable, yet I prefer the present system to the wild schemes of some reformers. The *Times* I consider the best paper in London, the *New Times* without exception the worst. I will add a few words with respect to my opinion of my friends & acquaintance. The sweet and pleasing countenance, the amiable disposition, the maiden modesty & the good sense of Harriet Gurney approach nearer to my idea of perfection than the character of any woman with whom I am acquainted, while the unyielding honor, the manly & unshaken firmness of her Father in his principles, notwithstanding the temptation of his elevation in rank, demand an equal though very different praise. The fine deportment of Maria [Gurney] cannot fail to excite admiration in strangers, while her generally pleasing manners make her much esteemed by those more intimately acquainted with her. The most striking excellencies in Aunt Gurney are her unvarying attachment to her husband, & her strong but well regulated fondness for her children. The lustre of her lady-like appearance & general affability is however occasionally slightly tarnished by a degree of *hauteur* not always pleasing. In Hampden may be discerned, below the rudiments of a well informed English gentleman, the inheritor of his Father's integrity & of much, if not all, of his talents. In Uncle Benjamin I see a man of warm temperament & strong feelings, almost exhausted by his unremitted attention to business. For his kindness to me he has a claim on my gratitude for the remainder of my life, notwithstanding the occurrence of a breeze or two. Of Aunt Benjamin I say nothing, convinced that it is not necessary to commit to writing anything respecting her in order to enable me at any future period to know what are now my sentiments respecting her. In Benjamin I fancy I see a character yet unformed. Time & circumstances will prove what he will be; of this I cannot judge; with a delightful flow of spirits & talent for conversation, he possesses however a haughtiness sometimes intolerable, which once very nearly occasioned a breach between him & myself. He estimates too highly his consequence in the family & the world, & sometimes entertains a contempt for those of inferior rank, by no means amiable. Uncle Thomas, without any very great exertion of body or mind, has risen to the station in life he now holds. He is kindly disposed to every one. His friends would think a little more attention to dress by no means thrown away by him. Were I to say what I think of myself, I should perhaps feel mortified at my own vanity. Without doing so therefore I hope that when I next peruse the above I shall be better deserving the good opinion of myself.

SOPHIA RUSSELL SCOTT *to her Brother.*

PORTSMOUTH, *May* 13, 1819.

. . . I think, my dear Russell, you should not feel Aunt Gurney's having given Benjamin a superior present as arising from a preference, or one from Maria and Harriet as implying partiality, but recollect the handsome presents he brought them all from France—this is the way I should view it. . . .

RUSSELL SCOTT *to his Sister.*

BENNETT ST., *Dec.* 16, 1819.

MY DEAR SISTER, Although from the prolongation of the process of tea making (or rather of tea-drinking & of the mastication of bread & butter) & also from the protraction of the nap by which I usually refresh "exhausted nature," previous to the commencement of the operation of letter-writing, the time at which I usually consign my corpus to the precincts of the bed posts is arrived, whither my inclination or rather my laziness would have led me; the majority [illegible] legislative assembly have decided against any poss[illegible] the time of writing to you; the cabinet ministers [illegible] fol[illegible] Lord Castlereagh's example & have [illegible] wishes of the minority as to permi[illegible] culinary process upon a mince-pie in the mean-time. They were justly apprehensive that if this epistle were not written this evening it would probably be entirely omitted. I therefore proceed to act upon their determination.

I was much pleased, my dear sister, by the receipt of my yesterday's parcel & its contents; anticipating the arrival of something substantial, I desired Mrs. Reynolds to light my fire in the afternoon, & I came here to dinner after paying my cash into the Bankers'. The perusal of the letters (my mince-pie is most woefully burnt) occupied me the whole of dinner time. . . . My mince-pie, which has now shared the fate of thousands of its predecessors, was notwithstanding its mishap exceedingly good. To return however from all these digressions. Have the goodness to wait a few minutes while I stir my fire which is almost out. *J'oublie ce que je me suis proposé vous dire*—I must look at your letter. I see that fired with patriotic indignation you ask me how I feel amidst all the infringements on our liberties—nearly as I did before. If I take up the *Chronicle* or the *Times* at dinner, & I almost always see one or the other, I regret the fruitlessness of the efforts of the Opposition. If on the other hand I happen to look at the fulminations of Dr. Slop, I wish him at Constantinople, or some other place where he might practically find the advantage of his line of politics, & feel almost disposed to cram his newspaper into the fire; but with the exception of the very few minutes in the day when I am thus occupied, politics do not much employ my thoughts, & when they do, I do not feel my liberty much encroached upon by the bills now passing, particularly since the very important alterations which Lord Castlereagh has been compelled to make in them. The next point to which you direct your enquiries (& you see how anxious I am to solve them) is the delivery of a letter to Aunt Sarah which accompanied one to Miss Cox in a frank. You say she has "not received" it. [illegible] deny [illegible] fact; it came, I think, on a Saturday morning, [illegible] day I took both letters to Lavender Hill &

delivered one to Uncle Thomas & the other to Aunt Sarah. So much for your suspicions as to my 'punctuality' &c. &c. &c. I am much obliged to you for your congratulations on the frost; we had a large stock, but our market fell (just at the time your letter reached Bennett Street) about 2/6 p. Chauldron, in consequence of the change of the weather.

In a former letter you express your apprehensions lest the State secrets contained in your letters to me (I say it with all possible respect for them & their writer) should be divulged through my negligence of them. I beg you will not be disquieted on this account. That I have mistaken black currant jelly for raspberry jam I admit; that I sometimes mistake the slop-basin for the sugar basin I acknowledge, having done so this evening, & having once put the former in my closet instead of the latter; but that I ever mistook your letters for waste paper, I do most positively deny. I will tell you what process they undergo. After perusal they are placed upright in my waistcoat pocket for convenience of reference; two or three days afterwards they are deposited in my pocket-book until it becomes inconveniently filled. Now and then, upon emergency, one of them suffers martyrdom; the oldest however of the survivors takes up his final residence in the upper region of my closet. It is time that I left off, for you see I begin to talk nonsense, or perhaps you will say that I have been doing so all along. One word more & I have done. You are I believe [aware] of the geographical situation of a very useful recess in this apartment, called a closet; you are aware also that I am in the habit of depositing in it whatever good things happen to be in my possession. It is therefore fortified with lock & key. A breach has however been made in the walls (by gun-powder or other means) by certain four legged depredators, familiarly known by the name of mice, what Linnæus calls them I am sure I do not know, but you have probably heard of them by this name. I resorted to various means of preventing their incursions without success. I have been obliged partially to evacuate the fortress & to starve them out. I hope

I have succeeded in so doing, but am apprehensive of the safety of my ham. It is now quite time to wish you good night; the various topics contained in my other letters I must advert to when I write by the monthly parcel. As this inordinate quantity of nonsense will perhaps have tired your patience before you begin the second sheet, you will perhaps reserve that till the latter end of next week, which will answer the purpose of my writing a letter of ordinary length once a week.

Tell Papa that Mrs. Cory's sister, whose personal attractions & mental superiority so much excited his admiration, is come to London from St. Ives for a few days. I have not had the felicity of seeing her. I believe I could talk on till day-light but this will not do—so—Ever yours affectionately,

RUSSELL SCOTT.

SOPHIA R. SCOTT *to her Brother.*

PORTSMOUTH, *Dec.* 23. 1819.

. . . Say what you may in future, my dear Russell, it will be in vain to endeavour to persuade us that you have not sufficient variety of incident to fill a letter to us more frequently than you have hitherto done. You who can make so amusing a letter as you did on this day week out of so few materials, can never be at a loss for subjects; you have indeed been quite the life of our fireside of late, for certainly at no one time between or since the arrival of your two last letters to me, have we been so merry as on their arrival, & it is a source of great pleasure to us that you are so cheerful in your solitary room. You are very, very good, my Russell, to be so; indeed I scarcely know any one who deserves so much credit as my Brother. I am afraid you are grown rather too cool upon your country's weal, & are not quite so much of a patriot as you used to be. Individual feeling is nothing; but to live amidst so much misery & distress, to see it disregarded & insulted, instead of being sympathised with & alleviated; Oh! this harrows up the feelings to the highest point of indignation. . . .

SOPHIA RUSSELL SCOTT *to* MARY ANN TAYLOR.

Dec. 28, 1819.

. . . Our arrangements are somewhat uncertain. Aunt Gurney has been very desirous that Mamma should go to London this winter. She says, she shall not feel her house[1] properly warmed till Mamma has visited it, but Mamma is quite disinclined to leave home, & we are equally reluctant to part with her; for now that we are but three we are more than ever cemented together & as it were entwined around each other. To lose one appears to derange the whole, nor is my Mamma as well as I could wish her; she is equal to little, *very* little exertion or fatigue. . . .

We have an unusually heavy fall of snow here to-day; farther north it will probably be much heavier; it is rare for us to have any. To Russell it is, I dare say, a goodly sight; the coal markets are so much influenced by the changes in the weather, & they have a good stock. He complained sadly last winter of our having so little frost.—He is, dear fellow, very well & very cheerful. He writes me such cheerful letters when sitting in his solitary room that it is quite delightful. . . . His taste was not for business, nor were his habits suited to being alone, but he resolved to do, he determined to succeed, & the result has proved what the will can accomplish. But my dear Mary Ann I ought not to run on so to you, but I am sure you are interested in him & he is such a treasure to his sister. . . .

I shall I think always feel a melancholy attachment to Russell Square. It was you know the residence of Sir Samuel Romilly. Oh I shall never forget going to his house to view the furniture; it was full of persons attracted for the same purpose, but all was silence—not a word—not a sound above a whisper—it was a most striking & impressive tribute of respect to his memory.

What a distressing deplorable account is yours of the state

[1] Baron & Lady Gurney removed from Sergeants' Inn to Lincoln's Inn Fields.

of misery & wretchedness amongst the poor with you! These are indeed melancholy times; to live amidst so much distress without the power of alleviating or removing it; & to see those who possess the power insulting the feelings of the sufferers instead of commiserating & conciliating! In our town prospects are, I hope, rather brightening. We have certainly less distress this winter than for two or three years past. . . .

The "Peterloo Riot," in Manchester, had taken place in the previous August, occasioned by the suppression of a public meeting in favour of Reform, when the people had been fired on by the military, and when eleven had been killed and some six hundred wounded.

For J. E. Taylor's part in the affair, see Appendix, p. 457.

SOPHIA RUSSELL SCOTT *to her Brother.*

January 29, 1820.

. . . We conclude coals are now reduced to their usual price, as the weather is so mild. 70 shillings per ton did not astound us since I was in London in 1814 & then heard of five guineas.[1] . . .

I observed, my dear Brother, that you remarked "a vile Lavender Hill pen" when you were writing to me. I hope you did not make the same observation *audibly*, because I do recollect your doing so more than once, & I also recollect feeling a little hurt that you did not observe it made Aunt Sarah uncomfortable. Take a hint & say no more. I want you to observe how far little things render others uncomfortable, & manner will generally tell us. . . . Papa's & Mamma's love to you with the fond affection of your sister, S. R. SCOTT.

[1] That was the year of the great frost, when no coals could reach London. See letter from B. Hawes Feb. 7, 1814.

Mrs. Scott *to her Son.*

Portsmouth, *January* 31, 1820.

. . . I was very sorry, my Russell, to find by your letter you did not particularly enjoy the party at Lavender Hill. It appears unfortunately to have been at a time that your mind was much engaged with what you had to do, but I am very sorry for you not to be tolerably cheerful & happy in such parties. It is necessary to exert ourselves all we can to be agreeable, or we cannot expect to please. We know under all circumstances much is to be done by only making a little effort. You have full powers, my Russell, to be agreeable; do not let the disposition be wanting. We know not the vast importance it may be to us in life. I should be miserable were you to be led away with company & gaiety, but do if possible carefully avoid the opposite. Your not going to Mr. Brunel's[1] was unlucky, as it may lead to your not receiving an invitation again. It is of great importance you should mix a little in good company. I wished at the time you had written to your Aunt Sarah to have made your excuses, rather than intrusted them to Benjamin. . . .

I once observed to my mother that the letters showed that in the early years of my father's life in London he had not been at all on good terms with his cousins Thomas and William Hawes, especially with Thomas. She said it was so. They thought a great deal of wealth and position, and of themselves, and she believed they rather looked down on my father. He was very much set in his own ways, and he strongly disapproved of some of their ways. The consequence was they were anything but friendly. This was specially the case with Tom, who was inferior to William.

[1] Isambard K. Brunel, the engineer.

Mrs. SCOTT *to her Son.*

[1820.]

. . . In one of your letters, my Russell, which I intended answering, I was pained to find from you that Thomas & you did not appear to be on speaking terms. Do oblige me, my Russell, if you possibly can to avoid this let there be a passing word between you when you meet, however hurt you may be, or however wrong his conduct. The habit of not speaking will reflect on you, & you will be the censured person I am certain. How wretched, my Russell, should I be were you capable of the conduct you refer to in him. The slightest thing that is not right in you I feel most keenly, & I often think how much reason we have to be thankful your character is so formed as to conduce so much as it does to our happiness. Your Papa unites with me in Love. Ever most truly & tenderly,

YOUR MOTHER.

CHAPTER X

MISCELLANEOUS LETTERS

1820–1824

SOPHIA RUSSELL SCOTT *to her Brother.*

April 9th, 1820.

. . . I am almost doubtful, my dear Russell, whether you are as much interested as you used to be, or indeed as we wish you to be, in the events which have so much occupied our attention the past week. We have had a most gratifying meeting; indeed the progress Unitarianism is now making here is astonishing. Our congregations surprise us; Dr. Monsell of Brighton preached at our place on Wednesday evening to a *very* good congregation. We were quite delighted with him as a man and a preacher. They dined forty eight. Mr. Bristowe has remained and preached for papa to-day; our other friends are all gone,—we have had such a housefull. Thursday evening a Mr. Acton opened the Baptist Chapel[1] which was crowded up the pulpit stairs. It is a great pleasure to us to see the cause flourishing. Surely it is one of the most important that can exist, and to be in any way instrumental in promoting or supporting it would be a source of the greatest pleasure to me, and grieved indeed should I be if my brother's interest lessened instead of increasing with his years.

Business is no doubt of importance; it must be attended to, but the great object of our lives is and ought to be to prepare for another, and inasmuch as we are led to neglect this I think we are to blame. You, my Russell, will I doubt not agree with me in this, and I would not say a word to hurt your feelings, but I am alarmed at the idea that you are so completely engrossed by business. . . . Your affectionate Sister, S. R. S.

[1] Chapel of the General Baptists in St. Thomas Street.

SOPHIA RUSSELL SCOTT *to her Brother.*

PORTSMOUTH, *Oct.* 1820.

. . . Papa's lectures began on Sunday to one of the best, if not quite the largest congregation we have had. He received a request from some persons thro' John Handy to preach from John 17. 5. With this subject he opened his lectures. The persons who considered this text unanswerable were present. They last evening sent their thanks to Papa through John Handy & expressed themselves very much pleased & satisfied; they had not thought it possible so much could be said, & inquired for sittings. Papa certainly treated the subject very ably, & although he preached for an hour there was the most fixed attention. . . .

Tell Aunt Sarah that our new plan for the clothing at school succeeds better than I had any idea it could. We have collected nearly six pounds, & within the last week between twenty & thirty girls have bespoken frocks. . . .

SOPHIA R. SCOTT *to her Brother.*

PORTSMOUTH, *Nov* 5, 1820.

. . . I found your last letter at home on our return from dining at Mr. Crosley's. You will not I think be surprised that some part of it chased sleep from my eyelids. I wish I could talk over with you the subject to which it alludes. Warm & ardent as was the affection I before felt for you, my Russell, it were impossible it should not be increased by the lively interest you take in the most important act of my life.[1] When this is to take place, is I assure you, quite uncertain; it is an event which I can only view calmly at a distance. Were it to approach near I believe it would be overwhelming. Sometimes I censure myself for having ever yielded; I could have sacrificed my own happiness, I would even now do it if I thought it my duty; but another's is too much; yet ought I for myself, or for any one

[1] Until this time her brother had not been told of the engagement.

else, to lessen the happiness & comfort of those to whom I owe all that can be owed to earthly parents? Ought I to go far away from them when declining years may make any attentions I could pay them an increase of enjoyment, an alleviation to suffering? What kind, what tender attentions have I daily & hourly received, & shall I never repay any of them? Does it not wear the semblance of ingratitude? O my Russell, if you knew the struggle of your sister's feelings you would sometimes pity her. On the other hand when I am told by one to whom certainly I am not indifferent that he never did & never can love another, my courage fails, I hesitate, & hesitation you know is in these matters fatal. Yet even now, if I felt convinced what was the path duty pointed out & which I ought to pursue, I would not shrink from *any sacrifice*. But you know, my Russell, there are still other obstacles which remain to be removed; business is again less prosperous; there has been such a depreciation in the price of cotton that they know not where or when it will end. It is indeed very hard, very trying to him; all his "sunny hours for the last two years" he says have been those spent here. . . . How kind & good is our Uncle! [Thomas Hawes]. I do indeed feel increased love & affection for him; there are I believe few, very few men with so much feeling & kindness.

Papa is still preaching his "Devil Sermons," & it seems bringing conviction to many minds, though one woman said "he was a wicked man & not fit to live." We have excellent congregations. . . .

Addressed: "Mr. Scott, Messrs. Cory & Co., New Barge House Wharf."

SOPHIA RUSSELL SCOTT *to* RUSSELL SCOTT.

PORTSMOUTH, *Nov.* 23, 1820.

. . . You, I suppose, have seen in the paper an account of our demonstrations of joy at the Queen's acquittal. They were indeed very decided, notwithstanding all the means that were used by persons in authority to prevent it. Sir G. Campbell and *many* others sent round to their tradesmen threatening to withdraw their custom, if they illuminated, and every possible means was used to prevent the illuminations, which were very general. I never felt so relieved at the issue of any public event as this, and yet it is only since the storm has been so happily averted that one has felt fully sensible of the calamities which would in all probability have followed any other result . . . The shirt which accompanies this is for your approbation. The others are all waiting to be finished till we know whether you like this collar—therefore *be sure you tell us* & point out any defects or imperfections. . . .

SOPHIA R. SCOTT *to her Brother.*

Decr 31, 1820.

Papa has to-night finished his full, true & particular enquiry into the existence of his Satanic Majesty. It has excited surprising interest & sensation in the town. The most horrible things are written in various parts of the town, such as "Old Scott is damned," "Scott & the Devil are brothers" etc. etc. Indeed he is at present the most notorious person in the town. The writer of these denunciations turns out to be young Rood, a man of most abandoned character. He was discovered by a Jew, who said he thought "it was a shame Mr. Scott should be treated so" & took the pains to follow him one night through Portsmouth and Portsea. . . .

These lectures were afterwards published under the title, "The Scriptural Claims of the Devil," a copy of which is in my possession.

SOPHIA R. SCOTT *to her Brother.*

PORTSMOUTH, *Jany* 22, 1821.

I could ill describe to you, my dearest Russell, the pleasure your letter gave me on Friday week. It was so long, so very long since I had welcomed your handwriting addressed to myself, & at the moment unexpected, coming in too so *à propos*, just to welcome me downstairs as I was drinking tea below for the first time for some days; altogether it was almost too much for me. I felt its kindness very sensibly & I hope now to hear from you quite as often if not oftener than heretofore. How delighted were we to hear your fag was over. I scarcely know what we should have done had we known of your being exposed to the cold so early in the morning. . . .

Could you not spend your birthday with us? It is an important one you know my Russell, ushering you into the *twenties*. It was at that age you so affectionately gave me the seal & that little poetic effusion of which I never think without pleasure. *Then* we had you always with us, *now*, alas! we scarcely see you. I think you would find us improved in some things; for example, we always have wine and a dessert after dinner; no matter whether we eat or drink, there it is. To be sure the knocker is not mended, but if you will come we will get that done first. . . . Our chapel last evening was nearly as full as it *could be*. Several sat in the aisles. Papa preached one of the most interesting sermons I ever heard. Is it not a wonderful revolution, a wonderful improvement in public opinions? So many years as Papa has preached to a handful, & scarcely any durst venture within the walls, & now to see it full, evening after evening & month after month! The little persecution Papa endured is ended. . . .

Mrs. Scott *to her Son*.

February 18, 1821.

. . . I am much concerned about Tom. It is to me a very painful feeling that you are growing up, (for you my Russell I believe have not done growing), with dislike to each other. Such a disposition in him I tremble for the consequence in future life, & I am sure if I were not blind to it, it would make me miserable were he my son. [illegible] but one wish my Russell, that if he should be indu[illegible] properl[illegible] you, that you will then endeavour to answer him in the best way you can. Oh, sad, sad, in Russell Square![1] humble as is my situation I would not indeed change it. I could not meet it, were I either my brother or Mrs. Hawes.—Tenderly & with the most dearest wishes,

YOUR MOTHER.

SOPHIA R. SCOTT *to* MARY ANN TAYLOR.

PORTSMOUTH, *April* 22, 1821.

. . . Most grateful indeed do I feel to be so soon enabled to resume some of my accustomed occupations. Three weeks ago I little expected it; that I should ever do so appeared from my own feelings very doubtful, & Mamma has since said that at times she scarcely thought I should have strength to struggle with the severity of the attack. I have had a rheumatic fever before, but the suffering in this exceeded anything I ever remember. Every thing has been in my favour, the best of nursing, the kindest & most assiduous attention from Dr. Waller, coming always twice, sometimes 3 times a day. I was sadly afraid my Mamma's health would suffer, for the first ten days she had scarcely any rest night or day. . . . I hope, if I have no return, to be downstairs the end of this week. What a treat will it be after six weeks confinement to one room. . . . What a flying visit was Edward's, was it not? It was like a dream. Fortunately last Sunday was the best day I had had. . . .

Addressed:—"Miss Taylor, Mr. Scott's, Bridge Street, Bath."

SOPHIA RUSSELL SCOTT *to her Brother*.

PORTSMOUTH, *May* 8, 1821.

I assure you, my dear Russell, it requires very strong inclination to overcome my feelings of disinclination towards writing to-day, arising from my having had a considerable return

[1] The house of Mr. and Mrs. Benjamin Hawes.

of pain which makes me feel very poorly and renders the position of writing painful. . . . I enter on a subject which I was just intending to mention when I was taken ill.

You are perhaps not aware that it has been for some time felt both by Whigs and Reformers that a well conducted paper was much wanted in Manchester, one, to use Edward's words when he first wrote to me on the subject, 'which from its character either as a spirited vehicle for the promulgation of their political opinions, or from the tone & style of its literary execution could be considered worthy of the populous & intelligent district in which we are situated.' *Cowdroys*[1] derived its chief value from the part Edward frequently took in it. Under these circumstances, some of the most respectable & moderate persons in Manchester raised a subscription for the purpose of establishing a new newspaper, & they prevailed on Edward to become the Editor. Their view was public advantage; they were willing to take the risk without wishing to have any share in the profits. Edward's name does not appear, but it is generally known he is the editor, & indeed it was thought no one could establish a paper with equal prospects of success. It will not at all interfere with his business as there is a person to take the labour of it; besides which he writes and composes with greater facility than any one I ever saw. I expected you would have heard all this from himself, but he told me last week that he had omitted to mention it to you. . . . I send you a prospectus by which you will see the first number was published on Saturday. . . . Edward is very sanguine as to its success; indeed he has met with so much encouragement from all parties that it were impossible to be otherwise. It is indeed very gratifying to see how completely, amidst all the party feeling which has existed, he has won the confidence of all. This has been manifested in some very striking instances. I should much rather, my dearest Russell, have talked this over with you, but

[1] *Cowdroy's Gazette*, the only organ, it was said, which the Reformers then had in Manchester.

as there is now no chance of my seeing you till you come to us I did not like you should not know of it—indeed I wished you to do so long ago, for though I was once reserved with you it was not from choice. . . . Yours affectionately,

S. R. S.

ELIZA SCOTT *to* MARY ANN TAYLOR.

SHERBORNE, *August* 1821.

. . . I stayed with Mr. and Miss Scott [of Morden] one week; from thence I went to Ashford where I was quite concerned at the alteration in Miss Avice & Mrs. Gould. Mrs. Gould appears quite careworn. Miss A. Scott cannot move any part of her body without assistance & when touched by another feels extreme pain. She bears her sufferings with such patience and resignation that she is indeed a pattern worthy of imitation. Mr. Gould appeared just the same as when you saw him. . . .

Addressed: "Islington Street, Salford, Manchester."

Miss Avice Scott, mentioned above, was a great sufferer from rheumatism. Her death took place in 1825, after an illness of twelve years.

In the spring of 1821 Mary Ann Taylor and her cousin Robert Scott, one of the sons of Samuel Scott of Sherborne, were engaged to be married. Robert was a chemist, and had a shop at No. 7 Bridge Street, Bath, where his sister Eliza kept house for him, the living rooms being above the shop. Mary Ann had been paying a visit there of about a month, and at the end of that time the engagement took place. In the following December they were married. During the few intervening months it is clear from Mary Ann's letters that they were together only a few days, so that there could have been no intimate acquaintance previous to the marriage.

Almost all her letters written to Robert Scott during the engagement have been preserved, and that she was looking forward to her married life with very mixed feelings is evident. There are many tender expressions of affection, but her prevailing mood was one of doubt and anxiety. Except the first letter, all were written from her home in Manchester.

M. A. TAYLOR *to* ROBERT SCOTT.

TEWKSBURY, *June* 15, 1821.

We were just on the point of setting out for Malvern when I received your letter, dearest. . . . One sentence there was which forc'd tears to my eyes and embittered my ride there at least—You will guess I suppose that I allude to your father ***not even acquiescing*** in [your] selection. I told you from the first that I did not believe he would—and I told you too what I again repeat—that the want of his ***hearty approbation*** will form an insuperable barrier to any nearer connection with you. There were difficulties and discouragements sufficient in the way before —I wanted not this additional one—however my mind is fully made up. I wish to spare your feelings as much as possible—but my resolution is fixed—I will not think of leaving a comfortable home and kind friends—most kind—to be received with coldness by the head of any family—my own near relative too—else I should not care a straw about it. Your father I suppose (perhaps all your family) thinks me a good for nothing sort of personage. I am too proud to wish to undeceive them—You know I have thought I was not suitable for you myself. . . . Do not however think that I should make ***no sacrifice*** in giving you up—tho' I must confess it would if possible be a greater one to accept of you under the frowns of your father—why was he not more explicit at first—I ***cannot fathom*** it, but if you ***attempt*** to

conquer his prejudice I shall be *most seriously displeased*—my spirit cannot stoop to anything that would so humiliate me without any occasion. I am sorry to write anything that may distress the man I fondly love—but my pride is roused and I have as much as any of the Scotts when it is. . . . I am in some doubts whether after the resolution I have form'd I ought to give you my address at home—however I cannot entirely give you up all at once, so direct "Islington Street, Salford, Manchester." I must go and put this in the Post Office, for I will not disappoint my dearest of his Sunday visitor.—Adieu.

The same to the same.

MANCHESTER, *June* 29, 1821.

. . . You know well you are dear to me, how dear you cannot know, but I feel that you become most encroachingly so. I hope and believe that you will never give me cause to repent my attachment. Sometimes however when I read your passionate expressions the thought strikes me that it is possible—(mind I only say possible) I may one day be as much an object of indifference as I now am of affection. This I am told occurs most frequently with *ardent lovers*. . . .

The same to the same.

July 13, 1821.

. . . No woman I am certain could regard matrimony with more fear and apprehension than I do; when alone I become quite low-spirited. . . . You might almost wish to keep alive in my bosom the galling remembrance of your father's objections, for in every letter I receive from you they are in some way or other adverted to.

You appear to think it is impossible that you should alter in your sentiments towards me, forgetting that the alteration may in part be attributable to myself; for instance my person, of which you now think a great deal too much, may become almost disgusting to you—it is sadly changed for the worse since you

saw me—but you do, I trust, consider yourself quite at liberty to recede if you find I have lost my identity. Nothing could so supremely mortify me as to believe that anyone considered himself bound to me in honour, when inclination no longer attached him to me. . . .

The same to the same.

July 20, 1821.

. . . It is impossible for any woman, even engaged to the man she best loves, to anticipate less of happiness than I do. My spirits are depressed in a manner that I can scarce account for, but I think if I could set you down in a *cottage* in the *country*, and insure to myself plenty of your society and affection as long as we both should live, half the weight would be taken off my mind. . . . I have wished sometimes that I had never come to Bath, and often I think 'tis the height of folly in me to think of ever marrying. Do not however be so unjust as to suppose these thoughts have their rise in consequence of my diminish'd affection—far from it. You are dearer to me than ever, and were you with me I believe I should be happier. . . .

The same to the same.

[SALFORD] *July* 27, 1821.

. . . I almost hesitate whether to write to you or not for I have nothing pleasant to communicate, and what avails it to bore you every week with the recital of my melancholy feelings. In spite of all your sweet soothing, my dearest, this will have the ascendency. It is nothing in yourself that produces them, tho' I honestly confess there is a good deal I do not like in your business house, &c. We are accustomed here to see the gentlemen in the evening so completely at leisure (*if they are so disposed*) for walking with us &c. that I feel now more than I once did the deprivation I should experience in this respect. I am too once more in the midst of an extensive circle of kind, intelligent friends. At Bath I saw nothing resembling them. Again this connexion is so diametrically opposed to all my early prejudices and wishes, that I cannot quite reconcile myself to it. I always hoped fate would in some way or other fix me in the country, and married to a man some years older than myself. You are younger, and a passionate admirer of beauty. You are a relation too—another grand objection. Your father does not approve your choice—your whole family I believe wish it had been elsewhere directed. I feel more than ever fatigued with slight exertion, and this makes me angry with myself. Are not all these ideas, which haunt me like evil spirits, enough to make one feel disposed to break off a connexion which promises so little. You see something more than love is wanting to satisfy me, tho' *that* is indispensable too, & *yours* is *particularly to my taste*, because I hope and believe it is at once tender, ardent and refin'd. . . .

The same to the same.

Sepr. 7, 1821.

. . . I wish too I could by any means recover the light-hearted gaiety I us'd to feel ere I visited Bath. I cannot help fearing that the cradle of my love will prove the grave of my happiness.

In spite of her fears Mary Ann was married (Dec. 16, 1821), and went to her new home. Unhappily her apprehensions were in a great measure realized. When later we knew her and her husband there was no sign of married happiness in their home.

ANNA SELINA SCOTT *to* MRS. ROBERT SCOTT.

SHERBORNE, *Feb.* 4, 1822.

. . . I have not heard any particular account of the manner in which Mr. Hawes[1] has left his property, but from the newspapers which you have no doubt seen, his charities appear very extensive, & from my Uncle Scott's account he was quite dis-

[1] Benjamin Hawes of Worthing.

posed to do good. I hope with you, my dear Sister, that my Aunt Scott will receive a share of her Uncle's property. No family I think can be more deserving; their principal pleasure appears to be in doing good and relieving the wants of others. . . .

Addressed: "7 Bridge Street, Bath."

SOPHIA R. SCOTT *to* Mrs. ROBERT SCOTT.

August 16, 1822.

. . . I was particularly anxious to know how Mr. Scott was behaving. I rejoice most truly to find you are tolerably comfortable, & I hope it will increase. I should think you would have every attention and kindness from the female branches of the family, & you must try not to mind its head. He has indeed behaved shamefully towards you. Oh how angry I have been with him, but I dared not speak out when I was writing to Bath.[1] I have felt much, very much for you, my Mary Ann, and so longed to be able to have a chat with you. The reception you deserved on entering a family was indeed far different from what you received, but the love of money is the rock on which Uncle's good qualities have suffered a woeful shipwreck. . . .

Addressed: "Mr. Scott's, Sherborne."

SOPHIA R. SCOTT *to her Brother.*

December 18, 1822.

. . . Have you heard Papa's lectures have been answered by a Mr. Draper of Southampton? It is a small 2s. book, & more an attack on Unitarianism than a reply to Papa, for there are only two or three pages of argument in the whole. There is a good deal of show of candour & some compliments on Papa's character, but at the same time he gives him no credit for purity of intention or acting upon conviction,

[1] At Bath Robert Scott might expect to see letters addressed to his wife.

but asserts that Papa must know he was deceiving his hearers & asserting knowingly what is false. The subject is making a bustle at Chichester, it seems. A sermon in refutation of Papa's lectures is announced for next Sunday & Papa is styled the "Oracle of the South." . . .

Addressed: "Mr. Scott, Messrs. Cory & Scott, New Barge House, London."

SOPHIA R. SCOTT *to her Brother.*

January 10, 1823.

. . . You have been very gay indeed lately, quite keeping Xmas. I hope it agrees with you. We send you by this parcel part of our Twelfth Cake. We had a young & very merry party to keep that day & draw for King, Queen &c. . . . Did you think of us, dear Russell, as 1822 expired? We sat up as usual and thought of you. I do not know any year of my life which has so much added to my happiness as the last. You, my beloved Brother, stand prominent in this increase of Comfort. You have been in its progress settled in life as promisingly as you or we can desire, & still more grateful is it to the heart of your sister to feel persuaded you do indeed deserve every blessing which surrounds you. . . . During this year too we have the happiness of feeling that the comforts of our beloved parents are importantly increased, that they are now free from all cares & anxieties. I was scarcely aware how much money could increase my happiness till I felt its effects. . . . Do write soon to your affectionate Sister, S. R. SCOTT.

The above letter refers to my father's taking his place as a partner in the coal business. Mr. Benjamin Hawes, of Worthing, an uncle of my grandmother's, had recently died. He had been a blue and starch maker in Thames Street, and accumulated a considerable fortune. He left £35,000 to go to charities on the death of his niece, Lucy Hawes, and £80,000 to his nephews and nieces and their children. Of this sum £5000 came to my grandmother.

It had always been settled that on coming of age my father should have some share in the coal business. This most opportune legacy, however, with the £3000 belonging to my grandparents, which Messrs. T. & B. Hawes already held (mentioned on p. 154), sufficed to pay off their capital, and my father took their place as Mr. Cory's sole partner.

My mother once told me that Uncle Benjamin was unwilling to retire, as the business was a promising one. Uncle Thomas, however, was firm about it. This most kind uncle Thomas I have always regarded as the founder of my father's prosperity. I remember, when I was a child, seeing him as quite an old man, sitting in his dressing-gown in the window of his bedroom at Lavender Hill, his mind much impaired, but still evidently feeling very kindly towards my father, who brought me in to see him.

From this time forward my grandparents' means were much improved, as my father always paid them 5 per cent. on the capital they thus entrusted to him. He often spoke of the great confidence in him shown by his parents on this occasion.

I may mention here a [illegible]tle anecdote which my mother told me, and wh[illegible] doubt characteristic of these two uncles of [illegible]hers, who were in business toget[illegible] settled terms of partnership. [illegible]mas, an unmarried man, who li[illegible]and sisters at Lavender Hill, found that Uncle Benjamin, who had a large family and who lived expensively, was drawing considerably more than his share of the profits. Uncle Thomas made no complaint, but from that time forward whenever Uncle Benjamin drew a cheque, Uncle Thomas drew another of precisely the same amount, and so kept things even.

Rev. Russell Scott *to his Son.*

Portsmouth, *January* 10, 1823.

. . . One part of your letter, to which I was replying, remained unnoticed. I refer to that part of your letter where you express your hope & conviction that I shall never have cause to regret investing my money in your concern. If I had not entertained the same hope & conviction I should have hesitated more than I did before I made the proposal. And this I was led to do by the most anxious desire to see you in a way to become an useful & honourable member of society, & to provide for a wife & family agreeably to your wishes, as well as to secure your personal comfort as much as possible by confining the trade to Mr. Cory & yourself. And I rejoice most sincerely that it has been so effectually accomplished. . . . A part of what we obtain should be devoted to the purposes of religion and benevolence. And I feel much satisfaction in the persuasion that you possess the inclination thus to employ a portion of this world's goods. . . .

Sophia R. Scott *to her Brother.*

Portsmouth, *March* 18, 1823.

. . . They are having lectures at St. Johns Chapel to counteract the influence of Papa's. One of the lecturers, I believe from the great city, said the other day that the progress which had lately been made in overturning the Devil's Kingdom [illegible] him wrathful. . . .

SOPHIA R. SCOTT *to* MRS. ROBERT SCOTT.

Sept. 18, 1823.

. . . We did not visit the Valley of Rocks till the day before we left Devonshire, & getting up as we did morning after morning at 5 o'clock, walking or riding *all* day, I used to be so fagged at night that I really *could not* write. I did fully intend writing from Sherborne, but our few days went I scarce know how. I could not have conceived it possible to be out so long as we were without feeling a single hour's leisure; not *once* did I take up a book or work to occupy myself; there always seemed more to be done than could be accomplished. Had it not been for my beloved Papa's distressing & serious state of health, our journey would have been a constant source of enjoyment & delight. I thought my expectations high, but compared with realities they were as nothing. Such beautiful & delicious scenery as we beheld in some places, in others such extended, varied & lovely views; then again all grandeur & magnificence. I would not lose the recollection of them, the power of bringing them to my mind's eye, for a great, great deal. Dear Papa too at length grew better, & entered into everything with his wonted ardour, so that we had everything to make us happy, & most completely did we all enjoy ourselves. Although it has been a wet summer, I decidedly preferred it to a hot one. Extreme heat always makes me very languid; it is to the cool weather I feel in a great measure indebted for my great increase of strength; indeed I never was so well as now. Mamma says my improved health is worth all the journey. However this is not all, for she is very much improved also, & Papa too I am full of ho[illegible] permanently better. . . .

It is evident that this ex[illegible]
by the late increase in the f[illegible]
one of the party. Summer h[illegible]
spent in the Isle of Wight or a[illegible]

J. E. TAYLOR *to* SOPHIA RUSSELL SCOTT.

Dec. 1823.

. . . I am indeed, my love, most thankful to hear of your good health & I sincerely trust it will be preserved through the winter. When the shortest day is over I always think we are beginning to get towards Spring, but this year I know I shall think that Spring approaches very, very slowly. I hope indeed that this will be the last year of our lives on which we shall enter separated from each other, & I trust that each succeeding year will find the bond of affection & confidence more strongly uniting us. Shall you be up to see the New Year in, dearest? I shall, I have no doubt, & my last thoughts in 1823 & my first in 1824 will be of & for you. If you have time on Thursday, dearest, will you write to me, if it be only a *little* letter, just to send me a New Year's gift, & I will write to you as soon as I can, & tell you how I have got into my new house &c. . . . How I wish, my love, that I could make the wings of time wave faster to bring the 4th of May here sooner than it will naturally come. . . .

J. E. TAYLOR *to* SOPHIA RUSSELL SCOTT.

ISLINGTON STREET, SALFORD, *Dec.* 28, 1823.

I am writing to you, my dearest Sophia, for the last time (in all probability at least) not only in this year, but from this house—a house in which nearly one half of my life (at least more than fourteen years) has been passed, & which is therefore associated with numerous & interesting recollections. My sister said in one of her late letters to me "it makes me quite melancholy to think of your leaving Islington St."; & I will confess that in a certain way & to a certain extent it almost [illegible]kes me melancholy too. . . . Many of the years which have [illegible] I have been in this house have to me been very [illegible]e term of my residence in it comprises far the [illegible] portion of my life. When I came here my

Father was alive & in health, with peculiarities, certainly, resulting from his religious views, but possessing a fund of information & of general conversational talent, such as I have since met with in very few men indeed. He was too, all full of kindness to his children & of anxiety for their welfare, & attached to the memory of his wife, perhaps more than almost any person ever was who had so long been a widower. Here too it was that we saw so sad a contrast; his mind broken & his temper irritated by disease, until his faculties became so dreadfully shattered that even his death seemed a relief from a worse alternative, & the tears which natural feeling induced us to shed over his grave were quickly dried, from a conviction that neither to himself nor to his friends could his life, in the state in which he was, & was likely to be, be a thing any longer to be desired.

In this house too it was, dearest, that you came to see us; here it was that you first taught me to love you, & that my eyes often spoke & the pressure of my hands repeated language which it required a constant effort to make my tongue forbear to give utterance to. When I look back upon your visit to us, my Sophia, my falling in love with you seems like a thing of course. If I were to answer the question why I fell in love with you, I should say, because I could not help it, & if asked why I could not help it, my answer would be felt by myself, but I could not clothe it in words. And I do not think my love for you would be worth much if I could; for though I am sure it is ratified by my judgment as much as it exists in my heart, I have never been so methodical, so cool, I had almost said so cold-blooded, as to draw up even in my mind a catalogue of your good qualities & attractions. No, should the enquiry ever be made of me, I would reply to it by referring to my wife as a practical answer to it. Though I have many recollections of great pleasure associated with you, of which this house has been the scene, there are also others of great pain. Oh, what a sickening affair it was when every year seemed to increase the improbability of my being able to make you mine; when I felt restrained even by affection for you, & by considerations of prudence applying to us both, from asking you to quit the home of your parents for one perhaps of discomfort, arising from the uncertainty of competent income. Sometimes too I felt as though I had done you an injury. I knew that your most blooming years were passing away, & I could not help thinking that by engaging your affections I might have prevented you from forming a happier connection elsewhere. But I have said these things to you before, & why do I now repeat them? Simply because the circumstances in which I happen to be placed have forcibly recalled them to my memory.

From this house too it was that my sister, my only sister, the companion & friend of my childhood & more mature age, & whom, though I may at times have failed in the attentions she had a right to expect from me, I always tenderly loved & never was willingly unkind to, went forth to enter upon new relations & fill a new character in a distant scene. Though convinced that she was going to the protection of a kind husband, & that she had every prospect of worldly comfort, I parted from her with great regret, & my tears have never flowed since as they did when I returned into the parlour after she had just entered the chaise & drove off, & reflected that the link which had bound us together & made us—two orphans—almost all in all to each other, was broken for ever.

But there are other & livelier recollections, & this which I have just mentioned though it made me melancholy at the time, is in the common course of nature & therefore not a thing to be permanently repined at. Whilst I have lived in this house I have enjoyed much hearty sociality & much sincere friendship, & it is within that time too, that I have to date the commencement of that undertaking[1] to which I owe the means of being able to offer you, my beloved Sophia, I trust, a happy home & a permanent & comfortable income. However, my

[1] For the founding of the *Manchester Guardian* see the Appendix.

next home will be one more suitable for you, & therefore I have no doubt it will soon become dearer than this to me. I expect to be put in possession of the key tomorrow, & on Tuesday or Wednesday I think of removing. On some accounts it would be much more convenient to me to defer it a week or two, but on others I am anxious to get the job over as soon as possible. I think of asking Mrs. Shuttleworth to come & help me, as she has had a good deal of experience in the removing way, & you can't think how helpless I feel about it. Besides this I think I told you that I had promised to give my friends a treat as soon as I had passed the 100 advertisements, and this you see, my dear, I have now done at a hand-canter. . . . You would be astonished last week at the advert sements, weren't you, dear? I was at any rate. They kept pouring in so that I soon found there would be no room to spare for me, and therefore as my men were forward with their work I did what I have not done before on a Friday since I have had the *Guardian*. I went out to a 5 o'clock dinner, and stayed till 10 enjoying myself; then returned to the office, and left it for home at $\frac{1}{2}$ past 2. The profit that week was upwards of £36, and there was so little room for news that I wrote off on the Friday night about a quantity of smaller type to enable me to compress the advertisements into less compass. This will be an expense of £150 or £170, which I did not intend incurring at present: however, I cannot really say that I regret being obliged to do so. I was looking a little last evening at the result [illegible] half year, and I find the average of the advertisements [illegible] to be $73\frac{11}{21}$, and the average profit £21, 6s. 7d. pe[illegible] as I expect, the profit on the newspaper and the jo[illegible]s been sufficient to pay all expenses, that will ma[illegible]ofit on th[illegible] half year £550, and that is about what [illegible]nd. It wi[illegible] be a week or two, however, before I am [illegible] my stock-taking, and upon that week or two I d[illegible] look w[illegible] dread. . . .—Ev[illegible] ruly yours,

[illegible]YLOR.

SOPHIA R. SCOTT *to* MRS. ROBERT SCOTT.

April 8, 1824.

. . . And now, my dear Mary Ann, let me assure you that though I cannot deny some part of your first letter gave me pain, I at the same time fully appreciated & felt obliged by its frankness; & since it has been the means of removing uncomfortable feelings towards me from your mind, I feel most sincerely grateful to you for it. I am indeed very anxious to retain that place in your affections which it has been a source of so much pleasure to me to possess, & of which I trust no act of mine will ever deprive me. To be "peculiarly your sister" is indeed a delightful idea. I hope I should never love any one the less, but rather more, for telling me of my faults, for surely it is the greatest proof of true friendship; but on one point, my dear Mary Ann, you must allow me to make a little defence, & tho' you may not quite acquit me, I cannot help hoping you will perceive my conduct arose rather from the circumstances in which I was placed, than from a wilful deviation from that "straightforward sort of conduct" which you expected, & which I always wish to pursue. It was for a much longer time than six months after I left Manchester before I considered it at all beyond a *possible* thing that Edward & I should ever be more nearly connected; the distance from my home with all its consequences, & some other considerations, appeared to me to place an almost insuperable barrier between us. Could I then—was it not impossible—would it have been right to Edward to have told even his sister that such an event might *possibly* take place, but that I did not think it was likely? *More than this I could not have said*, & under these *peculiar*
[illegible] I do not see I had any alternative but *silence*.
[illegible] years before any one but yourself, except Papa
[illegible] of it; not even my own, my fondly loved
[illegible] was contrary to my wish, & he first heard
[illegible] ent channel. I always felt he had cause
[illegible] y good, tho' I know he felt it.

I will now tell you, as you wish it, when & how I was wounded; it was when you were here. From your manner then I certainly thought you disliked & disapproved of the connexion; this of course you were at full liberty to do; but I do assure you that if I had not had an opinion of Edward which nothing but fact could shake, things you said & hinted at would have broken off the connexion. Mamma has repeatedly said the same thing from what she heard you say. I often & often thought you must have some reason for what you said, some motive in saying it, & it made me miserable; it dwelt upon my mind; lessened my happiness, I think I may say, for years. I had no wish to enter into anything of this sort at such a time as this; I only did it because you expressed the wish to know my feelings. Believe me, my beloved Mary Ann, I think not now of these things; 'twas almost forgotten & will never I believe lessen the pleasure of our future intercourse, for I do indeed love you very much. . . .

Papa & Mamma have bought this house at last for £500; it is perhaps too much, but it is quite a relief to my mind. . . .

THOMAS HAWES *to* SOPHIA RUSSELL SCOTT.

[1824.]

I have not, my dear Sophia, been inattentive or indifferent to the Event now passing in our Family, in which you are so much interested. That it may be productive of every Happiness you expect (and which the uniform amiable conduct you have always shewn as a Daughter, Sister, and to all with whom you are related deserves), I most sincerely and truly wish. On an occasion like this, that naturally draws forth some expression of Interest and Kindness from those by whom it is felt, I have been much at a loss to select some Token of my Regard that was likely to be useful and acceptable, and have this Morning only been informed that what I had fixed on is in a great measure anticipated.

Fearing I might not make the best choice, I have determined to request you will take this trouble off my Hands into your

own, & when writing to Lavender Hill say whether (as there appears some purchases going forward here) I shall pay to your Aunt Sarah £100, or enclose it to you.

Remember me affectionately to your Father and Mother & believe me to be Sincerely your Friend & Uncle,

THOMAS HAWES.

SOPHIA RUSSELL SCOTT *to* J. E. TAYLOR.

Last letter before marriage.

PORTSMOUTH, *April* 26, 1824.
(My Papa's birthday.)

I am indeed, my beloved Edward, truly thankful to be enabled to send you tolerable tidings of my health, for the last has been a week of most painful anxiety to my Mamma, and of not a little to myself. But I am better, much better, and contrary to our expectations at one time, hope to present no obstacle to our long formed plans. . . . Unfortunate as this indisposition seems I almost rejoice in it from the good effects it has produced on my Mamma's mind; she has suffered so much from the idea of my being ill, that she says if I am but well, my going away seems comparatively trifling. She has, too, so much confidence in your care and watchfulness, and knows that if I can escape cold the journey will do me more good than anything. I am quite sorry, dearest Edward, you have so much to hurry you just at last. I quite agree with you that it would be a great pity you should spend Saturday in London, when it is so important you should be at home Friday. Never mind Russell—he only wants to have you. I do not think there can be any other reason. Sunday will be Faulkner's day. I hope you will come by the "Hero," but *do not be set down at the door*, for all our neighbours will see you. You can get down just outside the town, walk in, and have your luggage &c. sent up. And, my Edward, with respect to your journey from Manchester to London, I have one thing to beg of you, & for the *first* time. I *hope* you will be dutiful—*take an inside*

place. Ride outside as much as you please, but be able to get in if you feel inclined. You will oblige your Sophia, will you not, my own Edward? . . . I received another present this morning—a pair of silver candlesticks—the most massy and elegant I ever saw, or at least observed. They are from Benjamin and his brothers. . . .

I scarcely know how I feel at the idea that in this kind of intercourse, under my present character & signed by my present name, I am now about to bid you a final farewell. For nearly seven years the feelings your letters have breathed, the utterances of love they have borne, have been one source of my dearest, greatest happiness.

If ever woman had perfect, unlimited confidence in man, I have in you; if ever woman fervently desired to constitute her husband's perfect happiness, to be in every possible respect all he shall approve, to be the object of his fondest, tenderest love, this your Sophia does. And, my Edward, may God grant that our union be the source of that which is of all things most fervently to be desired—the improvement of our characters. May we so live that when either of us shall be separated from the other we may possess that greatest of all consolations—the hope of a future reunion in a state of superior intellectual and moral existence. Oh, it seems to me that if I could feel confident I was fit for Heaven, my cup of earthly happiness would be full and o'erflowing. . . .

Write *once* more, if it be but a few lines, by Wednesday's post. . . . Farewell! yes, I hope a last farewell from your very affectionate but almost expiring, SOPHIA RUSSELL SCOTT.

The marriage took place on May 4th, 1824.

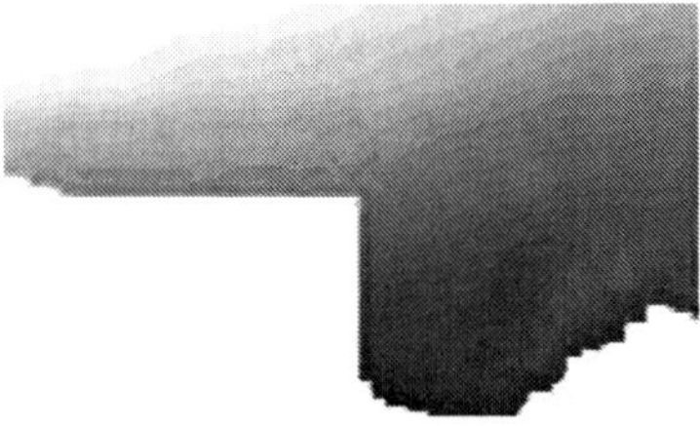

CHAPTER XI

MRS. J. E. TAYLOR'S MARRIED LIFE—DEATH OF HER MOTHER

1824-1829

Mrs. J. E. TAYLOR *to her Brother.*

MATLOCK, *May* 10, 1824.

I am quite sorry, my beloved Brother, to be within one day's journey of my new home without having written to you. . . . Writing home has completely occupied all our little leisure time, & this I could not neglect. I can scarcely believe it possible that a week has not yet run its little round since I saw you. It has indeed been an eventful period to me, involving such a change as would indeed be more than I could bear, if it had not been made for one whose qualities as a friend & companion will I believe compensate for all. I know not how I took leave of you, my Russell, nor indeed do I recollect that I took leave of any of you. I have tried in vain to recall it; the overwhelming feeling of the moment has made it as though it had never been . . . but of this I am sure, that nothing I could say could convey to you an adequate idea of the source of comfort & increase of happiness your interest & kindness on this occasion has been to my mind. . . .

The journey has surprisingly increased my strength, and I hope when you come you will be quite satisfied with your transplanted sister. When shall we have this happiness, dearest Russell? Your brother & sister are anticipating its near approach, the one with pleasure, the other with delight. Do write to me, very, very soon. You must not think, my dearest brother, because I have said nothing of home, that it is not in my mind.

Oh yes, it is indeed!—constantly & almost unceasingly there, exciting a poignancy of feeling which at times is agony; but 'tis done. Oh I trust not wrongly done! . . .

Russell Scott *to his Sister.*

May 15, 1824.

I must be permitted to commend you (now that all is past) for your very good behaviour on the 4th. I had no expectation that all could have passed off so well, for except the tragic scene just before you went, & a gloomy one for a very short time afterwards, there was little, while I was at Portsmouth, to give rise to painful feelings. . . . We made ourselves quite merry occasionally, as you would guess from the direction of your cake.

I scarcely know whether you were aware of the entertainment given on Wednesday in honour of a recent event . . . . a dinner at the Crown & Sceptre, Greenwich, being thought a more respectful mode of celebrating such an event than a supper at 12 Commercial Road [his lodgings]. I gave orders for a handsome one & a most pleasant afternoon we had. Aunt Gurney did every thing she could (& you know how much she can do) to make it so. Our first toast was of course "Mr. & Mrs. Edwd Taylor"; the next was "Success to Leap Year"—you will probably understand the allusion conveyed,—that as there were two marriages in the family last leap year, there ought also to be two this. I took occasion, to the great amusement of the party, although I ought not to say so, to allude to the station to which Harriet had become advanced by your secession, & suggested that Hampden should return thanks for her. "The junior branches of the family" was given, & much commendation bestowed on the excellence of Edward's choice, & hopes expressed that those present might be equally fortunate. I had to return thanks as the *senior junior* of the male part of the family, & was altogether kept pretty actively employed in my capacity of Chairman. We left about nine o'clock. . . .

Addressed: "Mrs. Taylor, Crescent, Salford."

Mrs. Scott *to her Son.*

Portsmouth, *May* 26, 1824.

I was, my dearest Russell, almost in the act of writing to you last week when we heard from your Aunt Sarah, to our no small astonishment, that you were really off for Manchester, & the next morning we had the satisfaction of hearing from yourself that you were arrived safely there. I think, my Russell, your Papa & I were almost as much pleased at your going as yourself, & as your sister & Edward were to receive you. I should like much your report of your sister, her situation & things around her. I long for such a sight as you have had, to think of her as she really is. Of Edward I feel no doubt but he will be all that is kind & affectionate. Nothing but the full persuasion of this supports me under the most painful loss I have sustained, but I am getting the better of the very distressing feelings I have experienced, & shall now be pretty much engaged till the time of our departure. In a little more than 6 weeks we shall be with her. . . . At Manchester we shall be quite at home. The change will I hope make your father quite well, & enable us to set off for the Lakes with full prospect of enjoyment. . . .

Be so kind as to order, to be sent to Hunter's for the monthly parcel, 2 pounds of 7 shilling tea, ½ lb. of 10s. black, 1 lb. of ground rice, ½ lb. of ginger. . . .

Hunter's was a bookseller's in St. Paul's Churchyard, from which a monthly parcel of books was sent down for the Reading Society, the members of which met at my grandfather's house. Letters were frequently sent in this way as well as many other things, as shown above. In other letters mention is made of the despatch of candles and of materials for clothing.

The expedition to the Lakes took place as planned. The party consisted of my grandfather and grandmother, their son and daughter, and her husband. A journal of the few weeks' trip remains.

Mrs. Samuel Scott *to* Mrs. Robert Scott.

Sherborne, *Jan.* 14, 1825.

. . . How many mercyes have been continued to us the last year, as a Family. We have many of us tasted the bitter cup of Affliction; but my beloved Robert has drank the deepest in that bitter cup. Afflictions draws a vaile over the prospects and pleasures of this short uncertain life, if we receive our Afflictions with a humble submition to the will of our heavenly Father they will open and enlarge the prospects of a better life, as Moses on the top of Pisgah saw the good land of Canaan before him while the wilderness was behind him. I sincerely hope that you will all live to see many returnes of this season in the enjoyment of the good things of life and in the prospect of more substantial and lasting blessings than can be enjoyed hear—I am, I thank God, as well as I can expect. When I look back on my life of seventy Years it seems to me as a variegated dream, a mear point, happy if it points to a blessed Eternity, that happiness I ardently hope, my beloved, we shall constantly keep in view, to this end may our Bible be our daily studdy and delight. I beg you to give a kiss to my dear babby for me, & am my dear Mary A. and Robert's truly affectionate

Mother.

Mr. and Mrs. Robert Scott had two children, Mary Downing Russell and Anna Sophia Russell. I have already mentioned this Mary, under her married name of Mrs. Elliott.

Mrs. J. E. Taylor *to her Brother.*

Tuesday morn, *March 8th*, 1825.

. . . Thank you, my brother, most affectionately for all your interest and solicitude for me at this time. The kindness I have experienced would amply repay me for a vast deal of suffering, if I had not in addition my darling babe hourly and minutely to reward me. I feel indeed that I have so much, so very much to be grateful for, that my chief fear is I do not feel as deeply as I ought to that Being who has not only spared my life, but blessed us with such an inestimable treasure in our infant—It was perhaps natural that a thousand anxieties should present themselves to the mind—now all are removed—a healthy, perfect child was all we desired or thought of; we have indeed one who seems to promise everything we can wish. I had no idea what delight there was in a mother's feelings till I became one. . . . Our little boy is to be a namesake of yours, Russell Scott; how I wish you could see him as I do at this moment, and hear his grandmamma talking to him as she has been doing while I have been writing. . . .

Mrs. Scott *to her Son.*

PORTSMOUTH, *Oct.* 16, 1825.

. . . You ask me, my Russell, if I am coming to town this winter. I think not this winter, but it is probable early in the Spring, unless it should run on to the time of your father's coming at Whitsuntide; but I do think, if all goes on as I wish, I may pay an annual visit as well as your father. You say, my dearest Russell, in this letter, you will not allow us to say "one word about expense because you know we have an adequate income if we will but spend it." I know, my Russell, you like to prove what you advance; now do prove to us that we have yet saved. We are fully sensible of the great kindness of both you & your sister, for wishing us every possible comfort we can enjoy & we do hope to live quite comfortably; as far as I am concerned I have no wish to save. I profess not to wish it, but we must look to the time when the £400 [1] will be all we shall have to defray our annual expenses—not very adequate,

[1] That is to say, when the time should come for my grandfather to retire from the ministry.

such times as these, & when either your father or I may be obliged to expend no small sum in medical attendance; but if your father is inclined to meet your views I am willing. I have urged him to borrow £100 of you to get quite clear of all our debts before Xmas. Your plan would I should hope make us begin the next year clear. We have desired to have our bill for painting, & and are afraid to look upon it; but enough of these things my dear Russell. I must hasten to conclude or this will not be with you tomorrow morning.—I remain most tenderly and affectionately your mother, S. S.

Mrs. Scott *to her Son.*

PORTSMOUTH, *November* 26, 1825.

I have not, my dearest Russell, returned an answer to your letter of Tuesday morning so soon as the contents of it demanded. We, my dearest Russell, feel it most tenderly and affectionately, & are confident you would act up most strictly to all you propose for us, but we trust it will never be put to the test. It has however this good effect upon my mind, to feel at perfect ease for the future. Respecting the sum you propose sending to us at Xmas, your father will have all his bills in by that time, & then determine the sum it is necessary for us to have which will set us easy for the next year. After that I hope we shall be enabled to adopt your plan of saving, and feel ourselves perfectly easy in spending as much as our wishes & wants require. What I have said, my dearest Russell, will I hope be perfectly satisfactory to you. I feel I ought to say more after such a letter from you. You may one day know how we must feel under it. . . .

J. E. Taylor *to his Brother-in-Law.*

MANCHESTER, *Dec.* 18, 1825.

My dear Russell,—I was indeed very much gratified by the receipt of your letter on Friday evening, for to say the truth I had been most anxiously wishing all week to hear from you, more especially from the time I heard of the severe run upon Lubbocks & Co. I congratulate you however on their having weathered the storm so gallantly, & I may also I hope congratulate you now that its violence is abated, on your having even whilst it was raging shown such confidence as not only not to withdraw your balance, but to increase it from day to day. It is perhaps scarcely possible but the late most extraordinary convulsion must have affected you directly or indirectly. I hope however you will suffer little if at all, from its consequences. I could scarcely help reproaching myself at times during the last week for having diminished your resources at such a period to the amount of £600, but if, as we may surely believe, the hurricane has spent its force I am willing to flatter myself the loan will not prove seriously inconvenient to you. . . .

J. E. TAYLOR *to* MRS. ROBERT SCOTT.

Jan. 19, 1826.

. . . I certainly should have written to you whilst these terrible tumults in the money market were proceeding, had it not been that I assured myself you would be aware of my anxiety, when the panic extended to your city. . . . I attended repeatedly, day after day, at the post office in the confident expectation of hearing from you, & much disappointed I frequently was at the non-arrival of a letter. However at last I welcomed your handwriting, & glad I was to do so. . . . I was very uneasy until I heard from you to know how Robert might be affected by the banks. However though of course it is unpleasant to lose anything, yet I think £40 is as little as under the circumstances he could expect to suffer. . . . I will confess to you, my dear Sister, that I have been far less concerned to hear of this loss of Robert's than I was a few weeks ago to learn from Russell that all his experience of speculating in foreign stocks had not cured the propensity, but that he had again bought when in London in the Autumn both in the Spanish & Columbian funds, & that at prices enormously higher than their present or probable value. I do really feel exceedingly mortified that having suffered so much as he has before, having injured his health so much, & made all his friends so uneasy in consequence, having seen & had urged on him the *great disadvantage* at which any person a hundred miles from London must be in buying into any of the Stock Exchange bubbles, (for I call them no better) or even into the English Funds unless it be for permanent investment, Robert should persist in running into fresh losses & in laying up for himself fresh stores of anxiety. How infinitely better it would have been to invest his money safely, even at a lower rate of interest, than make ducks & drakes of it in this kind of way. Perhaps I am saying too much; I am sure however that I am not saying a word but what is dictated by the kindest feelings & the sincerest wish that what is worked hard for should not be lightly thrown away. If you had now the money which has been wasted on these absurd speculations it would have made a very pretty addition to your income, & enabled you to allow yourselves with perfect propriety indulgences in various ways from which I sometimes think that a wish to be economical now too much excludes you. But I should not have thought the first loss without its use, if Robert had learnt wisdom from it. . . .

Our little darling is as good-tempered & merry as possible & the number of his engaging little ways is very great. He has wakened up to-night & is now (half past ten o'clock) shouting away in the nursery as merrily as if it was noon-day. He seems to possess as much intelligence as he does vivacity, & it often interests & astonishes me to see the signs of thought & ingenuity which he exhibits. . . . In many respects his taste strongly resembles mine. Sophia says he is his Father's own boy; he is not fond of sweets, will hardly touch a bit of pudding or pie, but eats dry bread or bread & cheese with great relish & enjoys exceedingly sucking an orange; he is allowed a part or a whole one every day. He was in the season equally fond of apples.[1] . . .

Mrs. Scott *to her Son.*

PORTSMOUTH, *March* 15, 1826.

. . . How very concerned I was, dearest Russell, to hear the views that were likely so much to influence the future character of that sweet and lovely girl Louisa [Gurney]. What can have led to it? Are any, they are in the habit of associating with, in that connection? We cannot but regret that so much that is amiable & pleasing in character is likely to undergo a change, & that at her time of life she should feel it a duty to give up the innocent amusements of life, without an error or failing in thought, word, or deed. I never was more astonished. If you hear any more about it tell me. . . .

The younger Gurneys all joined the Church of England, and some of them became very "evangelical." They had been brought up as Unitarians. My mother told me that it was the influence of a governess that led to the change. Hampden Gurney became a clergyman. Louisa afterwards married a missionary (Mr. Start), and went to India, where she died a few years later.

During the autumn and winter of 1826, Mrs. Scott suffered from repeated attacks of illness, which gradually became more severe. The letters of Mrs. J. E. Taylor, written in the spring of 1827 to her brother, of which we have many, show the greatest anxiety and distress on their mother's account.

[1] He was at this time only eleven months old.

Mrs. J. E. Taylor *to her Brother.*

Manchester, *April* 2, 1827.

. . . O my Brother, if I could but have the fondest, the most anxious wish of my heart which is connected only with this world accomplished, by having Mamma & Papa removed hither, then I should indeed hope that if not quite strong she would be cheerful, happy & at ease. How constantly has my mind dwelt on this ideà ever since our marriage, but all this winter still more anxiously. I could then watch over & attend upon her; the children would afford her amusement without exertion, & to me my home would be like a little Paradise. Edward was saying only yesterday that perhaps we might be able to get a house of which Papa & Mamma could have a part, or at all events there would be little difficulty of getting one very near us. I am anxious to know what you think of our strongly urging this plan. You could do it best. My only fear is about Papa, but I think he would find abundant sources of occupation, interest & usefulness here. He is much known & as much respected, & I cannot help feeling sanguine he would be cheerful & happy. To you, I hope the change would not be a lessening of enjoyment; *we* should see you oftener, but I know you would not let self influence you. . . .

Mrs. J. E. Taylor *to her Brother.*

Manchester, *May* 6, 1827.

I was indeed, my dearest Brother, most truly grateful to receive from you an account of the continuance of that improvement in our beloved Mother's health. . . . I was so completely distressed with your report this day week that I resolved nothing should any longer interfere with my going to Mamma as soon as possible. . . . Mamma however appeared so decidedly to wish me not to go at present, that I of course relinquished this plan. . . . The first part of your letter yesterday made me feel quite myself again. My prospects seemed once more full of hope & gladness, & fancy was instantly picturing Mamma here again making us happy. Judge then how thunder-struck I was to find that any possible opposition could be made to her coming to see me & my children, that with every comfort about me, with the means of contributing to her comfort in every way, with a husband who would make any sacrifice for her good, I am likely to be deprived of the greatest happiness I could experience. I really scarcely felt myself. If Mamma could not undertake the journey we must submit, but if she be able as I now strongly hope she may, on what ground can it be opposed? Heaven knows I would sacrifice any personal wish or pleasure that I thought could interfere *possibly* or in the least with her recovery, but I am *sure it would do her good. I know she has always been better when with us;* everybody remarked how she improved last summer, & now I could be *devoted* to her, take her out for rides or do anything that could be of service to her. And is all this to be denied me? Are parent & child to be separated from the influence of any one? O my Brother, surely this happiness to which I have in anticipation so fondly clung is not to be denied me; but why should I thus write to you? You will do all you can that is good & kind, I know. But really I cannot help expressing a portion of my feelings. *I know not what to do*, how to act; I should be afraid to say much to Mamma lest my contending feelings might injure her. I did however write strongly before I received your letter. Could you not ascertain Mamma's wishes & feelings? Judging from her letter she quite looks to it. What an idea that she should not wish it! What a monstrous idea that Papa might oppose it! I should not hesitate a moment in going to Portsmouth if Mamma could not come here, but I should hesitate much if Mamma could come & did not, for it would be a serious thing to be away from Edward & my children, & I also know that it would be very serious to Mamma to part with me, under the idea of a long separation. Now if they came here shortly I could then go down for a visit some months hence,

& the prospect of this would prevent Mamma suffering as I feared she did last time from the separation. I should like to know on what grounds the objections rest & what course you think I had best take. Do tell me in your next what can possibly have given Aunt [Sarah] so strong a feeling upon it. . . .

In reply to this letter Mrs. Taylor appears to have heard from her brother that their mother, who was staying at Lavender Hill, was too ill to take the journey.

Mrs. J. E. TAYLOR *to her Brother.*

MANCHESTER, *May* 16, 1827.

. . . I had intended writing to you either to night or to-morrow, my beloved Brother, before I received your letter of this evening. Since its arrival I have felt almost unequal to doing so, yet I must write; I have scarcely been more deeply distressed by any account of Mamma than by yours tonight. I had so buoyed myself up with the hope that she was really getting better that I almost felt confidence about it, & began to be quite in spirits, for every day that I did *not* hear, I fancied was a confirmation of my hopes. My mind was dwelling upon the idea that to-night's letter would give me a fair prospect of having her here, but how different are my feelings now! I have hitherto borne up wonderfully. I have felt perhaps more sanguine than I ought, but now I am [illegible] sufficiently cast down. These returns [illegible] appear to me extraordinary as [illegible] couraging. . . . I thought you [illegible] myself too strongly in my last [illegible] myself upon reflecting on it, but [illegible] some excuse for a short-lived [illegible] how many months has my mind [illegible] my Mamma here this [illegible]mmer. [illegible] be perfect in happiness; with what increased delight have I looked at my children, thinking how Mamma would love them. If these loved anticipations cannot be realized it is my duty to submit, but that they should be disappointed without absolute necessity seemed too much to bear. . . .

Mrs. J. E. TAYLOR *to* Mrs. ROBERT SCOTT.

LAVENDER HILL, *June* 23, 1827.

I am most truly thankful to be enabled to give you a much better account of my beloved Mamma, than I had feared I should do. For the last fortnight she has been decidedly improving . . ., & she has not had a return of that distressing & alarming weakness which she so frequently suffered from before. . . . She is, alas, in person almost a shadow of what she was. I cannot fix my eyes upon her for it makes my heart misgive me, but still the expression of her countenance is such as to give me strong hope of a restoration to health. O my dearest sister, I am indeed now tried, for I feel now I am here, how shall I leave her, & yet what claims upon my tenderest love have I miles & miles away. . . . We left Manchester 8 minutes before six [P.M.] & arrived in London at five [P.M.]. I bore it very well. If Mamma continues mending, I have no doubt I shall get quite well, but while at home I had so much anxiety it was scarcely possible I could be so. . . .

Rev. RUSSELL SCOTT *to* Mrs. ROBERT SCOTT.

PORTSMOUTH, *August* 5, 1827.

. . . The plan of your Aunt's returning home last week was changed for a short residence at Little Hampton—a very retired [illegible]llage on the Sussex coast, between Arundel & Worthing. [illegible] Aunt, Miss Hawes & Sophia arrived there on Tuesday [illegible] in Mr. Hawes's carriage. Your Aunt bore the journey [illegible]pected, but she has become rather worse [illegible]s to return home on Wednesday. . . .

Russell came down last week, as a member of our Corporation, in order to wait on the Duke of Clarence with an address on his appointment to the distinguished & important office of Lord High Admiral, & afterwards to receive him at dinner. By Wednesday evening the great bustle & noise occasioned by the frequent parading of the military & the firing of cannon will have nearly subsided, as the Duke & Duchess of Clarence leave on Thursday morning. It never would have done for your Aunt to have been in Portsmouth during the last week & the beginning of this.

The party returned, as arranged, and Sophia appears to have remained at Portsmouth with her mother till the middle of October. Mr. Taylor and my father in the meantime paid a short visit to Paris.

Mrs. Scott *to her Son.*

[Portsmouth, *October* 18, 1827.]

We, my dearest Russell, took it most kind & feeling of you to take so much pains to prevent our being uneasy about you. . . . Edward's journal made us travel most pleasant with you till that time I parted with your sister on Monday evening. I could not consent to her staying after that time, desirous as she was of it; but the parting must come, & whether now or a few weeks hence it only required resolution to meet it. . . . Having lost her, I give you my word I am perfectly comfortable in being without any one else. Do not therefore be the least anxious about your aunt's [Sarah] arrival. I shall be much hurt if she were to make herself anxious to come to me before she has settled in things with comfort for Brother, & I will promise to write if I need it, which I have not the least expectation of. I can only expect to go on in my poorly lingering way, & thank God I can meet it. When you can run down, so as not to interfere with business, I shall be most glad to see you. I have thought perhaps you might come down in the day of a Saturday, or on Friday night & return Sunday night, or any plan you can best think of to be absent but a little time. Your sister is I suppose to-day at Bristol, to-morrow intends setting off for Birmingham, home I trust safe & well on Saturday afternoon. With every kind feeling & full of affection, ever tenderly your Mother.

Assure yourself I have every attention and every comfort about me I can desire. I am, when up, in the library on the sofa with your papa.

Evidently Edward returned from Paris by way of Portsmouth and took his wife home.

It will be noticed that Mrs. Scott speaks of "Brother." Thomas Hawes, of Lavender Hill, being the eldest, was always called "Brother" or "Uncle" without a Christian name.

Mrs. J. E. Taylor *to* Mrs. Robert Scott.

Manchester, *November* 23, 1827.

. . . I have not taken our Boy to Chapel yet, my dearest Sister, nor have I any intention of doing so for a long time. I think if you take a child early it must be irksome to them & they acquire the habit of sleeping or fidgeting which is not easily broken; by waiting a little & making it a privilege to go you have the advantage of early association in making the attendance upon public worship more highly valued & enjoyed through life; at least thus I trust we shall find it, if our lives are spared to witness the formation of their characters. Oh, what depth of anxiety is there in the thought of what our children will be in character & conduct! What responsibility there is in becoming a parent! I feel it more & more. Where you have but one child I think it alters the case much with respect to taking them to Chapel, because you must keep some one at home to take care of them. . . .

J. E. TAYLOR *to* MRS. ROBERT SCOTT.

MANCHESTER, *January* 13, 1828.

. . . I had heard from Russell when he came down for Sophia of Robert's hasty trip to London, & I must say I am very sorry he will keep running after some new thing. However I am glad he has had the discretion not to commit himself with Gurney's carriage at present, for though I have no doubt that steam carriages will ere long be introduced I think it very probable they will be far from profitable to those who first put them on the roads. At any rate my motto would always be in Robert's situation & my own "Security with a small return, rather than risk for the temptation of a large one" . . .

MRS. J. E. TAYLOR *to* MRS. ROBERT SCOTT.

PORTSMOUTH, *Ap.* 7, 1828.

. . . I arrived here on Thursday evening, & found my beloved Mamma very ill indeed. She is more altered & reduced than I thought it possible she could alter. . . . She does not suffer much from actual pain, but a great deal indeed from weakness, sinking & exhaustion. . . . I pray we may all be supported under this great affliction. Some months ago I should have thought it more than I could have supported, but we know not what we are enabled to bear till the time of trial comes. . . . I heard from my dearest Edward yesterday. Excepting being very dull & desolate he is very well. He says he finds no use for his tongue when he goes home now. Our children are at Lavender Hill. . . .

Mrs. Taylor brought her children up from Manchester, but left them at Lavender Hill, in readiness to go to Portsmouth if their grandmother should wish to see them.

Rev. RUSSELL SCOTT *to* Mrs. ROBERT SCOTT.

PORTSMOUTH, *April* 8, 1828.

. . . You are right, my dear. The first division on the repeal of the Corporation & Test laws[1] was such as no one I believe did anticipate. It bespeaks a spirit of liberality in the rising generation which is truly cheering. All the young members in the House of Commons voted for the repeal, & two of them made most excellent maiden speeches on the occasion. I am surprised that no petition for the repeal has gone from Argyle Chapel [Bath] & still more so that Mr. Jay should not think it incumbent on him to inform the minds of his younger hearers at least on the subject. When my congregation met last year to petition for the repeal of these laws I thought it my duty to make my audience acquainted with the subject, aware that very few of them could know any thing about it, as the subject had not for so long a period been brought under public discussion. The hour & half I devoted to the subject was well repaid by the interest which my congregation then took in it, as well as again this year. . . .

ELIZA SCOTT *to* Mrs. ROBERT SCOTT.

LONDON, *April* 14, 1828.

. . . I thought my letter would be more acceptable if I deferred writing a little longer until I could give you some little account of your nephew & niece. I was quite disappointed at not seeing Sophia. Had I known the day she would spend at Lavender Hill I should certainly have taken a ride to have seen her. When too late Russell regretted that he had not made the communication, but he is not very apt to think of those things; but I have not much reason to complain of him. I went to Mr. Hawes's on Wednesday, when I was introduced to my

[1] The Test Act passed in 1673, and repealed on May 9, 1828, required as a condition of holding public offices, the taking of the Sacrament in church, and a declaration against Transubstantiation.

little cousins who are two of the finest children I have seen a long time. They have beautiful complexions, fine dark eyes & eyelashes, & are remarkably upright. The boy is like Papa, the girl Mamma. Russell's hair curls over his forehead; he told me the hairdresser curled it for him. . . .

Mrs. J. E. Taylor *to her Brother.*

PORTSMOUTH, *April 21st*, 1828.

I have only, my dearest Brother, a continuation of the same melancholy account to give you respecting our beloved Mother's now truly distressing state. I do not think she has been herself one quarter of an hour since the middle of the day yesterday; her mind is either rambling or highly delirious. She has scarcely slept & I may say scarcely laid down, but is almost continually sitting up in bed feeling about after things she fancies she sees. O my Brother, this is indeed a time of trial, but I am supported under it better than I could have thought possible. Mr. Thompson . . . does not think there is any immediate danger, but I cannot think her feeble frame can long struggle with the effects of the artificial strength fever now gives her. . . . I do not know how you will decide, my brother, as to coming down. I dare not buoy myself up with the hope she will be better than she is. At present I think she would take little notice of you, but in what way she may change, we of course can form no opinion. . . . She fancied you were here last evening & said "O Russell, love!" What has most dwelt upon her mind for the last 24 hours is the children. She is continually fancying they are come, & thinking it is the time for them to arrive, or thinking she sees them, & in her moments of recollection she is planning things for them & ordering things to be done against they arrive. Mr. Thompson said this morning he thought if she were to be disappointed of seeing them her mind would quite go. How I regret I put them off one day; it was the only part I took about their coming & little did I think it would be of so much importance. . . .

Three days after this letter was written, on April 24, Mrs. Scott died.

MRS. J. E. TAYLOR *to* MRS. ROBERT SCOTT.

PORTSMOUTH, *May* 21, 1828.

I am very sorry, my dearest Sister, your letter has remained till this time unanswered, but you will scarcely be surprised that I know not how to summon resolution to write upon a subject which is indeed almost ever present to my mind, but which is more forcibly and painfully impressed upon it when answering such a letter as yours. For all the kindness and sympathy of that letter, my dear sister, my heart most warmly thanks you. I knew well how much you would feel for us. I know how much you loved & how highly you appreciated the beloved being we have lost, & your affection for her binds you closer to her daughter's heart. But I *dare not dwell* upon the extent of my loss, which I feel more & more poignantly every day. My feelings at first were nothing compared with what they now are, for I saw my Mamma live till I felt almost thankful when that life was suspended, & the extraordinary pleasure & interest she felt about our beloved children is the only bright gleam which calms the recollection of the last few days; for tho' not a murmur or complaint escaped her I am sure her sufferings were great, & they were indeed most agonizing to those who witnessed them. It were impossible for a family to have greater sources of consolation than we have—for her we can have no anxieties—the loss is only ours & the respect which has been shown to her memory, the high & universal appreciation of a character whose peculiar excellence was of the retired & unobtrusive kind, has consoled us more than any other earthly comfort could have done—it has been far beyond our expectations. For myself I feel indeed I ought not to sorrow too much. I have indeed lost one great blessing, but what inestimable blessings have I left, blessings for which I never can be sufficiently thankful. . . . I do not know, my sister, whether you are aware our children only arrived on the Tuesday preceding our loss, & after we had thought her so ill that almost all prospect of her knowing anything of their coming was over; but to my astonishment she revived, ordered the minutest things for their comfort, a cake to be made for them, what was for their tea &c., & at five o'clock she said after scarcely speaking for hours "They will be here in half an hour" & she listened for the coach as I did. When they arrived I said "I shall not bring them to you Mamma, till you express a wish to see them," "Let them come directly," she replied, & she certainly was made as happy as could be by the sight;. she made minute remarks upon them as to their countenances & resemblance. She continued to see them often—said they did not disturb her the least—that she liked to hear Boy's "sweet prattle" & this to the morning of the day that closed her life; & when her power of speech was nearly gone I could tell by the words I could catch that she was talking of them. I trust all her wishes were gratified. She was very desirous to see Edward, & this also was accomplished. My sweet Boy's grief at finding she was dead was beyond any conception I could have formed of grief in a child. I did not tell him for a week; he was daily asking when he might go in to see his Grandmamma, & at last I told him; it was nearly an hour before we could pacify him & his expressions were quite heart-rending, such as, 'Give Grandmamma physic,' 'Send her Boy's kisses,' 'Boy has no Grandmamma, take Boy home,' & others of a similar nature, & it is still the constant subject of his thoughts. . . . I stay here till the 9th of June, for Papa is not in a state of health or spirits that I could possibly leave him till he can also go. He accompanies us to London, stays ten days, then returns & sets off for the West; after he has paid his visits there I hope you will be sufficiently recovered to enjoy him. . . .

Rev. Russell Scott *to* Mrs. Robert Scott.

Portsmouth, *June* 23, 1828.

. . . On Thursday evening I returned to a very sad, sad home & have been suffering from my melancholy solitude ever since. I leave it again at 2 o'clock for Poole, & then to Evershot,[1] afterwards for Sherborne; & then towards the end of July I trust for Bath, that is if you should be well enough to receive me. These changes I hope will be beneficial to me, & enable me to return to my solitary habitation with more comfort than I have now done. I had the satisfaction of hearing yesterday morning that my beloved Sophia set off on her long journey very comfortably the preceding evening. I feel it very, very long before I can hear of her at Poole, on Tuesday morning. I am very anxious on her account, but I trust I shall receive a favourable report of her progress. . . .

J. E. Taylor *to* Mrs. Robert Scott.

Manchester, *July* 2, 1828.

. . . I do not know whether you had been at all apprised of our plan, which was to take the inside of the Defiance London Coach. . . . The children made capital travellers. Our little Sophia never uttered the least syllable of impatience during the whole journey, & the most her brother said was, when we had got within 30 or 40 miles of Manchester, "Boy begins to be tired of this coach," when she replied "You had better lie down, Brother" which he did & went to sleep. In a quarter of an hour after they got in they were both as busy with their playthings as they were likely to be on first getting up in a morning, & when Boy was summoned to dinner he said he "could not spare time to come." So that on the whole I think we got through our journey quite as satisfactorily as could be wished. . . .

[1] The home of Mr. and Mrs. Petty.

The boy at this time was three years and four months old, and little Sophia one year and ten months.

In the following August another son was born to Mr. and Mrs. Taylor. They gave him his father's name, John Edward. He lived only six months, and during that time needed constant care and nursing.

MRS. J. E. TAYLOR *to her Brother.*

MANCHESTER, *Jan.* 20, 1829.

. . . My anxiety for him to recover is certainly lessened from the great apprehension I have lest his head should in any way be wrong. Mr. Whatton says if he were his child he could not wish it; but O my brother, when I see an occasional though faint smile gladden his countenance, when I look at his eye watching for me, and turning wherever he hears my voice, when I watch over his sufferings and his uncommon patience, can I feel otherwise than that it would indeed be happiness to save him? But I am resigned. I have borne too much these last two years not to be able to support this trial if it be the will of Heaven. . . .

In February the baby died. Mrs. Taylor's health never recovered from the fatigue of nursing him, following as it did on the long strain of her mother's illness and death. She wrote to her brother that she was almost worn out with want of rest.

MRS. SAMUEL SCOTT *to* MRS. ROBERT SCOTT.

Novr 19, 1828.

As Mr. Scott, my dear fellow travelour for nearly fifty years, is going to send a parcel I will write a line to my dear Mary Ann. We ware surprized and very glad to see my dear Robert looking so well and he gave us a good account of his family at

home. Surely we are surrounded with goodness and mercy. May they lead us to the founting from whence they all flow, Anna came home safe and well. We are all enjoying a comfortable share of helth. I hope my dear little granddaughters and their Parents will continue to enjoy their health for you have now another blessing added to your cares, and O may your care to traine up your tender babes for God be crowned with success, they will then be eternal blessings. I shall always be happy to receive a letter from my dear Daughter . . . you must not impute my silence to forgettfullness, for I cannot forget my beloved family for the hope of meeting them in a better world is the sweetest consolation in this state of tryal. . . . I hope my dear Robert had a safe journey home, beg my love to him and to my dear Mary, and I hope that she will love her dear little sister for my sake, farewell my dear Daughter, from your affectionate Mother G. SCOTT.

Rev. RUSSELL SCOTT *to his Son.*

PORTSMOUTH, *Jan.* 18, 1829.

. . . If you have seen Eliza Scott lately, you will of course have heard from her of the death of Mr. Scott of Morden. . . . By the Portsmouth paper of this day, I see it is reported that he has died worth £200,000, & that having died without a will his property will go to his sisters Mrs. Gould & Miss Scott & his nephew Mr. J. S. Gould. . . . That he has died without a will I think is most probable, which I dare say will be a great disappointment to some distant relatives at Bath,[1] where I believe considerable expectations had been cherished; but certainly without any just grounds. . . . His landed property, I suppose will go to Mr. Gould by inheritance & his personal be divided between the sisters. . . . I think also that Mrs. Petty had expectations, & certainly with more reason. . . .

Dr. Lardner has written against the Arians. Neither Sir I. Newton nor his learned friend & associate Hopton Haynes were

[1] Mr. Robert Scott.

Arians. Locke was more of a Socinian than an Arian. Milton I have not read, but from extracts that I have seen, he does not appear to have departed so much from the system advocated in his *Paradise Lost & Regained* as Arianism. . . .

CHAPTER XII

LIFE OF RUSSELL SCOTT—*Continued*

1829–1831

MY father was now twenty-eight years old, and in a position to marry. He wished to make his cousin Sarah, daughter of his uncle Benjamin, his wife and received much encouragement from her father and brother.

Mrs. J. E. TAYLOR *to her Brother.*

MANCHESTER, *Nov.* 11, 1829.

. . . How I wish I could but see Sarah, provided I might converse about you, for I am completely at a loss to conjecture in what state her mind is. I have had some very uncomfortable fears since your letter last evening, whether she might not be startled almost by a tone of feeling & expression on religious subjects differing so widely from her habits & education, & form erroneous ideas of you. Of her, you know I know nothing. The fears I have had since last night were that I should not hear from you tonight, & I knew not how to wait 24 more hours. Little did I expect so painful a letter, yet the more I reflect upon it, the stronger hope I feel that ere this reaches you, you may be under more happy feelings. . . . Most anxiously & affectionately, my beloved brother, yours, S. R. TAYLOR.

Mrs. J. E. TAYLOR *to her Brother.*

MANCHESTER, *Nov.* 14, 1829.

. . . Far from minding your not coming, my beloved brother, I was exceedingly relieved when Edward came alone, for we

hoped the result of Uncle Benjamin's visit had been favourable to your wishes. Your letter therefore has disappointed us, as though I trust it is auspicious, still it does not appear so much so as we hoped when we did not see you. I think however you are quite right to remain on the spot. With respect to writing to Sarah, I need not tell you how gladly I would do anything you should wish or that could by any possibility promote a favourable feeling in her mind, but I am so totally at a loss in what sort of way or to what in you or your letters she objects, or whether it is from herself, or she is influenced by others, that I could not—unless you can give me some information upon it, or express a wish that I should at all events write to her,—I could not feel any confidence that I should be doing you any good. I of course do not know Sarah, & I in fact know nothing how matters stand, but from what I do gather I certainly cannot comprehend her conduct, & I must *feel* cordial to write so. She knows you, & she ought to appreciate your character if she is to be my sister, & as to merely urging or persuading, I think it would be hardly consistent with the high estimation in which I hold the dignity of your character. You may feel very humble just now, but I do not for you. I am delighted at Benjamin's cordiality. Do endeavour to let us know a little how things are, especially the result of uncle B.'s visit. I trust you are quite well, but I cannot but feel very uneasy at the state of mind in which you are kept. Do not be hurt with me because I may feel a little disposed to blame Sarah. . . . Most affectionately your sister S. R. TAYLOR.

J. E. TAYLOR *to* RUSSELL SCOTT.

MANCHESTER, *Nov.* 23, 1829.

MY DEAR RUSSELL,—I cannot but hope that what has passed with Mr. Cory & his little techiness may have the effect of inducing you to give up the notion of living at the West End, at any rate for a few years. If Sarah is (& I assure you I do not in the least mean to question it) a woman of the good sense you

attribute to her, I think she will be quite desirous to promote your sedulous application to business; and I think she will not be disposed to quarrel with a part of the town in which her brother & sister both reside. Mr. Cory's apprehensions that your attentions to a wife would be inconsistent with what he deemed necessary attention to business, would I fear be in his opinion quite in the way of being realized if he found you taking a house at the West End, & what he would consider as a necessary consequence, indulging in West End habits & expenses. You are a young man, & successful as you have been the caution may seem needless, but it is still a valuable one—that it is infinitely easier to rise than to descend—that you could lose nothing (not in a pecuniary point of view only) but in the consideration of those whose good opinion you ought to value, by not setting out immediately upon marriage in the style you might (I hope) very properly assume a few years afterwards. Take a little time to see how you are going on, & pay that attention to business in discharge of an obligation to your partner which you would wish him to pay to it in discharge of an obligation to you. . . .

Mrs. J. E. Taylor *to* Mrs. Robert Scott.

Manchester, *Dec.* 6, 1829.

I am sorry, my dear sister, you have been so uneasy about Edward; he is I am most thankful to tell you now quite well. . . . He had a series of colds, one after the other, till at last they ended in a serious illness . . . & before he got strong he went whisking through the air, at an immense velocity, on the Liverpool railroad, without a great coat, which Mr. Whatton called "a very young trick." . . .

This is the first notice we have of an affection of the throat from which Mr. Taylor suffered from this time forward. It very gradually increased and eventually led to his death. The Manchester and Liverpool Railway

was not opened till September 15, 1830. This journey of Mr. Taylor's was on a trial trip, in an open car.

The following letters seem to show that Mr. Cory, my father's partner and the head of the firm, had reason to feel that this uncomfortable love-making was not conducive to attention to business on my father's part.

WILLIAM CORY *to* RUSSELL SCOTT.

NEW BARGE HOUSE WHARF, *Nov.* 19, 1829.

DEAR SIR,—You have sometimes accused me of too sanguine a disposition, but I believe that has not been the case of late upon most matters, tho' there is one affair in which I fear I have for some time indulged hope too much; partly probably from my natural temperament; but principally from a feeling of respect & esteem for you; & tho' I have often felt personal inconvenience in consequence of what I have conceived to be a want of proper attention to business on your part (on which subject I have addressed you more than once) I have been disposed to think no more of it, when I have found you again affording me that assistance, which you are so well able to do, in particular parts of our concern, but which upon a retrospective view of some years appears to me to have been irregular & uncertain, nearly always making attention to business, and consequently my comforts, a secondary object—& I must confess that I conceive your late visit to Manchester partakes strongly of this character. . . . I think it was nearly in the last conversation which took place between us on the subject of your attachment that you stated you had not for some time past felt any interest in business, because you considered you had money enough—Now I am ready to acknowledge the candour of this declaration, but as the man who has rendered you some assistance in getting this money (& who thinks he possesses some share of your friendship) has a large family dependent upon him for support, & is of course desirous to increase his property, I think a little interest might have been felt upon his account; but this declaration in addition to another—that in the event of your proving unsuccessful you should quit London—seems conclusive on your part, & now I feel bound in justice to you & to myself to make a declaration equally conclusive on my part—viz., that nothing shall induce me to place myself in a situation where there will be a possibility of my affairs ever again being in any way subject to the control, influence or interference of the Gentleman who destroyed the letter you had intended to send to me, & which I have no doubt was a very proper letter to be sent. I receive this as an earnest of what I might expect; indeed of what I feel certain would be, in the event of the alliance between you & him becoming more closely cemented, & which if your happiness depends upon it I sincerely hope will be the result.

With this view of the case then I have only to add that it is my wish that as speedy a termination should be put to our partnership as an equitable arrangement will admit of & I feel convinced that we shall both be governed by friendly feelings in carrying it into effect.

The "gentleman who destroyed the letter" was no doubt my father's uncle, Benjamin Hawes.

WILLIAM CORY *to* RUSSELL SCOTT.

COMMERCIAL ROAD, *Nov.* 27, 1829.

. . . I shall rely with confidence on your not permitting Mr. Benj. Hawes to interfere with our affairs & the gentleman you have named as your exor., [J. E. Taylor] in the event of what may be considered a very remote contingency, satisfies me that I should still be safe, & therefore I am willing to consider that matter disposed of. From what you have stated to me in conversation on the subject, & from the contents of your letter, & I will add from what I think I know of your disposition, I have every reason to believe that you are inclined to make such an arrangement with me as may enable me to do justice to my family, & if my thoughts are correct on this point I do not anticipate any difficulty in settling the matter to the satisfaction of both parties. I know of no person more capable of forming a correct view of the subject (except yourself) than Mr. Taylor because I consider that his head & his heart are right.

I think I need not say more at present to satisfy you of my feelings & wishes.

I believe my part of our articles is locked in a drawer of which I some time since lost the key, but in case of need I can refer to yours. One new clause I shall propose which is "that William Cory & Russell Scott mutually agree to attend at the counting house alternate months after dinner." I have a vile pen & cannot see to mend it.[1]

William Cory *to* Russell Scott.

December 15, 1829.

Dear Sir,—In reflecting upon the observation in your last short letter to me, that you could not answer mine (which was nearly equally short) in writing, & also in reflecting upon the short interview which took place at your request upon the subject of it, when you stated that it appeared as if I wished to hurry you, & I think said something about my wishing to take advantage of the circumstances of your situation, I am driven to what I feel to be a necessary but most unsatisfactory result; but before I state to you this result I shall trouble you with a few observations which now must be considered as free from self interest, & I assure you are not intended to give offence. I begin with the period when I was applied to by your uncle Benjamin on the subject of a partnership with his brother & himself in the coal trade, when flaming promises & assurances were given; when he undertook to sell as many coals in the year as I

[1] Quills only were used at this time and for many years later.

did; after ascertaining that my expected quantity was 30,000 chauldron; when in consequence of my belief in his promises, & by his I may almost say sole advice, I built a house the cost of which was extremely inconvenient to me. In full reliance upon him & confidence in what I had myself undertaken to perform, an expensive wharf was taken, a large stock of Barges, Horses, Waggons etc purchased, every way commensurate with a grand concern. How woefully I was deceived I need not tell you; for four years I was in misery; my health & spirits broken; my little all nearly vanished & I almost within a step of being a ruined man. But about this period I was released of a hated connection & you became my partner; from a variety of causes the scene was most providentially changed, & a more pleasing picture presented to my view, & I am happy to acknowledge that considerable success has attended our efforts ever since.

I am now going to advert to circumstances which as I have before stated must be stripped of the suspicion of self interested views by the conclusion of this letter. You have more than once or twice said to me that you were getting too much money, or words to that effect, & at our last balancing you most strikingly alluded to this circumstance at a period when the figures were before you, which must have shown you how differently I was situated. I must confess at that moment I felt, if our situations had been reversed, how easy a method as well as pleasing, I could have discovered to ease myself of a part at least of the incumbrance of too large an income, by a proposition which must have been gratifying & beneficial to the individual principally instrumental in it, & who had for years sacrificed his time, his health, & his property in laying the foundation of the business out of which it arose. I should have felt that I was doing an act of generous justice to a man who knew how to value such an act. But to draw to a conclusion; I will not have it said that I am disposed to take advantage of any man under circumstances of peculiar delicacy, tho' that man may have time to devote with avidity

& zeal to the interests of parties whose claims may not be quite so strong upon him as I think mine are, whilst my interests & comforts seem to be considered a fit subject for postponement & delay. With these impressions then I have no wish whatever that your visit to Manchester should take place at a period when your time may be employed to advantage at home, & it is my desire that the subject may be altogether dropped with this very particular request—that you will endeavour to discharge your duty by me as I hope to do mine by you during the remainder of our term of partnership, & [I hope] that it will be your good fortune hereafter to meet with a man that will treat you better than I have done, & mine if I should ever have another partner, to meet with one of equal integrity with you.

P.S.—I have no wish whatever for an answer to this letter or that any change should take place in our behaviour to each other.

Mr. Cory had not always found his partner's "integrity" quite to his mind. My father told us once that in the early days of his partnership he had insisted that coals advertised as "twice screened" should actually be twice screened. Mr. Cory, who was sitting with him, thereupon lifted his hands and three times brought them down with a slap on his knees, exclaiming, "Then we are ruined! Then we are ruined! Then we are ruined!" My father introduced much greater strictness into the business methods of the firm.

We may suppose that after the date of Mr. Cory's letters, my father, by attention to business, gave him greater satisfaction as the partnership did not come to an end till about nine years later.

Mrs. J. E. TAYLOR *to her Brother.*

MANCHESTER, *December* 27, 1829.

. . . I know it would be wrong to repine, otherwise I could not help it—to have such men as Dr. Carpenter & Dr. Hutton preaching to-day & tomorrow & Mr. Robberds on Christmas Day & be unable to attend either service. What a source of high enjoyment would it have been to me had I been well. . . .

The same to the same.

MANCHESTER, *Dec.* 20, 1829.

. . . I want sadly to hear from you again to know the reception you have since received from Sarah for I can scarcely help calling her naughty for being so reserved and distant. This I agree with you is more than is necessary to prevent your entertaining false hopes, but of course you think she is quite right. . . .

No letters of this period from my father relating to Sarah Hawes have been preserved. It is clear, however, that he now became aware that his hopes were not to be fulfilled. Happily the disappointment was not a severe one, as letters which follow will show. My mother, fifty years later, said to me that she always believed the affair was of the head rather than of the heart.

Mrs. J. E. TAYLOR *to her Brother.*

MANCHESTER, *March* 10, 1830.

. . . It has been an eventful period to us both,[1] my dearest brother, since this hand last conveyed my thoughts & feelings to you. What were then your fondest, dearest hopes are all,

[1] Her youngest child, another John Edward, was born February 2 of this year.

alas, full of hope no longer; your silence had in a great measure prepared me for unpropitious tidings. . . . Your letter was far more full of comfort to me than I could have imagined under the circumstances, but I am very anxious to be again assured that there is no reason for the anxiety I cannot still avoid feeling about you, & I am of course very anxious to know a little more of the circumstances which have produced such a revolution in your feelings; but for this I must wait till I have again the happiness of seeing you, resting in confidence & thankfulness that the blighting of your hopes has not produced effects upon you which I so much feared would result, provided you were obliged to give up your suit. . . .

BENJAMIN HAWES, Junior, *to* RUSSELL SCOTT.

May 1830.

. . . Sarah has written me a note to say that all your Letters are burnt—and that she has received your packet. . . .

The following letter is given as a specimen of the letters of Miss Scott of Morden. A good deal of friendly intercourse was always kept up between the members of the elder branch of the family and the Scotts of Sherborne and Bath.

Miss SCOTT *to* Mrs. ROBERT SCOTT.

MORDEN, *July* 1, 1830.

MY DEAR Mrs. SCOTT,—I have long thought of writing but hearing from Sherborne that you was all well except the baby but I hope that this Summer that she will be able to walk. Russell Scott [of Sherborne] was heare at Whitsuntide, and he said that his S [illegible]s was gone to Bath for a Month, so it must have been [illegible] pleasant for you. Are they gone home? We [illegible]e [illegible] different Weather for Hay Making, not three [illegible] rain [illegible] that when it was 'most Dry the rain [illegible]—[illegible] we have spoiled any, but it keeps it a good while in hand, and it hurts the flowers and makes the Weeds grow. I wish Mary was heare that she could pick up the Apples in the Garden as she did last yeare. My love to her and tell her she must come next year if please God I live so long. I am much oblidge to you for your kind invitation to Bath and I hope if nothing happens to come and see you in September if it is convenient to Mrs. Petty as I do not like travelling by myself. I have wrote to her have had no answer yet. I goes out very little have not been to Taunton this year. I dont know how Miss Scott thought so much of my going to Portsmouth. Your Uncle very kindly ask me to come and see him but the journey was too far for me and I am so poor a walker that it would be no pleasure. . . . The Death of the poor King I supose have made the People very busy at Bath. I believe he was a great sufferer. The papers often say that he was better. He often put me in mind of my Dear Brother and died of the same age born one year after him but it is what we must all come to. I cannot expect to live long and hope that I shall be prepared when the time comes. Now I do not ask *you* but we shall be very glad to see Mr. Scott to spend a few Days, and as he has got a partenner he can come very well. Now I hope that you will write me a long letter soon and let me hear all about you. I hope Mrs. Taylor is got pretty well and her little Family. Sister Gould and John joins me in best regards to you and Mr. Scott, and our love to Mary and tell her that I want to see her & am Dear Madam Your sincere Friend

M. Scott.

Mrs. J. E. Taylor *to her Brother.*

Manchester, *September* 29, 1830.

. . . Uncle Benjamin, Aunt & Sarah arrived per railroad on Thursday; they dined with us. The first meeting between Sarah & [illegible] was, as you may suppose, rather awkward. I saw her [illegible] she saw me; she looked very uncomfortable

& in a moment, as her eyes met mine, I saw her cheeks become as red as I should think they could do. However this passed off soon, but I certainly thought her quite out of spirits the whole of the visit, though she was very pleasant & attentive & very kind to the children. . . . This morning Edward went down to take them to Chapel . . . from Chapel they came up here. . . . Sarah was more at ease to-day; she was quite disposed to be cordial & I felt as if I should quite have enjoyed her, if I had not had my mind constantly impressed with the recollection of the way in which she had treated you. I scarcely know how to believe she could act so to you. . . . As far as I have had an opportunity of judging, I certainly think you have over-estimated Sarah. I think her very pleasing & unaffected, but I cannot see anything very superior about her. . . .

They must have come from Liverpool. The Liverpool and Manchester Railway had been open only a fortnight.

RUSSELL SCOTT *to his Sister.*

October 12, 1830.

MY DEAR SISTER,—I dined on Sunday at Russell Square, Sarah being at her sister's. They seemed pleased with their visit to Manchester & spoke most highly of your little Sophia. I am glad that they went, and that you received them as you did. Nothing has passed which you need resent, even were all circumstances known; but for myself I think it will be long before I meet Sarah Hawes when I can conveniently avoid it, or treat her with more than distant & formal politeness when I do meet her. I am quite of opinion with you that I over-estimated her, but I doubt whether you could see her otherwise than at a disadvantage. The circle of my acquaintance is unfortunately a small one, but I cannot say that I know any other young woman of one & twenty whom I can consider her equal. Perhaps you think me not impartial, but my want of impartiality (if any) would be likely to bias me against her, for I assure you

I am out of all patience with myself, when I recollect any of the innumerable foolish things which I said, & did, & thought, & wrote in the months of November, December & January last. I told you, perhaps you remember, of some lines I wrote on her birthday—I believe it was on the first day I had a fire in my room that I popped them into it; luckily no mortal has seen them, & I had not patience to read them through myself. I do hope & believe that if ever I should again be in love, I shall preserve a larger portion of what little sense I possess. . . . Yours ever affect[ly] RUSSELL SCOTT.

Mrs. J. E. TAYLOR *to her Brother.*

MANCHESTER, *Dec.* 2, 1830.

. . . Aunt Sarah says she thinks you have changed your servant much for the better. I hope you find it so.

There is one sermon in Dr. Channing's own book on preaching Christ that I think will be a treat to you. The other new pieces are mostly short, & though very delightful there is nothing characteristic of his most superior mind. I had such a loss on Sunday in not being at Chapel. Mr. Robberds preached one of his most beautiful sermons. I do so envy Miss Rackett, for she goes to Chapel twice a day* & I have only been once for five weeks. . . .

Addressed: "New Barge House."

Rev. RUSSELL SCOTT *to his Son.*

PORTSMOUTH, *Dec.* 17, 1830.

. . . I trust Lord Althorp will not be disappointed in his expectations of establishing a government without patronage. It will indeed be a great gratification to me to have been permitted to witness so glorious an event. It is no small consolation to have read the declaration of one of the principal officers of the Government declaring that our country was no longer

* That is twice. In Dissenting chapels there was

to be governed under the influence of patronage. I think he would scarcely have made such a novel declaration if he had not strong reasons for making it. In what an eventful period am I closing my scene of action! How gratifying the prospect for those who are young, that they are likely to witness a rapid & effectual amelioration in the state of mankind generally. . . .

In 1832, when the Reform Bill was pending, only two years before his death, my grandfather hired a post-chaise and drove to Winchester, taking four others, in order to record their votes. It was a drive of fifty-two miles, and must have cost him at least £5. County elections at that time were held in county towns.

RUSSELL SCOTT *to his Sister.*

LONDON, *Feb.* 4, 1831.

. . . Last evening I again mentioned it [the subject of the partnership] & the matter was pretty nearly arranged. . . . The term is to be three years. . . . I am not to be allowed to have more than £20,000 in the concern but my father's £8,000 is to remain in addition. I have inserted a clause providing for my absence during one sixth of the year, being determined to have a full right to this privilege, & to avoid not merely the expression of dissatisfaction on this score, but the suspicion I have frequently entertained (sometimes perhaps erroneously) that dissatisfaction has been felt, though not expressed. I have claimed & intend to insist upon an extra month for a trip to America. . . . The matter has been very good-humouredly discussed between us on the whole, though certainly the budget was opened stiffly enough.

I should have been glad to see Miss Carpenter whose praises are not new to me, although I have never seen her. I am sorry you have had the misfortune of falling in love with her, and would recommend you to give up all expectation of any other sister-in-law than your husband's sister; remember your brother is between thirty and forty years of age and may well consider himself *shelved*. . . .

This alludes to Miss Mary Carpenter, with whom my father later in life established the Kingswood Reformatory, and whose successful work for the children of the "perishing classes" in England, and on behalf of women in India, is well known. She was the eldest daughter of Dr. Lant Carpenter, and the sister of William Carpenter, M.D., F.R.S., LL.D.

RUSSELL SCOTT *to his Sister.*

LONDON, *March* 7th, 1831.

. . . I am pleased, but not so much pleased as you appear to expect, with the reform plan. I have one very strong objection to it, that the qualification is much too low. In London the labouring classes will have a majority of votes—many of our coal porters & 21 of the Barge House soap men among the number; in fact it would have been the same thing in effect to have given votes to all householders. I looked with anxiety for the *Guardian* this morning, & was glad to find the £10 qualification approved there, because it tended to make me think I had over-estimated the danger. Danger however I cannot but think there is, especially if the clamourous advocates of the ballot should carry their point. I think I have heard Edward say that a £20 qualification would give between 4 & 5,000 votes for Manchester; quite enough I think for any good purpose. I rejoice that the reign of the boroughmongers is at an end, but I fear that in the intoxication of the triumph we are in danger of forgetting a yet more formidable enemy, the demon of democracy. . . .

I had a note from Benjamin on Wednesday, to inform me that the affair between his sister & John Curtis had that day been definitely settled, & on Thursday I had a sort of official communication to the same effect from my uncle Benjamin, immediately on the receipt of which I sent a letter of congratulation on the occasion to Sarah. It would appear that they were all as little prepared for my doing this, as I was for the very great credit I obtained in consequence. At a party at Mr. Sweet's the same evening I was spoken to by my Uncle B, by William & by Sarah herself on the subject. In a tone & manner that evinced considerable feeling she assured me that she considered it particularly kind on my part to write to her on the occasion. There was nothing amounting to embarrassment on either side. I soon afterwards asked her to dance a quadrille & we conversed with ease & cheerfulness. . . .

Rev. Russell Scott *to his Son.*

Portsmouth, *March* 8, 1831.

. . . I was very glad to find that you enjoyed your excursion to Manchester, & particularly to & from Liverpool by the steam carriage. What a delightful mode of travelling it is! You had 150 fellow passengers I find; what a number to travel by the same conveyance! What eventful times have I lived to see! Such a plan of Parliamentary reform I never expected to see submitted to Parliament by any ministry as that proposed by Lord John Russell this day week. I was perfectly astounded & thought it impossible when I first knew it. It appears to me to be so good, as to make me fear it will not be realized. It is scarcely out of my mind day or night. For every night it has been occupying my mind in dreams. Mr. Edward Carter was so good as to send me over the *Morning Chronicle* which you sent to him on Wednesday by the Rocket. I found it on my table when I returned home to tea, with a message that I would return it when I had done with it. I accordingly read the leading article containing the outline of the plan, & then hastily looked over Lord John Russell's speech, when I returned it. I borrowed it the next morning to look at it more leisurely, not receiving any myself, & then sent it to Dr. Waller, requesting him to return it to Mr. Carter. This morning the Portsmouth Corporation met & unanimously voted a petition to the House of Commons, stating their great desire that the plan of Parliamentary reform proposed by the King's ministry might be adopted & passed into a law. After this an address was unanimously voted to the King on the same subject. . . .

RUSSELL SCOTT *to his Sister.*

LONDON, *June* 25, 1831.

. . . I am exceedingly glad to hear, though not through you, that Russell is going to Mr. Beard's & should be still more so if I could hope it would lead to his education being carried on at school. I could say much on this subject if I had time & space & a prospect of being favourably listened to, but I know parents think bachelors no judges of anything relating to children, & in my turn I think parents, & more particularly those who are most anxious for their children's welfare, not the best judges on a point of this sort. . . .

MRS. J. E. TAYLOR *to her Brother.*

30 PARK STREET, LEAMINGTON, *June* 28, 1831.

. . . As you are so anxious for me to stay here as long as Dr. Jephson wishes I thought I would write & tell you we have determined on doing so, which is till next Monday. . . . In my general health I am very well now. He expresses himself delighted at my appearance, though when first he saw me he was certainly very nearly as uneasy as Mr. Whatton, whom you may remember I was uncharitable enough to blame for his anxiety about my having grown so thin. . . . Sarah & Anna [Scott] have been as anxious for me to stay as possible, & are most kind in making themselves as happy & pleased with the arrangements as can be. I enjoy them very much. Anna is quite devoted to my little Sophia—I never met with anyone excepting Anne Street who so completely laid themselves out for attention & accommodation to everyone around her, without apparently a thought for herself. . . . I assure you, my dearest brother, I am completely tired of my confinement here; I am not allowed to stir out. . . . Thinking I should be out enjoying myself all the time I made no preparation for employing so many leisure hours. We subscribed to the library one week; I read one novel but I could read no more—I have an utter aversion to this method of killing time. . . .

I fully intended to tell you, my dearest brother, our Russell was going to school after the holidays. It has certainly been a serious determination for me, tho' I think it for the best; but I certainly have felt & do feel very anxious to keep him as much as possible under my own eye, till he shall have attained a sufficient knowledge of right & wrong to prevent his being as likely to follow the example of others in the one as the other. At present he certainly does appear to me to have a very quick sense of & a great desire to do right. God grant it may continue. But you know not, you can scarcely conceive a Mother's anxiety for her children, especially her boys; it can only be moderated by full reliance on the over-ruling providence of God, after we have used our best exertions. I assure you, my brother, I am not at all disposed to undervalue your opinions on education. I only think you feel the disadvantages of your own, without sufficiently also feeling its advantages. This would make you most decided in sending children from home, whereas I should be inclined to steer a more moderate & middle course. You feel all your disadvantages, but what are they? what do they appear to me when I think of you, compare you with others, & reflect upon what I wish my boy to be? They are all of an earthly nature. What are they compared to the excellence of your principles & your actions? What will they be in a few years? I have had so much cause to look to another world, I perhaps think less of the advantages of this than many. Could I but possess the hope I were fitted for it, my joy would indeed be complete, for few, I believe very few, enjoy such a happy lot as mine; but alas! I feel more & more how little I am what I ought to be, & sometimes I feel desponding, but I trust I may have time to improve. . . .

At about the date at which we have now arrived in our history, my father wrote, or rather began to write, a "brief memoir" of himself. It is dated November 1830. Some extracts from it may be given; they take us back again to his early life at Portsmouth.

After stating that during the first twelve years of his life his mental faculties had been somewhat injuriously forced, he continues:—

"Unfortunately I had no one of my own age to associate with—as I write however I remember that Hampden and Russell Gurney, the one a year & a half only, and the other three years younger than myself must have gone to Portsmouth about the end of 1807 or the beginning of 1808—but I believe I considered myself too important a personage to join them, as much as it would have been desirable that I should, in amusements suitable to my age. Instead of which my chief attention was directed to matters of which it would have been quite as well if I had not known anything for several years. I remember that every Sunday evening I went into my father's library not merely to repeat my catechism, but to be instructed in controversial Theology, and I believe that at seven years old at latest I fancied myself as well acquainted with the objections to the [doctrine of the] Trinity as I do now. I was moreover vastly well acquainted with politics. I can remember the principal political circumstances of the years 1809 & 10—the Archduke Charles' battles, Bonaparte's marriage, the Walcheren expedition, the taking of Flushing, the attempts to turn out the then administration, the duel between Lord Castlereagh and Mr. Canning, and the motion with respect to the conduct of ministers made by Mr. Whitbread and carried by a majority of 7 (I do not know that I have read or heard of it from that time to this). Such being the subjects of my thoughts instead of the amusements suitable to my age, I associated much with those older than myself and my mind became a sort of hot-house plant, the strength of which was not a little impaired by the artificial and undue excitement to which it was subjected.

"In 1811 Benjamin Hawes went to Portsmouth, and I believe the two years he passed there to have been very valuable to me. Although four years older than me he was quite disposed to treat me as an equal, being sensible of the greater advantages I had had; indeed I can well remember the extravagant encomiums he used to bestow both on my disposition and my abilities, and the protests I made against them on the ground (and I have no doubt I was sincere) that he would make me vain, which he in return declared to be impossible. A most intimate friendship was formed between us. Many are the alternations it has since undergone! . . .

"With the exception perhaps of these two years, I do not think I was happy as a boy, and this may perhaps have arisen in part from the causes I have referred to. I believe I was not a little impatient of restraint which I always persuaded myself was injustice and oppression, and this was manifested not by any violence of temper, from which I believe I was always free, but in a way perhaps still more objectionable—by frequent murmurs and complaints — and by complying, when I was sometimes obliged to comply, in a way which showed that I did it *because* I was obliged to comply. I was certainly also much less attached to my parents than might have been expected, and I am not a little at a loss to account for this, especially as regards my mother, who must have been I am sure at all times, what I can so well remember her to have been for the last ten years of her life, extraordinary even among mothers for tenderness and affection. Yet there are instances which occur to me, and I cannot hope they were exceptions to my general conduct, in which I have replied

to what she said in a way that must have wounded, and indeed I know that it did most severely wound her feelings. Painful indeed would be the recollection that, even at this period of my life, I should thus have treated her, had I not had opportunities, of which I trust I have not been altogether unmindful, of atoning in some measure for conduct of this description.

"I must say that I have a strong impression that the course adopted in my education was in many respects very injudicious. . . . In some respects, indeed, the plan adopted was adopted from necessity, for economy rendered it necessary to educate me at home. The evils resulting from this however were not mitigated as they might have been. There were for several years three or four of the Haweses & Gurneys at Portsmouth, but I was placed in authority over them, a course which was objectionable as regarded them, as there was no difference of age sufficient to justify it, but indeed more mischievous as respected myself. Instead of being looked up to in the way in which as their senior I probably should have been if a different plan had been acted upon, I was naturally regarded with aversion; instead of having associates, I felt myself isolated; and when my decrees were reversed, as of course they often required to be, by a higher tribunal, I had no resource but to go and shut myself up in my own room. . . .

"Another great mistake, as it appears to me, which was made was that of repressing observations upon a great many matters of secondary importance. Not a syllable of reference was ever allowed in my hearing to personal attraction or to dress, or if such subjects did happen to be alluded to by any one who might come to the house the folly of speaking of such things was sure to be commented upon afterwards. With respect to dress I never have recovered and never shall recover the faculty of observing it; and with respect to beauty, when I did become sensible of its charms, which I think was later by two or three years than most men, I never could very particularly describe even those who most struck me. Indeed

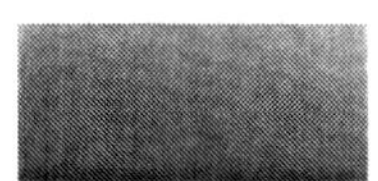

my deficiency of observation in general has been my greatest misfortune, and it has been so remarkable that it would not be fair to set it all down to the want of early encouragement. If I had made better use of my eyes, even though I had made less of my reflecting faculties, I should have appeared to far greater advantage than I have done.

"When Benj[n] Hawes left Portsmouth I was twelve years old — the time when most begin to store their minds with important knowledge — but it was unfortunately the time at which I almost left it off. Few have made so little use of the most valuable period of their lives as I did. The absence of the stimulus afforded while he was at Portsmouth had probably something to do with this, and the position in which I was placed with respect to his brothers and the Gurneys something also. My own idleness, unless indeed this were rather an effect than a cause, would also operate, but I believe an important reason to have been that my father was not fully qualified for the higher branches of education. At all events it would have been highly desirable that I should at that time have been removed to some good school. As it was, it is certain that I employed four years with but little profit, and at sixteen I came to London.

"Anything like study was now out of the question. For the first eight months I resided at my uncle's at Lavender Hill, or rather slept there, for I left it at 7 in the morning and did not return until 9 at night. . . .

"On the 1st January 1818 at 6 o'clock in the morning the firm of Will[m] Cory & Co. commenced business, and on the same day at the same hour commenced also my acquaintance with the coal trade, an acquaintance which I have cultivated with various degrees of zeal at different periods, but of which, at the time I am writing, I have for some time been tired and which I suspect to be drawing to a close. I entered upon it with earnestness, was disappointed at finding there was in the first instance so little that I could do, but when this ceased to be the case, I rendered most important service to the concern.

The first stock-taking was managed by Mr. Cory, the second, at Midsummer 1819 by myself, and it appeared that up to that period there had been not merely no profit realized by the concern, but a slight loss sustained. Convinced that this ought not to be, and that a cause must be discovered and also a remedy, I set about a pretty thorough investigation of the affairs and although I believe no very great importance was at first attached to my labours I soon detected serious miscalculations to have arisen in more ways than one, and numerous expenses requiring retrenchment, & I am certainly of opinion that I was in a great degree instrumental in rescuing the concern from approaching ruin. My entire attention was now directed to a single object, for when, at half past 8 o'clock in the evening, I used to return to my lodgings, I was too much exhausted to be able to think of anything worth thinking of. I believe that at no period have I felt so strong an interest in everything affecting the welfare of the concern, as when I was receiving from it a fixed salary of £100 p. annum. . . ."

My father then states that it was his habit to spend the Sunday very frequently either at Mr. Gurney's or Mr. Addington's, and continues:—

"I dined too at Serjeants' Inn [Mr. Gurney's] two or three times a week, & occasionally spent an evening there also. It was at this period and in this way that I acquired a taste for a different kind of society from that to which I had been accustomed, and an unfortunate disrelish for all such as I deemed inferior to that which I now & then met with there. I remarked to my mother in one of the delightful conversations I had with her very shortly before her death, that I thought my intimacy with the family of the Gurneys had been mischievous to me in its effects, however pleasant it was to me at the time. She said that she and my sister had often said so to each other. Certain it is that I raised my standard too high. . . .

"One circumstance which contributed to make what I saw at Serjeants' Inn my standard of what ought to be, was the high admiration I entertained towards Harriet Gurney. I hardly know whether I ever fancied myself in love with her, but I rather think that I sometimes did, and I know that others thought me so. . . . I remember writing some verses on the occasion of her "coming out" which I showed to Benjamin Hawes and requested his opinion upon them. This was, that the only good ideas they contained were very far from original, and it so much damped my poetical ardour that I do not believe I again attempted rhyming of any kind until last Spring. . . .

"In the year 1822 I came of age, and the death of my mother's uncle happening about the same time furnished the means of paying off my uncles' capital and placing me in their stead as a partner in the concern, to the no small satisfaction of Mr. Cory, by whom I was then considered the very perfection of a partner. I believe this change, as of course it gave me more importance, also gave me more confidence, but I nevertheless remained in this respect at a heavy discount, so that even on the Coal Exchange there were few to whom I was in the habit of speaking, and none, I apprehend, who at all anticipated that I should acquire the sort of standing there which I have more recently attained. . . .

"In the year 1824 my sister was married, and I was not a little elated by the event. I was probably the more gratified because I had much regretted the length of the attachment which preceded it. I expended upwards of £200 in presents on the occasion, and invited the members of the family residing in London to a dinner at the Crown & Sceptre, of which I retain very agreeable recollections. A visit to the Lakes was my summer excursion.

"My sister's marriage may be considered as having given me another lift, or perhaps I should rather say that about this period I made another step, though I had still an abundance and a great superabundance of gravity and sedateness. Prior to this time, at least for the two or three preceding years, I had had to encounter not a little of repulsiveness from Mrs. Gurney. The suddenness with which it disappeared, and the complete return of the kindness with which I had been treated by her when I first came to London, struck me as quite remarkable. I could not—nor can I now—disconnect it with a circumstance which took place at about the same time, Harriet Gurney's matrimonial engagement."

My father's memoir here comes to an end. It is evidently unfinished. As to his remark that at the time of his sister's marriage he still had a great superabundance of gravity, I doubt if he quite knew the impression he made on others in this respect. Three years earlier, Mary Ann Taylor, in a letter to Robert Scott, had said, "You and Eliza will, I think, be pleased with Russell—at least I was last year—he is lively, intelligent, and affectionate." In later life his children did not feel him to be specially grave. He probably at no time had high spirits, and he did not *make* fun, but he fully appreciated fun in others, and he had a most hearty laugh.

His want of observation of trifles, and of almost anything that did not interest him, was always a most marked trait in him. It seemed to arise partly from his mind being occupied with subjects of more importance, but was chiefly constitutional. One consequence of it was a very unusual amount of indifference to small personal comforts and discomforts.

After his marriage it was my mother who arranged all the minor details of every-day life for him and for their children. Questions of dress, food, and even of health he felt to be quite beyond his sphere.

CHAPTER XIII

RUSSELL SCOTT IS ENGAGED TO BE MARRIED—DEATH OF HIS SISTER

1831-1832

THE letters of this period are not very numerous. We next come to those relating to my father's engagement to my mother.

Not much more than a year after his final rejection by Sarah Hawes he met my mother at a dance, at the house of Mr. Crowley, of Lavender Hill—a near neighbour of his aunt Sarah's. This was on March 30, 1831. He had felt but little inclination to go to this dance, but had gone influenced (as he used to tell us) by a remembrance of some words of his mother's. She had spoken to him of her great wish that he should marry, and had desired him to go more into society where nice girls might be met with. Thinking of this, he went to Mr. Crowley's. People at that time were greatly interested in the unhappy condition of the Poles, there having lately been an insurrection in Poland, and my mother, on this first introduction, talked eagerly about them. My father was delighted with her enthusiasm and greatly attracted by her. They subsequently met at another house, and then my father spoke to his aunt Sarah, who immediately made the acquaintance of Mr. and Mrs. Prestwich, in order to enable him to visit there, and afterwards in every way gave him what help she could.

Personally my mother was always beautiful, and her bright intelligence and sympathetic nature made her most attractive. She was the eldest daughter of Mr. Joseph Prestwich, a wine merchant, living at No. 8 The Lawn, South Lambeth, descended from an old Lancashire family. A genealogical table of this family is in the Appendix, and further information as to my mother's immediate relations will be found in Chapter XXIII. of this book, and in the "Life" of her brother, Sir Joseph Prestwich, by his wife, published in 1899.

RUSSELL SCOTT *to his Aunt*, MISS SARAH HAWES.

LONDON, 9th *Aug.* 1831.

MY DEAR AUNT,—You will probably not receive this for some days, but I write without waiting to hear when you will be at Liverpool. You would infer from what I said in my sister's letter that I had not found the family returned when I called at The Lawn on Tuesday. On Sunday I called again & saw them all—one of the party was certainly looking better than I have ever seen her. This morning I sent a note to Mrs. Prestwich to the effect that I should be much obliged if she could favor me with an interview, but that if it were more convenient I would do myself the pleasure of calling on Mr. P. at his counting-house; my man was detained full an hour & half; he brought back a letter written in very friendly terms, apologizing for not seeing me, & referring me to Mr. P. I then wished & still wish I had called in Mark Lane in the first instance. I of course went there immediately & said what I had to say. Mr. P. was not disposed to say much & I cannot say his manner pleased me; he said it must be left entirely to his daughter; that he could have no objection, being perfectly satisfied as to my own respectability & that of my connections; that his daughter was at present only 18 & that marriage was at present not to be thought of; that he did not

believe she had ever bestowed a thought on such a subject; & that he & Mrs. P. would be glad to see me whenever I liked to call; & he concluded an interview of less than 5 minutes by begging I would excuse him. You will perhaps think me fastidious that I was not satisfied, but it was not anything that he said that I did not like; his manner conveyed no impression that he was gratified by the avowal I had made, & neither that nor anything he said could be supposed to imply that it would give him pleasure if the connection should take place; nor do I know that I shall be invited to the house, although I can hardly imagine that Mrs. P. will not do this.

I wish now that I had not been so much in a hurry, for which it is pretty clear there was no occasion. When I see Mrs. P. I shall say to her that I think it better not to name the subject just at present to her daughter, provided that is, that it be not already done, which is not improbable.

I have now told you as far as I can how matters stand; you will judge whether I ought to wish them to stand better; however that may be, I certainly do wish you were close at hand, instead of 200 miles off. . . . Very affectionately yours, R. S.

Miss Sarah Hawes *to* Russell Scott.

Liverpool, *August* 14, 1831.

. . . My first object on arrival was to go to the Post Office, & my promptness met the reward I wished. I most truly welcomed your Letter, & I sit down to answer it immediately. As far as I can judge you ought to be satisfied & perfectly so. All Mr. P. did say was enough for you to feel the hope with great certainty of success. If you can but gain the affections of his Daughter, they will make no objection. This surely is all at present [illegible] wanted to know; that she at present [is] disengaged, & [illegible] Father to be assured that you are the first [illegible] think perhaps what you did not feel [illegible] Mr. P. proceeded only from strong [illegible] think you are a little unreasonable in [illegible]

Remember how little acquaintance [he had] with you, previous to making the proposal—I have much regretted my separation at this very interesting time. Your Uncle went out when I went for the letter & is not yet returned, therefore I shall now wait & give you his opinion before I write on other subjects. Pray for once put confidence in yourself & I trust all may terminate as you wish; & what can you want more [than] that he & Mrs. P. would be glad to see you whenever you liked to call? That at first seems stronger than a particular invitation.

When your Uncle returned he concurred in every thing that I had wrote without my giving any opinion to him; he also wished me to say how glad he felt at no one but ourselves being acquainted with this affair. He hopes you will remain of the same opinion to all the London circle, till you are sure of her consent; he is very interested to hear progress. We leave here *Wednesday*—don't forget that we desire to hear by return of post. Brother desires his best wishes with every earnest wish for your future happiness. Your Sister & I was talking and rejoicing at your having got over your feeling for Sarah. She finished by saying, "how I wish he would think of some one." . . .

Miss Sarah Hawes *to* Russell Scott.

September 2, 1831.

. . . I am now fully satisfied that every thing is as favourable as you ought to wish at present. I give you very great credit in procuring Mrs. & Miss P. such a very great gratification.[1] You were very clever to be able to accomplish it. I am very glad you did, as the attention was a very marked one. All *parties* there must understand the cause, which I now think is quite necessary [illegible] your feelings it should be so; they cannot be too decided to [illegible] subject. I conclude you have been at The Lawn more [illegible]tion. It is very certain you are approved by both [illegible]er or they would not have allowed such attentions

[1] [illegible] that this was a visit to the House of Commons to

to be accepted. I am very sure Mrs. P. would not give the least encouragement that was not approved by him. . . .

The Prestwich family belonged to the Church of England, but no objection was raised to the engagement on the score of difference of religious opinions.

In October my father paid a visit to Manchester, and no doubt then told his sister of his hopes, as from her letters previous to that time it does not appear that she knew anything of them.

BENJAMIN HAWES *to his Nephew*, RUSSELL SCOTT.

Wednesday [*Nov.* 16th, 1831].

. . . I thank you for the intelligence, tho' late, & I suppose to-night would let the secret out. I congratulate you on the approaching event & assure you I most sincerely wish your happiness, & shall always remember with pleasure the very kind & conciliatory conduct you pursued. Marriages, they say, are made in Heaven; could they have been made on earth by my influence, Miss P. would not have ended your bachelor's reign. I have always regretted it, but I hope it is *all* for the best. You will recollect my words and prophecies. I am glad they are so soon realized. . . .

RUSSELL SCOTT *to his Sister*.

LONDON, 17th *Nov.* 1831.

MY DEAR SISTER,—Having been not a little occupied since my return to town, I did not think it necessary to write to you sooner than you would expect, & I believe this was the day we named. I believe that when I left you, I rather intended postponing speaking to Isabella until after the party of last night; this however I did not do.

Of course I was at The Lawn in about an hour after the arrival of the Red Rover, which, by the bye, was more than 22 instead of 21 hours on the road. On Sunday I dined &

spent the evening there; on Monday I called on Mr. P. who quite agreed with me as to the needlessness of further delay, & even suggested my naming the subject that evening when I told him I should pass it at his house. I preferred however my own plan, & on Tuesday morning sent a note to Isabella enclosed in a cover addressed to her mother, giving her about two hours notice of my intention. From what her father had said, I felt scarcely a doubt of her acquiescence in my wishes that I should be allowed to announce the affair as settled. In this I was disappointed, & at first was not a little under apprehension that I had miscalculated. After a long silence on her part she startled me by speaking of being "quite unprepared" for what I had said—the meaning of which I suppose was, though I could not conceive what it could mean at the time, that she did not expect it so soon. However I do not know that I ought to give even to you full particulars of such an interview, but after a considerable time I learned the nature of her only objection, which was "the difference in our religious sentiments." I found upon enquiry that she had not any exaggerated idea of the extent of that difference. We were interrupted & went downstairs to lunch, & afterwards adjourned to the garden where we had a walk by ourselves for nearly two hours, in the course of which I obtained an acknowledgement that she did not consider it as a matter of *duty* to act upon the objection she had raised; so that you see the difficulties are not likely to be serious. However it is still "Mr. Scott" & "Miss Prestwich" & all that, which I want much to get rid of & hope I soon shall.

Under these circumstances, thinking further concealment neither necessary nor desirable, or practicable either, I wrote to my Aunt Gurney & my Uncle Benj^m^ & spoke of the affair as being as nearly settled as possible, although not actually announceable. I requested it might not be named out of the family—& accordingly it was named to Miss Foy by a lady whom I had never seen or heard of, & congratulations came in upon me on all hands. I do not think, however that all the parties had their information from my side of the question.

Isabella did not interpose any objection to my being in attendance nearly all the evening. I thought she looked exceedingly well, & she was certainly much admired. "Upon my honour, you *are* a lucky fellow" said Russell Gurney. William Hawes wrote me a letter with which I was much pleased, & concluded it by hoping for similar good fortune for himself & saying he could not but envy me. Sarah was most cordial in her congratulations & in her praises, & I had a letter from my uncle Benj[m] lamenting that my bachelorship should not have been terminated as he wished it, instead of by Miss P. It is to be hoped after all this nothing untoward will arise, but I think there cannot be much danger. . . .

The party was probably at Lavender Hill, as so many of the Hawes family were present.

RUSSELL SCOTT *to his Sister.*

LONDON, 23rd *Nov[r]* 1831.

The arrival of your letter this morning, my very dear sister, gave me much pleasure. Knowing the affectionate interest you feel in all that is materially interesting to me I had fully relied on receiving a letter from you on Monday morning, more particularly as I had strongly expressed to you when I left you how desirous I should be to hear how you were going on. But really I do find it difficult to impress upon you as fully as I wish the idea that your silence does frequently make me uncomfortable; be so good as to tell Edward that the next time he interferes to prevent your writing to me, I trust it will be for a better reason than he could assign upon this occasion.

I should certainly have written to you this evening, if I had not had the pleasure of hearing from you, as I am now enabled to communicate the agreeable information that Isabella Prestwich has given me her final consent to become Mrs. Russell Scott. I did not intend to fill so large a part of my sheet before I put you in possession of the intelligence, but I have not time to re-write my letter. When I wrote to you last I thought there could scarcely be a doubt of my success, & on Sunday none at all; still however I wished for such an assurance from her own lips, & this I obtained yesterday. I remained at The Lawn to dinner, & therefore had no opportunity of writing to you.

I very much regret that another malady should have succeeded those you have hitherto encountered. I beg that I may hear from or of you *not later* than this day week; of course I shall be very glad to hear as much sooner as you please. I trust most sincerely your expectations of amendment may be realized. . . . Ever affectionately yours

RUSSELL SCOTT.

Mrs. J. E. TAYLOR *to her Brother.*

MANCHESTER, *November* 24, 1831.

Indeed, my dearest Brother, I cannot lose a post, much less let nearly a week pass, before I tell you how truly thankful I feel that your best, fondest & most ardent hopes are fulfilled, that your anxieties & doubts are dispelled, & all your prospects are full of joy & happiness. I cannot write much for I really have not the power, but I trust you can appreciate the fervour of my feelings. I fancied the good news would come to-night & I was not disappointed. I did not however wait to read two sides, for as I opened it I saw the words "Mrs Russell Scott."

This cough has sadly weakened me again; the night I wrote to you I was not conscious of getting any sleep till 6 o'clock, but it is now nearly gone & I hope to-night I may sleep better. Good night, my dearest Brother. My hopes, wishes & prayers are with you for the realization of all the happiness you can enjoy in this world. I should like to send a pretty message to Isabella, but I am too poorly to please myself; assure yourself my feelings towards her are as cordial as they must be from a sister who loves a brother as I love you. May God bless you both. . . .

Her husband adds:—

"I join my beloved Sophia most heartily in my congratulations on your joyful prospects, & in best wishes for your full & lasting happiness in the married state. May your wife resemble mine—I cannot offer you a better wish—in every thing but her very delicate health. The latter however I am sanguine in hoping we shall soon see much better." . . .

Rev. RUSSELL SCOTT *to his Son.*

PORTSMOUTH, *November* 24, 1831.

Hoping that Wednesday's or Thursday's post might bring me the much wished for intelligence communicated in your letter of this morning, I have deferred writing to my brother in order that no time might be lost in making the communication to him. For I did not like to be writing on purpose to tell him of the event & I have no doubt of their soon hearing of it from Bath. I have accordingly just sent off my letter, so that tomorrow morning about 10 o'clk they will all be perfectly astonished; especially as they have so very lately seen me & talked about your getting married. I gave them not the most distant hint that you had even any object of your affection in view. I merely said it would be a great satisfaction to me to see you well & comfortably settled, & that as you were only 30 last birthday I did not know that there had been much time unnecessarily lost. I did not introduce the subject until after I had given an account of my journey. I should like very much to be present tomorrow morning when that part of the letter is read. . . . I should like to send my love to your Isabella; for I am disposed to love her for accepting of you. I may I think send my friendly remembrances to Mr. & Mrs. Prestwich, if you think it proper to be the bearer of such an article. . . .

Mrs. J. E. Taylor *to her Brother.*

Manchester, *December* 11, 1831.

. . . The first impulse of my feelings, my dearest Brother, on receiving your letter was to write immediately, for I was both delighted & gratified by it in no ordinary degree, but alas now-a-days mental inclination must yield to bodily debility, for it is rarely I feel the power of writing a letter, yet I do not like to give up writing to you regularly. Two or three days last week I fully determined upon writing to you, but my mornings were taken up with friends' calling & in the evening I am generally unfit for every thing either from pain or fatigue.

I trust indeed, my brother, your Isabella will love me; I feel I love her already for the new & overflowing current of happiness she has poured in upon you. I feel much more hope the last two or three days that I may know her. I believe I have no organic disease, but that general debility is the great cause of my distressing feelings. . . . I could not express to you the relief it was to my mind you were at Portsmouth last Sunday. I really felt alarmed about Papa, but he tells me he is well. I have not been to Chapel since the Sunday after you were here; this is a trial to me. I do not know how to write more. I will write you again in about a week if I am able. . . .

The same to the same.

Manchester, *Dec.* 21, 1831.

. . . Yesterday Russell's fate was decided; he brought home the *first* prize in the junior class with a degree of ecstasy which I think you cannot conceive. He seemed as if he could think of nothing else all day & as if he could scarcely contain himself. When he laid down in bed he said to Miss Rackett "I shall sleep to-night—I shall not have to think." I knew he had laid awake a good deal, but I did not know that this was one cause. I am quite proud of his first half-year; he has not been turned back in one lesson, nor has he I may say been scarcely found fault with. A difficulty of fixing his attention is his great fault. "I hope Mamma" he said yesterday "you will live to see me grown up good and wise." Thank you for your letter my dearest brother; I hope I need not tell you how interested I am in every thing relating to your Isabella. . . .

SAMUEL SCOTT *to* REV. RUSSELL SCOTT.

SHERBORNE, *January* 5, 1832.

MY DEAR BROTHER,—We are now arrived at the commencement of a new year, which has set in with fine seasonable frosty weather, not extremely severe but very pleasant for walking, which I avail myself [of] by taking some hours in a day of that beneficial exercise, if not overdone by too much exhausting the frame. I frequently think of you walking in your warm passage enjoying your pipe, when I am going from the front to the back door in the Vestibule, in the cold evening air. . . . I have pretty good proof I think that the air of Portsmouth does not altogether suit my constitution. The place itself is very inviting with all its accompanying scenes, varieties & gratifications and kind attentions, which I experienced during my visit at Portsmouth. I have to thank you too for your early communication of the result of your journey home, with your safe arrival, without experiencing any uncomfortable effects therefrom. . . . Our Christmas party was small this year—NO PARSON, & Mr. Gould did not come till Tuesday morning, having an engagement the preceding day. He staid till Friday. Mr. & Mrs. Petty desired their kind respects & are both well. What an alarming disease this Cholera [illegible], which is so fast spreading in this country, & how fatal [illegible] hear of its being any where in the Western or Sou[illegible] the kingdom but we can scarcely expect to escape it. You must feel a good deal on account of your beloved family at Manchester, which is so much nearer the spot from whence it originated. I rejoice to hear of the prospect my cousin Russell has in view, which I hope will in due time be compleated to the entire satisfaction of all parties & the mutual happiness of the more interested ones. My kind love to my Nephew when you write. With wishing you many happy returns of the present season, in which I am joined by my wife, adding our love, I conclude my dear brother (writing in the dark almost) Yours affectionately SAM[L] SCOTT.

I have to beg your acceptance of the usual Xmas package[1] which does not I am sorry to say come to their former size since Mrs. Turp's inability to attend them, and her husband too is in a declining state of health. A few sparrows killed Tuesday evening, a moorhen a day or two before, the turkey yesterday. Farewell, hoping you are well.

Mrs. J. E. TAYLOR *to her Brother*.

MANCHESTER, *January* 8, 1832.

. . . May will soon be here, my dearest brother, before, I fear, I am able to undertake the journey or can be otherwise than an invalid, & under these circumstances I would never consent to go so far from home; so that I think all probability of my seeing your Isabella either before her marriage, or at the time, is over. My feelings have been so very distressing for a long time that I have never looked forward to any thing. I thank God these feelings are now much alleviated, but my health is too completely impaired to anticipate any powers of exertion within these few months, if they ever should return. I said to Dr. J. "I have had a very distressing time since I saw you." He replied "You have no occasion to tell me that, I can see it in your face."

I suppose you know Uncle William & Mrs. Hawes spent a

[1] A turkey was sent every Christmas to Portsmouth.

few days [here]. I was confined upstairs the first day, but got down & quite enjoyed them the last two or three. I was very glad indeed they came. I am very much pleased with Mrs. Hawes, & Uncle I think so improved. You would have been somewhat pleased to have heard Mrs. Hawes's eulogiums upon your Isabella. She knew so much of her character from both the Miss Lawrences. From Miss Lawrence, with whom she corresponds, she first heard of the proposed marriage, & the way in which she spoke of Isabella is quite delightful. . . .

The Miss Lawrences, Civil, Elizabeth, and Anne, were cousins of my mother, being nieces of Mrs. Elias Prestwich, her grandmother. My brother Lawrence was named after these cousins, who were always very intimate with my mother's family. They did not marry. The youngest sister died in 1887 at the age of eighty-five.

RUSSELL SCOTT *to his Father.*

LONDON, *March* 14, 1832.

. . . If I do not go to Portsmouth next week I must avoid being away on the 30th, as on that day I am to give a little party in commemoration of the anniversary of the day on which I first met Miss Prestwich, at Mrs. Crowley's at Lavender Hill. Mr. & Mrs. Crowley are to be of the party. Suppose you come up & join it. Be so good as to let me hear from you as soon as you can, if you can write without inconvenience, & if not ask my Uncle William to write for you.

Isabella was very much obliged to you for your kind messages. She is quite well. My uncle Benjamin sent her a very pretty present of a cabinet yesterday. . . .

Mr. William Hawes, my grandfather's brother-in-law, with his wife, had most kindly gone to live in Portsmouth in order to be near my grandfather and

lessen the solitude of his last years. They remained there till after his death.

The little "cabinet," mentioned in my father's letter, was many years later given by my mother to her grand-daughter Isabel.

Rev. RUSSELL SCOTT *to his Daughter.*

PORTSMOUTH, *March* 19, 1832.

. . . Not having been able to be out for the last two Sundays, I had no opportunity of ascertaining the wish of my congregation respecting the cholera fast on Wednesday. After the morning service I requested those who were present, & we had a pretty full attendance, to remain for a few minutes. I told them it did not appear to me to be necessary on that occasion to acquaint them with my views respecting this, or any other fast by proclamation. What I was desirous of knowing was whether it were their wish to have service on the following Wednesday, & if they did whether they would also have a collection for the poor. On putting the question whether there should be service on Wednesday morning, not a single hand was held up; I was surprised & therefore put the question whether it were their wish that there should not be a service on Wednesday morning, when hands were held up from every part of the chapel. . . . I expect your brother down on Wednesday afternoon by the Rocket coach which is usually in by 5 o'clock. I shall have a cold fowl in readiness for him after his journey, although it will be a fast day, so that he may drink tea with me, and eat his dinner at the same time. . . .

RUSSELL SCOTT *to his Sister.*

April 2, 1832.

. . . I much wish I could see you for two or three days & Isabella is quite desirous that I should, but with the prospect of a long absence in the summer I do not think it would be at all well to leave town now. I assure you, my dear sister, it is not without painful feelings that I not unfrequently contrast the happy circumstances in which I am already placed, & the prospect of happiness which is before me, with the sad deprivation of enjoyment which your long illness occasions, & I believe & indeed am certain that my Isabella fully participates in these feelings. She considers herself to be already very much acquainted with you, having of course heard a good deal of you from myself, besides hearing the greater part of your more recent letters.

The time of our marriage is not yet very definitely fixed. Isabella leaves the matter entirely to her parents. This day week I shall get possession of my house and ascertain when it will be ready, and I shall probably then have the day fixed. We have determined to go to Paris after the wedding, whether beyond it or not must depend on circumstances. Isabella is very desirous to go to Italy, but I know she will cheerfully relinquish the idea if I should think it necessary. . . .

RUSSELL SCOTT *to his Father.*

LONDON, *April* 16, 1832.

. . . I shall hope to meet you in good health & spirits this day week at Lavender Hill. On the following day I suppose you will dine with my friends at The Lawn, either there or at Lavender Hill. Isabella was saying this morning at breakfast, in the absence of her sisters, that they would be delighted to see you & she added in a whisper to me that she should also. So you must be sure to be very agreeable as everybody says you can be & realize the expectations entertained of you. . . .

I do not know whether I told you, but I suppose I must have done so when I saw you, that I have a four-wheeled chaise or phaeton building, Mr. Prestwich having been very much afraid of his daughter riding in a two-wheeled vehicle, which he considers exceedingly unsafe. He was very uneasy about her yesterday, when I drove her out before dinner, & happening to take rather a longer round than I intended, was a few minutes after time for dinner. It is not yet quite settled when I am to be married. If you would like to be present I hope you will arrange accordingly. If the ceremony were one in which I could feel greater satisfaction I should be more desirous than I am that you should be present, but if you would like to be present I shall be very glad to see you on the occasion. . . . I have not heard of my sister for a fortnight. I think it is hard that I am not to be allowed to hear of her more regularly & more frequently, but I have not for a considerable time said anything about it, as I find it is of no use. I think if my sister had been well enough to write to me herself she would have done it & I therefore fear she must have gone back since I heard last. . . .

My father's objection, mentioned above, was chiefly to the wording of the Marriage Service as it stands in the Prayer-Book—partly also, no doubt, to being himself married in a building of the Church of England.

RUSSELL SCOTT *to his Sister.*

LONDON, *April* 20, 1832.

. . . My wedding day being now fixed for the 2nd June I wish to give you the earliest information of it, persuaded that it will not fail to be interesting both to you & Edward. I should like much to write you a long & cheerful letter on the occasion, but it would be in vain to attempt it. Not that there is the slightest cloud on my prospects of happiness in my expected marriage, but that I am checked by the persuasion which presses itself upon me that there must be some cause for the evident disinclination to comply with my wish to be less seldom informed of your state of health. I did not at all intend again to mention the subject, & I have done it only to avoid the abruptness of concluding my letter with simply telling you the day fixed for my ma[illegible]. Of course I shall hear of you when I see my father o[illegible]nday. Unfortunately I have not had a letter from him this month. He comes to town chiefly, as I suppose you know, to see my Isabella, who is looking forward to meeting him with very great pleasure. . . .

Mrs. J. E. Taylor *to her Brother.*

MANCHESTER, *April* 21, 1832.

. . . If you knew, my beloved brother, how I have thought of you, how often day after day & hour after hour I have wished, "oh that I could write to my brother," you would not, you could not think anything, but that completely overwhelming feelings of utter powerlessness could have prevented my writing; but your letter has even overcome this. I feel I must write instantly to one I love as I love you, my own & only brother, to remove as far as I can an impression from your mind which it makes me quite miserable should exist there. I never should have written to my father if he had not seemed always to expect it, & often have I laid thinking of it the whole day & not till night made the effort. I caught cold the day after I heard from you, was first confined to my bed & only one day before this have walked downstairs, or been able to put my feet down off the sofa. My cough is very troublesome, my nights very bad —always wakeful & at times, even with anodynes, almost sleepless. Yet Mr. Turner says I am really better, & if we could get some warm weather & I lose my cough, I should improve rapidly. God grant I may, for the sake of those who have suffered so many deprivations for twelve months for me. Often have I thought, I never scarcely shall see my brother again, but still I do hope I may get well again. Your last letter made me indeed love your Isabella. I felt so gratified by her wish you should come. I indeed should like to see you more than I can express, but do not let my feelings influence you, if you think it best not to leave home. I do wish I had a prospect of seeing your Isabella. Remember me to her with the greatest regard. Edward has been led on the last fortnight, thinking every day I should write. May God grant you every happiness in your delightful prospects, & I entreat you do not let your sister be a cloud over them for an instant. Oh, I entreat you, do not.—Yours S. R. T.

RUSSELL SCOTT *to his Sister.*

LONDON, *April* 23, 1832.

I can scarcely forgive myself, my dearest sister, for having caused you to take the exertion of writing to me at a time when I am sure you ought not to have done it; you indeed much misunderstand me, but it was my fault not to write more explicitly. I did not for a moment doubt you would write to me, if you were well enough to do it, & I have always been most willing & indeed most anxious to forego the gratification of receiving a letter from yourself, provided I could hear of you & know how you were. . . . I do assure you it never entered my contemplation that my sister was disinclined to write to me, or that she would suppose from what I said that I thought her so. Many thanks to you for your most kind message to my Isabella. I know she will be very highly gratified to receive it; it was only yesterday she was calling you *her* sister & expressing her anxiety to see you, but when & how this is to be I am sure I hardly know.

We think of a visit to the Continent for our wedding trip, and have spoken of a journey to Manchester on our return. For myself I scarcely know what to say. I have been so much reproached for neglecting business lately, that with my wedding trip in prospect, I can hardly venture to leave town previously. I shall not decide any thing until I hear again from Edward, which I hope will be *soon*. The Prestwiches dine at Lavender Hill tomorrow & Isabella is to remain there tomorrow night.

I hope Edward & your dear children are all well. I trust the genial weather which we may now expect, & which indeed may be said to have commenced here, may have a good effect on you & gradually restore your strength; a rapid improvement we must hardly look for. I know I need not ask forgiveness, except of myself, for writing so unguardedly to you. I hope

most sincerely the exertion of writing has not seriously affected you. Hoping in some way or other to see you at no very great distance of time, I remain, my very dear sister, Most affectionately yours, RUSSELL SCOTT.

My father never ceased to regret that he did not go at this time to see his sister.

J. E. TAYLOR *to* RUSSELL SCOTT.

MANCHESTER, *April* 30, 1832.

It is with the most poignant grief, my dear Russell, that I have to communicate to you the distressing intelligence of the death of my beloved wife & your beloved sister. This awful event has come upon me quite unexpectedly & suddenly. Early in the last week Sophia suffered from an attack of pain in the side which tried her a good deal, but it yielded to the means which were applied, & since Wednesday she seemed to be rallying rapidly. . . . She felt rather poorly, more so I mean than usual this morning . . . but when I left at 10 o'clock for Chapel she was dressed, sitting in the easy chair. . . . She walked down stairs with my arm about one o'clock. . . . After dinner she took a few turns in the dining-room with my arm, but felt feeble, so that I stayed in the house with her all afternoon. . . . Between 6 & 7 this even[g] she expressed a wish to go upstairs & as she appeared feeble still, I carried her up in my arms. On sitting down in the easy chair she said "Oh, I've come up delightfully." And in about ¼ or ½ an hour, she said she felt quite comfortable & begged I would go out for a little walk, which she was sure would do me good. As she seemed better I at length assented, went out & returned a little before 8. She had just then gone to bed but did not seem worse. As she said she wished not to go to sleep at once, I read & took a little supper in our bed-room, & it was not until past 9 that I thought, or that she thought, she became materially worse. I then ran [illegible]ss to Mr. Beard's to get him to send some person to Mr. Turner's for him to come up again. . . . On going back into the room, she said, "Oh don't leave me, my own love." . . . Finding shortly after that she got worse I sent for our neighbour Mr. Nursaw, who came a little before 10. Soon after she saw him she said "Oh don't you think I'm dying, Mr. Nursaw?" . . . He told me she had spasms in the chest, & after he had been there perhaps half an hour, not having found any of the means he had then used—hot brandy & water, ether or hot water to the feet—produce a reaction, he said he considered her in great danger, & told me to prepare for a change. . . . Mr. Turner did not get here until about 11 & at ½ past 11 or thereabouts, it pleased God to take our beloved Sophia to himself. The last hour or more she was not able to speak; indeed I may say she never was after I had been apprised of her imminent danger; but she returned my pressure of her hand, which I was holding, within 10 minutes of her death. Her death took place with such stillness & composure that neither I, nor Miss Rackett, nor Jane, who were all hanging over her could ascertain the moment of her departure. Our beloved children know not yet of their orphanage. They were in bed & asleep before our alarms were excited. Oh my dear Russell, what can make up to them for their loss. I have a comfort unspeakable, as far as my Sophia is concerned, in my knowledge of her excellencies & my consequent conviction of her happiness. For my own loss I trust God will grant me fortitude & resignation, but this is an awful cloud come over the prospects of my children, for the loss of their Mother, & such a mother, nothing on earth can compensate them.

I have thought a good deal about the best mode of communicating the afflicting intelligence of this unexpected dispensation to your dear Father. And the best that I can think of is for you to go down to Portsmouth & break it to him. Of course I shall want you both here as early as possible. Your Father will travel better with you than alone, or I would have asked you to come to me at once. Write to me by return, dear Russell, if you please & let me know what you determine on. . . . I do not know—I felt I could not—rewrite the details I have here given you. I enclose therefore a short letter to your Father which you will please to give him with this, or, if you decide not to go down on Tuesday, send them either to him or to Uncle William, or somebody who will break the matter kindly & judiciously to him, by Tuesday night's post. . . .

My grandfather must have felt his solitude much. He had been most tenderly cared for by both wife and daughter, and both were now gone. He continued to live at his house, 124 High Street [now 125], till his death.

Rev. RUSSELL SCOTT *to his Son.*

May 22, 1832.

The purpose of my writing to you this morning is to acquaint you that Mr. & Mrs. James Carter took their leave of Portsmouth yesterday morning. . . . I called at their lodgings on Saturday evening & took my leave of them. It was to me a very painful meeting. I am becoming more & more a solitary being. I am losing in one way or other all my friends; at least the friends to whom I have been closely attached. . . .

Rev. RUSSELL SCOTT *to* J. E. TAYLOR.

PORTSMOUTH, *May* 14, 1832.

MY DEAR EDWARD,—As it was your wish that I would not delay writing to you beyond this evening's post I sit down to comply with your kind request without the ability to do it. It is the day in which I have been accustomed to write & chat with my & your very dear, most beloved, & deeply lamented Sophia. She is gone where we can no longer hold converse with her. She has been summoned to leave those to whom she was attached by the strongest bonds of affection, which have been suddenly broken, & which in the rupture have very severely wounded those who remain to deplore the early separation.

There have arisen already several little incidents which I should naturally have communicated to the child of my heart, & to whom I was in the habit of narrating every occurrence in which she could feel any interest, as they arose. But to you they would be entirely without interest except she were by your side to explain them. . . .

I had a very comfortable journey to London where I arrived soon after 10 o'clock. Miss Hawes & I left Lavender Hill at 2 o'clock in the carriage & reached Godalming soon after 7. We started the next morning at half past seven & reached my house at a quarter before five. . . . Mr. Maurice[1] preached for me yesterday. I did not feel myself fully equal to the duty. I found a letter from him at Lavender Hill, offering to do so if I was in the least desirous of it. I hope I shall be better able next Sunday. It is a great comfort to have Miss Hawes with me at this time. . . . She desires to be kindly remembered to you. . . .

RUSSELL SCOTT *to* J. E. TAYLOR.

LONDON, *May* 14, 1832.

. . . When I arrived at The Lawn last Tuesday evening, I found Miss Prestwich in mourning for my sister—I was glad to find that it was consistent with etiquette that she should put it on. . . . Isabella was gratified at your giving her a mourning ring & expressed herself very much so at receiving from you the ornaments which I formerly gave my sister. She assured me she should value them very highly. I told her you had mentioned that you feared there might have been a change in fashion since they were new & enquired if that were so.

[1] Rev. Michael Maurice, a Unitarian minister at Southampton, and an old friend of my grandfather's. His son was the well-known Rev. Frederick Denison Maurice.

She said that bracelets (I think) were now worn narrower & I proposed that they should be altered, but she said she should prefer to let them remain exactly as they were. She has written a letter of two sides to Sophia which I should hope will please her; but I suppose you will be obliged to read it to her. I hope you will very soon write & let me know how she & her brothers are, & what plans you have adopted & are pursuing. . . . Yours ever R. S.

J. E. TAYLOR *to* RUSSELL SCOTT.

May 19, 1832.

I am pleased to find that Miss Prestwich was in mourning for my poor wife, & that she has been gratified in receiving the ornaments. God grant her long life & health to wear them, & may He grant further, my very dear Russell, that your union may be long & happy, that you may never feel the pang on either side of the untimely disruption of a connexion, the nearness & intimacy of which none but the married can fully appreciate, & the pain of the severing of which, none but those who have loved each other as my Sophia & I did, can comprehend in its true extent. My little Sophia,—alas, my only remaining Sophia—was exceedingly gratified by Miss Prestwich's letter to her, which I received on Thursday. I read it to her twice & she was running up & down the house with it in her hands that evening & yesterday morning, saying "My letter, my nice letter." . . . I have not formed any decided plan with respect to Sophia's studies. In this respect you know that unfortunately I cannot have much aid from Miss Rackett; & it is almost as much as I can do to take care that Russell learns his lessons properly, not that I wholly overlook my little girl however. I endeavour to get a reading lesson once at least daily with her & you know she reads with interest & intelligence. . . . I am, dear Russell, very truly yours, JOHN EDWD. TAYLOR.

J. E. TAYLOR *to* Rev. RUSSELL SCOTT.

May 23, 1832.

MY DEAR SIR,—. . . To you I need not describe the void which the death of our beloved Sophia has made in my house & in my heart. Often still does the whole affair seem to me as a painful dream. I seem at times to fancy her *only absent* from me. . . . I have a great source of comfort in my fondly loved children. Though the feeling of my responsibility as regards them is at times almost overwhelming, their caresses, their ardent love, which I believe I possess, are a great consolation to me. I trust the Divine Being will strengthen & bless my resolution to endeavour to make them as much as possible what their departed Mother would have wished that they should become.—Most affectly. yours,

JOHN EDWARD TAYLOR.

J. E. TAYLOR *to* RUSSELL SCOTT.

June 14, 1832.

It is past midnight, my very dear Russell. For the last three hours I have been engaged in putting in order some of my book shelves in the breakfast room, where I have met with so many things to remind me of my beloved lost one that I know not how either to go on, or to go to bed; if I did the latter I could not sleep. I have therefore taken my paper to write a few lines to you in hopes I may find the employment a somewhat soothing one. You were right in deciding to write to me, for you did owe me a letter & I was wishing much to hear from you. . . . Mr. Beard showed me a passage in a letter of Mr. Fox[1] referring to Sophia to the following effect:—"I cannot write about that admirable woman. For some years I have seen little of her. She was a sweet & noble creature. Poor old man, he must long to go."—Ever very affectionately yours, JOHN EDWD. TAYLOR.

Addressed: "New Barge House."

[1] Rev. William Johnston Fox.

Rev. RUSSELL SCOTT *to* J. E. TAYLOR.

PORTSMOUTH, *July* 4, 1832.

I returned home from Worthing very unwell, & was under the necessity of writing to postpone my journey to Sherborne. Though still unwell I ventured to undertake it on the 11th of June in the hope it might prove beneficial to me. In this I was disappointed; my nights were disturbed & restless & in the day my headaches were severe. Every night I had regularly a visit from our beloved Sophia & her dear Mother, who entered my room hand in hand. These imaginary nocturnal visits naturally deprived me of sleep & affected my head, & also produced such a depression of spirits as I do not remember ever to have experienced before. The constant endeavour to check & to conceal it when with others made me feel it the more I think when I was alone. My journey therefore did not produce the effect I expected from it, and when I returned home on Saturday week I was almost overwhelmed with depression & headache; I had however the day before me to compose myself & I went through the services of the following day better than I feared. . . .

CHAPTER XIV

MARRIAGE OF RUSSELL SCOTT—JOHN EDWARD TAYLOR'S SECOND MARRIAGE

1832–1835

RUSSELL SCOTT *to his Father.*

LONDON, *July* 21, 1832.

MY DEAR FATHER,—I have been much longer than I like in replying to your last letter. I was saying so this morning to your intended daughter-in-law, & I told her I should look to her in future to make up in some degree for my deficiencies in attention to you. This she very readily promised to do, & said that she should take part of the correspondence upon herself, which she should have much pleasure in doing from the great regard she entertained for you, & the kindness you had shown towards her. She also expressed her hope that you would pay us a very early visit after our marriage. . . . This reminds me that I have to tell you that a day is once more fixed for our marriage.[1] If nothing intervenes again to prevent it, it is to take place on Wednesday, the 12th of September. I hope that will not prove an inconvenient day for you to be in London. We do not at present say anything about the day, though I suppose it will be quite in vain to attempt to keep it to ourselves. I should like to do so if it were practicable, & prevent what I consider the intrusion of those who will otherwise come uninvited to see the ceremony. Where we shall go afterwards I do not know. It will depend chiefly I believe upon the state of the cholera. We wish much to visit Paris, but unless it be in a much more healthy state

[1] It had been postponed in consequence of his sister's death.

than at present it will not be prudent to do so. . . . The cholera has been much more prevalent in London than the newspapers would lead you to suppose. I have no doubt the deaths have more than doubled the average number. It has taken off 3 or 4 with whom I have been on speaking terms, several others whom I have known by sight, & very many indeed whose relatives & friends I have been acquainted with. About a fortnight ago the medical computation was about 50 or 60 deaths per diem, but I have no doubt that since that time it has reached 100. . . .

Rev. Russell Scott *to* J. E. Taylor.

Lavender Hill, *Sept.* 12, 1832.

I am but just returned, my dear Edward, from The Lawn, & have only time to tell you that Russell was married soon after 10 o'clock this morning. The service was made very unnecessarily long. There were present the Father & Mother, Uncle & Aunt [Blakeway] & two sisters & a brother of the bride. Russell's two uncles & aunts Hawes, & Sarah Hawes [Aunt Sarah] & cousin Benjamin & his wife. I believe these were all. At the breakfast we were joined by Mr. & Mrs. John Donkin, Sarah Hawes that was & her husband (I forget the name at this moment) Wm. Hawes, & Russell Gurney. Russell & Isabella started for Sittingbourne soon after one o'clock; tomorrow they proceed to Dover; on Friday morning they hope to cross over to Calais, & if they arrive there in time they propose to proceed immediately for Dunkirk, where they are expected on Friday & Saturday by a brother & sister of Isabella's, who are at school there. From Dunkirk they proceed to Brussels, from thence up the Rhine to Switzerland & from thence to Paris, returning by way of Havre to Portsmouth by about the first of November. . . .

My grandfather was much pleased with his son's marriage, and was most kind to my mother. After a

visit to Portsmouth, my father and mother began their home life at 6 Upper Stamford Street, Blackfriars (now 88 Stamford Street), that house having been chosen as being conveniently near to New Barge House Wharf.

My eldest sister was born here in June the next year, and my grandfather came to town to baptize her by the dear name of Sophia Russell.

RUSSELL SCOTT *to* J. E. TAYLOR.

LONDON, *June* 10, 1833.

MY DEAR EDWARD,—. . . Our child will be named Sophia Russell Scott. This has been long settled between Isabella & me, provided it should be a girl, & it is my ardent hope that in future life she may possess in some degree the qualities of mind & heart which distinguished her who once bore the name.

Your children will, I dare say, be pleased at having a little cousin. Kate & Eliza Prestwich are most highly delighted & you would be amused to hear the various perfections they have already found in their niece. . . .

J. E. TAYLOR *to* RUSSELL SCOTT.

MANCHESTER, *Nov.* 23, 1833.

MY DEAR RUSSELL,—I feel that the time is come when I ought not any longer to delay apprising you that I contemplate at no very distant period being married. In making this communication to you (the first person to whom I have made it) I hope I need not assure you that my regret for the loss of my beloved Sophia, my attachment to her memory, & my high estimate of her character, have undergone no diminution whatever. But it has pleased Providence to sever our connexion, & it has therefore become my duty to consider what course is most calculated to promote my own happiness & the welfare of my dear children. My habits you know, & I am thankful such is the case, are very domestic; & the death of my Sophia created a void in my circle of which the lapse of time has not made me less sensible, & which indeed seems at times to make me feel almost more lonely this winter than the last. . . . With warm feelings & I hope an affectionate disposition, & with spirits not naturally high, I want a companion, a cheerful constant companion, to be interested in all my concerns, to whom I can speak unreservedly & whose attachment to me I could especially rely on seeing exhibited in the way I should most value it, by undeviating & I may say maternal kindness towards my children. Such an one I believe I have found; & I believe that if it were possible for my departed Sophia to express a wish on the subject, she would desire both for her children's sake & for mine, that I should form the connexion I have in view. I have always rated too highly the various excellencies of *her* character to expect—it would be unreasonable that I should expect—to meet with her equal. But I believe in sweetness of temper, in natural cheerfulness of disposition, in good principles, & in attachment to me & mine, the lady to whom I am alluding will be every thing I could desire. She is a Miss Gaskell an own cousin of Mrs. Edward Tagart (whose maiden name was Bourne) a second cousin of our minister. . . . My Sophia, who slightly knew Miss Gaskell, had been very much pleased with what she had seen of her. Some six months or so before Sophia's death Miss G. called on her in company with Miss Sanderson (now Mrs. Alex[r] Kay) whom you have seen at our house; & I well remember the warmth with which, when I came home to dinner, Sophia said "Oh Edward, Miss Gaskell has been here with Miss Sanderson, I do *so* like her." I believe it was the strong recollection of these words which when I was thrown repeatedly into Miss Gaskell's society, during a visit of some months which this spring & summer she paid to Mrs. Kay, first excited in me the wish to become better acquainted with her, & ultimately led to the attachment which now subsists between us. I have told her that this was the case. Often &

often has she heard me describe in terms of the warmest regard the leading points of my Sophia's character, thoroughly is she aware of the deep veneration in which I hold her memory; & I am fully convinced she has no higher ambition than to endeavour to imitate her. I was over at Warrington the beginning of the present week, & though the time is hardly finally settled, it is at present probable that our marriage will take place on the 31st of January, on which day Miss Gaskell will complete her 31st year. . . .

I hope my dearest Russell, you will do me the justice to believe that this connexion will not in the slightest degree detract from the sincere regard & interest I feel, not only for you & your Father, but generally for the relatives of my Sophia. My brotherly affection for you, my anxious desire for your welfare & prosperity & that of your family will be as warm as ever; & I trust I shall not have the pain of perceiving any diminution in your attachment to me & my children. I hope that our intercourse, whether personal or epistolary, will not become more infrequent than it has been, & on my part I can promise that it shall not be less cordial or affectionate. . . .

Russell Scott *to* J. E. Taylor.

London, *Nov.* 26, 1833.

My dear Edward,—You will hardly expect I think that in the interval between the arrival & departure of yesterday's post I should be able to find either sufficient leisure, or the necessary composure, to enable me to reply to the very unexpected & startling communication which your letter contained. Now however that I have both I will tell you without the least reserve the views I entertain of your intended marriage & the feelings to which its near approach has given rise. First then, I do not think it was desirable either for yourself or your children that you should suffer your attachment to my sister's memory to form an insurmountable obstacle to a second marriage, which I have sometimes thought of as an event in itself desirable, though it would have been long before I could have ventured to allude to such an idea, even if my own feelings had been less intimately concerned. The account you give of the lady who is to bear the name of her whom I so fondly loved, & to whose memory I am yet *more* strongly attached, is highly gratifying, & I cannot entertain the slightest doubt that your choice has been judicious. Independently however of what you tell me there is no man in whose soundness of judgment on so important a matter I should place greater reliance. But though I am far from objecting to your marrying again, & still farther from questioning the choice you have made, I must say that I am deeply grieved to find that 12 months had scarcely elapsed (probably had *not* elapsed) from the day of her removal before you entertained a wish to become acquainted with another lady, with a view of course to making her your wife, if your impressions respecting her were confirmed. I should not have thought this possible. I should have thought that if you had suspected yourself of an attachment to another at so early a period, you would have deemed the feeling inconsistent with the regard you entertained & which I am quite sure you still entertain for her memory. I am aware you had strong inducements to remedy, as far as possible, the loss you had sustained. I can appreciate I think the feeling of desolation which it must have required all your fortitude to support, but I should have thought you would have deemed my sister's memory deserving of more than ordinary respect, & that if any sacrifice were necessary to evince it you would not hesitate to make it. . . .

You have judged quite rightly in not informing my father of your intentions, nor will it be proper that the subject should be mentioned to him by letter, as it is quite uncertain in what state he might be when it should reach him, so much does he fluctuate from day to day. I shall go down on Friday week, which I had told him I might probably do before I received your letter, & shall consult Mr. Martell as to the propriety of mentioning the subject to him, of which I confess

I have some dread. The time of your marriage being so close at hand is a difficulty. Were it more distant he would think of it as an event not likely to take place in his life-time. I could say much more, but should probably be trying my own feelings & yours to no good purpose. I do not charge myself with this, as it is, for I should feel no satisfaction in concealment of my views from you, nor do I think you would wish me to suppress them. I will only add that you need not at all apprehend the slightest diminution of my attachment to your children; the contrary effect seems to me more natural, & that I shall still entertain for you that strong regard which your devoted attachment to my sister so necessarily secured for you in my mind, & which must always give me a strong interest in your happiness & welfare. . . .

J. E. TAYLOR *to* RUSSELL SCOTT.

MANCHESTER. *Dec.* 3, 1833.

MY DEAR RUSSELL,—You may probably have expected that I should reply to your letter before now. I will frankly confess that I have scarcely known how to do so. For although I have perhaps under the circumstances scarcely any reason to complain of the mode in which you have received my communication, yet there are one or two parts of your letter which cannot have failed to cause me considerable pain. You say you are "deeply grieved to find that 12 months had scarcely elapsed (probably had not elapsed) from the day of my Sophia's removal before I entertained a wish to become acquainted with another lady, with the view of course of making her my wife if my impressions respecting her were confirmed." More than 12 months had elapsed, but it was not a great deal more, so I do not dwell upon that. I was too "acquainted" with her & had been for years. If I had or could have gone coolly a wife-hunting (if I may use the phrase) I should have fully merited the censure this part of your letter implies, but the case was far otherwise. The feelings I entertain for Miss

Gaskell sprung up involuntarily on my part, out of an intercourse which undoubtedly was not in the first instance connected with any such anticipation. For a long time I had scarcely more than one topic of conversation with her; & that was the affliction I had sustained, & the character of the wife I had lost; & in the end the result was "I loved Her that she did pity me." I do think that this exact statement of the origin of our connexion ought to remove much of the feeling which you might otherwise justly entertain on the subject. With respect to the time of our marriage, I think I told you in my last that we had originally spoken of it between ourselves as to take place in the spring. . . . I proposed the 31st January, partly because it was Miss Gaskell's birthday, & I have a fondness (perhaps not a wise one) for such coincidencies, & partly because as I found contrary to my earnest desire, that the affair had become known, I almost thought that the sooner it was got quietly over the better. I do not like to be spoken to about it. Some people will joke, & jokes upon such a subject I hardly know how to bear. With the fullest confidence in the warmth of Miss Gaskell's attachment, & in both her disposition & her power to contribute much to the happiness of my home, I feel none of the elevation of spirits which, under common circumstances, the approach of marriage usually inspires. I almost shrink from the thought of its unavoidable festivities. I am only anxious for us to subside as soon as maybe into the quiet round of domestic duties & engagements. But the reason which rendered the period we had first thought of for our marriage ineligible, does not I presume render inconvenient its postponement to March, & in a letter which I had from Miss Gaskell yesterday after enquiring if I had heard from my friends, she, purely of her own accord, says that "dearly as she loves me & much as she values my society, she would rather resign it for a time, than I should be exposed to the slightest censure on her account, in case they should think it too early for me to enter into a second marriage."

The only thing I have ever much apprehended about the

affair is the effect it might produce on your Father, in the present critical state of his health; & respecting this I have felt a great deal. What I want now to suggest to you is this; if you have not arranged for going down to Portsmouth this week, that you should postpone it until next week. I shall go to Warrington on Saturday & I will have some conversation with Miss Gaskell on the subject, & I will endeavour to make up my mind what course under all the circumstances it is best to determine on, & write you again on my return home early in the week. There is only one other point I shall mention at present; it is with reference to the concluding part of your letter where you assure me of the strong regard "my devoted attachment to your sister so necessarily secured for me in your mind & which must always give you a strong interest in my welfare & happiness." This regard I sincerely value, & to it I feel that I possess a just title. God knows how ardently I loved my Sophia when living, & how dear her memory is to me now that she is no more; but my dear Russell, perhaps I am too sensitive, but I had hoped that I might have some *further* claims, from character or personal qualities, to a portion of your affection. You have many to mine *beyond* our relationship. I can never, I believe, cease to feel a fraternal love for you; & I had hoped that this feeling was in some degree reciprocal. I could not resign that hope without a pang that I trust I shall not have to encounter. . . .

RUSSELL SCOTT *to* J. E. TAYLOR.

LONDON, *Dec.* 5, 1833.

MY DEAR EDWARD,—I certainly had as you suppose expected to hear from you sooner, & that I had not received any answer to my last had given me some uneasiness, & I was therefore the more pleased to find from your letter which arrived this morning that there was no occasion for it. I do not like to lose a post in replying, more particularly as you propose going to Warrington on Saturday, but I have been engaged all day in attendance on a Committee which has left me very little time to write.

I regret that some parts of my last should have given you so much pain, yet I cannot blame myself for having said what I did, because I think that frankness in communicating one's feelings is almost essential to the preservation of such an intimacy as has subsisted, & I trust ever will subsist, between you and myself, & because also it has in the present case had the effect of occasioning such explanations from you as have very materially mitigated the feelings of grief & of uneasiness to which the announcement of your approaching marriage, not unnaturally I think, gave rise in my mind. I confess your first letter led me to fear that you had almost determined on a second marriage before the period when you were thrown so much into Miss Gaskell's society, & I am very much obliged to you for removing an impression so painful to my feelings, & so unjust to yourself. You propose a postponement of my journey to Portsmouth. This is quite impossible unless I were prepared to assign a specific reason, which of course I am not. My father has been looking forward with pleasure for a week past to my visit. I have twice written to him about it & I cannot disappoint him, but I may possibly postpone mentioning the subject of your marriage, in which case I believe I must go down a second time for that purpose. My chief fear arises from the notoriety of the matter in Lancashire & the possibility that in some way or other it may reach him suddenly. I have not told any one in London except my aunt Sarah & my uncle Thomas. I shall not decide until I have seen my father & consulted Mr. Martell. I had a letter from the former this morning, which rather confirms than allays my apprehensions respecting him. . . .

I must just notice what you say respecting the concluding part of my last letter. I assure you I by no means intended to imply that you had no other claims on me than those arising from your most exemplary conduct as the husband of my poor sister. I am quite sensible you have ot [illegible] claims on my regard & affection, although at the time I w [illegible] not allude to any less immediately connected with her memory, which was at that moment chiefly occupying my thoughts. Your own expressions respecting myself are highly gratifying, & I trust will last as long as we may live. With Isabella's kind regards, & our best love to the children, I remain my dear Edward, yours affectionately,

RUSSELL SCOTT.

RUSSELL SCOTT *to* J. E. TAYLOR.

LONDON, *Dec.* 10, 1833.

MY DEAR EDWARD,— . . . I am happy to say that I found my father much better than I had expected to find him, & that it does not appear that at any time since I was last at Portsmouth he has been so unwell as I had feared he had been,—indeed about a fortnight ago it would appear that he was as well as he has been at any time since his attack 12 months since. Under these circumstances I did not hesitate to inform him of your intended marriage. He was not in the least degree agitated—so far from it indeed that I was much surprised when he told me the next day that it would be painful to him to write to you on the subject, & that he should prefer that nothing should pass between you respecting it. I thought however that this could not be pleasant to you & therefore took an opportunity of mentioning it again, when he said his only objection to hearing from you upon the subject was the necessity he would be under of replying. He wished me to tell you that he was "quite satisfied" & that your marriage was what he "naturally expected." I give you his words & I believe that both expressions (certainly the former) were intended as messages. If I had been aware of the little effect my communication was likely to produce I would not have taken a journey to Portsmouth on purpose to make it. I am happy to be able to tell you that the legacy to your children will not be less than the £[illegible] mentioned in the letter* to my poor sister which you returned to me. I am very glad of this as the subject of it need not again be brought u[illegible]

* Evidently a letter from my grandfather to his daughter mentioning the amount which [illegible]

J. E. TAYLOR *to* RUSSELL SCOTT.

Dec. 19, 1833.

MY DEAR RUSSELL,—Your last two letters were a great comfort to me. . . . I was also particularly rejoiced to find that your Father had borne so well the intelligence of my approaching marriage & that he was satisfied with it. I trust it may prove & I believe it will, a step beneficial to my children as well as productive of happiness to myself. It is my earnest wish to bring them up as our lamented Sophia would have desired & I believe Miss Gaskell will not only be disposed but anxious to conform to my views in this respect. I wish to have as few changes as possible in my domestic arrangements. We contemplate Miss Rackett's continuance with us in the same situation she had formerly filled. I know this, under ordinary circumstances, would be a somewhat hazardous experiment, but with Miss Rackett's quiet, unobtrusive & amiable disposition on the one hand, & Miss Gaskell's remarkable sweetness of temper on the other, I do not anticipate any practical difficulty; & with the value I attach to Miss Rackett as an attendant on the children, particularly from her intimate knowledge of their poor Mamma's mode of managing them, I could not think of removing her. This I have told Miss Gaskell from the first & she has cordially assented to it. I hope & expect consequently that they will be quite comfortable together. Miss Gaskell has been at my house three or four times with the Kays & had had an opportunity of seeing Miss Rackett's attention, I may say devotion to the children, & had expressed a very strong opinion respecting it to me before any thing had passed between us & almost before I had thought of it. Remember me most kindly to Isabella & believe me, my dear Russell, with the best wishes for your mutual enjoyment of the approaching festive season, Very affectionately yours

JOHN EDWARD TAYLOR.

Addressed: "6 Upper Stamford St., London."

Rev. RUSSELL SCOTT *to* J. E. TAYLOR.

PORTSMOUTH, *Jan.* 22, 1834.

MY DEAR EDWARD,—You have of course heard from Russell of the decided character my complaint has taken, & that now from the extreme debility of my frame those active means cannot be employed which would otherwise be used to counteract & remove it. The consequence is that the disease is making rapid progress & this is probably the last letter I shall be able to write to you. It is not unlikely from present appearance but that in the course of the ensuing week I may be summoned to quit this period of my existence, in which I trust I have not been wholly useless. I look forward to a future with great tranquillity & composure, from the nature & character of that Being whom I trust I have faithfully served. . . .

And now my dear Edward, [allow me] to commend you & your dear children to the merciful care & protection of God's kind providence through the changing scenes of this eventful & constantly changing life. Permit me also to implore the divine blessing on the endearing connexion you are about to form, & at the same time to inform & assure you it meets with my most cordial approbation. Pray be careful that Miss Rackett be not invested with that authority & influence over the minds & conduct which ought to be entrusted only to her whom you select as their adopted parent. Indeed I have great doubts of Miss Rackett's adequacy in the management of such children as yours in any respects.—Yours most affectionately,

R. SCOTT.

My grandfather died three weeks after this letter was written—on February 14, 1834. He had sent a few days before an affectionate message to the congregation whose minister he had been for forty-five years. "May the God of love," he said, "bless you and lead you all to keep steadfast in every good word and work, and may we be united together for ever."

In the latter part of his life my grandfather was the leading Unitarian minister in the south of England. My father recollected Mr. Thomas Cook, of Newport in the Isle of Wight, saying, "In Mr. Scott's lifetime we had a bishop; now we are all equals." The High Street congregation had been Presbyterian, but gradually became Unitarian during his ministry.

My mother described my grandfather as a tall man of fine dignified presence. He was stout in later years, and his hair was thick and white. As a preacher he was much valued, and the congregation was a large and important one. Personal dignity, my mother said, was strongly characteristic of him; he was not a very clever man, but he saw clearly and held his opinions strongly. He was a very agreeable companion, talked well and was cheerful. She thought he must have been a slow man, for there was so much weight and dignity in his manner; it made all he said very impressive. She often spoke of his fine voice, and said that he read extremely well. He was blind of one eye, having been injured as a child by a squib, when taken on the 5th of November to see some fireworks.

We have a book of his collected lectures entitled the "Scriptural Claims of the Devil," as well as copies of several of his printed sermons.

Grace Downing Scott *to* Mrs. Robert Scott.

Sherborne, *Feb.* 18, 1834.

. . . I received a letter from my uncle containing an enclosure of thirty pounds, which he requested might be equally divided between yourself, Mrs. Petty & Eliza, Sarah, Anna & myself, & forwarded after his death for the purpose of assisting in the purchase of mourning. Our dear uncle wished & intended it to have been double that sum, & had his life been longer spared it was his design to have accomplished it, but he considered it his duty to make a provision for Osborne for her long-tried, unremitting & faithful services during his painful & trying sicknesses, especially the last 15 months of his life. Uncle has settled on Osborne an annuity of thirty pounds. It gave me much pleasure to hear that she will be so comfortably provided for. . . .

RUSSELL SCOTT *to* J. E. TAYLOR.

LONDON, *March* 15, 1834.

. . . You enquire respecting my father's sermons. He destroyed about 1000 of them, as Osborne informed me, in the three months preceding his death; there are a few left, & they were in the heavy box we brought up from Portsmouth.

I know that he destroyed a great many of your mother's and other letters written when he was young.

March 31.— . . . We packed 29 cases of books at Portsmouth which are coming round by sea. . . . Isabella is fitting up our back parlour as a library, and we are to occupy it in future. I have let the house to Mr. Slight, the surgeon, at 30 guineas p. annum. . . .

These sermons were written in shorthand, for which reason they have not been read. We still possess the silver plate brought from Portsmouth. The tea-service has the initials R. S. S. engraved on the three pieces, and has the hall-mark of 1808, and the spoons and forks have a small mark on the handles which stands for the word "Scott" in shorthand. Much of the silver which we still have, engraved with a griffin's head and the

motto *Nosce teipsum*, was bought by my father at the time of his marriage. This was not an old family crest, but was chosen by my grandfather, who used it only on his seal.

I cannot let the above mention of my grandfather's books occur without a word of true gratitude to him for this gift of a library. If I do not mistake, my mother said that 6000 volumes came from Portsmouth. Many of these were on theological subjects, and being now superseded, have in most cases been gradually disposed of; but a very large number of books on other subjects remain. We grew up amongst these books to our very great advantage. They were of course added to by my father and mother.

Charles Lamb says of Bridget Elia that "she was tumbled early, by accident or design, into a spacious closet of good old English reading, without much selection or prohibition, and browsed at will upon that fair and wholesome pasturage. Had I twenty girls," he goes on, "they should be brought up exactly in this fashion. I know not whether their chance in wedlock might not be diminished by it; but I can answer for it, that it makes (if the worst comes to the worst) most incomparable old maids." We do not rival Bridget, but we can bear our testimony to the pleasantness and profit of "browsing" among books.

RUSSELL SCOTT *to* J. E. TAYLOR.

LONDON, *April* 13, 1834.

MY DEAR EDWARD,—Isabella & I were both desirous of writing to you to-day & I therefore procured a frank this morning from Benj. Hawes. . . . I have already briefly adverted to the probable breaking off of your intended marriage. Your letter of Monday appears to intimate that you do not consider it as final, but from what Mr. Potter told Benjamin in the House I apprehend Miss Gaskell does. I should very much, more indeed than I know how to express, regret having reason to imagine that any supposed feelings of mine had had the least influence in altering your views. It is true I did expect, & I have lately heard that my father entertained the same idea, that you would not, at least for some years, be able to contemplate a second marriage. I do not at all mean to say that there was any sufficient reason why I should have thought so, & now that that idea has been dispelled, it is I assure you a source of considerable regret to me that your intended marriage is not likely to take place. I do not at all like to say anything about Miss Rackett, but I think I ought to say—perhaps ought to have said before—that my father had not lightly taken up the view he expressed in the last letter he wrote to you. It gives me pain, especially after your very kind letter, to say anything that may give pain to you, but I think my duty to my sister's children requires me to say as much as this. Isabella has answered your kind letter to her, but I must add that I am exceedingly pleased with both likenesses. They will be over the mantle piece in the library which we are fitting up. That of my sister I think I value more than if it had been taken at a later period; it recals to my mind what she was before she was married. What she was in the latter years of her life I must of course remember as long as memory avails me at all; & my father's likeness is admirable. I think it does the artist very great credit. . . I remain,' my dear Edward, yours very affectionately,

RUSSELL SCOTT.

The engagement was broken off. I understood from my mother that Mr. Taylor's wish to retain Miss Rackett in charge of his children was one cause of the rupture. His wife had had great confidence in Miss

Rackett, and he made the sad mistake of thinking that she could not be parted with. The portraits mentioned above are the silhouettes reproduced on the preceding page.

RUSSELL SCOTT *to* J. E. TAYLOR.

LONDON, *May* 12, 1834.

MY DEAR EDWARD,—I have adopted your suggestion of making an "evening job" of writing to you, & I have done it in the only practicable way, by waiting until Isabella & her sister, who is here, are both gone to bed. . . . I said nothing in my last, although Isabella did, about the wish you were kind enough to express that we should pay you a visit. I was talking over the matter yesterday with her & there really appeared no chance of our being able to accomplish it. To take the child with us would not at all do, for many reasons—the principal of which is that the journey would in all probability be very bad for her, as appears from the effect produced by riding a short distance over the stones in London; & to leave her behind, unless she were perfectly strong & healthy, would be out of the question with Isabella, unless from absolute necessity. She has been staying the last four or five days at The Lawn, which appears to have been of much service to her. Her Mamma sees her every day, & to day she tells me the spasms & the affection of the throat have entirely left her. We are going there ourselves on Wednesday,—& in a short time we think of taking lodgings, probably for two months, at a short distance from town, possibly at Barnes. This of course will involve a good deal of absence from business on my part & render a journey to Lancashire rather inadvisable on that score, but Isabella says it is quite indispensable for the baby. . . .

The child was extremely delicate and was reared with great difficulty. My mother believed in later life that she had been much mismanaged with regard to her food.

RUSSELL SCOTT *to* J. E. TAYLOR.

LONDON, *Dec.* 3, 1834.

. . . Our little girl will, I believe, be named Isabella Prestwich—certainly the former. We do not regret that she *is* a little girl. I prefer a decided preponderance of girls in a family & we think the two, if they live & do well, will be companions to each other. . . .

Next as to politics—be it known to you that I am likely to renounce my adherence to you, as a political authority, at least if the two last *Guardians* contain the sentiments by which you continue to be guided, & as you have long been the only political authority to whom I acknowledge any allegiance, it follows that henceforth I must endeavour to get on without one. Joking apart, however, I regret the tone of the two last *Guardians*. . . .

J. E. TAYLOR *to* RUSSELL SCOTT.

Dec. 30, 1834.

MY DEAR RUSSELL,— . . . I told you some time ago that I intended to be on the look-out for a lady to take the management of my children as governess. Within these few weeks a lady has been mentioned to me whom I consider from all I have heard likely to be extremely well suited for my objects. She is a Miss Harriet Boyce of a Tiverton family. She left a few months ago the family of Mrs. William Stansfeld of Wakefield. I think I may rely on Mrs. Stansfeld's account, & regard her as perhaps even peculiarly qualified, both morally & as an instructress, to superintend my children. She is a decided & zealous Unitarian, and has been accustomed to give that sort of direction to the minds & the pursuits of her pupils which my poor Sophia would have wished that her children should have. If I engage her I am to give her £100 a year—for me a considerable sum, but which I shall think well laid out if she prove to be what she is represented. My plan does not involve the parting with Miss Rackett. I think I can chalk out distinct lines of duty for them, which shall preclude the probability of any jarring or interference. I should give Miss Boyce the entire superintendence of their education & the formation of their minds & characters for the most part; & I should continue Miss Rackett as housekeeper & to superintend the clothes & the health of the children. This is my plan; if I find practically that it will not work I must modify or change it, but I confess I am very sanguine that it will. . . .

J. E. TAYLOR *to* RUSSELL SCOTT.

Feb. 16, 1835.

. . . I expect to see Miss Boyce and finally to arrange with her tomorrow. . . . I am more and more inclined to think Miss Rackett will not stay,[1] and I have now to a certain extent accustomed my mind to think of it. My impression is that I should allow her £25 to £30 per annum. I should think not less than the former. . . .

J. E. TAYLOR *to* RUSSELL SCOTT.

May 3, 1835.

. . . I continue very much satisfied with Miss Boyce's treatment of the children, and I think they are all already very fond of her. I trust she will acquire great influence over their minds and conduct. I have every confidence that it will be exercised for good. . . .

J. E. TAYLOR *to* RUSSELL SCOTT.

MANCHESTER, *July* 28, 1835.

MY DEAR RUSSELL,—. . . I have intended in several of my last letters to inform you that I am at length resolved on making my will & to ask you not only (which indeed I think I have

[1] Miss Rackett left.

already done) to permit me to nominate you an executor, but also to permit me to bequeath to you the copyright of the *Guardian* (which you are aware is my exclusive property) as trustee for my children. At one time this might have been an affair of some difficulty & danger to you, but with the present feeling in regard to the libel law, I do not think it is. There could be no danger of a trustee for infant children being prosecuted criminally for libel now-a-days, even were the *Guardian* at all likely to afford ground for such prosecution, & as to civil actions (which I hope also will be avoided) it could of course be arranged that all costs & damages in these should be chargeable on the trust funds. There would be no occasion whatever for your name to appear on the paper as the proprietor. It need only be given in at the Stamp Office. The property of course is far too valuable to be sacrificed at my death if I can help it, and to avoid it I find that I must bequeath the copyright to somebody or other, and of course there are not many persons on whom I should like to devolve such a trust. I shall be glad if you will give me your opinion on this when you write, as I am desirous now to complete the affair. I have not yet fixed whom to appoint executors along with you. . . .

RUSSELL SCOTT *to* J. E. TAYLOR.

LONDON, *May* 10, 1836.

MY DEAR EDWARD,—. . . I am happy to say Isabella is extremely well & the little one also, notwithstanding some heterodox departures from old established rules respecting infants, which her Mamma has insisted on with respect to her. As to her name I am not able to give you any information—we have decided that she is to have one, but not what it is to be.[1]

I am not sorry to hear you have reverted to your original plan of being married at Tiverton; if not *very* inconvenient, it appears to me the best plan. I should think you will now be

[1] This was my sister Catherine.

able to visit the Isle of Wight while we are there. We hope to reach it about the middle of June. . . .

I was much pleased with what I saw of Mr. Thornely; he is I think the only thorough radical for whom I have ever felt much respect. . . . Seven years ago I should have felt a sort of awe in the presence of four M.P.'s—but your modern M.P.'s are not the men to be frightened at. . . .

Mr. Taylor had previously announced to my father his intended marriage to Miss Harriet Boyce. Her home was at Tiverton, and the marriage took place on 1st June. She proved a wise and most loving mother to his children.

I hope especially that they behave well. Tell them this from me with my affectionate love & as many kisses as good children deserve. . . . When you go to Sherborne you will be good enough to remember me with all brotherly affection to my dear brother & sisters. It is unfortunate that you have not yet sent me the copy of my dear Father's will etc, because I am not able to write to my dear brother in America the more full account which I promised him & for other reasons. . . . Business seems flat at No 7 [Bridge St.] & there has been great depression in foreign stock & shares. I will now relieve you by signing my name.—Yours, etc. ROBERT SCOTT.

One cannot read the above letter without remembering the fears and anxiety expressed in Mary Ann Taylor's letters to Robert Scott before their marriage. Probably there may have been faults on both sides which made their married life, as we believed it to be, anything but a happy one. His temper, however, was such as would have severely tried any woman, and he had not enough of right feeling to treat his wife, after he had ceased to care for her, with proper consideration. His love of money too, no doubt, made further difficulties. We understood that he told his wife little or nothing of his affairs, and always kept her short of money, although certainly when we knew them his means were ample.

MRS. RUSSELL SCOTT *to her Husband.*

WALMER BEACH, *August 21st*, 1836.

MY DEAREST RUSSELL,—I was very glad to receive your letter this morning, and much obliged to you for its kind contents. I assure you my conscience had been reproaching me for the shortness of my last letter to you and I felt I deserved a scolding. I do not know how it was that I should write to *you* with so much brevity, but I believe I was a good deal tired, for I certainly feel quite as much pleasure in addressing you as I always do, notwithstanding that Kate is here; in fact that really makes no difference, for the society of no one, my dearest Russell, can make up to me for the loss of yours, and writing to you, although a very imperfect substitute for the pleasure of talking to you, is still my most delightful employment in your absence. Dearest love, I long to see you whenever I think of you, more especially on Sunday, for that is the day of all others when I most value and enjoy your company.

. . . Our dear children are quite well. I have not yet resumed my morning's walk with Sophia, though I hope to be able to do so tomorrow or the next day. Yesterday it rained almost without intermission—today the weather is delightful, though I daresay you would find the breeze rather too cool.

The message which I asked you to deliver at The Lawn, was to beg Emily to come down if she could without waiting for you, that she might have rather more of the sea breezes. . . .

You told me, dearest, that there has been a revolution in Madrid, but you did not inform me whether it was brought about by the Carlists or the ultra-liberals. I presume by the latter party, as it appears a likely sequel to the revolts in Valentia and the other place, of which I have forgotten the name; pray inform me of the principal particulars in your next, for I feel a considerable interest in the matter.

When you come down, dearest, will you bring with you Miss Aikin's Memoirs of the Court of Charles 1st; it is on the same shelf in the library as Turner's works. Kate & I have been thinking that when our party becomes so large it will be a good plan to read aloud every morning, and that is the book we have fixed upon, but if you can think of any other which appears to you better suited for the purpose, bring it instead. I had intended to have asked you for the "Natural History of Enthusiasm," but then it occurred to me that you had read it, & also that I did not exactly know where to direct you to find it. Bring down what "Society" books you can, or if there should not be any, bring down some of our own, for I have not any books here which will suit Sarah Blakeway & Emily. I am glad it has been arranged for Eliza to accompany them instead of Kitty Blakeway. Kate sends you her love as a proof of her mild & forgiving disposition. She also desires it to all at The Lawn when you next go there. Sophia sends you her love & a kiss, but Isabella says she has no wish to see Papa and has nothing to say to him; for myself I can only say my dearest husband, that I love you very dearly, and long for the time to come when I shall next see you.

By the bye, Sir, I have just been calculating that you have cheated me most unfairly of three days of your society. You had arranged at first to have left here today and to return again next Saturday, & when you settled to leave me last Thursday you assured me it should not make any difference in the time you meant to pass here, and that you would return proportionally earlier. Instead of that you have fixed to stay in London until the Saturday you had first fixed upon, and so have lessened your stay here three days; however I hope a little consideration will show you the hardship of my case, and that you will make a point of returning to me on Thursday. And now my own Russell, Farewell.—Ever your most affectionate wife,

ISABELLA SCOTT.

Remember I shall be very much disappointed if I do not receive a letter every other day.

RUSSELL SCOTT *to* J. E. TAYLOR.

HOTEL QUILLACQ, CALAIS, *Aug.* 15, 1837.

MY DEAR EDWARD,—I came over here yesterday fortnight, & passed the week before last at Dunkirk, where the female members of Mr. Prestwich's family have been staying for the last two months, & our little Sophia with them. I intended returning by the steam boat to London on Monday week & Kate Prestwich & myself had taken our respective berths on board, when I found it necessary to go on shore between

1 & 2 in the morning to obtain from the English Consul (who proved to be in bed and asleep) a passport for my companion which I had previously been assured was needless. I had a good deal of vexation & delay & did not again reach the port until the clock was striking two, which was the hour for departure. I ran on as fast as possible (leaving Miss P. with the *commissionaire*) & fell with great violence over an iron cable drawn completely across the footpath in a dark place. When taken up, it proved that my thigh was broken a little above the knee, & it afterwards appeared that I had injured the tendon of the leg, which seems to be scarcely a less important matter, with reference either to present pain or future danger of lameness. Of the former however, I have really had less than I should have at all expected antecedently, & M. Boulanger, my surgeon, affirms that with proper care I need not fear the latter,—& that in due time I shall be perfectly well able to dance, which however I never yet was. However I am exceedingly thankful that matters are no worse. I am quite sure I am very far from having had my average share of the pain & suffering allotted to mortals, & I am happy to be able to say that I have felt no disposition to repine at this little untoward incident; indeed it would be most unjustifiable if I had, for there is nothing in an accident of this nature that produces any depressing effect upon the spirits, as is so often the case with various diseases.

I believe I am pretty sure to be detained here until about the middle of next month. I expect Isabella to be with me tomorrow. She was desirous of coming sooner, but I prevailed upon her to remain. Her sister has supplied her place exceedingly well, & the people of the Inn have been most exceedingly attentive, so that I have been very comfortable. . . . Our little boy[1] seems to be a stout & hearty chap. Sophia is exceedingly well & her mind surprisingly developed since she has been in France. . . .

[1] My brother Russell, born July 24, 1837, at 8 The Lawn, my grandfather's house at South Lambeth.

RUSSELL SCOTT *to* J. E. TAYLOR.

HOTEL QUILLACQ, CALAIS, *Aug.* 30, 1837.

MY DEAR EDWARD,—. . . You may perhaps have observed that I have for some time avoided the subject of politics—I have thought it as well to do so. I found your sentiments in the *Guardian* differing widely, not merely from my own, but as it appeared to me from those I had been accustomed to find there,—& I certainly thought, (& am still rather disposed to think) not that you were becoming a radical, because every now & then, though certainly not very often, you let us know to the contrary, but that you were so devoted an adherent of the present ministry that they could neither do nor attempt any thing that should place them in much danger of losing your support. I feared therefore, that to touch on politics might be dangerous, and then again when I found such complimentary epithets as "besotted" &c. (epithets such as I think I used not formerly to find in the *Guardian*) applied to those who might have the misfortune to entertain certain sentiments —which sentiments nevertheless I did & do entertain & profess—I could not help thinking you were much too fierce upon such subjects for me to venture to attack you. However as you have commenced the assault—certainly in a way quite free from *fierceness* of any kind—I shall endeavour, if I can find space & strength, to parry your thrusts & to make some on my own account. . . .

I observe you greatly regret (by anticipation) my letter inserted in the *Times*. The "very name of the paper" seems to shock you. Now I will grant you at once that the *Times* is as thoroughly unprincipled now as it has been for the last 10 years. Its manners I think are a little improved, but this may be fancy on my part, & is not very material. . . . Now what would you have had me to do? Should I have sent it to the *Chronicle* or the *Globe*? or would you have inserted it in the *Guardian*? If I had thought that probable, you certainly should have had the opportunity. If you will insert it even now when there is no danger of its influencing a stray vote at the South Lancashire election, I will promise never again to send a communication to the *Times* until you shall have refused it. I am not likely to trouble the public with many of my lucubrations, but it is most unconscionable in you, who blaze forth twice a week in leading articles, to object to my occupying a little corner of the only paper of extensive circulation that would be likely to insert what I may happen to write—perhaps once in seven years. . . .

RUSSELL SCOTT *to* J. E. TAYLOR.

LONDON, *Nov.* 21, 1837.

When I last wrote to you, I was desirous that it should be the last time the subject of politics should be referred to by me in writing to you, & you appear to agree with me in wishing the subject to be dropped, but unfortunately you have introduced into your letter so many remarks addressed completely *ad hominem* that I cannot well avoid saying something. In reply to these & to some apparent misconceptions of my meaning I shall confine myself at present, being quite desirous to have done with a subject upon which, until some important change shall have taken place in public affairs, our agreement appears quite hopeless.

You begin by regretting the "extent of my deviation from the faith of my fathers." It seems you anticipated my denial of the charge. Surely then it was for you who made it to point out in what this deviation consisted. The questions which existed in former years are for the most part settled, & most assuredly I have no wish they should not remain so. On those which are not I hold the same opinions I did 10 years ago, & I cannot imagine what pretence there is for charging a man with having changed his principles because, after being a zealous supporter of Lord Grey, he is not a supporter of Lord Melbourne & the three or four other members of Lord Grey's cabinet who belong to the present Ministry. It always appears to me that most people's ideas are rather confused upon this point; conservatives sometimes express their satisfaction that I have "come over" to their views. I always say I have done no such thing—it is they who have been driven back to the position in which the moderate Whigs have always stood, & where most of them still remain. You seem to think that because we once agreed & now differ, *one of us* must have changed; this seems to me a hasty inference. The questions which divide political parties are entirely *new*, & those who agreed three years ago may therefore differ now without the least ground, as it appears to me, for calling in question the consistency of either party. . . .

I am very glad to find you appear disposed to come to London once more, but I object decidedly to your making it next summer. We should in all probability be then absent from London, as Isabella generally manages to be away for four or five months. Besides which, delays are objectionable & I think therefore you had better bring up Russell & take him to Mr. Malleson's when the school reopens after the holidays. I should really think you will not be likely to do better, & for him in particular that you would not be able to do so well. I want too to speak to you about two or three matters & also to see whether you really are so fierce & unreasonable a personage as you endeavour in the *Guardian* to make us believe. It is to the hope of seeing you face to face that you are indebted for the non-infliction of a longer discussion of politics in this letter, for there were several points on which I found it difficult to restrain myself from touching. Isabella & I are most anxious too that you should bring Sophia with you, whom we very much wish to see, & if you could leave her with us for a little while, hardly anything would afford us so much pleasure. . . .

RUSSELL SCOTT *to* J. E. TAYLOR.

LONDON, *April* 1, 1838.

MY DEAR EDWARD,—. . . I have said nothing whatever to Mr. Cory about the partnership since you left—& altogether my affairs are in the most delightful state of uncertainty imaginable. As to our summer excursion, we have travelled I believe full 300 miles in search of a house, & it seems at present rather more doubtful than ever where we shall locate. We have visited almost every house that has been advertized lately, that has appeared at all likely to suit us, but I really do not think we have seen one at a lower rent than £150 a year that has not been decidedly objectionable. . . .

With respect to your visit . . . Isabella & I shall be very happy to come to town during your stay . . . but we hope you will pay us a visit in the country also, in which there will not be any difficulty on our part, as we fully intend to take a house with plenty of rooms. I am sorry we are obliged to leave town before you come, but the two elder children are both much in want of country air, & indeed we are always obliged to leave town as early as we can on that account. . . . I wish you could arrange to leave Sophia with us for two or three months—Isabella would be very glad to do whatever she could towards keeping up her pursuits during her stay. . . .

At this time my father retired from business. His partnership with Mr. Cory came to an end in 1838, and was not renewed.* In speaking of this he said that his property at that time amounted to about £40,000, and that he believed that he should be able to improve it considerably by judicious investments. This proved to be the case. His investments were very largely in railway stocks. All the principal railways in England were built in his lifetime, and he shared in their growing prosperity, but this was not done without close attention

* The business which almost from the first had been a successful one continued to prosper. In 1896 it was acquired by a company and at the present time (1909), as was recently stated in an obituary notice of the head of the firm, the coal distributing house of William Cory and Son "is the biggest in the world in its own sphere of operation [illegible] 2,000,000 [illegible]

to this class of business, and the exercise of much sound judgment and prudence. His opinion in later life was much valued by his friends, not a few of whom sought his advice in financial matters.

RUSSELL SCOTT *to* J. E. TAYLOR.

LONDON, *April* 4, 1838.

MY DEAR EDWARD,—I am at last able to say that I have taken a house. It was advertised in last Friday's *Times*, to which I dare say you have the means of reference. The description was good, but for the first time in my experience we found the reality better; it is called Great Gaddesden Hoo, & is five miles from the Boxmoor Station. The rent being stated in the advertisement at £30 a year, I feared it must have been long unoccupied, & in a state of great dilapidation, & wrote to make inquiries on that point before I thought it worth while to go down. The contrary however is the fact in both respects, & the situation is in our estimation excellent. There is a farm-house adjoining, one of the rooms of which Isabella thought it advisable to engage for a nursery, by which means we shall have three spare bedrooms, so that we shall be perfectly well able to take you all in when you come up. I have engaged it for three years, & would have taken it for a longer time, but the party had found out that he had put a very low rent on it & would not let me. Isabella is gone down by this morning's 8 o'clock train with 300 yards of papering for the different rooms, & this, with a little painting, will be nearly the whole *necessary* expense to be incurred before we take possession. She is going to put the workmen to work immediately, & we expect to get in in two or three weeks.

I shall hope now soon to hear from you as to *your* plans.

Gaddesden Hoo, Great Gaddesden, Herts., was our home for six years. Here my sister Sarah was born. It was (and is) a charming old place, in our day partly used as a farm-house. A short account of our childhood here, written by Sophia in 1851, is in No. 4 of the "Summer Hill Repository," a little family magazine which I still possess. There was a park surrounding the house to which we had free access, and a good garden and lawn. My father kept a carriage and a pair of grey ponies, so that the station (Boxmoor) and St. Albans were within easy reach. Occasionally, too, I remember, we drove up to London.

Our coachman was George Martin. He remained in my father's and mother's service for fifty-three years, and was an excellent servant, faithful and attached. In his own department everything was left to his management. Before my father's marriage he acted as groom, my father driving his gig himself, and remained on as coachman, or as gardener when, at Bath, no carriage was kept. As long as we lived in the country he and his family occupied a cottage near our house, and in early days his children, five daughters, were our chief friends and playmates.

Gaddesden Hoo was an interesting and very old house, probably dating from the time of Queen Elizabeth. One part of the kitchen floor was raised a step above the rest, showing where in old times the family had sat at dinner a little above the serving maids and men, who sat at the lower end of the table. A deep well was under one of the outhouses, from which water was drawn by a donkey walking within a huge wheel, always climbing up it and never getting any higher. Since we left the wheel has been removed and a similar one, still shown in Carisbrooke Castle, is perhaps the last left in England.

RUSSELL SCOTT *to* J. E. TAYLOR.

LONDON, *May* 23, 1838.

. . . I am sorry you appear to entertain objections to our plans, for you are *not* wrong in supposing that I do not intend to have an establishment in London as well as in the country. This would be to draw rather too freely on my "handsome fortune"—which, although I think it sufficient to justify my remaining out of business, will nevertheless, due regard being had to future contingencies, require husbanding. As to the distance from our friends, it will certainly be 30 miles from the nearest of them, but as that will be only two hours journey, we do not expect to see much less of them than at present. Were it otherwise however I think we should probably consider the sacrifice desirable on our own account, & most particularly so on account of the children. With respect to my "leaving the Dissenters" because I leave London, I hardly know whether I rightly apprehend the sense in which you use the expression. If you think I shall associate less with them, that is hardly possible. Out of the Unitarian connection, the only Dissenter in our acquaintance is Mr. Winston, our medical man, who is a Quaker, & in it we know very few indeed, & visit only the Miss Martineaus. I trust however that my principles do not very materially depend on those of my acquaintance. It is certainly one of the principal objects of my anxiety to form & to modify them for myself, with reference only to those facts & arguments which may appear to bear upon them. You are right in supposing there is no [Unitarian] chapel near our future residence. There is one however at St. Albans, & if no serious objection present itself we shall be pretty regular attendants there; the distance is about 8 miles; & we hope to come to London on the first Sunday in every month to hear Dr. Hutton. . . .

My father, when he married, made up his mind that he would not in any way try to influence his wife's religious opinions. She had been brought up in the

Church of England. They were to attend alternately Church and Chapel. My father however found so much that he objected to in the services of the Church that this rule was kept to, I believe, for only a very short time. My mother, on the other hand, was quite willing to go to Chapel, and led no doubt partly by what she heard there, and partly by her husband's unconscious influence, she very soon came over to his way of thinking.

RUSSELL SCOTT *to* J. E. TAYLOR.

GADDESDEN HOO, *Nov.* 20, 1838.

MY DEAR EDWARD,—. . . . I think I can relieve the solicitude you appear to feel on our account & which I think you have expressed before. I assure you we are not "yet" tired of living "*so far*" in the country. On the contrary we fully expect to continue to find the winter here, as we have hitherto done, vastly pleasanter than in London. Last week the sun shone brightly almost every day; this week we have certainly not yet seen him, but Isabella & I have nevertheless had a two hours walk this morning. The difference in the facility & inducement for taking exercise is immense, for in London Isabella frequently did not take a walk, excepting on Sundays, for weeks together. As for the snow, which seems the chief calamity you apprehend for us, we really had been looking forward with pleasure to seeing the trees & the ground covered with it, & I certainly think it will look much better here than when covered with smoke & "*blacks*," & trampled upon by thousands of dirty feet. As to our "communications" being cut off by it I am not sure that I quite understand your meaning. I do not think I can remember the roads being stopped by snow for any considerable time between the years 1814 & 1836, but if we should have to forego the visits of the baker & butcher for a day or two, we shall be in no danger even of being reduced to live on potatoes & cabbages (to which however I should not much object for once in a way) since there are enough geese & fowls in the farm yard to supply our garrison during a long siege. Perhaps, although you do not say so, you think we may find ourselves *ennuyés*; of this it is perhaps too soon to judge, & Benjamin Hawes says the *second* winter will be the test. Isabella however seems likely to find abundant occupation, & for myself I believe it will only be by laying down & strictly adhering to a fixed plan, that I shall be able to read through the scores of unread volumes in the library, with which I wish to make myself acquainted. . . .

RUSSELL SCOTT *to* J. E. TAYLOR.

GADDESDEN HOO, *Jan.* 2, 1839.

. . . Russell [Taylor] is exceedingly well & in most excellent spirits, which is a matter of considerable satisfaction to Isabella & myself. I had had some fear that he might think this *very* quiet place a little *dull*, in the absence of companions of his own age, particularly as our little poney has been ruined by a fall. There seems however no danger of this. I assure you it is a great pleasure to have him with us, & I think this is saying a good deal, considering that he is at an age at which almost all boys are positively troublesome. I shall not anticipate what he himself will probably report as to his occupations, but I assure you he appears to me to possess that combined cheerfulness & contentedness of disposition which almost always ensures happiness to its possessor. . . .

KATE PRESTWICH *to* MRS. RUSSELL SCOTT.

THE LAWN, *Novber* 15, 1838.

MY DEAREST ISABELLA,—I have delayed writing to you until the return of my sisters from Hornsey as I did not hear from them during their stay there; indeed they had nothing particular to tell me until yesterday morning.

John Noble has been a constant visitor at Mrs. Price's, spent the whole of Tuesday and Sunday, and dined and slept there nearly every day.

I am sure you will be as *astounded* as we have been, when I tell you the object of his attentions has been *Eliza*, not Emily. Yesterday the offer was made in due form. Emily has thought all the time (that is to say this last week) that he paid at all events as much attention to Eliza as to her; but she did not herself, and when he did say his say she was quite overwhelmed and *excessively* annoyed. She never has for one instant thought of him but as a friend, and feels quite persuaded that she never can.

Mrs. Price it appears has always been in his counsels, and was quite surprized Eliza had no idea of it; Eliza said she certainly had none, and indeed that he had invariably paid both me and Emily more attention than her. Mrs. Price said that always was the way, but she knew that he always had preferred her to us, and that she was his first and only attachment. Eliza told her that she had been so long accustomed to look upon him as a friend that she did not believe she should ever have any other feeling for him. Mrs. Price asked her if she had any objection in any way, or if her affections were pre-engaged, to which she replied in the negative.

He comes on Saturday at 12 o'clock for his final answer which I quite think will be in the negative also.

She is in a state of the greatest discomfort as she cannot accept him, and feels exceedingly sorry for the pain she must inflict. I do not think myself he would suit her; in the first place I do not think him equal to her, and in the second I do not think their tempers would agree quite. I am very sorry for him. Emily says all the time he has been at Hornsey he has entirely lost his appetite, and yesterday evening looked *very* ill. Eliza was so faint she was obliged to lie down, and to-day is quite unwell; her predominant feeling is that of great annoyance. Pray write per return and give us your views of the matter; she begs you will as she wishes to have them before giving her answer.

I am writing in great haste to save the post, but suppose you will not be satisfied unless I let you know how I am going on.

Things are in just the same state as when you were in town. I certainly like him [Robert Thurburn] better than I did, which I suppose he perceives; but although he has had several opportunities, not another syllable has he said on the subject. The fact is he has no more idea of "making love" than a child of two years old. I am sure I am very kind and coming, but *I* cannot broach the subject. His nearest approach is grasping my hand (and such a grasp!), and heaving a sigh deep and loud enough for you to hear at the Hoo.

We go this evening to the Charltons, and sleep at the Collards where we remain until Saturday, but shall return in time for Eliza's appointment. I have not time to say any more. Therefore with our united best love to all and kisses for the dear pets, believe me, dearest Isabella, ever most affectly. yours,

KATE PRESTWICH.

Addressed: "Mrs. Scott, Gaddesden Hoo, nr Hemel Hempstead."

RUSSELL SCOTT *to* J. E. TAYLOR.

GADDESDEN HOO, *Dec.* 4, 1838.

MY DEAR EDWARD,—We are going to London rather sooner than we intended. . . . We are principally led to do this from wishing to see as much as we can of Kate Prestwich before her marriage, she having recently accepted a gentleman who has for some time been paying his addresses to her. His name is Thurburn & he is I believe principal managing partner in the house of Briggs, Thurburn & Co. of Crosby Square, Levant & American merchants & agents to the Pasha of Egypt. He is we think in every respect unexceptionable, & Isabella & I have for some time wished to have him for a brother-in-law. He has been here several times when Kate has been staying with us. . . . I am very glad to find you are less unfavourable to "postage reform" than when I conversed with you on the subject. To me the moral argument in favour of it has always appeared of paramount importance. I have heard you speak (& I do not differ from you) of the great moral advantage derivable from the increased facilities afforded to persons desirous to visit parents or relations by means of railways, but I think I speak within compass in saying that a penny postage would be of ten times the value in that respect. I say therefore it ought to be done, even if it were necessary to re-enact repealed duties to accomplish it, but my own impression is that it would not be necessary, particularly if newspapers were subjected to postage which I have long thought they ought to be. And since I have learned from Hill's pamphlet what an immense proportion of the *bulk* of the letter bags is occupied by them, the exemption has appeared to me still more unreasonable. It is however one consequence of the discontinuance of the sinking fund (a measure I never liked) that an experiment cannot be made of a plan like this without incurring the risk of a deficient revenue, although perhaps, were it actually tried, no loss whatever might arise. I suppose you did not express the doubts you intimated in the *Guardian* of Saturday, as to there being *any* revenue to be derived from a penny postage without having examined the subject pretty fully, but it appears to me that a penny postage would cover its expenses *almost without any increase at all*, & I have as little doubt of its doing so, as I have of the revenue of the London & Birmingham railway paying the expenses of that concern. . . . Unless the increase in the number of letters were so enormous as to make the plan absolutely a profitable one, I cannot see how any increased expenses are to arise under the new system. . . .

The weather here is delightful. Isabella & I do not at all like leaving, for mild winter weather in London is not (so far as my experience & recollection goes) in the least agreeable. I begin now to think the country as much preferable to London in December as in July.

I am much obliged to you for offering me my letters to my sister; some of them I should probably like to have an opportunity of seeing, & Isabella says she should very much wish to have them. I shall therefore be obliged to you to send them when opportunity occurs.

My father received these letters, and a number of others were sent to him later—I believe not long before Mr. Taylor's death. Amongst them were the letters from Mary Scott to John Taylor, given in Chapter V. of this book, as well as those written by Sophia Russell Scott to J. E. Taylor during their engagement.

As far as I can judge from old letters in our possession, at least half of them were sent in some parcel, or by hand, or were franked. Under the old system the postage from London to Portsmouth was 8d., and from London to Manchester was 11d. Any member of Parliament had the power of franking letters. He wrote his name outside in the corner, and the letter went post free. He was allowed to frank ten letters and to receive fifteen free of charge daily. Postage was always paid by the recipient of the letter, not the sender. As it was not necessary that the letter should be written either by or to the privileged person, this privilege of "franking" was much abused. Newspapers went free, and we often find that a line was written inside the cover of one in place of a letter. On one occasion S. R. Scott sent a newspaper to her brother addressed "Will. U. Knott Wright Esq. c/o Russell Scott," &c.

RUSSELL SCOTT *to* J. E. TAYLOR.

GADDESDEN HOO, *May* 30, 1839.

. . . I did not recollect not having said anything about our school. You will however hear full particulars from Sophia. It is a plan Isabella & I have contemplated for a very long time, as long I believe as we have entertained the idea of living in the country. Our present room, which will only contain 32, is full & we have applications from others. The scholars pay 3d. per week, which I consider a much better plan, when the school is not designed for the *very* lowest classes, than gratuitous admission. I believe we shall very soon build a school room for 100 boys & that Sir John Sebright [1] will defray one half of the expense, at least he offered to do so some time ago, & although he afterwards cooled a little & wished to wait until our present room was filled, I do not apprehend that he will be at all disposed to recede from his offer now that this is the case.

This school was not far from the village of Great Gaddesden. The master was John Goodland, a self-taught man and an excellent teacher. My mother said many years afterwards that he was a born teacher, who could not be happy in any other occupation. A few of his letters to my father have been preserved. They show how great his enthusiasm was, and also how great was the need at that time of schools in country districts. My father and mother used often to teach in the school, and found one of their chief interests in it.

The National School Society, which had been founded in 1811, no doubt provided schools in a certain number of towns, but there was nothing within the reach of the children of the agricultural poor. Great numbers of people strongly objected to their being taught even to read and write, believing that it would make them discontented and unfit them for their work.

RUSSELL SCOTT *to* J. E. TAYLOR.

GADDESDEN HOO, *Jan.* 21, 1841.

. . . We have done well enough here, notwithstanding the snow. Isabella & I did not once miss a day in going to the

[1] Of Beechwood, a near neighbour of my father's.

school, until the baby became unwell about a week ago. It was rather a violent cough, which happily did not last many days. . . . The depth of snow on our lawn, where of course there was no drift, was from 16 to 17 inches. . . . I like the notion of meeting you at Birmingham . . . but as for accompanying you back to Manchester, I should not be able to resolve on so strong a measure, even if Isabella were more willing than she is to be left. I am scarcely ever absent *one* night. I think that which I passed at Leamington must have been the only one for about two years. The only way in which I shall be able to accomplish a visit to Manchester will be by going down at some time when Isabella & the children are staying either in London or at Lavender Hill; & that we are not likely to do in future very frequently, for independently of the increased size of our family we have so many occupations here that we find it difficult to leave.

RUSSELL SCOTT *to* J. E. TAYLOR.

GADDESDEN HOO, *Feb.* 6, 1841.

. . . Surely your friends must have made up their minds to resign, before they proposed this £5 Irish franchise, for I cannot imagine they can expect to carry it even through the House of Commons, neither can I understand how the £10 franchise could be maintained in England, if such a concession were made in Ireland. I would not say so much on such a subject if I were not going to see you next week, which obviates all danger of controversy, nor if I were not afraid the *Times* of to-day might anticipate me in one or both notions.

I am very much obliged to you for thinking of me on the 3rd. We are now, you know, both between 40 & 50 & people can have no pretence for taking you for my *father* again. I had letters from Sophia & Isabella on Wednesday which, much to their delight, were smuggled into the letter bag. Sophia's was written by herself, & without any assistance in spelling. Of course there were many faults, but considering that she had had no instruction in reading or writing until about 3 months ago, & very little since, I was much pleased with her performance. The progress she makes confirms me in the idea, that there is nothing gained by beginning to teach a child of tolerably good understanding before it is six or seven years old.

RUSSELL SCOTT *to* J. E. TAYLOR.

GADDESDEN HOO, *July* 4, 1841.

Mr. Maurice, who came down to baptize our baby, gave an account of Portsmouth matters which rather surprised me. The congregation there seems to have fallen to a very low ebb. This indeed is not, I think, very much to be wondered at, for I do not think Mr. Hawkes at all well qualified for the pulpit.

My sister Sophia was always a delicate child, and early in the summer of 1841 she was sent with her little brother Russell to the seaside under the care of Mrs. Swatling, a nurse who was much valued in our family, and who through life remained attached to us. Sophia's letters from Worthing were carefully preserved by my mother. I give a few specimens. She was just eight years old. The letters are written by herself in a small flowing hand, which at first sight one could scarcely suppose to be a child's.

SOPHIA *to her Mother.*

[WORTHING, 1841.]

MY DEAR MAMMA,—I hope you are well and my dear little sisters and dearest Papa I was very pleased to have your letter and dear Papas I wish you would ask little Isabella to write in her own hand writeing I think that there are some faults wich I will try and correct and I wish to be corrected I miss your kiss dear Mamma too—when I have been diped I feel very warm and comfortable Mrs S thinks that it does me

a great deal of good I dip every other day at the time the water is right—I write from twelve to one I read after dinner when Russell is in bed I send my very best love to Grandmamma and Cousin Kitty pray give seven kisses and two loves to dear little Annie Thurburn and I hope she will have some of my strawberries when they are ripe I have received another letter from Mamma but it was rather a finding fault letter I will try and do better.

The same to the same.

[WORTHING, 1841.]

Please Mamma may we give my old bonnet away or must I bring it home again or give it to the poor woman that baths me she is very poor and only gets a shilling a morning and she has a great many children and she is very kind to me.

The same to the same.

MY DEAR MAMMA,—I thank you very much for you pretty little letter—I thank you very much dear Mamma for haveing a lady to help take care of us and I send her my very best regards and if she is kind I shall love her very much—dear Mamma if you are sorry for your fault[1] I will forgive you but you must remember not to do it again—dear Mamma I should like to see you and dear Papa and dear little sisters very much indeed again and is Grandmamma staying at the Hoo if she is I send my very best love to her and to you and dear little sisters and I long to see the dear little Queen [Sarah] so much that you cannot tell at all—dear Mamma when we come home are we going to the Hoo the same day or are we going to stay a night in London because Mrs. Swatling wants to know—dear Mamma Russell send a hundurd regards and hundurd loves and a hundurd kisses to all—I remean my dear Mamma your very affectionate little girl,

SOPHIA

[1] This refers no doubt to the "findi-

Mrs. Russell Scott *to* Sophia.

[Gaddesden Hoo, 1841.]

. . . My dear little girl must take pains with every thing she does, and you must ask Mrs. Swatling to arrange for you to do your reading and writing at a certain time every day—either in the morning, afternoon, or evening, whichever is the most convenient—and then you must regularly every day when the time comes sit down and do what you have to do as quickly, as attentively, and as well as you can. I also wish you to pay attention to what Mrs. Swatling says about your behaviour out of doors. Remember it is a very different thing playing on our lawn here and playing in the garden at Worthing; and now you are such a great girl you must learn to behave properly. You should not make much noise or take off your bonnet, or lie down or roll upon the grass; and when you walk on the road you must walk very quietly and steadily, and not run about. You may run in the garden and on the sands and beach, but not on the road. I think, my dear Sophia, you know what I should like you to do, and how I like you to behave, therefore I hope you will try and remember, and not give Mrs. Swatling more trouble than you can help. You must not have any more toys, as you do not take care of those you have already. We are all very well; Baby gets on nicely. I am very glad to hear so good an account of dear Russell. Give him our best love, and a great many kisses. Good-bye, my darling. Your Mamma who loves you dearly.

Mrs. Russell Scott *to* Sophia.

June 9, 1841.

My dearest Sophia,—You will receive this letter on your birthday, and with it, my darling girl, your Mamma's best wishes for your happiness both now and always. My Sophia knows the way to be happy—it is always to try and make others happy—and if she always does so, the older and more useful she becomes, the greater satisfaction will she feel.

I miss you, my dear child, very much, and Russell too—I hope when you come back again I shall see you both looking very well.

On Sunday, when Mr. Maurice was here, he preached two sermons in the library—one in the morning and one in the afternoon. Several people came to hear him, and there were prayers and hymns sung just the same as at chapel. In the afternoon Isabella and Katie begged very much to be allowed to come in the room, and as they promised to sit very still, we allowed them to do so. They sat very quietly, and although the service was a long one, liked it very much, and said they were not at all tired. I take Katie to the school with me almost every day—she does not read or write yet, she only works, but she will very soon begin to read. She is making a silk pocket handkerchief for Papa. Give my best love and a great many kisses to my precious boy. . . .

SOPHIA *to* CATHERINE.

[WORTHING, *Summer of* 1841.]

MY DEAR LITTLE SISTER KITTY,—I think you would like to have a little letter as you have not had a letter for a long time. I hope dear kitty when we come to Worthing again you will come two and help us dig on the sand and ride on the donkeys two and bathe in the sea and spalsh about with me and dip each another—dear kitty when we come home you may nurse my doll I have got a very nice little pair of scales to way her medicine when she is ill in bed—dear kitty Mrs. Swatling sends you some shugaplums—dear kitty Russell sends a thousn hundred best loves and a thousn hundred best kisses, from your very affectionate sister who loves you dearly

SOPHIA RUSSELL SCOTT.

CHAPTER XVI

A FEW MONTHS IN JERSEY—DEATH OF JOHN EDWARD TAYLOR

1842–1845

RUSSELL SCOTT *to* J. E. TAYLOR.

GADDESDEN HOO, *Feb.* 2, 1842.

. . . I believe I have mentioned to you that Mr. Prestwich's business has not been going on so satisfactorily as might be wished for some time. It had been hoped that there was good reason to expect it to be again in a satisfactory condition under Joseph Prestwich junr.'s management, who has had the main control for some time past; but it seems now to be more a work of time than had been anticipated, in consequence of which it has been determined that Mr. & Mrs. P. & their daughters shall remove to Jersey for a time. The house in town[1] is therefore to be let forthwith, & being in a good situation & well-furnished, is likely to let well, & I expect they will leave early in April. We propose going with them & remaining three or four months. . . . This is not exactly what I should have preferred, but Isabella's wishes are strong upon it & I have yielded to them. . . . We shall be near St. Helier's, as it will be desirable that Mr. Prestwich, whose mind is exceedingly active, should be furnished with as much occupation for it as possible. The business will go on as usual so far as the public are concerned. . . .

My grandfather Prestwich with his eldest son, were wine merchants in Mark Lane. The former was anything but a good man of business, and my uncle Joseph

[1] No. 10 Devonshire Street, Portland Place.

had great difficulty in working with him. In the year 1842 my grandfather was persuaded to retire, much against his inclination, and went to live in Jersey. From this time forward the sole management of the business was in my uncle's hands, and the maintenance of the family devolved on him. My father gave most generous help, putting so large a sum into the business that his own expenditure had to be considerably reduced. He was not, however, a "sleeping partner," as is stated in Lady Prestwich's "Life" of her husband.

RUSSELL SCOTT *to* J. E. TAYLOR.

MILLBROOK, JERSEY, *May* 8, 1842.

I duly received yours of the 17th ult., which I ought to have answered sooner, as you were kind enough to wish to be informed when we had fixed our habitation here. We have now been finally settled rather more than a fortnight. The house is about midway between St. Helier's & St. Aubin's & very near the sea. The sands are the finest I have seen. At low water they must be nearly half a mile broad & they extend along the whole of the bay, the curve of which is about 3½ miles. I think there appears to be more difference in the expense of house rent and furniture here than in almost any other branch of expenditure. Mme. le Capelain our landlady, asked us only £1 a week for the best part of a good house furnished. I doubt whether we should easily have obtained equal accommodation at this season of the year at an English watering-place under £3, 3s. per week. Mr. Prestwich's house is very well situated about a mile N. of St. Helier's & I hope the family will find themselves comfortable there. . . . I shall depend almost entirely on the *Guardian* for political news—for I have countermanded the *Times* in consequence of the newspapers arriving only twice a week, & although a friend of Mr. Prestwich's has put down my name for admission to the reading-room of (I think) the "Chamber of Commerce" I have not yet inquired where it is. . . .

RUSSELL SCOTT *to* J. E. TAYLOR.

MILLBROOK, JERSEY, *June* 6, 1842.

I am happy to tell you that your wishes as to Isabella's having another boy are fulfilled—the child was born last Friday morning. . . . He[1] is the finest and strongest child that Isabella has yet had, & makes more use of his eyes than any of his predecessors have done at the same age. . . .

Mrs. PRESTWICH *to* Mrs. RUSSELL SCOTT.

QUATRE BRAS, JERSEY, *Sep.* 14, 1842.

MY DEAREST ISABELLA,—I have not written for some time, but knowing you had constant accounts of the dear children from your sisters I was satisfied in remaining silent. I am thankful to say dear Katie and Russell are now surprisingly well. . . . I am glad to hear your babe thrives so nicely. Dear little Sarah, does she grow stronger? How glad I shall be to see them again! The time is now drawing near, but I shall be very sorry to part with the two I have. They are excellent children, and Russell possesses the sweetest temper and disposition imaginable. I had no idea what a lovable child he was. Katie too is very amiable and they agree well together. . . .

Mrs. ROBERT THURBURN *to her Sister*, Mrs. R. SCOTT.

HANOVER TERRACE, [*June* 2, 1843.]

Many thanks, my dearest Isabella, to you & to Mr. Scott for your kind and sympathising letters—they afforded us both much consolation. . . .

Yesterday I had a succession of visitors from eleven till almost

[1] This was my brother Arthur.

dinner time—visits meant in kindness, and which are certainly grateful to one's feelings, but which nevertheless, when from friends who really feel for us, unnerve me more than anything. I am thankful that what has happened does not appear to us the dreadful misfortune that it is evidently considered by people in general. I feel for Robert that he should lose all that he has earned with so much toil and harass; but for myself, dearest Isabella, I am sure *you* will quite understand that the loss of property, so that we can but earn a respectable livelihood *in England*, and pay our creditors, will be no real trial to me. With such a constant source of happiness and thankfulness as my dear husband and children are to me, I fancy that there are few sacrifices or privations that I may be called upon to make that would not appear light to me, and I trust that when the reality arrives, even if I should feel it more than I now think, the entire conviction that I have that all things are ordered for our real good, would enable me to bear the trial cheerfully. I am very, very thankful to be able to say that my dear Robert views things in the same light that I do, and thinks with me that adversity will probably promote our real welfare and happiness more than prosperity. I cannot express to you, my dearest sister, how much we have both felt Mr. Scott's great kindness and warm sympathy. We can never forget it. For myself when I think of all his kindness and affection ever since I have been able to call myself his sister my heart overflows, and I really am afraid to say what I feel lest it should appear exaggeration. Our relationship both to him and to you, dearest Isabella, we do consider as one of the many great blessings we have left. I rejoice to hear that you and your dear baby boy are going on so well. . . . Give my best love to dear Mamma. I hope that she will not make herself uncomfortable about us—there is really no cause for her to do so. . . . Believe me, dearest Isabella, ever most affectionately yours

KATE THURBURN.

My uncle, Mr. Thurburn, continued in business, and retrieved his position.

Mrs. PRESTWICH *to* Mrs. RUSSELL SCOTT.

JERSEY, *May* 16, 1843.

MY DEAREST ISABELLA,—I address this to the Hoo, for by the contents of your last letter I judge you are now arrived there. I sincerely congratulate you on so doing, and hope you and Mr. Scott and all the dear children are in health to enjoy the comfort and delight of returning to your own happy home.

My precious little Sarah, I am thankful to say, is quite well, and has been so ever since she came to us. . . . I cannot express how much I feel your and Mr. Scott's kindness in leaving her with us. She lessens the desolate feeling we experienced on your leaving us; it was indeed very dull afterwards, but the dear child's presence seems to bring you nearer to us. Though she cannot replace you, yet she amuses and occupies us more than I could have imagined. . . . I fear by your account that dear Kate looks by no means well. . . . In the course of a few months I hope all things will be settled and progressing comfortably. Poor Kate! It has been her first serious trial & trouble. If no greater assail her in life's course she will have reason to be thankful; with the blessing of health, a kind husband, and dear children she must be contented and happy. . . .

How did you think poor Joseph looking, and has he better hopes of business improving? Do you know whether anything is arranged or settled in regard to Edward? Poor boy! I suppose he is in a state of suspense. I hope he will conduct himself with steadiness and propriety, and under all circumstances be patient. I cannot express, dear Isabella, how much I think & how much I feel Mr. Scott's & your kindness to me and mine; yet I cannot help grieving you are taxed so heavily, and that the inconvenience and trouble has been a cloud so many years upon your happy married life. May time remove or lessen the evil, and may you both now and henceforward be rewarded for all your kind consideration and goodness. I often wish I could do something towards our maintenance, and in my mind devise many plans and projects, but it is difficult to decide and execute. . . .

We often talk of and often wish you here again; and with all the attraction of a pretty country it is not so pretty now you are all away. . . . Ever most affect[ly] yours C. PRESTWICH.

After the year 1842, the date of the last letter which has been given from my father to Mr. J. E. Taylor, there can have been but little correspondence between them. Mr. Taylor's health gradually failed more and more, and on January 7, 1844, his son wrote to announce his death.

Russell Taylor was then too young to take his father's place as Editor of the *Manchester Guardian.*

The following letters will show what were his step-mother's immediate plans for him.

The second MRS. J. E. TAYLOR *to* MRS. ROBERT SCOTT.

THE ROOKERY [MANCHESTER], *March* 6, 1845.

. . . I am contemplating a lengthened absence for her [Sophia] & Russell after Midsummer, a tour of six months on the Continent. I am most anxious that Russell should have the opportunity of seeing more of the world, & something of the governments, institutions, & manufactures of other countries, before he is called upon to take the important situation he must one day fill in Manchester. At the same time I cannot but feel that there is much risk of injuring the character of a young man by sending him on the Continent alone. Russell & Sophia are both anxious to share the pleasure together, & a sister I think must be a safe companion. I therefore hope to be able to make such arrangements as will enable her to accompany him & my sister also as a chaperon.

The same to the same.

June 6, 1845.

I have been in such a whirl of business ever since Mary left us, that though I have thought of you often I have been quite unable to write. . . . My long expected picture is come home, & in my opinion is a most faithful & beautiful likeness, & reminds us of the look he used to cast on his children when particularly pleased & happy, & the artist has given all the intellectual look to the head which must have been so difficult to express. The little ones sat down before it in perfect astonishment, & Mary Ann after looking at it for some time this morning said "Yes, it is, it is Papa!" Indeed I wish Mary could have seen it.

The children mentioned in the above letter were Mrs. Taylor's three little girls, Sarah, Harriet, and Mary Ann.

Mrs. Taylor unhappily did not long survive her husband. She died in 1845, an irreparable loss for the family, and in 1848 another blow fell in the death of Russell, the eldest son. Both were grievously missed. Miss Boyce, a sister of Mrs. Taylor's, came to share with Sophia in the charge of the younger children.

Sophia had been greatly attached to her brother. She was in Germany when the news reached her that he had been attacked by typhoid fever. She hurried home, but the illness had lasted only a very few days, and he died before she reached England. I remember that my father met her on her arrival in London, and it was his most painful duty to tell her that she was too late.

Russell Taylor had been married in the previous year to Emily Acland, a relation of his stepmother's, and a child had been born. This little daughter survived her father only four months, and the poor young widow returned to live with her mother. Six years later she was married to M. Delbrück, a native of France.

Russell Taylor was a young man of great promise. He probably acted as Editor of the *Manchester Guardian* for about two years. When Edward, the younger son, had finished his education, he took up the work.

RUSSELL SCOTT *to his Wife.*

BEECH HILL, CHEETHAM, MANCHESTER, *Jan.* 16, 1844.

MY DEAREST LOVE,—It was very good of you to make such a point of writing to me yesterday. . . .

I hardly know what to say to your self-reproaches, except that I am sure it is not for me to complain of you. You best know your own shortcomings, and I hope & believe you will be able to diminish them. What I know is that I never ought to forgive myself if I did not love you, and that among the many undeserved blessings which it has pleased God to bestow upon me, the foremost is the having you for the companion of my life, and the depositary of my thoughts & feelings. . . .

In September 1844 my father and mother left Gaddesden Hoo, as the situation of the house had been found not to suit my father's health. They were long remembered there. In 1876, when my brother Russell and I saw the house again, the family living in it received us most kindly, and assured us that the influence of my father and mother and of their work in the school was still perceptible.

One of our family party at this time was George Blakeway, an orphan cousin of my mother's. He had lost both parents when an infant, and was ten years old when he came to us. He was somewhat unruly

and troublesome, and seemed to be wanted by no one, so that his other relations were much relieved when my father and mother took him in. It was in fact an act of great kindness towards the poor boy. He remained with us for two years, and was then sent to school. When he visited us a few years later he spoke of those two years as the happiest of his childhood, and as almost the only time when he was under good influences.

Mrs. Prestwich *to* Mrs. Russell Scott.

Quatre Bras, Jersey, *Feb.* 20, 1845.

My dearest Isabella,—I was very much pleased to receive your nice long letter, though the portion of the contents relative to George vexed and annoyed me not a little. I fear he strongly resembles his grandfather Thiébaud in character and disposition, who I have always understood was a very obstinate morose old man. George certainly is not like either father or mother in disposition. . . . I have great apprehensions for him when again he goes to school; if with your kind and gentle discipline he is so wayward and obdurate, I know not what he will then become. . . .

I really rejoiced that the news of my poor mother's amendment came in time to prevent my journey to Shropshire, which under any circumstances I should have taken had she continued in the same state. I begin to hope from the letters I receive that, the danger having passed over, she may continue well for months to come; if so I shall delay going to see her until the autumn of the year, at which time if you wish it Russell and Sarah can accompany me to England, and I am anxious to keep them as long as possible, considering the permanent benefit it may be to their health; and between ourselves the idea of leaving them was very annoying to me, as of course there must have been great uncertainty about my return. Your father enjoys having them as much as I do, and I only fear we shall not like parting with them. . . . Isabella, when we were at Church on Sunday, was reading to Sarah the story of Abraham offering up his son Isaac, but when she came to the part where he was going to plunge the knife into his heart, Sarah could contain herself no longer, but burst into a flood of tears. Isabella then explained the remainder, and the dear child was quite satisfied with the conclusion. . . .

Feb. 24.—I had good news relative to my mother on Thursday evening from Jane Jackson; she says Mr. Fifield, the medical attendant, called on them the morning she wrote, and begged her to say how remarkably well my mother was—better than he or any of her friends could possibly expect. . . . Maria, her servant, she also tells me, is most attentive, and was in great sorrow when she thought she was going to lose her poor old mistress. My mother is very partial to her—more so than she ever was to anyone else—and considers everything she does quite right; how fortunate it is so, as it makes her latter days so comfortable. With united love to you & Mr. Scott, believe me ever dearest Isabella most affectionately yours,

C. Prestwich.

My grandmother's mother, old Mrs. Blakeway, died three months after the above letter was written, at Broseley in Shropshire, where she had lived since the time of her marriage. She was ninety-two years of age, and had long been blind. Her husband had died thirty-four years previously, at the same age, and she had frequently announced her intention of living as long as he did. There are a few particulars about her, showing her character, to be found in the "Life" of her grandson, Sir Joseph Prestwich, written by his wife.

The following short table is given that my nephews and nieces may know how their cousins on the Blakeway side are related to them.

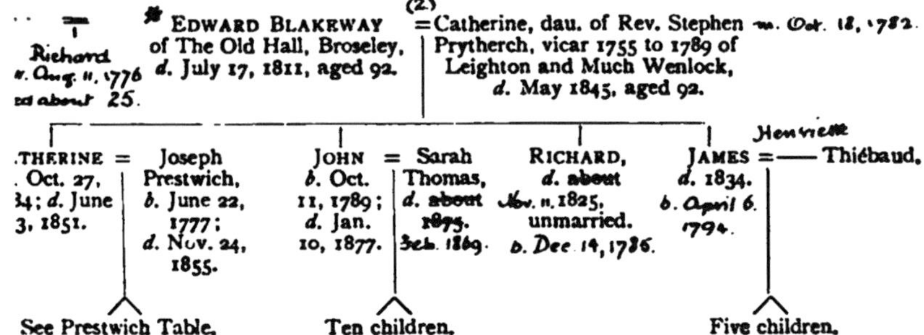

John and Sarah Blakeway had ten children and fifty grandchildren. Their descendants are our cousins of various names: Rouquette, I'Anson, King, Mushet, Hadwen; a sixth daughter was married to Mr. George Smith, the publisher, to whom we owe the "Dictionary of National Biography." The descendants of the sons are not known to us, except those of the youngest, William Evan, who married Mary, daughter of our uncle Tomkins. Our cousins Henrietta de Pury and George Blakeway were the children of James Blakeway. George was in business in Japan, married a Japanese, and died in Japan, much respected, leaving two children.

EDWARD PRESTWICH *to his Sister*, MRS. RUSSELL SCOTT.

7 CANONBURY TERRACE, *May* 3, 1845.

MY DEAREST SISTER,—I received your letter this afternoon & I cannot rest till I have answered it. I feel grieved that your kind sympathy for me should be the cause of pain & anxiety to you—that I should have that to add to my own. You have already too many subjects for painful reflection in our own family without my giving you any additional one. I have never received from you, whatever I may have deserved, one harsh word, one unkind expression, and it is inexpressibly painful to me to think the return I make. It was foolish, it was selfish of me, ever to

* Inscription on a Tablet in the parish church at Broseley.
Near this spot are deposited the remains of Edward Blakeway Esq.re late of Broseley Hall, who departed this life July 17, 1811, in the 93rd year of his age.
As a small tribute of affection to the memory of one of the best and

tell you what would give you pain, but with those we love it is ever difficult to impose a restraint upon one's full & free confidence, which from me you have always had. However in your letter you ask for it, you have a right to it, & you shall have it.

In the first place as to my position or, as "Pemmy" [Emily] would call it, my vocation. Without cant for or against, I feel that my great object in this life is to gather together honest pence & honest pounds; other subsidiary matters may naturally have a share of my attention, but *that* must & shall be the ruling feeling. In a worldly point of view therefore I am likely to do well, inasmuch as I am not likely to allow any foolish ideas to turn me from my pursuit; at the same time I shall not allow (and I think you know me well enough for that) my worship of the golden image, my religion, to interfere with my natural feelings & affections; indeed the former as you also know is merely a development of the latter, brought about by peculiar circumstances. Thoughts of family have already preserved me from many what would generally be esteemed rash & inconsiderate proceedings, and they are not likely to prove traitor to me now. This is the idea I am intently resolved to follow out through life, & call it what you will, it can go by no very bad name, when the end of it is to enable my uncomplaining Mother, my kind, tender, careful, thoughtful Mother to pass her last days in peace & quiet, undisturbed by any of the harassing cares & anxieties that now trouble her. If I *could* kneel & pray it would be to accomplish this. Without the good friends we have had to assist us, what I wonder would be our position now.

With regard to myself individually—in Crosby Sqre—matters are I think going on more smoothly; the old faults of want of method, thought, etc., still exist, aye flourish—but not quite so abundantly & obtrusively as formerly. Altho' they certainly never will be entirely eradicated I have reason to believe they may be considerably modified; the new clerk contributes not a little to this end. Before he came the multifarious minor objects that I had to crowd into my head were sufficient to distract the brain of a tyro, & such a tyro as myself, setting aside the feeling that I was overlooked by & driving half distracted one of the most methodical & orderly men in existence. The new clerk (this strictly privately—it mustn't go thro' Kate to her husband) is a Scotchman, decidedly *Scotch*, having a lively possession of the peculiarities of his nation. On the other hand he is sharp, industrious and—oh summa virtute!—highly methodical, & therefore no doubt pleases, altho' his master (I mean no disparagement here) *is* Scotch too. As to his other business qualifications they may be a *shade* better than mine, therefore nothing very wonderful. He is the head of the office "de jure"—£50 above me—but as to "de facto" I leave you to imagine whether I knock under very low.

After the letting of the house in Devonshire Street I returned to my old quarters in Canonbury. I was very glad to get back, & my Landlady was not sorry to see me, especially as I gave her 4 weeks' rent having been absent 10 weeks instead of the contemplated six. The paintings from Devon* St. are now in my possession & furnish the walls of my apartments most sumptuously. While my father is in town, & Joseph absent, I am obliged to spend a portion of my evenings in Mark Lane, to the great interruption of my *reformed* course of life, as when I return home late I feel tired & am not good for much. Nevertheless I struggle on & do as well as I can. I also am able to go to Ames occasionally—not very often—never more than I can help. I am weaning him gradually; I dont like to do it too abruptly, as he has done me many kind & friendly acts & latterly he has required my assistance in "*an affair*"—but that's a secret.

My reading is of a very multifarious description, from Butler's *Analogy* down to Comic Songs—both inclusive. I find the mixture not bad. It would seem that the mind of man like his body is adapted to & benefited by variety of food—at least it is so with me, for there are very few well written books, where the subject is not too long, that I do not relish. I think it is the case with all who are fond of reading. Believe me ever your sincerely attached brother ED. PRESTWICH.

"Crosby Square" was my uncle Thurburn's place of business, and Edward Prestwich was acting as a clerk in it. It will probably be understood that the faults of "want of method, &c.," were in himself, and the "most methodical of men," whom he was driving half distracted, was Mr. Thurburn. Edward was at this time twenty-five years old. His hopes as to making money were never realised.

JOSEPH PRESTWICH *to his Daughter* ISABELLA.

JERSEY, *July* 4, 1845.

MY DEAR ISABELLA,—Emily no doubt furnishes you with the logbook of your children's doings in this Island. To this I can add little, but however trifling it may be I know it will be acceptable. Imprimis, Russell is in excellent health—had he the dress of a yeoman of the guard he would present the beau ideal of that character. He continues to amuse himself in various ways and you continually hear his whistle, which, if it has not the varied modulations of the nightingale or the brilliancy of the thrush, shows a happy & contented mind; he is in fact a good boy, with an excellent disposition, and in the analysis of his character the percentage of *méchanceté* will be found as small as in any youth I was ever acquainted with. Sarah is now sitting near me—she has just returned from bathing, and looks as fresh and beautiful as a rose. This place most certainly agrees with both your children, and as it has decidedly improved their health you must consider it as some compensation for the sacrifice you have made in parting from them. Altho' I might say much upon her winning manners, her pretty smiles and her clear intellect, I must hasten to give you a sketch of her accomplishments as described by herself and *in her own words.* A few evenings since I ask'd her if she was acquainted with one *Sally* Scott. She said she was not, but that she knew a *Sarah* Scott. And what, I added, could *she* do? Her reply was "she could knit—she could sew—she could pod Beans—could dance a quadrille—could draw a square—could work in the garden—could pour out Beer, Milk, and Toast & Water—could clean silver—could water the Plants—could make beds and spell a few words." In these doings are comprized the useful & domestic, dancing, horticulture and letters—and if Music is not in the list of her acquirements, it is fully compensated by her ability to pod Beans & clean Silver! If a few years hence she should meet with this letter she will no doubt be much amused with the modest avowal of what she was capable of performing at the early age of five.

I am happy to find that you are so well pleased with your present residence. With children and those who are good and whom you love, scarcely any place can be dull. *Ennui* however may more easily be contracted in the streets of a populous town than amidst the glorious scenery of the Lakes. Your Mother would have been delighted to have participated with you in the enjoyment of your rural excursions. For this summer at least it cannot be—we sadly want her here. The garden is in perfect beauty, & we wish to have her before the summer is too far advanced. Our little kitchen-garden has produced an enormous crop of currants & apricots—the latter we are beginning to gather. Grapes, apples & figs are abundant. Pears but few, except upon a Tree of Jargonelles.

I think if you obtain Dr. Parry's house at Bath you will have one of the very best in that city.

With love to all your children & kind regards to Mr. Scott, believe me your ever affectionate Father J. Prestwich.

Addressed: "Mrs. R. Scott, Dalehead Hall, near Ambleside."

About this time my grandfather had an attack of illness, supposed to be apoplectic. My grandmother, who was in England, hurriedly returned to Jersey, accompanied by her son Edward.

EDWARD PRESTWICH *to his Sister*, MRS. THURBURN.

QUATRE BRAS, JERSEY, *Aug.* 11, 1845.

MY DEAREST KATE,—Upon our arrival at the pier of St. Helier's this morning you may conceive what our feelings were when we discovered my father awaiting our coming. During the transit from the steamer I had been indulging in a pleasant retrospect of the past when my father was ever found true to his post, hovering about in happy expectation of the arrival of any of his family. I was thinking of this & contrasting it with the melancholy cause of our hasty departure—of what awaited us upon reaching home—where *he* would be—in bed at least—when suddenly appeared the beaming blooming face of my father, looking through his spectacles—radiant with his wonted calm-looking smile of satisfaction! It must be said I was never so delightfully surprized in my life. . . . Ever affect[ly] yours

E. PRESTWICH.

This is the last letter we have from my uncle Edward. He was an affectionate son and brother. I remember my grandfather once saying, "Edward has the heart of a girl." But he was weak and easily led. He went to India, and was for many years in a house of business in Calcutta. He returned to England about the year 1865, I believe almost penniless. Where he lived then I do not remember, but I know that he was a source of anxiety to his family. In 1876 he died.

For about a year after leaving Gaddesden Hoo we had no settled home. The last six months of 1845 were spent at Dalehead Hall, Thirlmere, and by the elder children of the family this was always remembered as the happiest part of their early life. The house has not been altered since we lived there. It is now the property of the Manchester Corporation, by whom a dam has been built at the north end of Thirlmere which has raised its level; and our old boat-house, and the three little bridges which reached across the lake, and from which we used to fish, have disappeared beneath the water.

It was from Dalehead Hall that my mother wrote as follows to my father (who at the moment was in Manchester) on behalf of John Goodland, the former master of the school at Great Gaddesden already mentioned.

[*Autumn of* 1845.]

My dearest Love,—I enclose you a letter from poor Goodland. Pray answer it as quickly as you can, and if you could enclose him a five pound note, I am sure it would be a most acceptable present. I really am extremely sorry for him. Can you not write to Mr. Murch, who I suppose has by this time returned home, and ask him to forward him if he possibly can? It is possible that there may be an opening for a school of the kind at Bath. Something must certainly be done speedily, or the poor man will be ruined. Do pray, love, write immediately both to Goodland and to Mr. Murch, and say what you can to the latter in Goodland's favour. Will you also speak to Russell Taylor and to Mr. Robberds? It is possible too that Dr. Beard's congregation might furnish an opening for a school—in the districts too round about Manchester there are many Unitarians in the middling and lower classes, from whom he might perhaps get pupils. Unless he can get congregational introductions either at Bristol or somewhere else, I should think his case a very forlorn one. Pray, love, exert yourself to see all about this as soon as you possibly can, and write as friendly and consolatory a letter as you can to Goodland.

Darling baby has taken advantage of your absence to cut his first tooth. The children are all good & happy. . . .

Work was found for Goodland in the printing office of the *Manchester Guardian*. His wife died in Manchester soon after their arrival there, and he survived her only two or three years. Their three children were then removed to Bath by my father, who placed them in a comfortable home, and maintained and educated them. They all did well.

* The baby mentioned in my mother's letter was my brother Lawrence, born at Brighton on 21st June 1844.

* The child was named after my mother's cousin, Civil Lawrence, who, with her sisters, was warmly attached to my mother. They were great-nieces of Isabella Civil Wild, married in 1773 to Elias Prestwich.

CHAPTER XVII

FAMILY LIFE AT BATH

1846–1853

In January 1846 my father and mother removed to Bath, and settled at Summer Hill House, Sion Hill.

Bath was chosen partly because it was a place where such masters as we might require were to be had, and because we had already some connection with it, as our cousins, the Robert Scotts, lived there, but mainly because there was there a chapel and a minister liked by my parents. The house, garden, and fields were large and pleasant, and here we had most of the pleasures of a country life, although the house was only just outside the streets of Bath. No carriage was kept while we lived at Summer Hill, my father wishing, as I have already mentioned, to live inexpensively; and our former coachman, George Martin, became gardener, and attended to the cows, poultry, &c., as well as to our Shetland ponies. These were given to us by our great-aunt Sarah. Since we left it the house has been enlarged, and it and the garden and grounds are so much altered as to be scarcely recognisable. Our old home has disappeared.

In the spring of 1847 Sophia was sent to school at Leam, a house half-way between Leamington and Warwick. The school was kept by the Miss Fields, daughters of the Rev. William Field, formerly Unitarian minister at Warwick. The girls sent there were chiefly from Unitarian families; there were about sixteen of them. Lesson hours were short, and the life on the whole was very healthy and good. There was a large playground, a garden and fields.

I joined Sophia there in the beginning of 1848, and Catherine followed a little later, but we did not stay long.

RUSSELL SCOTT *to his Daughter* SOPHIA.

SUMMER HILL, BATH, *May* 5, 1847.

MY DEAR SOPHIA,—. . . Your letters have given very great pleasure to your mamma, to me, and to "the others" also, so far as they have been allowed to see them, but I think no one but Isabella was allowed to see your last, in consequence of what you said about the Minister, which we were exceedingly sorry to hear. . . . Are you sure that the terms you mentioned were applied not merely to the church services, but also to those who used them? I suppose it was to some particular part and not to the whole, that the remarks were applied. In either case they are not to be justified, but if, as I imagine must have been the case, the allusion was to particular expressions, I will just say in palliation of the language used, that there are parts of the church service—of the litany more particularly—which I cannot read without being shocked, and Dr. Channing, who was unquestionably not inclined to judge harshly of those who differed from him, and who possessed a mind of an unusually high order, and was far less under the influence of prejudices than most men, says the same thing. . . .

I do not know whether you may have heard of the fall which Uncle Thomas had on Good Friday. Aunt Sarah, thinking it very serious, wrote to me, and I went up to see him last week. His life appears to be in considerable danger, owing to his being too weak to withstand the effects of the fall, but he does not suffer, and may perhaps survive for a few weeks or months. . . .

We are expecting Miss Saunders and Willie [William Fox Hawes] here to-morrow, much to the satisfaction of all parties concerned. I do not know how long they are likely to stay. I wish you could be here to welcome them. . . .

I hope, dear Sophia, you will let your mamma or me have a long letter soon, if you can possibly find time. Your letters are much more interesting to us than you are likely to imagine; indeed, it would hardly be possible for you to write anything that should not be interesting to us. I remember this was what my own dear mother used to say to me, and at the time, perhaps, I could not very well understand it, but now I understand it perfectly, and I hope your comprehension is better than your father's was at the time I refer to, and that you understand the feeling I have expressed—your sex is in your favour for doing so.

Your Mamma desires her very best love to you, so no doubt would your brothers and sisters, if they were at hand. Baby[1] has improved vastly since you left, and if he does not fall off again before you see him, I think you will be quite sure to consider him a most charming little fellow. Good-bye, my very dear girl, I think I have been talking to you pretty much as if we were walking together on the upper terrace, as I hope we shall be once more in the course of a few weeks. In the meantime, and always, I remain your very affectionate father,

RUSSELL SCOTT.

RUSSELL SCOTT *to his Daughter* SOPHIA.

SUMMER HILL, *May* 20, 1847.

MY DEAR SOPHIA,—I returned from London the night before last. I was very much pained indeed to learn the

[1] My brother Charles, born 26th October 1846.

contents of your last letter to your mamma. I cannot justify Miss Field, & I will not therefore attempt it, but there are one or two things to be considered which I may as well mention, although possibly your mamma may have already done so. Unhappily a thorough love of truth is rare, even in parents; those who may practice it themselves are not sufficiently sensible of the importance & the practicability of inducing a strict adherence to it on the part of their children; so that probably Miss Field generally finds that girls attempt to deceive her when they first come to school. You will probably be surprised to hear—what I confess I am rather ashamed to tell you—that when I was your age, or very little younger, I used to think it very hard that my mother objected not merely to falsehood but to deceit. I had no objection to tell the truth *in words*, but I wished to be at liberty to mislead people a little if I wished, & thought I could manage to do so without actually saying what was not true. This of course is a confidential confession, but it may serve to satisfy you that that real love of truth, which it is our happiness to believe that our elder children possess, is very far from common. The next thing to be considered is, that the circumstances you mention really were rather unfortunate, & were calculated to inspire doubts, if Miss Field knew nothing particular of you before you went to school, which I imagine must have been the case. I must say I think she should have kept those doubts to herself, & have waited to see whether they were confirmed, & I am grieved that you should have suffered so much, & so undeservedly; but I hope that you have found out some one who knows you better than Miss Field appears to do at present, though I hope it will not be very long before she knows you better. Pray, my darling girl, do not allow any feelings of anger to arise in your mind. I am satisfied that Miss Field is a very excellent & estimable person. I was talking a good deal to your cousin Sophia about her on Monday on our way from Portsmouth to London.

I am very much pressed for time, & do not like to lose a

post in writing to you, so must hastily assure you once more that I am your very affectionate Father,

RUSSELL SCOTT.

In August 1847 my father went to Boppart for the sake of the cold-water cure, accompanied by my uncle Joseph Prestwich. In my aunt's "Life" of my uncle she mentions the visit to Boppart, but says nothing as to an event preceding it. My uncle had shortly before met in Dublin a young lady whom he greatly admired and much wished to make his wife. His father and mother however, as well as his unmarried sisters, were all dependent on him for a maintenance, and at the same time business was going on badly. For their sakes he gave up all thoughts of his own happiness. My aunt much wished to relate this circumstance in the "Life" of my uncle. She once said to me that it was the most telling thing she could have said of him, and that the picture of his life would not be complete without some mention of what she called "his great act of unselfishness."

His two surviving sisters, Mrs. Tomkins and Emily Prestwich, however strongly objected to her doing so, and she yielded to their wishes.

JOSEPH PRESTWICH, Junior, *to his Sister* ISABELLA.

DUBLIN, *July* 8, 1847.

MY DEAREST ISABELLA,—The fear of Mark Lane[1] has prevailed. I feel afraid to contemplate my liabilities and engagements. I have lost confidence in the result of the business, and dare not now incur fresh liabilities. This I had anticipated for some weeks past—still I had hoped that with

[1] His place of business in the City.

some little property on her part I might possibly have followed the bent of my feelings. I feel however that it is impossible, and I am wretched. Since I last wrote to you I have been in a state of miserable uncertainty—now resolving on one course—now on another—changing my mind every half hour—almost at one time resolving to act as my feelings dictated. A letter from Kate, reminding me of my unfortunate prudential necessities, reached me at this time. My mind is now made up. I have not seen Jane Maher again and I shall leave Dublin tomorrow. I am, I can assure you my dear Sister, most unhappy. I never felt so acutely the want of a slight independence or a small certainty—then I could follow my inclinations; now I must be miserably led by my means.—
Your affect: Brother J. PRESTWICH, Jr.

Does Mr. Scott still think of going to Boppart? I shall be happy to accompany him.

MRS. THURBURN *to* RUSSELL SCOTT.

July 10, 1847.

MY DEAR MR. SCOTT,—Joseph's letter is indeed a very painful one—your's will be most consolatory to him. It is but too kind—too little thought for yourself. No one could have given the advice you have, for no one could have felt justified in so doing. But I do hope & trust that Mark Lane may prosper, and poor Joseph still be happy.

I only hope that he will ascertain all about Miss Maher's previous engagement, and how it was broken off—by herself I hope. I really believe that Joseph will be as much better as happier, if happily married; that his welfare in every way will be so very, very much promoted by marriage; but he is very sensitive and a little suspicious, & it is most desirable that all things should be made clear.

My time is very short, it need be very long to say *how* very kind we feel your letter to Jo[illegible]e been. You [illegible] have another sister-in-law, but we can never, never have another brother-in-law like you. Best love to dear Isabella, yourself and the dear children, & believe me ever most affect[ly] yours,

KATE THURBURN.

This letter from my aunt Kate shows that in reply to my uncle's letter my father had advised him to marry, and had made an offer of some sort in the hope of enabling him to do so. What the offer was I do not know. I never heard the subject mentioned by my father or mother, and my aunt Kate's letter contains the only reference to it that has come down to us. We know, however, that my uncle made no proposal of marriage to Miss Maher.

The visit to Boppart did my father great good. From that time forward he had his daily cold bath, never wore woollen underclothing, drank only water at breakfast and at tea-time as well as at dinner, and almost gave up the use of a great-coat. He was a very much stronger man for the rest of his life.

MRS. RUSSELL SCOTT *to her Daughter* ISABELLA.

[SUMMER HILL, *February or March* 1848.]

MY DARLING GIRL,—I really am very sorry you were so much disappointed about your letter. I intended to punish you a little, but not so much as I appear to have done, for I thought your scrap of a letter was partly a joke, and partly or principally a piece of laziness; and I thought if I repaid you in kind it would be but fitting. I did not at all understand that you sent me the beginning of a letter you had not had time to finish, in order to show me that you had intended to send me a proper letter. However for the future I hope you will begin your letters in better time, and then I have no doubt you will be able to finish them. I expect that you are still rather a dawdle, and that you waste at least half-an-hour in making up your mind to write, then getting out your paper, saying perhaps a few words to Sophia, with a few jokes to the other girls interspersed here and there, until it suddenly occurs to you that you will be short of time, and then you sit down and write away in a great bustle, and after all do not get half through your letter. So, Miss Isabella, I hope you will amend the error of your ways—and ceasing to do evil, learn to do well—in the article of letter-writing first and foremost. However I daresay you think I have said enough upon this topic, and so I will proceed to more agreeable subjects.

I think you would be quite pleased to see how well dear little Charlie is looking; he is out of doors a good deal now, and it has given him such a bright colour and such a healthy look. He does not get on very fast with his talking, but he looks as bright and intelligent as possible, and as you no doubt can well imagine, is as interesting and engaging as it is possible to be. "No" and "Don't" are his favourite words, to which I should add "Go." With these three he makes his wishes very clearly understood. Arthur and Lawrie are also very well; they are dear little boys and very affectionate. Yesterday I was in the library with them, when I observed Arthur go up to Lawrie and say, "Lawrie dear, give me a kiss, it is such a long time since I have had a kiss of you," upon which they put their arms round each other's necks and gave each other a very loving fraternal hug and kissing, and then began to play together as merrily as possible. Lawrie behaves much better to Charlie than he did, and seldom knocks or hurts him now. Katie has been laid up for some days with a bad broken chilblain. I hope yours are not very bad. We are obliged to keep her foot constantly poulticed, and several days she has laid in bed almost till dinner-time in order to keep it quite quiet, so that her lessons have not gone on very capitally. Both she and Frank have had their quantity of Latin considerably increased in consequence of what Sophia told us of your achievements at school in that way. Pray do you parse much of your twelve lines, and are you required to be quite perfect in the translation? Sarah has begun French with me, and will be I think a very good pupil. She has struck up an immense friendship with Master Samuel Green. I suppose it is the moral qualities she finds so attractive in him, for his mental powers do not appear to me to be of a very high order, but she tells me that she likes to play with Samuel so very much, for that he always does whatever she asks him, and is so exceedingly kind. I endeavoured to lead her to perceive the desirability of adopting herself, in some degree, Samuel's mode of conduct; but like many other people I think Sarah finds it more agreeable and easy to avail herself of Samuel's good nature than to practise it herself. . . . The Sunday School goes on tolerably; last Sunday it was wet and I only had seven pupils, which considering that on one other wet Sunday when it really rained much faster, I had either thirteen or fifteen pupils, rather disappointed me. I am afraid the children have not derived much benefit from my teaching at present. . . . I think I get on rather better with the girls at the day school, but they are very troublesome and contrive to forget a great part of what I teach them one lesson, before the next comes round. . . . Next Saturday we hope to see your Uncle Joseph here. . . . We shall be very glad indeed to see him. The crocuses and snowdrops are all out in blossom and make the garden look quite gay; the primroses, too, in the shrubbery are coming out, so that it really looks like spring. Last week we had most delightful weather, and Sunday afternoon was like a summer's day. Let me know how you get on with your lessons. We all unite in best love to you and dear Sophia, and believe me, my dearest child, ever most affectionately your mother,

ISABELLA SCOTT.

RUSSELL SCOTT *to his Daughter* SOPHIA.

SUMMER HILL, BATH, 2nd *Mar.* 1848.

. . . You want to hear about the French Revolution. It is an extraordinary affair, and the French are an extraordinary people, unlike any others; although the Irish national character bears some resemblance to theirs. I know no more about it than everybody else knows I suppose, whether in Bath or Leamington, so that you might have had your information I imagine from Miss Field. I should except one important fact which reached me, and which I have not seen referred to in the papers, to wit that the poor Duke de Nemours arrived in London minus his moustaches, having been obliged, or at all events thought it most prudent, to dispossess himself of them on the road, in order to escape recognition.

Nothing had been heard of his father, the ex-king, up to the time of my leaving London last night, but I should think that neither he nor the queen were likely to be ill-treated. Charles the Tenth was allowed to depart quietly in 1830, and even the French can hardly persuade themselves that Louis Philippe is the worst of the two. I send you by this post yesterday's *Manchester Guardian*, which seems to contain a very good account of the whole affair. It would seem that it might very probably have all blown over on the afternoon of this day week, if some scoundrel had not gone up to the Colonel of some troops who were on guard at the Foreign Office, and shot him dead. His men immediately fired on the people who accompanied the man, and killed four or five of them; and this, in the excited state of people's minds, led to what followed. However it is evident that the Government was thoroughly disliked by almost all, and that it was likely to be overturned by the people upon the earliest provocation, or the occurrence of what they might deem such. What is to follow is difficult to say, but it is pretty clear that the present men cannot continue in power. They evidently think that the Government can and ought to maintain the people, by finding them constant work at good wages, an immense mistake and an impracticable attempt, calculated to paralyse industry, and thereby to create that very poverty proposed to be abolished. When this is discovered as it must be, discontent will be stronger than ever, and it is to be feared that worse disorder will arise, unless men's minds should be occupied by foreign war which is much to be apprehended. . . .

I am very glad you and Isabella are not disposed to give up walking together because some of the girls laugh at you. It is well for everybody to be laughed at sometimes, and I have often wished I had been more accustomed to be laughed at when at about your age. It would have saved me much discomfort in the ten following years. There is no cure so effectual for trifling faults and little peculiarities which may not be worth serious notice, and which it may nevertheless be desirable to get rid of. Your Mamma tells me it is not very usual for sisters to walk together at school. The reason must be that they are soon tired of each other's company, and I hope this is not likely to be the case with our girls. . . . With love to Isabella, I remain, my dear girl, yours very affectionately,
RUSSELL SCOTT.

MRS. RUSSELL SCOTT *to her Daughter* ISABELLA.

[SUMMER HILL, BATH, *March* 1848.]

MY DEAREST ISABELLA,— . . . We have been going on very quietly for some time at Summer Hill. Tonight however & tomorrow night we are going to Mr. Wallace's. Tomorrow it is to be a congregational party, that is to say a number of those members not usually on visiting terms are to meet each other in order to promote a feeling of union & good-will in the congregation. . . . I hope the party will be liked, & that it will be followed by others, for I should be very glad to see a stronger feeling of sympathy existing among the different members of the congregation. . . .

My mother's feeling about congregational life was very strong, and somewhat later she instituted "Working Parties" amongst the women of the Trim Street congregation, who met regularly at different houses to work for the poor. These gatherings were found so useful and so pleasant that they have been continued I believe to the present day.

RUSSELL SCOTT *to his Daughter* CATHERINE.

SUMMER HILL, 19th *March* 1849.

MY DEAR KATIE,—The time is drawing near for your return home [from school], & I strongly suspect that I have not written to you at all since you left us at Portsmouth. It is also more particularly incumbent on me to do so now, as your dear mamma is not able to write to you. You have had divers letters from your brothers & sisters, two or three of which I despatched this evening, but did not read. I do not think, however, that they told you how very unwell your mamma has been. For several days she had a good deal of fever. However this has passed off, I am glad to say, but it has left her very weak & I fear she will hardly be down stairs much before the time of your coming home. What a tribe of children we shall have when you return—nine of you at home! What do you think we shall do with you all?

I suppose you have heard that Aunt Eliza as well as Aunt Civil has been with us for the last fortnight. I have been very glad indeed to have her here while your mamma has been so poorly. . . . Sophia, I am glad to tell you, is really a great deal better. She seldom rides out in the carriage now, but has a Bath chair & rides in the garden or on the Upper Terrace. We are in great hopes that she will gradually gain strength now. I suppose you have been told that she walks a little in the room. Until the last day or two her leg seemed nearly well.

About six weeks ago I determined to see how often it happened that I had occasion to find fault seriously with my children. Of course I did not include Lawrence & Charlie, who do not yet very well understand what obedience means. I intended to put down everything amounting to a squabble, but I have not seen anything of the kind. Once or twice I have thought Sarah or Arthur likely to be angry, but on calling to them by name they have checked themselves, & when I asked Arthur the other day whether he endeavoured not to be angry when he found himself likely to be so, he said that *of course* he did. Once however, I was informed that he had been in a passion, & he could not deny it, so I put that down as a "black day," & there have been two others besides in the six weeks, but the offences were not very heinous. So I have come to the conclusion that my children have not given me very great cause for complaint.

I believe Isabella told you that the baby has not been well to-day—but I hope he will be in a day or two. . . .

In this letter we have the first mention made of Sophia's illness, which had begun a year before, and of which an account is given later. The ninth child of whom my father speaks was an infant son born on March 7 in this year, who lived only sixteen days.

The following letter needs a few words of explanation. My aunt, Emily Prestwich, had early in life become a Roman Catholic. She had joined a few years before this date a community of French ladies who had a *Maison de Bonnes Œuvres* in Paris, and a similar house at Clapham, where my aunt at this time generally lived. The members of the community were not wholly separated from their families; my aunt on many occasions was able to be at home for longer or shorter periods when specially needed. In 1850 my grandmother was taken ill, and was removed for a short time to Brighton.

EMILY PRESTWICH *to her Sister*, MRS. RUSSELL SCOTT.

ST. ANNE'S, CLAPHAM [1850].

MY DEAR ISABELLA,—I left Brighton because I could not do otherwise, I must have come up to town on Wednesday had I returned on the following day, but as it is Miss Thornton is so seriously ill that she cannot only not replace me, but is completely laid up. So long as she could replace me my duties did but devolve upon her, but now that she is ill they cannot be neglected. They are as positive in their nature as tho' I had been married, and as your's are, my dear Isabella. Eliza returns to Brighton the latter end of next week. Had Civil been much longer alone I should if possible have again returned, but if we consider, she has been in fact but a very short time alone since the commencement of Mamma's illness. Whilst they were at Clapham I always daily took my turn for watching with my sisters, and at Brighton she has had Eliza until within a little more than a fortnight. I know as you say that it is the monotony now, more than the anxiety of the illness, but you are mistaken in supposing that Civil is constantly confined to Mamma's room. When she is put upon the sofa and Papa has his dinner, Civil remains upstairs until Mamma goes to bed, which is from two to three hours. Then again while Miss Tomkins rubs her legs, another hour, after which comes supper and sleep. Then there is going out for a walk in the morning with Mamma, and with Papa in the afternoon. I mention all this merely to say that I do not think it quite so monotonous as you think, for even during Mamma's morning and afternoon sleep the children are out with Miss Tomkins, and Civil can read or do anything she chooses. Not but with all this *there is* still a weariness and little daily trials which Civil supports in a very admirable manner, but I do think that it will not do her health the slightest injury to support it for a little time. It is not as tho' she had not plenty of fresh air and exercise and a good long night's rest. That the cares & occupations she has had of late, have been of infinite service to her I have no doubt whatever; it has drawn out her activity and natural kindness of disposition, and no one could have seen the care and watchfulness with which she watched over Mamma during so many weeks of real anxiety without being greatly edified; as much as one deplored the utter uselessness of the life she was leading previously to sickness having fallen upon so many members of the family. When she used to rise late in order to make the days shorter, and spend them in utter listlessness. This was not what such a nature as Civil's was intended for, and if now Providence has given her constant and hourly occupations, altho' they may be wearisome and trying, I think that they will bring with them much that is beneficial. My dear Isabella, *voilà ma pensée*; we all have our duties, and we all have our trials; I here as well as anywhere else. You are mistaken in supposing that my present duties are such as I should have chosen; certainly the state of life *is*, but not my present position in it. Not but that I am certainly very happy, and so may everyone else be, in the midst of the greatest trials, if they do but strive to love God and walk in His presence, for in that alone is peace. So dear Isabella I will now say Good-bye. I like you all the more for saying what you really think, and although our views do sometimes differ, still I am always and ever shall be, your affectionate sister,

E. Prestwich.

My grandmother was brought home from Brighton to 4 Church Buildings, Clapham Common, where she died on June 3, 1851. How much she was beloved, and how deservedly so, is shown in the "Life" of my uncle.

We were always much attached to my aunt Emily, though we saw less of her than of the other sisters of my mother. She has often told us little anecdotes of our childhood; one that she related of Sophia is perhaps worth preserving. My father was rather proud of Sophia's aptitude for arithmetic, and once in her presence told his friend, the Rev. Charles Pritchard, of a problem which she had solved—a difficult one for her age. The gentlemen left the room, and my father on returning a few minutes later found Sophia in tears. She said: "O Papa, I wish you would not say such things. It makes me feel so proud!" "Was not that a tender conscience?" added my aunt.

My father and mother used to teach the children who were at home, and a governess attended daily. My father kept the teaching of arithmetic entirely to himself. Later we had a German resident governess, and a French governess who stayed three years with us. My brother Russell went for a year as day boarder to a school at Clapham, kept by the Rev. Charles Pritchard, afterwards Professor of Astronomy at the University of Oxford. Russell lived at this time with his great-aunt Sarah at Lavender Hill. When he came home a tutor was engaged, Mr. Frank Harrison Hill, who remained with us about two years, from 1851 to 1853, and his teaching we have always felt to have been most valuable to us. My mother was much occupied with the care of Sophia, and no longer taught us, but she decided on the course of our reading with Mr. Hill, and it included a good deal not usually taught in schools, and which we found very interesting.

My sister Sarah was too young to join in these lessons, and was besides prevented from having regular teaching by great delicacy of health. From the time when she was about eight years old she suffered from headache, from which she was never entirely free, and the cause of which was always obscure. These headaches have been a life-long trial, incapacitating her from much that she would have liked to do.

It was while we were living at Bath that Miss Mary Carpenter, with my father's assistance, established the Kingswood Reformatory School, near Bristol, one of the first reformatories in England. My father bought the house and land and gave them for the purpose. The school was opened in September 1852, and for some years he was much occupied with the part he took in the management of it. Letters remaining show how great were the difficulties met with.

CHAPTER XVIII

THE ROBERT SCOTTS OF BATH—THE MISS SCOTTS OF SHERBORNE

1851–1875

A VERY few years at this period made great changes in the homes of our cousins both at Bath and Sherborne. Of the cousins at Bath we saw a good deal when we lived there. Mr. Robert Scott was not a favourite with his young relations. My sisters and I, going to his house as young girls, always found him smiling and jocose, and he still talked much of love and matrimony, as was once reported of him by his cousin, S. R. Scott, after a visit which she had paid at his house in Bath. He paid us many extravagant compliments; but there were glimpses occasionally of the very different manners which he used towards his wife and daughter in private. In his love of money he too much resembled his father. His daughter Mary was treated much like a child as long as he lived. Fortunately for her, her mother was of a very different character, and there was strong affection between them. It was to her that her father addressed the following curious letter:—

ROBERT SCOTT *to his Daughter* MARY.

BATH, *Aug.* 28, 1859.

MY DEAR MARY,—I suppose you will like to receive a line or two of thanks for your letter. . . . Last evening I was in Mr. Tyler's shop . . . when who should come in but Mr. P.'s enamorata. She appeared to be in a most heavenly state of mind, & enraptured with the brightness of her future prospects, to say nothing of the agreeableness of the present. What very winning creatures the ancient gents of 3 score & 10 or 4 score are, so that their money bags are full enough to keep the line perpendicular! Can there be sovereign delight in possessing sovereigns? Alas! no, no! They are useful servants but despicable Idols. Virtue excelleth them all. . . . Your affectionate Father ROBERT SCOTT.

Mrs. Robert Scott had wider interests than her husband and more cultivation of mind. This was specially noticeable before her marriage. In her father's house she had had books and a good deal of intellectual companionship; in her husband's she had little of either; and my father said that no one seeing her in later life could have guessed how much mental superiority she had shown in youth.

Anna Sophia, the second daughter of Mr. and Mrs. Robert Scott, was several years younger than her sister. She was deformed and always sickly, but had a most grateful, contented, and affectionate disposition, and was fervently loved by her father, mother, and sister. She lived to the age of twenty-two, dying in 1851, and most of the happiness of the home seemed to be lost with her.

MRS. ROBERT SCOTT *to* ANNA SELINA SCOTT.

March 25, 1851.

You have now, beloved Anna, received the confirmation of our worst apprehensions for our beloved child. Her pure angelic spirit has escaped from its cumbrous clay tenement, & is now I humbly trust with its great Creator and Redeemer.

Nothing could be more gentle than her dismission from the body; life seemed quite to evaporate; & not till Mr. Skinner had convinced himself of the fact, could we believe that our sweet Blossie had for ever closed her eyes on this world. . . . Not a murmur at her increasing afflictions ever escaped her; she was patient & even cheerful, with heartfelt gratitude for every attention. Her beloved sister was chief nurse, & I could not have believed it possible that Mary could be so watchful, so gentle, so self-devoted as she has proved herself to be, well & fondly as I knew she loved her dear fragile sister. It is pleasant too, to see how the dear child is & has been appreciated by *all* who in any way, however slightly, came in contact with her. I cannot be too thankful for the privilege of being the mother of such a child, & of having been so little separated from her during the 22 years that she has been lent to us. I do thank you, my dear Anna & our loved Sarah, from my heart for all the many kindnesses you have bestowed upon her. How pleased the sweet creature was with the basket which you so kindly sent her & above all with the letter, the beautiful letter, from "dear Aunt Anna." . . . Cousin Russell has been every thing that is kind to us in this affliction. Tomorrow I shall hope we may welcome a letter however brief from you. We are not so absorbed by our own more particular sorrows as to be unmindful of others, & trust that you may be able to report some improvement in dear Sarah. Your brother has hitherto borne up very tolerably, but to day he is very poorly both in mind & body. He unites with me & Mary in best love to dear Sarah & yourself.—Believe me your affectionate, sorrowing sister M. A. SCOTT.

MRS. ROBERT SCOTT *to* ANNA SELINA SCOTT.

April 1, 1851.

We were much gratified by your kind and soothing letter to dear Mary yesterday, my beloved Anna. To write to the dear girl in such a manner, & under such trying circumstances, is only consistent with your usual kindness, of which we have had so many demonstrations. Until after the last melancholy solemnities, when she gave way sadly, & on the Saturday when, to make it a little less *triste* for dear Edward, we had Cousin Russell and Mrs. Scott to an early dinner, the dear girl was quite unable to join us. It is *her* first heavy trial, & one which will be long & deeply felt by both parents as well as by herself, for a more affectionate, obliging & obedient child never existed, & had her physical organization & powers been stronger, her mind would have been of no common order. Her tastes & pursuits were all elegant & good & she was exceedingly accurate. . . . She is now I humbly trust far happier than our fondest wishes could ever make her, but a dreadful void & blank is left in our little household. . . . Dear Edward is by no means well, though he carries off his indispositions with graceful cheerfulness. . . . Cousin Russell, Mrs Scott & all our friends here, have been very kind. My husband has been wonderfully supported. Edward's coming down was a very good thing for him, & in some features he does so resemble our lost loved one. God grant that you may be able in your next letter to say that our dear Sarah has made some little advance towards convalescence. . . .

Sarah Scott died at Sherborne five days after the date of this letter. She was said to be the clever one of the family. She was an invalid during the greater part of her life, and was tenderly cared for by her sister Anna. One of her few amusements and pleasures was that of collecting shells. These were kept in a beautiful inlaid cabinet, which after cousin Anna's death Mary Elliott gave to my mother. It now stands in my house, and the shells are still in the drawers. One brother, Russell, never left the family home, being unfit for any business. He continued to live with his sisters till his death in 1846.

My sister Catherine and I paid a visit to Sherborne in 1852, and I remember cousin Downing telling us of a happy visit she had paid to her uncle, my grandfather, at Portsmouth (the visit mentioned in letters at the beginning of 1801), before she lost her sight; and then she began to repeat a great number of verses, finishing by saying, "I have not thought of those verses for forty years!" They were some she had made about the little incidents of her visit and the people she had met in Portsmouth. There were then living Downing, Eliza, and Anna. We liked them all, and received great kindness from them.

The eldest sister, Mrs. Petty, was married. She and her husband lived at Evershott, about ten miles from Sherborne. It was perhaps a fortunate thing for the other sisters that her home was not with them, as she had unfortunately a temper somewhat like her father's. Her husband, one of the gentlest of men, had sometimes to leave the house in order to escape from her. There is a story that on one of these occasions he heard a cock crowing, and it seemed to him that the bird was shouting, "The ladies is missus and master *too*, down here." An answering crow from a distance replied, "And so they be everywhere." Mrs. Robert Scott, in telling the story, used to repeat the words with an amusing imitation of the crowing of a cock.

About a year after our visit cousin Anna was left alone, through the death of her two sisters. She was greatly liked and respected in Sherborne.

She was a timid, retiring woman, not unlike "Miss Matty" in "Cranford," extremely gentle and kind-hearted. She was warmly attached to her sister-in-law, Mrs. Robert Scott, and to her niece Mary, who frequently stayed with her.

Robert Scott did not long survive his two sisters. He died at Bath in 1861, when his daughter Mary inherited a considerable fortune, amounting probably to £60,000. He left nothing to his wife, which made my father very indignant, and he persuaded Mary to settle £400 a year on her mother at once. Mrs. Scott survived her husband thirteen years.

As I may not have occasion to mention these cousins again, I will add a few words as to what happened to them after Mr. Robert Scott's death.

Mary lived with her mother very happily for ten years, and then she was most unfortunately induced to marry Dr. Rowland Elliott; she was then fifty years of age. The marriage turned out far from a happy one. At the end of ten months Dr. Elliott quietly bade her good-bye, as if for an absence of a few days only, and never returned. The shock was a severe one to Mary, and greatly embittered her feelings towards him. They never met again.

Mrs. Robert Scott died in 1875, a few weeks before her sister-in-law, our cousin Anna. Mrs. Elliott thus lost at once her mother and her aunt, her only near relatives—a loss that she felt most severely. After that she lived alone, often much depressed in spirits. Her means were large, but she continued to live very simply, and gave away large sums, both to her poorer relations and to charities. She put a stained glass window in Bath Abbey, and did other things for the beauty and convenience of the town. She frequently made little journeys to different parts of England and visited her cousins. These were some of her chief pleasures. It was with her that I made the first of my journeys into Somersetshire, mentioned in this book. My sisters and I always felt very affectionately towards her. She had great peculiarities, which at times were rather trying, but her great goodness of heart and genuine kind feeling towards us made it easy to overlook these failings. The solitariness of her later years made her cling to the relations who were left to her.

The house in which the greater part of her life had been spent, 5 Duke Street, Bath, continued to be her home till the end. She died there on June 1, 1891, at the age of sixty-eight. She was the last of our cousins of the name of Scott.

The house in Long Street, Sherborne, so closely associated in our minds with our cousins, now belongs to my sister Catherine and myself, having been left by cousin Anna to my father, to come to him after Mrs. Elliott's death. It is held by a form of tenure now uncommon, for three lives; the lives being from time to time renewed, on payment of a fine. My sister Catherine's is now the only life on which the lease depends, as the law no longer allows the renewal of lives. Her name was put in the lease when she was six years old. A yearly quit rent of £1 is still paid by my sister and myself to the Master and Brethren of St. John's Almshouses, Sherborne, to whom the house will revert at her death. Eastbury is the name given to it by the last tenant. Some cottages adjoining it, the fields and a portion of the garden, are freehold, and belong at present to my sister and myself.

CHAPTER XIX

MALAGA

1853–1854

THE chief sorrow of my father and mother's married life was the long illness and early death of their eldest child. Consumption had developed in Sophia while at school, unperceived by any one, and on her return home in June 1848 she was in a state which alarmed her parents much. She was taken to London for medical advice; there her strength suddenly failed, and they were overwhelmed with grief on being told that she had probably not six weeks to live. With great difficulty she was taken to Ventnor, where she passed the winter of 1848–49. She gradually improved in health, and for a time her parents were again hopeful. For five years she lingered, growing constantly more and more dear to all her family, and showing a beauty of character that made the deepest impression on all who knew her.

Something of this will be seen from the following letter from Mr. F. H. Hill. Though written after her death, it will be most fittingly inserted here.

"Such acquaintance as I had with Miss Scott was almost exclusively confined to what my duties as tutor to your children occasioned. But it was impossible, even under such circumstances, not to observe and admire the patience and forbearance, the thoroughly chastened tone of mind and character which always manifested themselves in her; and the recollection of which, except as inevitably mingled with the feelings of bereavement, must always be delightful to Mrs. Scott and yourself. It must be a matter of indifference to you to learn, though I cannot refrain from telling you, how highly I was led to estimate Miss Scott's merely intellectual endowments. It was a real and great pleasure to me to meet her when she joined her sisters in the Logic lessons. And it was often a matter of regret to me that any personal peculiarities of mine, should have rendered free and open conversation on other opportunities with her and others, so difficult to me." . . .

Few letters exist written by Sophia after her return from school, as she was constantly at home from that time.

The following letter was written two years after the commencement of her illness, soon after a visit to London. The doctor who had been consulted there had given no hope of more than temporary improvement. No doubt she had inquired as to the doctor's opinion, and my father's letter told her no more than she already knew, which was apparently that her life must henceforth be that of an invalid.

RUSSELL SCOTT *to his Daughter* SOPHIA.

SUMMER HILL, *6th October* 1850.

MY DEAR SOPHIA,—You will easily suppose that I must have been deeply pained by what your mamma told me last night of the view taken by so eminent a man as Dr. Williams of the nature of your case. I was much grieved, too, that circumstances had prevented me from being with you, as I should have made a point of being, if I had at all anticipated that the sanguine hopes we have lately been led to entertain of your being once more restored to health and strength were likely to meet with so much discouragement—I should have wished to speak to you, not only of the future, but of the past—of the day when I took you to the Isle of Wight,[1] when my apprehensions were first aroused, and when you complained of my silence, and of my thinking so very much about Aunt Sarah—of that sad day when we were sent for to London, to take you to Ventnor—and of all the anxiety which your dear mamma, in particular, went through during our stay there, and for some time subsequently. I believe now—and I partly believed at the time—that we might safely have communicated to you what our apprehensions then were—and that we should have had the comfort to see that you were prepared to submit to whatever your Almighty Father might see fit to appoint—but considering how young you then were—how completely prostrated in bodily strength—and how fatal the effects of mental agitation are likely to be, when life hangs upon a thread, as yours seemed to us to do, I think we could hardly do otherwise than as we did.

I must not omit to tell you, my darling girl, what indeed it was my chief object in writing to you to say, that what your mamma tells me of the way in which you appear to have so soon reconciled yourself to the idea of living the life of an invalid, has given me a degree of satisfaction, which it would indeed be very difficult to express. It has done what I should hardly have thought possible—it has deepened the feelings of attachment which your father entertains towards you. It has I trust deepened the feelings of gratitude which he entertains towards the Great Giver of All Good, who has given you to him for a daughter—and it has given him the strongest hopes that you will derive real and solid benefit—and therefore real and substantial happiness from a state

[1] This was in 1847, immediately after Sophia left school, and before she returned home.

of circumstances, which to too many I fear appears devoid of almost everything that makes life worth possessing. But you have not to learn how little external circumstances have to do with an inward peace—and I venture to hope for you somewhat—perhaps even much—of that satisfaction which is derived from the consciousness of not having lived in vain. . . . I remain ever, my dearest girl, very affectionately your father,

RUSSELL SCOTT.

In 1853 Sophia's increasing illness made my father and mother decide to try what a winter in a warm climate would do for her. In October of that year they took her to Malaga. Catherine and Charles, then a little boy of seven, went with them.

Mrs. RUSSELL SCOTT *to her Daughter* ISABELLA.

HAMILTON TERRACE, ST. JOHN'S WOOD [*October* 1853].[1]

MY DEAREST ISABELLA,—. . . My thoughts are almost constantly with my dear children at home, & I cannot bear to think of you as solitary & unhappy—but you have all of you plenty of occupation & so I trust that tho' the winter months may seem long in prospective, that they will not prove quite so much so in reality—& the winter once over you may rest assured my dear children, that nothing but absolute necessity, will prevent our re-union. I suppose we must not hope to meet again until the mild weather has fairly set in, but I hope & pray we may then once more enjoy the blessing of being all of us together & I trust I may have the happiness of finding you all in good health & benefited & improved in character by the responsibility devolving, of course principally upon you, but also in a considerable degree upon Sarah & the two boys. . . .

Monday.—I wrote the above yesterday, since then it has been

[1] My aunt Kate's house.

determined for us to go by way of Folkestone & Boulogne—& we shall have to sleep at both places. . . . Sophia had a better night last night, & I hope will be tolerably rested for her long journey.

I have no time to write any more, so with best love to all my darlings, believe me ever, my dearest Isabella, most affect^ly^ yrs. ISABELLA SCOTT.

The journey was by rail as far as Châlons-sur-Saone, and then by boat down the Saone and the Rhone. By far the most trying part was from Marseilles to Malaga, as the steamers were small and very uncomfortable.

Malaga suited Sophia, and she was better there than probably she would have been in England. My father came home before Christmas, after seeing the party safely to Malaga. The drawback to the place was that carriages were not to be hired, so that drives could be taken only when a private carriage was borrowed; but this was the less felt because Sophia much enjoyed being out in a boat, which could always be had. The boatmen carried her down from the hotel. She took much pleasure in the beauty of the climate and the sea.

SOPHIA RUSSELL SCOTT *to her Sister* ISABELLA.

FONDA DE LA ALAMEDA, MALAGA, *Nov.* 30, 1853.

MY DEAREST ISABELLA,—I do not know if Mamma will find room for this in her next letter, but I will write a few lines on the chance of it. I think I will give you a little domestic news. Charlie is at present in bed nursing a troublesome cough. He was told he might get up after he had finished his breakfast, but he preferred staying in bed, and reading a French book to which he has taken a fancy. Mamma bought him a story book, but he did not at all care for it, and declared he did "not like stories about M. le Beau and all that, but something dreadful like the Bible"! I suppose it is owing to the notice taken of him during the journey, and indeed since, that he has grown the most good-for-nothing bold little fellow imaginable, with twice the spirit and self-importance that he had at home, but it is no doubt also owing to his excellent health. Notwithstanding his cough he grows quite fat and strong.

Loder has a very great desire to learn French. She picked up several sentences during the journey & she has a very good opportunity here. Don Carlos speaks French, the cook also, and one or two waiters. Charlie offered to give her lessons, and for three days he gave them regularly; on the fourth the following scene occurred:—

Loder. Well, Charlie, I said your French to them downstairs and they all laughed at it.

Charlie (exceedingly red in the face). And pray what did you say? Tell me, now!

Loder. I said so and so—

Charlie (marching up and down, and not knowing what to do with himself, he felt so angry). You stupid thing! Of course they laughed. It should have been so and so. You stupid creature! Now I will never teach you again.

Loder. Well, perhaps someone else will, as well as you, or perhaps even better.

Charlie. No, you will never get such a good master as me. I have been very regular and punctual with you. You will never find any one to take so much pains as me.

Do you know he actually remained firm to his resolution for about ten days. He would not answer the slightest question relating to French. I enquired of Loder as to the nature of the lessons; she said that one day it consisted in learning the following dialogue:—

Loder. Voulez-vous vous promener avec moi?

Answer. Si vous voulez.

Loder. Où est ce que nous irons?
Answer. Où vous voulez.

Another time Loder said that she often wanted to ask the cook for something. What should she say? Charlie taught her the following sentences:—

Loder. Voulez-vous me donner quelque chose de bon?
Answer. Je ne veux pas.
Loder. Je commence à pleurer.
Answer. Je suis bien faché.

Loder it appears turned this lesson to good account. She went up to the cook, tapped him on the shoulder, and repeated her phrase. He was so delighted (being a Frenchman) that he took her instantly to the larder, and heaped her plate with the best of everything. The maid-servants here are a curious set, usually merry, but looking so black sometimes. Don Carlos is not married and they have no mistress to look after them. They take their work tolerably easy, playing at cards together in the evening, etc. The waiters wash up the dishes with cigars in their mouths! One day one of the Spanish maids to amuse the English servants went all the way down stairs on her hands, leaving her feet to drop down stair after stair. When she had concluded this singular amusement, she looked up and said, "Very good? Very good?" so they replied, "Oh, yes, very good." I went this morning to be weighed; I was only 80 Spanish pounds, which we should have imagined to be nearly 90 English, but Mr. Loring (the cousin) told us it was only about 81½ English. A dreadful reduction from 110, my last measurement. Tell Papa that Mr. Loring has gained three pounds in the last fortnight, and that he went out in the boat with us yesterday (a coldish day) and was no worse whatever, and said he enjoyed himself very much. This seems a very shabby letter to send such a long distance, but crossing is not permissible. I will only just add that I went on horseback a few days since for

half-an-hour, and felt but very little tired. With very best love to all at home, I remain, dearest Bell, your affectionate sister,

SOPHIA R. SCOTT.

CATHERINE SCOTT *to her Sister* ISABELLA.

MALAGA, 1853.

MY DEAREST ISABELLA,—. . . It is very funny to go out with Mamma shopping, for we go in & point to the things we want, only saying "quanto" (how much), and yesterday we made a poor fellow blush most painfully, so as to be quite visible through his dark skin, by laughing somewhat because when we asked for some elastic he brought us down some men's flannel waistcoats. We are still without our boxes from England, they are performing quarantine at Gibraltar. . . . I find Mamma a terrible person to learn with. We have had two lessons from a Don Gregorio, or Don Roderigo, as Papa persists in calling him, and Mamma wants me to learn such an awful quantity between times, as is enough to drive one distracted; in fact I cannot possibly do it all, and both she and the Don must learn to be contented with less. . . .

MRS. RUSSELL SCOTT *to her Daughter* ISABELLA.

MALAGA, *Jan'y 27th*, 1854.

MY DEAREST ISABELLA,—. . . This afternoon Katie, Charlie & I, went with Miss Hayward & Flora Stiebel a long walk into the mountains, & we did not get back until ½ past six, & since then I have been fully occupied; first in taking tea, which as we were extremely hungry & had had no dinner, was a very long affair; & since then in attending to Sophia. We had the most delightful walk possible & we were only sorry that we had not longer time, tho' as it was we were home much later than we ought to have been—it having been quite dark for half an hour before we reached the Hotel, & we had to pass through a very disagreeable suburb. But Miss Hayward, who was guide, rather miscalculated the time & the direction. It is the first time Katie & I have been in the mountains, for we never have liked to leave Sophia before for more than a short time, & in the morning when we have to be back for the boat by a given time it does not do to go exploring very far; besides which it would not be safe for two ladies alone. In fact I expect we should have been considered very venturesome by many for going the walk we did to-day, altho' we were four, without an escort. However we saw nothing whatever to alarm us, & as I said, enjoyed it exceedingly, & quite intend to take a similar excursion before long.

Dear Sophia, I am happy to say, goes on satisfactorily. She was weighed this morning & had gained a pound since her last weighing four weeks ago. I certainly thought from her appearance she had gained more, but however it is satisfactory that she has so far improved & I hope next month it may be a little more. . . . Her appetite is still bad, but I think it improves slightly, & she has less fever & her pulse is improving, & she looks very well—such a nice healthy color, & so bright & animated. She has finished two sketches, each of which took two days. Yesterday she said she felt too idle—it was a very warm & oppressive day. . . . My very best love to your Papa & all my darlings, & believe me ever, my dearest Isabella, most affect^{ly} yrs. ISABELLA SCOTT.

Until the beginning of February, Sophia continued to appear to do well, but a change came then, and the end was near.

The following account of the last days of Sophia's life was written by my mother, and was first seen by us forty years later, after my mother's death :—

" My dear Sophia during the end of January and the beginning of February had appeared to improve considerably. Every one remarked on the improvement in her appearance. . . . During the greater part of January the Terral wind had prevailed, and this suited dear Sophia better than any other. . . . About

February it began to blow very constantly from the Levant . . . and there was certainly a change for the worse. . . . On Sunday, Feb. 12, she did not go out, it being rather too rough at sea. She was in very good spirits, and there was nothing whatever to indicate an approaching change. . . . On that day we were speaking of Miss Coates, who had recently been pronounced to be in a decline. My darling child said to me, 'Mamma, I don't know & I can't tell—I don't know whether it is any consolation to parents to feel that they are the only sufferers.' 'What do you mean, my love?' I said. 'Why, Mamma, if Miss Coates dies her parents will be left & of course it will be a great affliction for them, but for Miss Coates herself surely it would be better to die.' Again in the evening we were talking about her own long illness, about the many alleviations she had had. She said she had had a great deal of happiness. She often thought that even if she had been well she should scarcely have been happier, perhaps not so much so. She should never have known how much she was loved.

"On Monday when we went out she said, 'Now, Mamma, it is tolerably calm; let us go straight out to sea; I will try & take that sketch of Malaga. We shall be going before long & if I do not make an effort I shall not do that sketch at all.' We chose a place & I tried to draw also, but it was too rough for me. My dear child however did not seem to feel it. She drew very steadily for about an hour, & then said she would finish it another day. She found it a troublesome sketch, there was so much detail. We then rowed about for a time. A fishing vessel attracted her attention, & she sketched it in a variety of positions, in order she said that she might have a collection of boats ready for foregrounds, for when she wanted one there were never any to be seen. On our return, as soon as she had finished her dinner, she got her drawing again, & drew till dusk & again while we were at t[illegible] She put in all the outline neatly & a little shading; this l[illegible] [illegible]ould rub out again, she did not like it, but [illegible] to let it stay. I did not like her having so m[illegible] [illegible]hing & said when she got in the rest of the shading she would be a better judge how it looked.

"That night there was a large discharge of matter from the lungs. When I went to her on Tuesday morning, she told me what had occurred in the night with perfect composure. She got up as usual, but while I was dressing her she observed that I was unhappy. She kissed me & began to cry, but it was only for a minute or two. She said to me, 'You must not be unhappy, dear Mamma, you know the only thing which grieves me is to see you unhappy.' That afternoon she sat a good deal on the sofa with me by her side to support her. She found that a comfortable position. I was kissing her and telling her what a darling child she had always been to us—what a comfort & happiness—always such a good child. She burst into tears, & said, 'Oh Mamma, pray do not speak so, you make me feel as if I were so hypocritical.' On Wednesday she asked me what I had written to her Papa. She hoped I had been very careful not to alarm him unnecessarily. She burst into tears, & said, 'It is such a disappointment to me, Mamma. It had made me so happy to think what a pleasure it would be to dear Papa to find me so much better when he came back. I had been thinking about it so much.' I observed on Friday that she was a good deal weaker, but there was no other change. She was as usual quite cheerful. When Dr. Bunsen came he asked her if she felt any pain. She answered, 'No, only a little tightness across the chest & a difficulty of breathing.' After he was gone she said, 'I don't think I said quite enough about it, Mamma. I do feel just a little pain, tho' nothing to signify.' During Friday night I had an easy chair in her room & another by the bedside, but whenever I went to sit by her she always told me she wished I would go to the other, she was sure I should be tired, and she did not like that."

Catherine was always with Sophia in the early mornings, and was with her as usual that morning. She had changed much during the night. About nine o'clock Sophia asked her to call their mother, and from that time till the end Catherine was almost always in the room.

My mother goes on to say:—

"After I came down on Saturday morning she seemed almost unable to swallow and could scarcely speak. I said to her, 'Do you think, dear, you can listen if I read to you?' She answered, 'I will try, Mamma.' I read to her portions from the New Testament & Psalms (I think). After a little while I left off, thinking I should tire her, but she said, 'Read me some hymns, Mamma.' This I did for a little while, but her breathing became rapidly worse & I feared she would be unable to speak. I said to her, 'My darling, when I write to your Papa this evening have you any message to send him.' She paused for a little while & then said, 'Give my best love to my dear Papa—tell him he must not grieve too much, but must try and submit. Give my love to my brothers & sisters, tell them they must be a comfort to you.' I asked her if she would like to kiss Charlie; she said 'yes,' and I sent for him. She kissed him, & just then Dr. Bunsen came. It was most painful to see the expression of her eyes as she followed him about the room—she seemed to be imploring relief. After he went & when she was a little easier, I spoke again about her Papa. An expression of great pain crossed her countenance & she said, 'You must comfort him, Mamma.' I continued to read to her, as I thought she could bear it, verses from Scripture & part of hymns. She was raised in bed into a sitting posture. She sat with her eyes fixed on mine. Once, when I was kissing her hand & stooping down, she began stroking my head with her other hand. It was her last caress. As her breathing became worse again she whispered, 'I trust in God. I know He sends this.' We moistened her lips occasionally with a little water; once I tried to give her some tea; she took two or three spoonfuls but she did not wish to drink.

"The time wore on. About twelve or half past she asked me to send for Dr. Bunsen again to see if he could try anything else for her breathing. Dr. B. came in about half an hour & gave her some medicine, but it was of no use. She asked me if I thought it could last much longer. I told her I did not know at all. She told me to ask the Dr. He gave some kind of an evasive answer. I told him she wished to know. He said he did not think it could. I told her what he said. She said in a whisper, 'Would that it were over.' Soon after the Dr. went Mr. Brereton sent to ask if we would like to see him. It was then I think a little after one. I asked her whether he should come in or whether she liked best to be alone. She whispered, 'Alone—alone.' I read to her what I thought would help & comfort her. Her eyes remained fixed on me. The expression of her countenance seemed to me exactly described by Christ's words in the garden. A little before two I felt her extremities becoming cold & her pulse very faint; her breathing was less trying. I said to her, 'My darling child, Good-bye—for a little while we shall be separated.' What more I said I do not remember, but I tried to comfort & help her. She said very faintly & at considerable intervals—her head was leaning on my hand for she could not then support it, 'Good-bye, my dear Mamma—Good-bye, my dear Papa—Oh how dearly I love you! Good-bye, Good-bye' —& then she seemed becoming unconscious; she repeated Good-bye a few times, & then her voice became inarticulate, tho' her lips continued to move. She lay quite still in the same position for a few minutes, the breathing gradually becoming weaker & weaker. Once she moved her arms forward & drew herself up a little—after that she lay quite still with her eyes closed, until she expired. This was at a quarter past two o'clock.

"She was buried between ten & eleven o'clock on Monday morning, Feb. 20th."

In writing to my father, my mother said:—

"I write to you from the bedside of our beloved child. No longer the bed of pain and suffering, for she is at rest. I am comforted when I look upon her, for all is peace. . . . She lies so peacefully, so calmly—the struggle over. When I look upon her I feel that God has granted a last final blessing, and removed her, with a struggle painful for a few hours, but soon exchanged for perfect rest & peace. May you be comforted, my dearest husband. It is so great a grief to me that you should not have seen her now and at the last. . . . Would that we were together! . . ."

Most of the English gentlemen of the town (merchants and others) came to the hotel for the funeral. The coffin was covered with the English flag, and was borne on the road to the Protestant Cemetery on their shoulders. This cemetery was the only one in Spain (except one in Madrid) in which Protestants were at that time allowed to be buried. It is a beautiful spot, full of trees and flowers.

Mrs. RUSSELL SCOTT *to her Daughter* ISABELLA.

MALAGA, *March* 9th, 1854.

MY DEAREST ISABELLA,—Every day I have been wishing to write to you, & every day I have felt unequal to the exertion. Not that I am otherwise than well, but I seem unable to occupy myself in any way. However I feel better able to do so than I did. We take long walks every day & they do us a great deal of good. The country is so interesting, the weather so delightful. We go out directly after dinner & walk till dusk. I cannot bear to come indoors again; our evenings, when we are alone, are so very melancholy. But our friends here are very kind, & very urgent we should not stay in our own room in the evening. . . .

Mrs. RUSSELL SCOTT *to her Daughter* ISABELLA.

MALAGA, *March* 11th, /54.

MY DEAREST ISABELLA,—I was very much pleased with dear Arthur's letter, & I had another very affectionate one from him the same day, written after he had heard of our great grief. Dear boy! He is a most loving & affectionate child, & I trust & fully believe will always be a blessing & a comfort to us—& this, my dearest Isabella, I have the firmest confidence you will all of you be. This great affliction which God has sent us will bind our hearts together even more closely than heretofore, & will also I humbly pray & trust draw us more closely to Him, & incite us to more strenuous efforts in the path of duty. God bless you all, my darling children; how much I long to see you all again.—Ever, your most affectionate mother,

ISABELLA SCOTT.

My mother remained at Malaga a few weeks with Catherine and Charles, till my father joined them, which he did as quickly as possible. They then came home.

Only once again did my father and mother visit Malaga. This was three years later, in November 1857. At the end of a letter written home on this journey, and dated from Malaga, my mother says: "Except to come here I could not have made up my mind to leave you all for so long and for such a terrible distance. I am 1600 miles away from home. But this journey I have thought of and wished for for so long a time. I think I shall be happier afterwards, and that my dear child's grave will no longer seem to me so solitary and so distant." And in another letter, written to my father after the lapse of seven or eight years, she says: "That graveyard is the only spot of ground on earth to which I feel really bound. I trust that I may have life and strength to see it once more at least." But this was not to be.

CHAPTER XX

REMOVAL TO LONDON AND VISITS ABROAD

1855–1863

MR. PRESTWICH died in November 1855. My father was trustee under the marriage-settlement of his wife, and it was to him as trustee that my aunt Emily wrote the following. Her previous letter is missing.

EMILY PRESTWICH *to her Brother-in-law*, RUSSELL SCOTT.

KENSINGTON, *Monday even^g^*.

MY DEAR MR. SCOTT,—I think it better to write a few lines by this evening's post, to say that I am perfectly satisfied with all arrangements that may have been made, relative to my poor mother's property.

It was foolish of me not to ask for an exact statement before I made my request, which was of course founded upon a mere supposition. You may also be quite sure that I cannot think any letter disagreeable which is kindly written and kindly meant. All I can do is to thank God for the little disappointment; it is all for the best, and so that His holy will is accomplished it matters so very little what happens.

What I do know and shall always feel, is that you have always been the kindest and truest of friends to my poor father and to us all, and had it not been for your assistance in the hour of need, we might have suffered real poverty, which one feels more for the sake of those who are gone than for aught else. And now I will say good-bye, hoping to see you and dear Isabella to-morrow morning. I ought just again to say somewhat more clearly that what I asked for was, if possible, an advance of my dear mother's property, but which of course I should not have done if I had understood the exact rights of the case; therefore all is ended, and all is quite right, and I am happy and satisfied.

My love to dear Isabella and the children, ever my dear Mr. Scott, affectionately yours, E. PRESTWICH.

We did not remain very long at Bath after Sophia's death. We had no society there beyond a few friends belonging to the little congregation of Trim Street Chapel, which we of course attended. In such a place as Bath, Unitarians could hardly expect to be visited by those of a different way of thinking. My father and mother considered that we were too much isolated. In 1855 they took us for three months to Paris, and for a further three months to Switzerland, an immense pleasure to us all. Lawrence was left at Neuchâtel after our visit to Switzerland, and remained there for a year at school. He was twelve when he came home. The M. Godet mentioned below was the head of the school, and M. de Pury was a cousin, Madame de Pury being by birth a Blakeway.

ISABELLA SCOTT *to her Sister* CATHERINE.

SOUTHEND, *Sep.* 19th, 1856.

MY DEAREST KATIE,—Lawrie is come. He arrived about an hour and a half ago, somewhat to our surprise, for we did not know there was any train at the time. Mamma and I were sitting in the drawing room, and Charlie was on the balcony, when we heard a knock at the door—I did not believe they could be there, but I went to see, and there was Lawrie standing in the hall—I rushed down, and he received me with one of his own desperate hugs. A moment after Mamma appeared, and he hugged her, and then with an arm round both he began kissing us alternately. His smiles as you may fancy were bright enough, but he did not seem able to muster a word of English. Then I took him up to Charlie. He sprang out on the balcony and caught him in a tight squeeze for an instant, and then arm in arm they walked to the end of the balcony smiling at each other, but not speaking. In fact he has the greatest difficulty in expressing himself in English. He uses no abbreviations and has a decided French accent. He speaks French very fluently and gesticulates violently (at least for an English boy). When Mamma asked him if they had not had a good deal of wind in crossing, he gave a regular French shrug and said, "Voila! passablement." And when Harris introduced herself to him, he made her a funny little French bow quite gravely. His pet phrases are characteristic—"Tant mieux," and "Ça m'est égal." He is enthusiastic about the Revolution. He watched it all from a hill, "et j'ai cru que les royalistes avaient gagné et puis j'étais content." M. Godet is "caché," and M. de Pury "n'a rien à craindre."

He is not more grown than the other boys, and not very brown, though he looks well. There is not the least difference in his dear face, and he is just the same sweet, simple hearted fellow as ever. Papa says he was in a great state of excitement all the way and extremely impatient to be moving towards home. He has brought presents for us all.

Later.—The boys are gone to bed, and I have just discovered to my dismay, that Mamma has caught me up in a novel we are reading and has taken my volume, so I will devote the rest of the evening to finishing my account of Lawrie.

We think that he is greatly improved. His ideas now seem to flow as rapidly as his tongue can utter them, and I am constantly surprised by remarks which make him appear at least two years older than when we left him. He is also more observant than he was. When Mamma was lamenting that he had not been able to [illegible] 1 on board the steamer (they crossed in the middle of Thursday night), he answered, in French of course—"Why how could I sleep when I had all the boat on my hands and everything to examine?"

Saturday, Sep. 20.—I have had a walk and a long talk with Lawrie this morning, & I have been very much pleased with what he has told me of his goings on at school. It appears that he is more trusted by the master of his class than any other boy, and is always chosen by him to take messages, etc. One anecdote he told me is a striking illustration of the master's confidence in him.

Lawrie one day saw a certain miserable little Adolph being very much ill-used and flew to his assistance. Rather a serious battle ensued, in the midst of which a man appeared who separated the combatants, and then reported them to M. L'Inspecteur. During school hours M. L'Inspecteur made his appearance and called up Lawrie and his opponent to answer for their conduct. The Swiss boy gave a very untrue account of the matter to prove himself not to have been to blame. But Lawrie stood up and said, "Pardon, Monsieur, ce n'est pas vrai ça; moi je vous dirai la vérité," and then gave his account. All the boys clamorously declared Lawrie to be telling stories, but he was believed nevertheless, and the affair ended by the "Inspecteur" telling them that whoever attacked Lawrie in future or called him names should be severely punished.

Dear Lawrie is now sitting by my side, industriously copying out his English dictation, for he is extremely anxious to get on with spelling while he is at home. He says he is so horribly backward. It is not often that he is so quiet. His merry laugh is constantly heard ringing through the house. Yesterday evening especially his mad antics kept us in roars of laughter. I never saw so much hugging and kissing as there has been since he has been here. Even Arthur's dignity gives way before it, and Charlie evidently likes nothing better than to be fondled & stroked and called "dear little Charlie, poor little fellow." I wondered how he had kept his heart so warm, and asked whom he had to kiss at Neuchâtel. He would only confess to kissing

Mme. de Pury sometimes, and laughed and snorted contemptuously when I mentioned Mme. Godet, and his little friends. It would have been a very great disappointment to him if he had not come home. He says he often longed to be with us, and he wishes it were not necessary to go back.

Lawrence did not return to Switzerland.

Catherine was at this time for fifteen months in Dr. Martineau's house in Liverpool (1855-56) studying with his daughters. Russell had been for two years previously at University Hall, London, attending lectures at University College. It was intended that he should go into business, and his father and mother wishing to make a home for him, we settled in London.* Our house was No. 10 Cornwall Terrace, Regent's Park, where we lived for eighteen years.

We all enjoyed the change. My father found occupation in various undertakings for the public good. I may specially mention the "Metropolitan Association for improving the Dwellings of the Industrious Classes," of which to the time of his death he remained a director. One of their blocks of buildings is named after him. In all that related to the Unitarian body he took a generous interest, and he was a warm friend to the "London Domestic Mission."

Both he and my mother had many relations as well as friends in London. My father made a practice of breakfasting at Lavender Hill with his aunt Sarah every other Wednesday morning. He seemed almost to take the place of a son to her. She consulted him on most occasions, and he managed her affairs for her. His mother had been her favourite sister, and *her* children remained, amongst all the nephews and nieces, the ones

* June 1856

to whom she was most attached. Aunt Sarah was then living alone, uncle Thomas having died in 1849. For many years her house was a centre of union for the whole family of relations, her nephews and nieces and great-nephews and great-nieces. She lived to see the descendants of her father number more than a hundred.

It was her habit to keep open house on Sunday for such members of the family as might like to come, and there was always a little gathering. Towards the end of her life "Company Sunday" came only once a fortnight. On Christmas Day and Good Friday the number who gathered round her was always considerable. We ourselves went regularly after our removal to London.

Aunt Sarah had, with great kindness of heart, a good deal of force and originality of character. This, with a habit of very plain speaking, gave her much weight and ascendency in the family circle. She took a lively interest in all, and those who lived in London were familiar from childhood with her and her delightful home. The garden was greatly enjoyed by the children; there was a summer house there and a pond, and a rockery near the pond, on which were collected numerous curiosities in the shape of shells and fossils and most interesting little images in crockery ware or wood. Once I remember in very early days, we took these wooden images and floated them on the pond as boats, on each of which a frog was sent off on a voyage. This however was too much for aunt Sarah's patience, and we were pretty severely reprimanded.

In the summer of 1859 my father was invited by friends in Boston, Mass., to pay them a visit. He took

Catherine and me with him, and we spent four months in travelling in the United States and Canada. In New Brunswick we visited my father's old friend from Portsmouth, Chief Justice Carter. This journey was to Catherine and me the most delightful we ever made. To us, as to other English people, the Americans were especially kind and hospitable; the times too were very interesting, as it was just before the American Civil War. Our friends, Judge Loring and his family, were anticipating the war in the event of Lincoln's election in the coming November. They threw themselves heart and soul into the cause of the North. When later on in consequence of the sacrifices they had made, their beautiful home at Beverley (where we visited them) was for sale, their fellow-citizens bought it and gave it back to Judge Loring in testimony of their admiration of him.

About this time it was that my younger brothers went to school. My father objected to sending his boys to public schools, and Arthur, Lawrence, and Charles, each in turn, went to Hove House, Brighton, a school carried on by the Rev. J. P. Malleson, minister of the Unitarian congregation at Brighton, an excellent man to whom the boys were much attached. Arthur subsequently went to University Hall, like his elder brother.

MRS. RUSSELL SCOTT *to her Son* CHARLES.

10 CORNWALL TERRACE, *Octr 26th*, 1860.

MY DARLING CHARLIE,—I ought to have written to you last night, but I hope this note will be in time for you to receive it to-day. How fervently & lovingly I wish you many, many happy returns of your birthday I am sure, my dear boy, you know full well, & I think my Charlie knows how happy birthdays are best to be ensured. Your fourteenth birthday, too, is rather a special one, for it is supposed somewhat to mark an important epoch in life—a transition to another stage of youth, when childish things are gradually put away & the last preparation is made for the active duties of manhood. That you may do this successfully & in a right spirit, always setting before you the highest standard of religious motive, & living a life of true manliness, is, my darling boy, the strongest desire, the dearest hope I can possibly have. May you have strength given you to fulfil it.—Ever, my dearest Charlie, your most affectionate Mother, ISABELLA C. SCOTT.

The winter of 1861–62 was spent by us in Algiers, in a most beautiful Moorish house, the Château d'Hydra. It is in Mustapha Supérieur, a delightful suburb, on the hills overlooking the town.

In 1863 my brother Lawrence went to the Royal Agricultural College at Cirencester to learn farming.

Charles had left school after spending two years as a weekly boarder at the Clapham Grammar School under the Rev. Charles Pritchard, an old friend of his father's, who was afterwards for many years Professor of Astronomy at Oxford. Not being very strong at this time, he was placed with the Rev. Arthur Watson at Cowes, who prepared him for going to Oxford.

CHAPTER XXI

LETTERS FROM RUSSELL SCOTT TO HIS SON—WINTER IN CATANIA

1863–1875

THE next few letters were addressed to Charles at Cowes by his father.

10 CORNWALL TERRACE, REGENT'S PARK, *Oct.* 16, 1863.

MY DEAR CHARLES,—I had no time yesterday to say anything about reform in Parliament, nor is it a subject to be disposed of on a sheet of note paper—but I will just say this—that unless you adopt the principle of universal suffrage, which is class representation of the very worst kind, you must either tolerate existing anomalies, or introduce new ones; & when anomalies are introduced or tolerated, the franchise cannot be treated as an absolute right in each individual case, but must be viewed rather as a trust and a privilege; and the question to be considered before making a change is whether the distribution of power among different classes is on the whole a fair one; & if not, whether the proposed change involves a principle which must be carried further; & if so, whether the carrying it out would be just to all parties, or whether some other & fairer mode of distributing power can be devised & carried out. I am not satisfied with the representation as it stands; still less am I satisfied with any alteration that has been proposed. I think the working classes ought not to be so nearly excluded from the representation as they are at present,—but I think that for the present, and for the next 30 or 40 years, they ought not to have more than an eighth or a tenth of the representation; and that even when they have become far better qualified than they are at present to judge of questions of political economy, & other important matters, a third or a fourth will be as large a share as they will be fairly entitled to. As to the mode in which additional influence should be given to the working classes, I will say nothing now, seeing that I have already filled one sheet; but I think it may be done in a satisfactory manner, with the aid of a partial application of the principle of single voting. Certainly I am not an advocate for "sweeping change" even prospectively. We have within the last 35 years effected greater reforms than have ever elsewhere been accomplished in the same or in a much longer period with or without bloodshed, & I hope those to be effected hereafter will also take place by means of the gradual changes in public opinion.

There can be no doubt that any considerable "accession of radicalism" would very seriously impede any reforms which should not be popular. It is the great vice of democratic institutions that nobody is trusted long; no man's character or reputation stands so high as to lead people to say—"this man must have well considered the subject, & he is certainly honest—probably he may be right, though his views are not in accordance with those generally entertained on the subject"; on the contrary, the more the suffrage is extended the more surely are candidates pledged to some favorite notion or notions, & the more does a man's willingness to give up all independence of thought become essential to his success. . . . Ever, dear Charles, your affectionate father, RUSSELL SCOTT.

RUSSELL SCOTT *to his Son* CHARLES.

DUBLIN, *Oct^r* 25, 1863.

MY DEAR CHARLES,—I am desirous to write a few lines to reach you on your 17th birthday, though I could wish for more of leisure, of quietness, & some other advantages, in doing so. The period from 16 to 18, the middle of which you will reach to-morrow, is probably by much the most important of a young man's life, and very glad should I be if it were in my power to render you any important assistance in the endeavours which I fully believe you are making, & will make, to pass it well. But it is not much that I can do in that respect; although it may I hope help you in some degree to know, as I hope you do, how earnest are the wishes of your parents that you may hereafter have as little as possible with which to reproach yourself for time misspent, or opportunities lost, or temptations not sufficiently withstood. Should this be so, it will be a small matter if you should be known hereafter only in the circle of your own friends; you will still help on, according to the measure of your opportunity, the great cause of human progress; & have the satisfaction of feeling, that (to however small an extent) the world is the better & not the worse for your having lived.

One thing more I will just say, for unfortunately time presses—that is, if in the formation of your opinions, you should be led to the adoption of views materially different from mine, it will be to me a matter of but slight regret, provided only I can feel a perfect conviction that your views, whatever they may be, are fairly arrived at. That no fear of the world's opinion, or even of the world's scorn, no deference to a majority, no shadow of influence from considerations of what may be most conducive to your own interest, your own advancement, or even to your own opportunities of being useful, has, consciously or unconsciously, determined them.

And now, dearest Charles, I must stop, for as I said time presses. I need hardly tell you I wish you many happy birthdays, many happy years. I should like to say something about dear Sarah — but this another time.—Your ever affectionate father,

RUSSELL SCOTT.

RUSSELL SCOTT *to his Son* CHARLES.

10 CORNWALL TERRACE, N.W., 26th *June* 1864.

MY DEAR CHARLES,—Although I still hope to pay you a visit at Cowes I do not like any longer to delay answering [your letter]. . . .

You say that you cannot understand how it is that men whom you recognise as in many respects your superiors should in some matters appear such children. I think you will understand this much better as you get older; you will find that even among the higher class of minds the love of truth seldom occupies the first place; that patient and persevering thought is rare; that the feelings with which a man has grown up, the mental atmosphere to which he has been accustomed, personal considerations, the desire to retain, or to attain, a position in society, sadly interfere with & disturb the conclusions to which a man might otherwise arrive. From all which I derive this consoling reflection, that if a man will but do what in him lies to preserve such faculties unclouded as it may have pleased God to give him—will use them steadily & perseveringly & will do his very best to maintain a judicial impartiality—he may fairly hope to reach conclusions much sounder than those of men gifted with powers much greater than his own, and may sometimes even see his way clearly when men whom he knows to be capable of doing better than himself are enveloped in darkness. . . .

RUSSELL SCOTT *to his Son* CHARLES.

10 CORNWALL TERRACE, REGENT'S PARK, *Feb.* 27, 1865.

MY DEAR CHARLES,— . . . Probably you are not aware that the Govt are about to bring in a bill for union rating, which Sir Jas. Graham & others tried to accomplish 20 years ago. It will go far to get rid of the *close parish* system, the greatest evil I think within the control of the legislature. I told you some time ago that you & your contemporaries would not be able to do so much as your predecessors, . . . and now here is another serious evil in a fair way to be nearly cured. I suspect that the next generation will have to take care quite as much that mischief is not done, as that existing evils are remedied. There is however the Irish Church for you to get rid of. I do not much expect to see an end of that.—Yours, dear Charles, ever affectionately, RUSSELL SCOTT.

My father was mistaken. The Irish Church was disestablished in 1871, nine years before his death.

RUSSELL SCOTT *to his Son* CHARLES.

10 CORNWALL TERRACE, 21st *May* 1865.

MY DEAR CHARLES,—I enclose you a letter from Mr. Davey;[1] he seems to think you fortunate in obtaining admission to Corpus. I wish we could remove Oxford to the Isle of Wight; if a million or two would accomplish it, the money would be exceedingly well expended. But as the wish is rather a vain one, I will content myself with the more modest and reasonable hope that you will lay in a stock of health at Cowes that shall last you for some time after you go to Oxford. But neither at Oxford nor anywhere else are you to risk injury to your health. That I hope you feel would be a breach of duty to your mother and to me, whatever else it might or might not be.

We dined the other day at Dr. Rees', where we met Dr. Roget. It was a great treat to meet him and to talk to him about his uncle, the great and good Sir Samuel Romilly, who died when I was just your age, but whom I seem to have known by reputation during a great many years. I think you have read his Memoirs—if so, I need not tell you how great and good a man he was. I felt the deepest interest in his election for Westminster in 1818, when he was returned at the head of the poll, without having asked for a vote, although

[1] Mr. Horace Davey, afterwards Lord Davey, and a Judge of the Court of Appeal.

that was just the time when my interest in politics was lower than it had been, and than it has been since; & his death seemed almost the greatest public calamity within my recollection. We have no such man now, but then such times as the present are not those which produce great men; it is adversity which brings out great qualities, and England has of late been prosperous, and there has not been very much to stir men's souls, although there is no danger that those who desire to leave the world better than they have found it, will not find plenty of occupation. And if we have no Romilly now, we have what is better than a succession even of such as he—a public interest in the detection and reformation of abuses such as he would have rejoiced to witness.

My conversation with Dr. Roget brought once more to my mind what has often occurred to it before—the idea how little Louis 14th knew, when he revoked the Edict of Nantes, what he was really doing; & how little such as he do know how the effects of injustice recoil upon themselves and their successors. It is hardly too much to say that the national character both of England & France has been permanently affected by what he then did.

Dr. Roget is a remarkable and very interesting man in himself. He gave me an account of his narrow escape from being sent to Vendome in 1803, & told an amusing story which illustrated the physical effect of fear. On his homeward voyage in that year most of the passengers were very sea-sick in consequence of being tossed about in the North Sea; a frigate, supposed to be French, came near to them, when every man rushed on deck, perfectly free from all effect of sea-sickness. He is now 87 years of age, but he remained standing, while talking to me and others, for an hour and a half after we left the dinner table. . . . Yours ever affectionately,

Russell Scott.

If you have not read the Memoirs you will not be likely to understand my allusions. If you have, you will probably remember that Romilly's ancestors were Huguenots, one of whom was driven from France.

At the time the following letter was written Charles had very recently gone to Oxford.* My father had much difficulty in finding a college willing to receive a Unitarian (as extant letters show), but Charles was finally entered in Corpus Christi, where rooms were assigned him on the result of the Scholarship Examination.

RUSSELL SCOTT *to his Son* CHARLES.

10 CORNWALL TERRACE, *Nov.* 4, 1865.

MY DEAR CHARLES,—I have just posted to your address the *Times* of Thursday last, containing one of Mr. Gladstone's best speeches, which I hope you will find time to read, as I do not think your time is at all likely to be better occupied than in reading it. Indeed I consider, as I have no doubt said before, such reading to constitute a very valuable part of your education. The *Spectator* says the House of Commons is doubtful whether to worship or to distrust him. If so, I trust they will soon make up their minds; for they have had no such leader, no one I mean by whom they have been so worthily led, in my time. Canning may have had as much brilliancy; and no man can have a more earnest desire to do right than was entertained by "honest Lord Althorpe"; but no one I think can fairly say that any leader of the House of Commons has combined these two requisites to the same extent as Mr. Gladstone, during the half century over which my recollection extends. And with the responsibility which will now be thrown on him, I cannot doubt that he will evince such a measure of tact and discretion as will suffice to fit him for his post. The *Times* attacks him to-day, as they attack everybody in turn, for the shorter of the two speeches reported on Thursday. I read it with satisfaction, and am quite disposed to augur from it a really good Reform Bill. . . .

* Oct. 13 1856.

RUSSELL SCOTT *to his Son* CHARLES.

10 CORNWALL TERRACE, *March* 14, 1866.

MY DEAR CHARLES,—I was glad to find that you seemed to feel ashamed of your long silence, since it showed that we took similar views of our duty as to that matter, as I trust we do as to many others. I had myself felt something like shame at not having written to my son Charles.

I showed your letter just now to Mr. Gilpin, the Quaker M.P. for Northampton, who takes very great interest in the question of capital punishment. . . . My own views I am afraid are very ultra on the subject of punishment altogether. I go so far as to doubt whether a large number of men (dignified by being called the State) have a right to inflict punishment on individuals either by way of retribution, or for the sake of deterring others (a very difficult matter I think in most cases) from the commission of offences. People have a right to protect themselves, & may therefore of course lock up thieves, & I do not say anything about the infliction of fines, which may be considered as levied by way of compensation for injuries done. But I doubt whether A. should be tormented, in order that B. & C. may be frightened. The punishment dreaded above all things, that of being disgraced in the eyes of his own associates, is one that necessarily follows the exposure of misconduct, even though no judicial punishment be inflicted. . . . Ever, my dear Charlie, your affectionate father,

RUSSELL SCOTT.

So I hear the money goes apace—do you not apprehend the paternal indignation? I fear not—perhaps I hope not.

In February 1866 my father's aunt, Miss Sarah Hawes of Lavender Hill, died at the age of ninety-three. From that time forward the various families of cousins who used to meet at her house saw much less of each other. We now rarely meet any of them.

"Aunt Sarah" was quite blind and very deaf for the last few years of her life. A kind and attentive servant waited on her.

The old Lavender Hill houses, including aunt Sarah's, have now all been pulled down, and the district is covered with small streets branching off from the main street of the Wandsworth Road. Lavender Hill is a gentle rise sloping up from Clapham Junction Station towards London. It was at the top of the hill, where the road is level, that the old house stood.

RUSSELL SCOTT *to his Son* CHARLES.

10 CORNWALL TERRACE, *May* 27, 1866.

MY DEAR CHARLES,—By all means write to Mr. Watson, and make what arrangements you like with him. The plan has your mother's special approbation, on account of the benefits she anticipates that you will derive from the air of Cowes.

You will be very wrong if you should suppose that because I have not particularly replied to your letter of the 1st of this month, that therefore I have felt little interest in its contents; perhaps I should have been more likely to reply to it if I had felt less. I have read it oftener probably than I should think it necessary to state, if I were able, and it is one of the very greatest pleasures I have to watch the expansion of your mind, the direction of your thoughts & the development of your tastes & feelings. But I seem to be living in a perpetual hurry, & to be quite incapable of doing anything like justice to such subjects as you write to me about. I am finishing this when everybody is gone to bed, and when bed is the only place for which I feel in the least fit. . . . Ever, my dear Charles, your very affectionate father,

RUSSELL SCOTT.

RUSSELL SCOTT *to his Son* CHARLES.

10 CORNWALL TERRACE, *Sep^r* 27, 1866.

MY DEAR CHARLES,—. . . I perfectly agree with you, I think, as to infant baptism, but somehow or other, my dear Charles, I find that I do agree with you more closely than I ever did before with anybody else. Your dear mother and I never can agree when we talk about war.[1] I do not know that we differ much about other matters, except that I am sometimes unable quite to coincide with her when she ascribes all possible perfections to her offspring. As to infant baptism however I see no Scriptural evidence for it; I know of no historical evidence; and in the absence of these, although it might still be held to be fit and suitable, it cannot fairly be considered to be in any sense necessary. I am particularly glad that you should be able to speak as you do as to its omission in your case, because I have thought and am still rather of opinion that we were running too much risk in omitting it, since you might when old enough to have an opinion of your own, have thought that it ought not to have been omitted, except on conscientious grounds, which did not exist. . . .

The following letter, received from Mr. Edward Enfield, whilst Charles was at Oxford, was very gratifying to my father. Mr. Enfield was intending to send his son Ernest to the same college, Corpus Christi.

June 13.

MY DEAR SIR,—I think you will like to see the following, which is the Postscript to a Letter I have just received from Mr. Furneaux of Corpus.

"I think young Scott is in every respect one of the most

[1] My father was strongly opposed to war, and a constant advocate for the settlement of disputes between nations by arbitration. He considered the Crimean War to be a blunder and a crime.

satisfactory young men that we have ever had in the college. He may not get the highest Honours, but will do very well, and few indeed of his age have such force of character and earnestness. If your son should do like him he would be indeed an acquisition to us." . . . Yours sincerely, E. ENFIELD.

Mr. Furneaux was Senior Proctor of the University.

Ruddington, where my mother was staying when she wrote the following letter, is a village near Nottingham, where my father had recently taken a farm for my brother Lawrence. The farm was called "Moor End."

RUDDINGTON, *October 8th*, 1866.

DEAREST CHARLIE,—Your father sent me some days ago a letter from you which has been a source of much comfort to me. The letter I refer to was mainly on *Ecce Homo*. What you said on the subject of baptism, especially with reference to your own case, has relieved me from one occasion of self-reproach. My own views on the subject are & long have been much more in accordance with those of the Quakers, than with those of the writer of *Ecce Homo*. But as I had no defined objections to the rite—on the contrary had always considered it a most pathetic & impressive ceremony, totally however without sacramental character, I have felt that I had been very reprehensible in overlooking what might be the claims of the child. I say *I* in all this, because I felt that I was so very much the more in fault, & that your father, sharing my opinions as to the character of the rite, left all arrangements as to time, etc., to me. Circumstances had prevented Arthur & Lawrence from being baptized in infancy. When you were born we talked about it; then my dear Sophia was taken ill & it was postponed. We agreed after the birth of my last child that you should all be baptized without delay, but the child died, & after that the subject dropped for some time; & then you seemed to be growing too big. One difficulty always was that Mr. Murch was a Baptist, & we did not like his successors in the ministry [at Bath]. Then too I always had it in mind that you could if you wished it be baptized when you were grown up; & so, my dear Charles, I feel that I was not only negligent, but forgetful & inconsiderate, & your letter as I said has been a source of comfort & thankfulness to me.

I have been reading & re-reading *Ecce Homo*. It is extraordinary the hold that book takes of the mind. I do not altogether agree with some of the writer's assumptions—nor altogether with his conclusions—but I feel that I want to think a great deal more about it; and also to know more, before I can see clearly where & how much I differ. I have been reading the Testament over, very rapidly, to see what impression a kind of bird's-eye view of its contents will have upon my mind. I cannot say it has modified my previous opinions so far; it has brought out some things very clearly and forcibly.

A great difficulty to an ordinary reader is the fact that so many words have acquired a technical meaning, which is often very different to that which they bore in the minds of Christ & his apostles. A knowledge of the original writings would not be sufficient to enable one rightly to understand these words; there is also wanted a knowledge of the literature & of the general tone of thought & expression of the age of the gospels, & also of that which preceded it. Christ says, "Upon this rock will I build my church"—(though I don't understand the object of his saying this to Peter because he said Christ was the Messiah; it had been said by others before). What did Christ mean exactly by the word "Church"? I wish you would tell me what you consider to be the force of the word? Does it mean or is it the same word as that which is translated "congregation" in the Psalms? (I have always been told that Church means congregation.) One of the books which many years ago, when I was about your age, gave me the most satisfactory explanation of some of the Epistles was Locke's *Paraphrase*. I do not think it has been at all superseded by the advance of critical knowledge. I shall look at it again when I go home, & also read Jowett.

In 1868 an event took place which was the cause of much happiness in the family. This was the marriage of my brother Russell to Jessie, daughter of Mr. William Thurburn of Keith.

Charles remained at Oxford till 1869, when he took a first class in Honours in "Greats." He was still there when his cousin, John Edward Taylor, expressed a wish that he should join the staff of the *Manchester Guardian*, and he consequently went, on leaving college, for a year to the office of the *Scotsman* in Edinburgh, to learn practically the details of the work of a newspaper. He went to Manchester in the spring of 1871, and a year later, at the age of twenty-five, he was made editor of the *Manchester Guardian*.

It is by no means my intention to give even in the briefest way a history of my brothers' lives, but of Arthur, as but little is to be learnt of him from the letters, I will give a few particulars.

Arthur was somewhat shy and retiring, and was especially devoted to our mother, more so she seemed to feel than any other of her children, from the time when, as she once said, he lay as an infant on the hearthrug and followed her constantly with his eyes as she moved about the room. He gave his parents no anxiety at any time except as to health, and even this was good for the first twenty-four years of his life. There was great uncertainty when he left University College, London, as to what business he should pursue; his real vocation was not for business at all, but for art. Eventually he joined Mr. Elijah Helm as a cotton broker in Manchester. The partnership was satisfactory on both sides, but as Arthur's health failed after a very few years it was not of long duration. In 1868 he broke a blood-vessel on the lungs. His mother went to Manchester to nurse him, and removed him to London, and he never returned to Manchester. In October of that year she and his father took him to Catania for the winter, and after that some years were spent by him in the search for the health that never came.

ARTHUR SCOTT *to his Brother* RUSSELL.

GRANDE ALBERGO, CATANIA, 1st *Jan'y* 1869.

MY DEAR RUSSELL,—I am sure you will believe that I have been very anxious to write to you for a long time past, and that nothing but my continued want of strength would have prevented my answering sooner your very kind and affectionate letters. . . .

I have been very happy, dear Russell, to receive the proofs of affection and sympathy you have given me, and assure you they have been a comfort to me, though I never doubted your warm-hearted feelings, nor can I recollect that, as you seem to suppose, you ever gave me the least cause to do so.

I send you and dear Jessie my best wishes for the new year we are now entering upon, and pray for your happiness both in this and those to come. . . . We may trust that there is a bright future in store for you.

Your hopes have been fulfilled, and you have gained a good and loving wife, such as it falls to the lot of few men to win. . . .

We had a hollow mockery of a Christmas dinner here, at which we drank the healths of all your party. I feel quite ashamed of having divided the family at such a time, and also I am very sorry to have deprived you and Jessie of my dear Mother's society all this winter. I value it so much myself that I feel how great a loss it must be to you. It is such a happiness to have my dear Mother so constantly with me that I look upon my illness as quite a blessing. . . .

All here send their love and best wishes for the new year, & again wishing you the same myself, I remain, dear Russell, your very affect^e brother, ARTHUR SCOTT.

After wintering in Catania, Arthur went with Catherine to Gleichenberg in Styria, in order to try the waters there, and my mother returned home.

CATHERINE SCOTT *to* ISABELLA SCOTT.

FELSENHAUS, GLEICHENBERG, *Thursday, June 24th*, 1869.

DEAREST ISABELLA,—In spite of having passed almost a fortnight without writing to you, I don't find that I have much to say, so you must forgive a short letter. Arthur continues to go on well. Dr. Weiss called to see him a few days ago & was satisfied about him. The last few days however have not been quite so good as the previous ones. He has felt his chest a little more & has been tired. This was brought on by attempting to sketch, which he must not do again. We have almost alternate fine & wet days; the wet ones *very* wet & the fine as charming as you can imagine. I doubt if this great changeability of weather is likely to be good for Arthur. He is out of doors a great deal, & walks far more briskly & for a longer time than he did in the winter & spring.

We were very glad to get your letter of the 18th; thanks for the enclosure to me. I have of course wanted to be at home constantly, but perhaps less than you would imagine, knowing my usual habits of mind. But uncertainty is what is most difficult to bear, and as long as home seemed almost as far off as heaven I could be content away; but it is different now that there is a good prospect, but no certainty, of our going home a month [illegible] In consequence of this the days are just n[illegible]

The [illegible] Charlie, now a month old,

reached us a few days ago. They had lingered at Rome & Trieste & finally lay four days in the Post Office here. . . .

Arthur has the room which I called Mamma's when I sent you the photograph. I have a bed in the salon. We both get up about 6.30. Arthur goes down to the springs at 7, and I follow soon after, leaving Marie, the servant of the house, to do our rooms & set out the breakfast. Arthur & I walk a little in the intervals of his tumblers of water & talk to the few people we know, & pay a visit to the postman's stall for the chance of finding a letter or newspaper for us there. The old man always delivers as many letters as he can at the springs where nearly everyone comes, & no doubt saves himself many a walk by that irregular proceeding. Then I buy a few currants for our breakfast & engage a little flower girl to fetch goat's milk & fresh eggs for us from a sort of farm near. I go home a little before Arthur to see after breakfast. This is never ready, so I dust the room & set it in order, & give Marie a scolding, which after a time takes effect, & the cups & plates appear. Then I heat the water for our tea at our spirit lamp, & get a big basin of cold water in which to give all the breakfast things a final wash & polish before using them, for Marie's ideas on the subject of cleanliness are utterly insufficient. Then comes the child with the milk & hot eggs (cooked to perfection & costing less than ½d. each) & breakfast is ready at last. After breakfast comes letter-writing or reading or anything indoors or in the garden, followed by a walk. Dinner, which we get fairly good at the "Restauration," is a little before two. After that comes a little walking & perhaps a little sketching for me. At five o'clock Arthur goes to the spring for more waters, & I go indoors, & after a while get tea by as lengthy a process as I got breakfast. After tea I remake Arthur's bed and my own & put his room straight for the night; then he goes to bed at about half past eight, & I sit in the garden a little while before going too, or at least going into my room; I can't say I go to bed till a good deal later. We both read the newspapers, & Arthur besides reads a French book he has got, &

I, Gervinus; but I have read very little since we left Catania. . . . My sketch ought to be very pretty but it is very difficult. I shall be glad to take home one view of the country here. The sketching place is very near the house & in a charming situation just at the outskirts of a beautiful wood. Arthur sits by me & watches the birds & all the creeping things while I paint. I hope to persuade him to do little or no painting himself. . . .

RUSSELL SCOTT *to* RUSSELL SCOTT, Junior.

10 CORNWALL TERRACE, *Feb.* 3, 1870.

MY DEAR RUSSELL,—I am much obliged to you for your congratulations on my birthday, contained in the very gratifying letter which I have received this morning. The affection of those who are near to us is *the* great blessing of life, and it always retains its value, which is more than can be said of the greater part of the pleasures & enjoyments to which in early life we are led to attach importance.

I will not pretend to say that I should not like to recover somewhat of my "old activity." I used to like to contrast myself in that respect with other sexagenarians, many of them very much my juniors; but it is said "that pride shall have a fall," & mine has been rather a heavy one. But really I cannot consider myself entitled to credit for bearing with what you call "philosophy" that which seems to me the very mildest ailment I could have. I have often sustained far more discomfort from a bad cold, before I took measures to relieve myself from such visitations, than now falls to my lot; in fact, I think I have scarcely more than enough to remind me how uninterruptedly I have enjoyed health ever since I was eight years old. Real gout might perhaps put me to too severe a test.—Ever, my dear Russell, yours very affectionately, RUSSELL SCOTT.

RUSSELL SCOTT *to* EDWARD I'ANSON.

Probably written in 1870.

MY DEAR SIR,—I hope you will not consider it very intrusive on my part that I should write to you on a matter connected with your approaching marriage, which not unnaturally I think occasions some anxiety in my wife's mind, and in the minds of other relations of your late wife, as to the future of her children.

Although the lady to whom I learn that you are to be married next month is entirely unknown to me, I feel that I can be doing her no injustice in assuming that the change *must* be one which will place your daughters in a situation of great difficulty, unless you should, previously to its taking place, put them in an independent position. This is what I have myself done for my daughters to a considerable extent (and I intend to do so fully before long), because it appeared to me to be right that at the age they had attained they should have means at their disposal considerably beyond mere necessaries; and that the best way of carrying this out was by the transfer of property, the interest of which should provide them with such means. I long ago determined in my own mind that if I should live to be old, I would divest myself of a considerable part of my property in favour of my children, for I never liked the idea of a man's clinging to that which he does not require for himself until it is wrested from him by death.

This of course does not apply to you so strongly as to me, because you are many years younger than I am; but on the other hand your intended marriage seems to supply a very cogent reason why your daughters should be as independent as it is in your power to make them, without imposing upon yourself a very serious sacrifice of your own comfort. In fact it seems to me that they ought to have the means, if either now or at any future time it should be their wish, of maintaining a separate establishment. This is what a much-esteemed friend of mine did for his daughters when he married a second time, although the eldest of them was some years younger than your daughter

Catherine is now; and I must say that it seems to me to be the only way in which a man who marries a second time and who has grown-up daughters, can ensure for them a comfortable home; for I do not think it is too much to say that there are very few women indeed who would succeed in making their husband's grown-up daughters happy in a home so changed. And when the lady has children of her own who are themselves grown up, or nearly so, the difficulty becomes of course greatly increased, and may be almost insurmountable.

I trust you will give this matter your *very* serious consideration. I hope indeed that you will deem it your duty to do so if you have not well pondered it already, out of regard for your late wife's memory, to say nothing of your love for your children, of whom everything I hear (though I scarcely know them), leads me to think that they must be very much what she would have wished them to be.

Let me just add that if your daughters should not wish for a separate establishment now, it cannot but be a matter of satisfaction to them to know that they can have one whenever they may wish it hereafter, and that the more their minds are at ease, the less will be the difficulty which they will find in reconciling themselves to the change which is about to take place, and which cannot I fear but be a painful one to them at best.

Mr. I'Anson took this letter in good part, and made arrangements as far as he could according to my father's suggestion. His daughters in after years frequently expressed their thankfulness for what my father had done. Mr. I'Anson's first wife was Catherine Blakeway, a first cousin of my mother's.

RUSSELL SCOTT *to his Son* CHARLES.

10 CORNWALL TERRACE, REGENT'S PARK, *Oct^r* 25, 1871.

MY DEAR CHARLES,—When this finds its way to your hands a quarter of a century will have elapsed since your appearance in this world. Often have I reproached myself (I believe I did so at the time) for saying what I did when I heard upon that occasion of another boy. I thought & said that I should have preferred a girl. But we know little what is to be desired, and I certainly do not think it probable that a daughter would have been more loveable than you have been—while, in the existing state of the world, I could hardly venture to hope that a daughter of mine should have an opportunity of being as useful in it as I trust you may be. May life and health be spared to you, my dear Charles, long after the time when I cease to be numbered among the living—but, if it be God's good pleasure, it will be no small blessing to be your contemporary for a few years longer.—Ever, my dear Charles, your affectionate father,

RUSSELL SCOTT.

RUSSELL SCOTT *to his Son* CHARLES.

10 CORNWALL TERRACE, 21st *Oct.* 1872.

MY DEAR CHARLES,—I beg to tender my especial thanks for your letter from Blackpool. I will not say that it amounted to a complete set-off against the vexation which has recently fallen to my lot—but it was at least an ample, and more than ample, compensation for Mr. ——'s shortcomings. . . .

It is no small satisfaction to me, my dear Charles, that you should be able to express yourself as you do with respect to the "intangible" benefits you have derived from me, and that I am able, with your mother's assistance, to persuade myself that those benefits are not entirely imaginary. To believe that I have in any degree contributed to make you what you are, and that I shall have contributed something towards your becoming what I think you will be, would indeed have been a reward for almost any amount of toil and sacrifice. Yet there is nothing that I have consciously done that has not been a pleasure in itself.

I do not think you need fear for me anything like weariness. I have never found so much time for reading as I have wished, and have always intended, whenever I might have sufficient

leisure, to teach myself algebra, which I have always regretted not having learned (except the very beginning) when young. It strikes me that I ought not to find it difficult. So that you see I have a satisfactory occupation in reserve in case of need. . . .

RUSSELL SCOTT *to his Son* CHARLES.

10 CORNWALL TERRACE, *Nov^r* 26, 1872.

MY DEAR CHARLIE,—There were two things which occurred to me soon after you left which I wished to mention to you—after a brief sojourn they both vanished from my memory—the consequence was a very persistent and long continued rummage of my brains, and the result, I am glad to say, the discovery of one of the two lost topics in some recess or other—if the brain has recesses. At all events it has come within my grasp, and I will proceed to give you the benefit of it. The other has hopelessly disappeared, but I doubt if I should value it much if I could remember it ever so well.

You were saying that electoral districts, by which of course is meant the assigning of representatives in as nearly as possible exact proportions to the population, might not be very objectionable if minorities could be properly represented,—to which I replied in a way that might lead you to think that I entertained the idea that such a system would be an improvement upon any plan that has hitherto been adopted or devised. But, as Toqueville not infrequently says in his notes upon Senior's reports of their conversations, *celà va plus loin que ma pensée.* I should prefer that our representative machinery should be let alone for another generation, but unfortunately it seems to be certain (at least everybody seems to agree that it is so, which alone is enough to make it so) that this is impossible. And it was because, in my own mind, I assumed that impossibility, that I so warmly welcomed your idea. If minorities could be represented in proportion to their numbers the [illegible] of Commons would, I think, always be an assembly, a [illegible] [illegible]ich men having the desire and the ability to be use[illegible] [illegible]ntry might [illegible]xpected to be willing to occupy. For though Odger & Potter & Bradlaugh would all be sure to be there, with not a few of their followers, the better class of members would not be without influence in the House, and they would gain access to it with far less temptation to forfeit their own self-respect than they now can; and though really good men might not be in a majority on a majority of questions, they would probably be strong enough to prevent much mischief, since they would be likely to form an important phalanx, which would be reinforced when any unusually extravagant or unjust measure were proposed by defections from the side generally opposed to them. . . . Did I speak to you about reading Senior's letters from & conversations with Toqueville? They were both such sound and sensible men, and so little influenced by the spirit of party, that every one interested in the politics, whether of the past, present, or future, ought to read them.—Ever, dear Charles, your affectionate father,

RUSSELL SCOTT.

Addressed: "Guardian Office, Manchester."

RUSSELL SCOTT *to his Son* CHARLES.

10 CORNWALL TERRACE, 30th Decr 1872.

MY DEAR CHARLES,—I have been purposing to write to you ever since you left, chiefly because I did not find an opportunity of making myself fully understood as to your money matters. I have no objection to your retrenching a little, if there be room for it, which I can quite imagine that there may be, but I strongly object to any retrenchment which may, however indirectly or remotely, affect your health—as for instance not taking a cab when you may have reason to think that you may be tired by walking, or economising in diet when your appetite may not be good, or in any of the ways which I might be able perhaps to enumerate, were it not that having always felt myself strong I have never thought of such matters.

I was very glad to hear of your party, not only because I am pleased that you should enjoy yourself but because I have no doubt that mental recreation is physically good for you.

With respect to that £100 which you had of me I do not know that there is any reason why you should not refund it, if at the end of 13 months you should be in tolerably affluent circumstances. In the meantime you may consider it carried to a suspense account, and I would much rather carry it at once to the debit of "Private Expenses" than that you should not consider yourself, as I hope you do, perfectly at liberty to expend the whole of your income of 1873 during that year, and to come to me for a little more in case of need.

I was very much pleased with your article on Mr. Gladstone —none the less so because it embodied my own views as to him & his speech—although I certainly should not have succeeded, if I had made such an attempt, in expressing them so well. I suppose you are right as to his having been once intended for the Church. I do not remember having heard of it, notwithstanding the great interest he always took in Church matters. What I do remember hearing said of him very soon after he entered Parliament as M.P. for Newark in 1832, was that Gladstone was a young man whose abilities would be likely to lead to his attaining a very prominent position, if it had not been for his extremely High Church views.

We are going to Bath by the 9.15 train to-morrow morning, to be present at Mary's [Scott's] wedding, where it seems I am to play the part of *father*. It had not occurred to me until a day or two ago that this was an obligation likely to devolve on me. Russell is also to be present, as you may probably have heard. He tried to avoid it, but Mary would evidently have been very much disappointed. I hope she will be happy. If her husband should be as kind to her as Dizzy appears to have been to a woman 15 years his senior, whom he married under somewhat similar circumstances, except that, from what I have heard, Lady Beaconsfield can hardly have been so suitable a wife for him as I think Mary is likely to be for her intended husband, there seems to me no reason why she should not be happy. Indeed

I believe she would be grateful for even a moderate amount of kindness.

We shall be very glad to have you at our party on the 7th. About 90 have accepted, but there is unfortunately a short supply of gentlemen, although I understand about equal numbers of them and of ladies were invited.—Ever, dear Charlie, your affectionate father,

RUSSELL SCOTT.

Letters between my father and brother became less frequent after Charles left Oxford, but my father took the greatest interest in all that my brother wrote as a journalist, and in the steady advance in influence and public usefulness which the *Manchester Guardian* made under his editorship. Charles was married in the spring of 1874 to Rachel Susan Cook, daughter of the late Dr. John Cook of St. Andrews. She had been a student of Girton College, when that college was at Hitchin, before its removal to Girton, and was one of the first half-dozen students who entered on the foundation of the college, and is named in the college song which celebrates the fame of "Woodhead, Cook and Lumsden, the Girton Pioneers." She took a second class in Honours in the Classical Tripos of 1872. That remained the highest distinction obtained by a woman student for a good many years. At that time Latin was not taught in girls' schools, and Rachel knew nothing of Latin and Greek till within a few months of going to college.

CHAPTER XXII

LAST YEARS OF RUSSELL SCOTT AND OF HIS WIFE

1875–1894

MY father's age and failing health had made my mother anxious that he should have the greater quiet of a country home, and she was happy in being able to rent the Manor House, an old and delightful house, about a mile from the sea, at Old Eastbourne. We removed there in April 1875. Here my dear brother Arthur died. The lungs had healed, but an affection of the brain gradually showed itself, which caused much suffering in the last months of his life, and put an end to it at the age of thirty-three—on January 10, 1876.

In stability and uprightness of character he resembled his father, as well as in his affectionate and generous disposition. In illness he was perfectly uncomplaining and very thoughtful for others. As long as his mother was near him he asked for nothing more, and his last months were spent with her.

At Eastbourne my father spent the last five years of his life. He greatly enjoyed the beautiful garden, in which he passed much of his time. Many friends and relations came to stay with him. My uncle Joseph and his wife came as often as they could, and children and grandchildren were about him. I remember his saying to my aunt Kate, "Is not this a pleasant place, Kate, in which to spend one's closing years?"

To my aunt Kate he was much attached, and indeed to the whole of my mother's family he took the place of an elder brother.

My mother never left him at this time for more than a day. During all their married life her companionship had been essential to his happiness, and it was indeed well for him that he was able to have it to the end.

My father was greatly interested in the last year of his life in my brother Lawrence's settlement (November 1, 1879) as a minister at Denton, near Manchester.

Having decided to train himself as a minister, Lawrence gave up his farm at Ruddington in the year 1875, and studied in Manchester College, London, under Dr. Martineau. The college had not then been removed to Oxford. It was a special satisfaction to my father that one of his sons should be a minister.

RUSSELL SCOTT *to his Son* CHARLES.

THE MANOR HOUSE, EASTBOURNE, 9th *Oct.* 1875.

MY DEAR CHARLES,—You judged rightly that I should be likely to take an interest in your article of Thursday. The subject of it is one which always interests me, and on which I hold rather far-going views, likely enough to be deemed very absurd by many people. I believe it will prove perfectly practicable—whether in one, two, or more generations I will not say—to extirpate professional crime. I mean that the time will come when there will no longer be a class of persons living without work, and supporting themselves by the plunder

of the community, unless that word be taken in a very wide sense, so as to include frauds of various kinds. I remember mentioning the idea to Matthew Davenport Hill, when he called at Kingswood one day in the year 1853, and I understood him to acquiesce in the probability of its being realised, as did Sir Walter Crofton, when I spoke of it to him much more recently—and he remarked that it was what he and others were aiming at. Perhaps you would say that, however great may be the reduction in the number of criminals, it is too much to expect entirely to get rid of even professional thieves, but I believe that whenever the number shall be brought very low, the total extinction of professional crime will be close at hand, for these people seem to require, even more than others, associates like themselves, and it is not surprising that it should be so considering that they know themselves to be held in abhorrence by the community at large. I daresay you have heard me speak of what I learned at Kingswood of the pains which the young thieves take to induce other boys to follow their own evil example. . . .

RUSSELL SCOTT *to his Son* CHARLES.

THE MANOR HOUSE, EASTBOURNE, *Oct.* 11, 1879.

MY DEAR CHARLES,— . . . I agree with you that there is much to be said in favour of the patriarchal system. It would be more pleasant no doubt for a man who is incapacitated from habilitating himself to be able to rely on his sons than to depend on a serving man. But I daresay you will agree with me that it is best upon the whole that the sons should quit the l roof, and have roofs of their own. If they did not, I afraid the world would soon have to accommodate a patriarchal rate of income and expenditure.

But we must n sons are missing, their sisters are often at h can render much valuable aid to o as I am at present. There is your youngest for instance who when with us, bandaged my feet, according to Mr. Sass, very much as an experienced hospital surgeon would have done. And since she has been gone, Katie has I believe done it nearly, if not quite as well (you do not seem to be aware that she has been here for a considerable time, and indeed appear to be altogether uninformed as to the personel of our present household). She leaves us, I am sorry to say, on Thursday. Isabella is to leave Jessie and return to us on Tuesday. From each and all of them, and I hope one will always be here, I can rely for an immense number of services, which, if some of them are small, are all important, and in the aggregate most valuable to me, and all the more so because I flatter myself that they are rendered, as well as received with pleasure.

As to my "serving-man" I cannot say that he displays much brilliancy, and he is rather wanting in promptitude. I got a heavy fall the other morning in getting out of my bath, which I think he might have prevented, but it seems that I cried out lustily when I found myself falling, and by that means scattered his wits. Fortunately I was not in the least hurt. He is however decidedly zealous, and I often observe that zeal supplies the place of ability to a great extent.

I am glad you are able to give so good an account of Rachel and her youngest. We shall be very glad when you and she, and the three little ones, are able to come and see us.

I should like to say a little more, for there was much in your letter provocative of a reply, but I can tell you this is a very long letter already, as measured by the time it has occupied me.

I am rather puzzled to make out how it is that I am able to write at all, considering the difficulty I have in what seems the easy task of putting my bread and butter in my mouth, and I find that either time or goutiness or both have decidedly checked the flow of my thou [illegible]ts, so as to make letter-writing [illegible] longer process [illegible]dependently of mechanical difficulties.

Give my lo[illegible] Rachel. . . .

The following is probably the last letter that my father wrote. It is an answer to one from my brother Charles received on his birthday, February 3.

RUSSELL SCOTT *to his Son* CHARLES.

THE MANOR HOUSE, *Feb.* 5, 1880.

MY DEAR CHARLES,—I have discontinued writing my own letters since about Christmas until yesterday, when I wrote a few lines to your aunt Kate—and to-day I must do so again.

Many thanks for your most kind and affectionate letter. It is clear to me that you have formed an exaggerated view of your indebtedness to me—intellectually you can owe me very little. . . . I remember that, when you were under four years old, you asked your mother whether God could make something out of nothing, illustrating the question by another, "Can God catch hold of nothing and make it into something?"—a problem which, as Mr. John James Tayler remarked when I told him you had propounded it, has exercised the greatest minds. I am always thankful that you should be what you are, and it seems to me that I can have had but a small share in the result.

You see I am little fitted for letter-writing, and I will not add more.

Give my love to Rachel, and remember that I am always (what it would be bad indeed if I were not) your very affectionate father, RUSSELL SCOTT.

A few weeks' illness, with little or no pain, preceded my father's death, which took place on April 18, 1880.

Once when I had been reading to my mother a description by Carlyle of his father's character, and remarked that in some respects the elder Carlyle reminded me of my father—"Yes," she answered, "you

see they had both the same simplicity and strength, great veracity and strong natural religiousness of mind; and both had great tenderness and depth of affection." I made a note of her words at the time.

My mother remained at the Manor House till October 1880.

When the following letter was written my uncle was Professor of Geology at Oxford.

JOSEPH PRESTWICH *to his Sister*, MRS. R. SCOTT.

SHOREHAM, 24th *Aug.* [1880].

DEAREST ISABELLA,—We returned here on Saturday night last after a very pleasant and successful trip to the Channel Islands and Normandy. Here we intended to remain till the October term, but having obtained in the Channel Islands the evidence I required respecting my diluvial theory we are going to Swansea to bring it before the British Association, of which my old friend Ramsay is President this year.

I think I am now in a position to show that the south of England, France, and probably the greater part of Europe have been submerged during the early human period, and that palœolithic man was thereby destroyed (in great part). It revives in a curious way the tradition of the Noachian deluge. I have long had cause to suspect this, but hesitated even to mention so unexpected a result until I was sure of the facts I obtained in the Channel Islands. After my return from Swansea I may possibly go to the meeting of the Geological Society of France at Boulogne.

There is one thing I regret in all this, which is it postpones the arrival of the many visitors we looked forward to in August and September. I suppose Russell & Jessie are back. Where are they now? Are they all well & you too? I shall look forward to seeing you and them about the middle of Sepr.

I the more hope this as I fear we shall hardly be able to visit Eastbourne. Grace sends her best love to all, & I am, Dearest Isabella, your affect[e] brother,

JOSEPH PRESTWICH.

Where is Kate now? We have had no family news for weeks. The main paper itself I reserve for the Royal Society in Nov. or Dec. as soon as I can get it ready.

Of our dear mother we ought to be able to say a good deal, but my sister and I find it most difficult to do so. Fortunately many of her grandchildren, for whom (and their descendants) this account is written, knew her well, though only in old age. Until my father's death her life was absorbed in that of her family. Certainly in her were combined excellences that are rarely united. An unusually quick and clear intelligence and great decision of character were united with a deference towards others, a willingness that they should carry out their own plans and live their own lives, which made all about her feel free and happy. The sweetness of her temper was unfailing, her affections were deep and strong, though they were rarely expressed in words, and in her unworldliness she was like my father. It is a happiness to think that she had joy in all her children. She had very great readiness of mind and a retentive memory, which made her a very interesting companion, though she was never a great talker. My father used to say that he never went to her in vain for information; but he often complained of her silence. My sister remembers Dr. Clarke (afterwards Sir Andrew Clarke), the well-known physician, saying to her, "Your mother is a wonderful woman — a *wonderful* woman."

She took great interest in all that my father did for the public good, and carried out many kind plans of her own. For twenty-one years she maintained and managed a little holiday house at Woodford Bridge for the benefit of the people attached to the London Domestic Mission, and when this house was given up on her removal to Eastbourne, she took cottages there (in Warrior Square) to which the missionaries could come down, or send any of their people, keeping them ready for their use at all times.

After my father's death she was able to do more. My brother Lawrence being settled as minister at Denton, Lancashire, she removed to his neighbourhood, staying for three years at Norcliffe Hall, Styal, and for eleven years (until her death) at Broomfield, South Reddish. These years were mainly occupied in building and managing (with my brother's help) the beautiful "Russell Scott Memorial Schools" at Denton, and (towards the end of her life) the "Lads' Club" near it.[1] I was with her during those years, and of course many other members of the family came frequently to stay with us. She taught regularly in the Sunday School attached to the Wilton Street Chapel, of which my brother Lawrence was the minister, and entered fully into the congregational life of his people, who regarded her with the greatest affection and admiration.

My sister Sarah was married in 1885 to Mr. H. E. O'Neill, a son of the Rev. James O'Neill, Vicar of

[1] The People's Hall was built by my brother Lawrence.

Luton. Mr. O'Neill had spent several years on the East African coast as a lieutenant in the Navy, engaged in the suppression of the slave-trade, and was subsequently appointed to the Consulate of Mozambique, where the same work was continued. While there he did a large amount of geographical work on the coast and in the interior of East Africa, and he was the first European to pass through and lay open the Makua and Lomwe countries lying between Mozambique and the Nyassa. In 1885 he received in recognition of the value of his work the gold medal of the Royal Geographical Society.

Four years later my brother Lawrence was married. Both these marriages gave my mother much happiness. My brother was married by Dr. Martineau in Rosslyn Hill Chapel, Hampstead, to Mary, daughter of Mr. James Banks, of Cork. I may insert here the kind little note which Dr. Martineau wrote to him on this occasion:—

35 GORDON SQUARE, LONDON, W.C., *Nov.* 21, 1888.

MY DEAR LAWRENCE,—I have so long shrunk into my shell of retirement, that I am hardly fit to come into the light of day on an occasion of such memorable interest as your marriage to Miss Banks. But few things can be more welcome to my heart than to be associated in any way with the happiness of your life. And if, on your wedding day, you will both be content to accept so feeble a presence and blessing as mine, they shall answer to your call, so far as it is right for me to register a promise across the boundary of another year. I need hardly say that I have no pre-engagements which can interefere with your choice of time; and I shall render my new Diary auspicious and bright by a first red-letter entry for Tuesday, Jany 29th.

Minor particulars of time and place you will report to me in due course.—Believe me, ever, your affectionate old friend,

James Martineau.

Rev. Lawrence Scott.

Dr. Martineau was at this time in his eighty-fourth year. He lived to be nearly ninety-five.

My mother's health throughout life was very good, but so early as 1875 she had threatenings of paralysis, and in later life she had slight seizures which disabled her from much walking, though they did not affect her speech or mind. In her old age she spent much of her time out of doors, sitting in her bath-chair in the garden at Broomfield, summer and winter, while novels were read to her often for many hours in the day. At this time she was nearly blind, having cataract in both eyes, but she never even spoke of this as a privation. The end came on August 23, 1894. She was buried in the same grave as my father and my brother Arthur in the St. Marylebone Cemetery at East Finchley. In her coffin her head rested (according to her own desire) on the pillow on which had lain my sister Sophia's head in her last hours. During the forty years that had passed since the death of this beloved child this had been one of my mother's pillows in use every night.

From amongst all the letters I received when my mother died I insert but two—one from a member of my brother Lawrence's congregation at Denton, and one from my uncle, which shows in part what the life-long affection was between him and his sister.

212 ASHTON ROAD, DENTON, *Sep.* 24, 1894.

DEAR MISS SCOTT,—I would like to thank you for the Beautiful Photo of your Dear Mother, which I shall keep as long as I live. I can never look on that Dear face without feeling that we have indeed lost a sincere Friend. I can never forget the many kindnesses that your Dear Mother and yourself have done to my Family and myself in the past. I am sure we feel very much for you in your great Loss of such a Mother. There is one consolation when we lose our dear ones—it is that we shall meet them in Heaven.

Dear Miss Scott, I often think of the morning that your Dear sister was married at our chapel. Your Mother came to me & shook hands and kissed me. That and many other little kindnesses I shall never forget.—I now remain, yours respectfully,

MRS. LETITIA WOODALL.

JOSEPH PRESTWICH *to his Niece* ISABELLA.

SHOREHAM, *Aug.* 23, 1894.

DEAREST ISABEL,—How deeply I sympathise with you all on your great and irreparable bereavement, and how deeply I share your sorrow I need not say. My life-long companion, helper and adviser in all early troubles, is now no more. But what a beautiful life it has been—what good it has effected and what an example it has set! It has descended as a blessed inheritance. Our thoughts for days past have been with you hourly, and how I regret I could not have been with you personally. I share lovingly with you all in your great affliction, and I am, ever your affectionate Uncle, JOSEPH PRESTWICH.

The portrait of my mother, by G. F. Watts, reproduced as the frontispiece of this book, was painted in 1874. Fine as it is as a painting, it does not fully express her character. It suggests more stateliness and far less sweetness than were hers. The photograph given here is an admirable likeness, as is also that of my father. The paper held in his hand is the *Economist*, a newspaper to which he was specially partial. These photographs were taken when my father and mother were at the ages of 73 and 67 respectively. A portrait of my father was painted by W. W. Ouless in 1875, but is not a satisfactory likeness.

CHAPTER XXIII

THE PRESTWICH FAMILY

A FEW pages must be given to records of my mother's family, but fortunately the "Life" of my uncle, Sir Joseph Prestwich, written by his widow, makes it unnecessary to say much. An interesting pedigree, too long to insert here, of the Prestwiches of Hulme, near Manchester, is to be seen in Part XXII. of the History of the County Palatine and Duchy of Lancaster, by Edward Baines, a new, revised, and enlarged edition, edited by James Croston, F.S.A., and published by John Heywood, Deansgate, Manchester, in 1888. This pedigree gives names and dates from the time of Ralph de Prestwych, who was living in 1434, and many particulars of the families into which the Prestwiches married, to which is added information as to the lands they owned.

Sir John Prestwich, whom Croston mentions as the author of "Respublica" and other works, was first cousin once removed to my grandfather, to whom he left his papers. He was an archæologist. It was he who furnished the design for the Great Seal of the United States. The War of Independence was going on at the time. Congress had for six years tried in vain to obtain a satisfactory design, and John Adams, then in London, knowing Sir John Prestwich as an antiquarian and a warm friend of America, sent the design he suggested to Washington. It was accepted by Congress, and remains in use to the present day.

Sir John Prestwich was much interested in his family

history. In a manuscript in his handwriting now at Darent Hulme, Shoreham, he says that the "family of Prestwich of Prestwich and Holme were in the times of the Saxons and after Thanes and Lords of Prestwich, Lords of the Manor of Hulme, Manchester, and great benefactors to the Collegiate Church of Manchester, and to divers others in this kingdom, particularly in the counties of Devon, Sussex, Leicestershire, Cheshire, Yorkshire, Northumberland, Lancashire, &c. &c., and also in Airshire, in the Kingdom of North Britain, now called Scotland." Sussex shows one memorial of the family in the fine brass of William Prestwyk, Dean of Battle, A.D. 1436, still to be seen in the Church at Warbleton in that county.

Croston gives a drawing of Hulme Hall, near Manchester, the seat of the family, which was in the possession of Ralph de Prestwych in 1439. He relates that in the reign of Elizabeth, the Queen wrote a letter to Edmund Prestwych, Esq., calling upon him to contribute £50 by voluntary contribution to the necessities of the State. His grandson Thomas was for his services to Charles I. created a baronet, April 25, 1644. In consequence of his losses in the royalist cause, he had to mortgage his manor of Hulme in 1654, and sell it in 1660.[1] The Dowager Lady Prestwich encouraged her son to continue faithful to the royal cause, under an assurance that she had hidden treasure with which to supply his wants. The depository of this wealth was supposed to be about Hulme Hall, but the old lady being taken speechless before her death, which happened suddenly, the secret was never discovered.

[1] See last page of Appendix for further particulars.

In recognition of his services, Charles I. gave a small gold medal to Sir Thomas, which is now at Darent Hulme. Sir Thomas died in 1689, leaving no male descendant, his only son (Thomas) having died before him. A cousin, Thomas Prestwich of Hulme, had a son Elias who held the title, whether legitimately or otherwise, and it descended, according to Croston, in his line.

In the Appendix will be found a portion of the pedigree given by Croston, to which I have added particulars as to the immediate ancestors of my mother, which are not given by him. This I am able to do in consequence of a clear statement of the facts having been left in the shape of an affidavit made by Catherine Prestwich in 1808. This Catherine was my mother's great-aunt on her father's side. Her affidavit is preserved at Darent Hulme, Shoreham, and runs as follows:—

COUNTY OF THE CITTY OF DUBLIN.

Affidavit of Catherine Prestwich of the s^{d} Citty, Spinster who came before me this day, One of His Majesty^{s} Justice^{s} of the Peace for s^{d} Citty and maketh Oath on the Holy Evangelist That she is a sister of the late Elias Prestwich of Broseley in the County of Shropshire, England, deceased—and that the said Elias Prestwich was the True and Lawful Son of Joseph and Hannah Prestwich and that the said Joseph Prestwich was the elder and only brother of the afs^{d} Elias Prestwich late of the said Citty of Dublin, Baronet.

Sworn before me this 11th day of August 1808. (SEAL.)

her
CATHERINE X PRESTWICH.
mark

WILLIAM STAMER
Alderman.

The word "aforesaid" in the above is clearly a clerk's error, and should been omitted.

It will be noticed that Catherine's grandfather, Sir Richard Prestwich, was a baronet, and that her father, who it is believed settled in England, did not continue the use of the title, although the eldest son, but left it to be used by his younger brother, who remained in Ireland in "the Citty of Dublin." Nothing is known as to his reason for doing this. This affidavit was probably procured at the instance of my grandfather, who sometimes had thoughts of resuming the title, and who might need his aunt's testimony to prove his right to it.

There is a tradition that Sir Richard Prestwich impoverished his family through neglect of his affairs in geological pursuits. This may well have been so, for he was living after the time of the Restoration, an age which, according to the historian J. R. Green, was "distinguished by the wonderful activity of its directly scientific thought"—when "the pursuit of physical science became a passion."

Catherine's father appears to have settled in Broseley. A cousin, who in early days visited the family there, in writing to my uncle Joseph, mentions in a letter that still exists, that she understood that his grandfather (Elias) inherited the business at Broseley from *his* father.

Catherine's brother Elias, my mother's grandfather, was married at St. Margaret's, Westminster, to Isabella Civil Wilde, of Newbury. The following is copied from the register of St. Margaret's:—

Ely Prestidge of this pa Batchelor and Isabella Wilde of this parish Spinster were ried in this Church by Banns this seventeenth day of April in the year One Thousand Seven Hundred and Seventy-three

By me, J. MORE, *Curate*.

This marriage was solemnized between us { ELY PRESTIDGE. ISABELLA WILD.

In the presence of FRANCIS GAY.
JOS. FFOX.

It is clear that at that time our great grandfather was not particular as to the spelling of his name. My mother said that her grandmother, Isabella Civil Wilde, was lady-in-waiting to some lady of title before her marriage. Hence, no doubt, it is that she too is said to be "of this parish." Portraits of both are at Darent Hulme, Shoreham.

Their married life was entirely spent, as far as we know, in Broseley, Shropshire, where Elias carried on the business of a wine merchant. It was in Broseley that both Elias and his wife died, leaving an only son (and only child), my grandfather, Joseph Prestwich, and in Broseley that son married,[1] not long after his parents' death. He and his wife must have visited Malvern on their wedding journey, as the tradition remains that on that occasion they ran, hand in hand, all along the top of the Malvern hills. Of some of their various homes in London mention is made in Sir Joseph Prestwich's "Life." It was from No. 8 The Lawn, South Lambeth, that both my mother and my aunt Kate were married at St. Mary's, the Parish Church of Lambeth. This house was occupied later by Mr. Fawcett, the blind Postmaster-General, and after his death it and the seven adjoining houses were pulled down, and the lawn in

[1] See Appendix, Table VI.

front and gardens behind were purchased by public subscription, and devoted to the public use in memory of Mr. Fawcett. Vauxhall Park is now its name.

Just before this happened, my mother, my uncle Joseph, and I visited the old house—a very interesting visit, although the whole neighbourhood was so changed that it could scarcely be recognised. The house itself was unchanged. The rivulet, the "Effra," used to run at the foot of The Lawn, and in those days was called the "Creek." It has long since been covered in. In the United States and Canada and in Australia the name "creek" is still given to a small river.

Of my uncle Joseph and his wife I need not say much, as his "Life" has been fully told; but I may mention here what my aunt could not say in her narrative, that she was a perfect wife for him and the kindest of friends to his relations. They will never forget the delightful welcome that each and all received at Darent Hulme when they went there.

Aunt Grace was a niece of the palæontologist, Dr. Hugh Falconer, whom she assisted in his investigations, and she was thoroughly able to enter into her husband's pursuits. Practically all his MSS., after his marriage, were penned by her. It was said at the time that she wrote out my uncle's book, "Geology, Chemical, Physical, and Stratigraphical," three times. She contributed many articles to periodicals, and wrote two novels of Scottish life—"The Harbour Bar" in 1875 and "Enga" in 1880.

My uncle was knighted in January 1896 in recognition of the value of his work as a geologist. He was in declining health at the time, and died in the same year. His wife survived him three years, and just lived to see the publication of her memoir of him. At her death the house which my uncle built at Shoreham in Kent, and which he and his wife occupied to the end, passed to my brother Russell. A memorial window has been put by Messrs. Morris & Co. in the church at Shoreham from designs by Burne-Jones in their possession, my uncle having left money for this purpose by his will. A good portrait of him is in the Geological Museum in Jermyn Street.

My aunt Eliza survives, the last member of the elder branch of the Prestwiches. There is a younger branch which is still numerous, but the degree of relationship is not known and must be very distant.

My aunt Emily died in Paris in 1904, in the Community in which she had spent the greater part of her life.

Only two of my grandfather's children left descendants—my mother and her sister Kate, (Mrs. Thurburn), three of whose children married and are still living. Their names will be found in the pedigree of the Prestwich family, given in the Appendix.

My aunt Eliza (Mrs. Tomkins) has no children, but has had all a mother's interest in her step-children and their descendants. To the whole family she has been invaluable. Through many troubles she has been their great support, and now in old age she is surrounded by those who love her. Her husband died many years ago.

CHAPTER XXIV

Mrs. C. P. SCOTT—LAURENCE PRESTWICH SCOTT—RUSSELL SCOTT

My sister Catherine and I had not intended to carry on this history beyond the date of our mother's death. From that time forward, for a good many years, there was no further break in our family circle, and we did not mean to write of any who were then living. Before the book was ready for the press however the death took place of three other members of the family—my brother Charles's wife, his eldest son, and my brother Russell.

In all three cases some notice of their lives appeared in newspapers, and considerable extracts from these notices may be given here.

From the *Manchester Guardian* of November 29th, 1905, I take the following :—

"We record with deep regret the death of Mrs. C. P. Scott. It took place peacefully at her home, The Firs, Fallowfield, on Monday evening [November 27th].

"Mrs. Scott, whose maiden name was Rachel Susan Cook, was a daughter of a family active for many generations in the service of the University of St. Andrews and the Church of Scotland. Her father, the Rev. John Cook, D.D., was Professor of Ecclesiastical History in the University, and had been Moderator of the Church; one of her grandfathers had held the Chair of Biblical Criticism; a great-grandfather, the Very Rev. Principal

Hill, had written on divinity with distinction, and had held the headship of St. Mary's College in the University. The youngest of five daughters, Mrs. Scott was born in 1848, passed her whole girlhood in the beautiful city, half fishing village and half university town, that was once the eye of mediæval Scotland, and that still inspires in those who best know it a kind of chiding love for its grey stones and mist-laden sea winds. She went to school at the ancient Madras College; then she received some private tuition, and in 1869, when the College for Women that was afterwards to grow into Girton was opened at Hitchin, in Hertfordshire, she was one of its seven original students. In 1872 she took the Cambridge Classical Tripos, being the first woman who had ever attempted honours in it, and she was placed in the second class. For one who was but a beginner in classics on entering the College, and who had to contend with all the difficulties that then confronted women students, the achievement was considerable, and it was long before it was surpassed; but it gave no measure of the personal impression that Miss Rachel Cook at that time made upon her contemporaries at Hitchin. George Eliot said of her that she was the most beautiful woman she had ever seen, and there still remains in the minds of those who knew her then a memorable picture of her uncommonness, her dramatic instinct and critical quickness, and her eagerness and radiance of mind. On leaving the College—on whose governing body she served for some years after its removal to Cambridge—Miss Cook had some thoughts of the stage as a profession. But in 1874, when she became the wife of Mr. C. P. Scott, the idea was abandoned. She came to live in Manchester, and thenceforward gave all of her powers that she could to the service of this city.

"Soon after coming to Manchester Mrs. Scott joined the Committee of the Girls' High School. Of this she remained a member for many years, and one of the last times she spoke in public was at the Free-trade Hall gathering of the school and its friends on July 26, 1900. But what was perhaps her chief work was done for the university education of women. In April 1877, when the Owens College had refused to admit women to its classes, Mrs. Scott brought together a number of friends of women's education, among them some of the professors of the Owens College, and initiated the scheme for the giving of university teaching, or its equivalent, to women at a house in Brunswick Street. As honorary secretary to the Committee of the new College she laboured unwearyingly to secure its success and prepare the way for its incorporation in the Owens College; and in 1883 the new institution was taken over by the old, at first for five years on probation, and then permanently. In 1890 Mrs. Scott was appointed a member of the Manchester School Board, to fill the vacancy caused by the death of Miss Becker. At the School Board election in November 1891 she headed the poll, and in 1894 she was again re-elected to the Board. In January 1896 she resigned. 'During the five years of her work on the Board,' writes one who was throughout that time her colleague in its work, 'Mrs. Scott was one of its most active and influential members, and her interest in all its details was unflagging. Education, she always said, was not a luxury, but one of the first necessities of civilised life, and she protested against the notion that the provision of it should be left to chance, or that its quality should be left to the decision of contending factions.' It is remembered that she was chiefly instrumental in the first appointment of a woman as a School Board officer, and that before free education was secured, or partly secured, she was its warm advocate. Mrs. Scott was also one of the founders of the Withington Girls' School, and she followed closely the fortunes of the Ladybarn House School, in which the successful co-education of boys and girls deeply interested her.

"In politics Mrs. Scott was a keen Liberal, though a strong critical faculty always kept her from mere unexamining acceptance of party programmes. In 1900 she was elected president of the Lancashire and Cheshire Union of Women's Liberal Associations in succession to Mrs. Jacob Bright. She retained the office until failure of health compelled her retirement in

1903, and it was largely through her tact and judgment that the obstacles to the amalgamation of the Liverpool Federal Council with the Union were overcome. She had the true actor's gift of speech; her voice had a clear resonance that filled the Free-trade Hall without perceptible effort; she spoke fluently, but with nothing of the formlessness and diluteness common in easy speakers; her own critical sense would have been impatient of anything like facile verbiage, and in all her relations with others she had an innate respect and sympathy with their intelligence which rendered it impossible for her to give them anything but the best of which her clear intellect and true sense of form were capable. Some of her speeches at School Board election meetings were models of what can only be called intellectual virility—that is, of strict logical connection, verbal directness and spareness, and aptness and economy of illustration. At her husband's elections both in North-east Manchester and in the Leigh division of Lancashire she was an unfailing and invaluable helper. In speaking, as in everything, she was wholly fearless and honest, never hesitated to forego a party cheer by making a concession required by fairness to an opponent, and would speak at her very best at meetings where violent opposition was offered or threatened, as at Mr. Cronwright-Schreiner's meeting in Manchester during the South African War, and at the famous meeting held in the Queen's Hall in London with a mob rioting at its doors.

"In 1885 Mrs. Scott published anonymously a translation of the *Agricola* of Tacitus, which competent judges praised warmly. Some years later she contributed a translation of the *Lettres de Deux Jeunes Mariées* and *Une Fille d'Eve* to Professor Saintsbury's edition of Balzac in English. In 1887 she published, also anonymously, a brief guide to the pictures in the Manchester Jubilee Exhibition of that year. She was also, until the last few years, a very frequent contributor of critical and other articles to the *Manchester Guardian*. But her published writings, and even her speeches and public addresses, give only a blurred impression of her glowing animation and vigour of mind and of her intense affection and sympathy, not for her personal friends alone, but for humanity and all great human interests."

Laurence Prestwich Scott survived his mother two and a half years, dying on May 16, 1908, of consumption, at a sanatorium in Aberdeenshire. He was thirty years old.

The following memorial notice appeared in the *Manchester Guardian* :—

"We deeply regret to record the death, at Banchory, near Aberdeen, of Mr. Laurence Prestwich Scott, a member for the last seven years of the staff of this journal.

"Mr. Scott was the eldest son of Mr. C. P. Scott, and was born at Kersal in 1877. For some years of childhood he went to the co-educational school founded by the late Mr. W. H. Herford at Ladybarn House, and then carried on by his daughter, and this early training counted for much in the boy's later growth. He went on to Rugby, and thence to Corpus Christi College, Oxford, of which he was an Exhibitioner. Taking his degree in 1900, with a First in Classical 'Greats,' he then went to Paris to work at the Ecole des Sciences Politiques. There, also, he formed a keen interest in the drama and in the history and criticism of painting, which was deepened during a period of some months passed in Italy between the close of his stay in Paris and the beginning of his professional work. Towards the end of 1901 he joined the staff of the *Manchester Guardian*, on which his work, so far as it consisted in writing, was chiefly critical. Until his disablement by illness at the beginning of last year, almost everything written in our columns on painting and sculpture—apart from London exhibitions—was by him. To this and to all his literary work he brought, from the first, a fastidious scholarship, humour, and a delicate exactitude of statement. . . . At the time of his death he had won the full command of a literary method wholly individual and of rare sincerity and distinction, and a career of high achievement was anticipated for him by the few exacting critics who watch for fine gold among journalism's river sands.

"Soon after taking up his work in Manchester, Mr. Scott became warmly interested in the enterprises of the University Settlement in Ancoats. For about a year he lived at the Men's Settlement, and he always spent much of his leisure there, or with the members and friends of the Settlement on their country expeditions and at their games and athletic sports, in all of which he would take most vigorous part; for he was a man of great stature and bodily strength, had rowed for three years in his college eight, and was an enthusiastic and almost untirable mountaineer who, to climb a peak that attracted him in the Alps, would walk for fifteen hours through soft snow and under a hot sun without visible sign of weariness. He had no trace of what sometimes passes for the philanthropic spirit, being quite unable to conceive of himself as a beneficent force to be directed upon objects qualified by poverty or want of education. This was perhaps one reason of the deep affection with which he was regarded by his many intimate friends among the members and neighbours of the Ancoats Settlement. He was of so perfect a kindness, simplicity, and humbleness of heart, that many of his friends will feel that they owe to their comradeship with him their fullest knowledge of the meaning of those words."

From an address at the funeral, by the Rev. C. S. Christie of Cults, near Aberdeen, the following extracts have been made:—

". . . We have come to do our last homage to one whom we have known and loved. We have to think of a career of great promise cut short, of a character of great beauty removed from us, and of a blank, not describable in words, left behind him in the hearts of those he loved. . . . And, talking of the character of our friend, I can only speak out of a limited acquaintance. It covers only the last seventeen months of his life—those months when, moving about among the fir woods of Deeside, or from his chamber looking out upon the Grampians to the south, he was leading the life of the invalid. During so short a time, and under such circumstances, it was only with certain of the qualities of his character that I could become acquainted.

"But character entered into one of the very first things that struck one who met Laurence Scott, and that was the singular charm of his personality. A manner entirely natural had something to do with it. But one felt that behind that were the substantial moral qualities, and that his charm was not something on the mere surface of his nature. At the centre one soon came to find that there were two of the high ethical qualities—a passion for righteousness and a passion for man. Those can speak more at length concerning the latter of these two qualities who knew of his work at Ancoats, which he continued nearly as long as his health permitted, and perhaps a little longer. But with regard to the former no one could even in thought associate anything that was base or impure with him; the moral atmosphere of his mind was clear and keen. . . .

"Compared with moral qualities of this kind, it is almost trivial to talk of intellectual qualities. Yet one noticed the promptness with which he saw the bearing of a new idea, the soundness of his judgement upon literary matters, the trust in his own critical faculties, and the clearness with which he could give a reason for his preferences. These all went to make up the sum of his personal charm, because of their unconsciousness, and because their owner never seemed to think that in respect of them he was different from other people.

"Only one word can be said upon another point, but to leave it unalluded to would be to omit a main feature of his character—and that is his attachment to his friends. Less ready, perhaps, than many others to make friends, he held to them all the more tenaciously on that account, and his eye used to brighten when their names were mentioned and the chance teristic smile used to flicker upon his lips when he talked of some member of his own family circle.

"Reflections of this sort, by dwelling upon the excellence of what we have lost, may seem to increase our regret at losing it. But in time it will be otherwise; it will be just those qualities, that charm, that sound ethical and religious basis, that loyal warmheartedness that hereafter we shall remember with pleasure and pride.

"May we not in conclusion fitly express all the love and longing and regret that mingle in our adieux in the words of the greatest of living poets:—

"'Farewell! why should not such as thou fare well?
Though we fare ill who love thee and who live,
And know whate'er the years wherein we dwell
May give us, thee again they will not give.'"

Within a few days of the death of my nephew, my dear brother Russell died, May 27, 1908. The following obituary notice is from the *Inquirer* of June 6th:—

"RUSSELL SCOTT.—In the third generation, we have now sorrowfully to record the death of the bearer of this honoured name. In February 1834 *The Christian Reformer* recorded the death, in his seventy-fourth year, of the Rev. Russell Scott, for forty-five years minister of the High Street congregation at Portsmouth. In April 1880 his eldest son, Russell Scott, for many years resident in London, and latterly at Eastbourne, passed away, at the age of seventy-nine. Now again the eldest son, of the same name, is taken from our midst, not an old man, as his friends knew him to the last, for it came as a surprise to many when they learnt that he was in his seventy-first year. His death was quite unexpected. He had, indeed, suffered some little time ago from a serious fall, but he was making a good recovery, and had been enjoying beautiful days out in the garden of his house, Darent Hulme, Shoreham, in Kent, when an internal trouble, only indirectly, if at all, due to his accident, suddenly supervened, and after two days of suffering, in the evening of Wednesday, May 27, he passed peacefully away. The loss is keenly felt, as a personal sorrow, by many who were associated with him in offices of public trust, as in private friendship, and not least by this journal, of which Mr. Scott had been for the last six years one of the directors, and latterly chairman of the board.

"He was a Hibbert Trustee, a governor of Willaston School, and for nearly twenty years had been a member of the Committee of Manchester College, Oxford. For many years also he was treasurer of the International Arbitration and Peace Association, in which capacity he attended last year the Peace Congress at Munich. His work for Willaston School was only a part of a very wide and practical interest he took in improved methods of education, an interest happily renewed in his children. In politics he was a staunch Liberal, like his father, who had fought in the old battles for reform and for the repeal of the corn laws. When he removed a few years ago from Hampstead into the country, it was only to find fresh opportunities of service. He took an active part on the executive of his district association, and was this year's president. He was keenly interested in the development of small holdings under the recent Act. His practical interest in social problems was no less hereditary than his zeal for civil and religious liberty. He served on the committee of the 'Metropolitan Association for Improving the Dwellings of the Industrious Classes,' of which his father was one of the founders. He was formerly treasurer, and was one of the chief promoters of the 'Home Colonisation Society,' which now survives under the name of the 'English Land Colonisation Society.'

"Born in 1837, Mr. Scott was educated privately and at University College, London, and for the rest of his life was engaged in business; but the above record may show in part how much of his time and strength he gave to other interests. In these, as in his business concerns, he manifested the same quiet steadfastness of principle and unfailing kindness; there was always the same spirit of consideration for those with whom he worked and who worked for him. We may say of him, as it was said in these columns of his father at the time of his death, that there was 'the same uprightness, the same scrupulous and exact regard for every obligation of duty and of honour, the same humanity shown in a thousand acts of consideration and kindness, the same warmth of affection and friendship and earnest zeal for the public good.' They came, father and son, of sturdy Nonconformist stock, going back to one of the Ejected of 1662, while the father of the Rev. Russell Scott, of Portsmouth, had his house licensed as a place for public religious worship. Each in his own generation, with the new duties which new occasions brought, maintained the same high tradition, and we think now, with sorrow indeed, but with great thankfulness for all that it has meant in the highest things, the things that abide, of this finished life.

"The funeral service was at Rosslyn Hill Chapel, Hampstead. The service, both there and at the graveside in East Finchley Cemetery, was conducted by the Rev. Henry Gow.

"In the course of an address in the chapel, Mr. Gow said: 'He whose body lies here in this place, which was so long his religious home, needs not many words of praise and honour. We bring the tribute of respect, of friendship, and of affection as we think of him to-day. We remember his long and faithful service in the various important offices he held, his attention to detail, his uprightness, his cheerful kindliness and courtesy. We remember his idealism, his firm convictions, his independence of thought, his work on behalf of the great principles of freedom and of justice in politics and religion, his fearless support of unpopular causes, and we remember how genial and tolerant he was towards those who differed with him in opinion, while never yielding from his own. We remember him in his home—his hospitality, his affectionate kindness, his wisdom and his goodness. It was a true and beautiful home life in which he lived, and which he helped to make with those whom he loved best.'"

Perhaps, in the above notice, hardly sufficient prominence is given to the keenness of his interest in the political life of the country, and the steadfastness with which he upheld certain unpopular causes. The cause of Peace and Arbitration was with him almost a passion, and after having championed it for twenty or thirty years, when it seemed to most men chimerical and ludicrous, he lived to see it obtain a world-wide measure of recognition in the Hague Conferences.

He took a lively interest in all questions of the day and held definite opinions on them, and was warmly interested in the fortunes and welfare of the Liberal Party itself. A fellow-member of the Sevenoaks Liberal Organisation writes: "The cause of Progress, Liberty, and Reform will miss not only his counsels at the board, but, what is more, his *sympathy* in the cause to which he was so devoted. He did so much to *encourage* us, especially in these days when courage seems to be so much needed." And these same qualities of sympathy and courage were also most characteristic of his private life. Not only to his nearest circle did he show a spirit of helpfulness strong and wise in no common measure; many with whom he was brought into contact in various ways bear grateful testimony to his interest in their concerns.

He took pleasure in useful activity of all kinds, and in walking and in country life generally—though not as a sportsman. Art and the artistic side of things, as well as natural beauty, appealed strongly to him. [illegible] scope was given him in this respect by the planning and decorating of his house at Lyndhurst [illegible] and of an addition to Darent Hulme, both of which were not only a source of great pleasure and interest to himself, but yielded much enjoyment to others. It may be well, too, to give a few additional particulars as to the outward facts of his life.

On leaving University Hall (see p. 384) he spent a holiday of a few months in Italy with certain artist friends of his early days. Val Princep and Leighton were of the party. It was a delightful and somewhat Bohemian holiday, to which he always looked back with much satisfaction.

After a short connection with one or two business concerns, he became a partner, in 1872, in the Corticine Floor Covering Company, with which he was occupied for the remainder of his life. His marriage, as already mentioned (see p. 400), had taken place in 1868, and he made his first home at No. 10 Winchester Road, N.W., near the Swiss Cottage. In 1877 the family moved to No. 1 The Chestnuts, Branch Hill, facing Hampstead Heath. Here they remained for thirteen years, the children, who were then young, finding in the Heath a delightful playground. In 1889 he acquired a quarter acre of leasehold ground in Lyndhurst Gardens, Hampstead, where he built a roomy house named "The Hoo," in remembrance of Gaddesden Hoo. This house was ultimately sold in 1904. On the death of Lady Prestwich, in 1899, he removed to Darent Hulme, which came into his possession in accordance with the will of his uncle, Joseph Prestwich, and it was here that he spent the remaining years of his life.

APPENDIX

THE ACT OF UNIFORMITY

It seems worth while to give here a short account of the contents of the Act of Uniformity of 1662, and of the reasons which chiefly influenced the two thousand ministers to decline subscription to it. I take the account from Calamy's Abridgment of Baxter's "History of his Life and Times," second edition, 1713, chapter [illegible]. —

"It is not to be supposed," Calamy says, "that Two thousand men, pick them where you will, should be all of a mind. Among the excluded Ministers there was a diversity of Sentiments. Some could have gone much farther than others in compliance with Authority: But as the terms of Conformity were settled, they durst not yield, some upon one Account, some upon another, and several upon many Reasons at once, fearing they should thereby have offended God. . . .

"The things impos'd upon them, if they would keep their Livings or Lectureships, or any Post of Service in the Establish'd Church were these Five.

"1. They must be Re-ordain'd, if not Episcopally Ordained before.

"2. They must declare their unfeign'd Assent and Consent to all and every thing contain'd and prescrib'd in and by the Book of Common Prayer and Administration of the Sacraments, and other Rites and Ceremonies of the Church of England; together with the Psalter and the Form or Manner of Making Ordaining and Consecrating Bishops, Priests and Deacons etc. . . .

"3. They must take the Oath of Canonical Obedience and swear Subjection to their Ordinary, according to the Canons of the Church.

"4. They must abjure the Solemn League and Covenant.

"5. And they must also Abjure the taking Arms upon any pretence whatsoever against the King, or any commissionated by Him.

"These Things were all strictly enjoin'd, without any Thing to qualifie or soften them, or room for a Dispensation. . . . I'll view them distinctly, in the order in which I have mentioned them. . . .

"*First.* Re-ordination. This affected by far the greatest part of those who came into the Ministry after that *Diocesans* were put down in *England* by the Power of the Parliament. For they were Ordained by an Assembly of Senior Pastors, who were then in possession of that Power: And tho' after due Examination as to their Qualifications, they were solemnly set apart to the Sacred Ministry by Fasting and Prayer, and Imposition of Hands, and had the Blessing of Heaven for many years attending their Sacred Ministrations, they must yet now be doomed to Silence, unless Re-ordained by *Diocesans*. This was what they could not submit to because it would, in their Apprehension, be a nullifying of their pass'd Ordination. This seemed not to them a light Matter, but very Momentous: in as much as the Peace of their own Consciences, the Credit of the Reformed Church Abroad, and the good and welfare of the People among whom they laboured, were all very nearly concern'd in it. Their Consciences would not allow them to play with Holy Things; in pretending to be moved by the Holy Ghost, to take upon them the office of a Deacon, when they knew themselves already fix'd sufficiently in the higher Office of Presbyters. . . ."

In addition to the Declaration before mentioned of "Unfeigned Assent and Consent," etc., which all in Holy Orders were required to make by word of mouth on some Lord's day before the 24th of August 1662, the Act required them to subscribe the following words: "That the Book of Common Prayer and of ordaining Bishops Priests and Deacons containeth in it nothing contrary to the Word of God and that it may lawfully be used: and that they themselves would use the form in the said Books prescribed in Public Prayer, and Administration of the Sacraments, and no other." As to this, Calamy says:—

"But they could not herein concur for two Grand Reasons: 1st. Because very few of them could see the book before the time limited by the Act was expired. For the Common Prayer Book with the Alterations and Amendments (for so they are called) made by the Convocation, did not come out of the Press till a few days before the 24th August, so that of the 7000 Ministers in England who kept their Livings few, except those who were in or near London, could possibly have a sight of the book with its Alterations till after they had declared their Assent and Consent to it. . . . 2nd. When they had opportunity to peruse the Book, they met with several Things there, which after the strictest search they could make, appear'd to them not agreeable to the Word of God; For them under this Apprehension (which it was not in their Power to alter) to have gone to declare their Satisfaction that there was nothing Contrary to the Word of God, and nothing but what they could both Assent to (as true) and Consent to (as good to be used) and to have subscribed this with their Hands, had been doing Violence to their Consciences, and attempting at once to impose upon God and Man. They could not but observe the Comprehensiveness of the requir'd Declaration: That there must be not only *Consent* but *Assent* too; and that not only to all in General, but to every Thing in Particular contain'd in and prescribed by the Book of Common Prayer. Words could scarce be devised by the Wit of Man, more full, and more significant, whereby they might testifie their highest Justification and Commendation of every Point and Syllable, ever Rite and Ceremony, every Matter and thing contained in the whole Book, and in every Page and Line of it. A Man might almost be tempted to imagine that the Framers of this impos'd Declaration and Subscription had had this Book of Common Prayer dropping down amongst them immediately from Heaven, and that they look'd upon it as nothing else but a continu'd Oracle from First to Last. . . ."

Calamy goes on to mention various passages in the Baptismal Service, in the Burial Service, and in the Ordination Services to which they had "many exceptions to bring in, which appear'd to them of great Weight and Consequence," and further he says :—

"They must Assent and Consent to St. Athanasius his Creed, in which Creed there is this Expression, 'which Faith except every-one do keep whole and undefiled; without doubt he shall perish everlastingly.' This to our Fathers seemed very harsh. Though they approved of the creed in general as heartily as their Brethren, and esteemed it an excellent Explication of the doctrine of the Trinity, yet could they not look upon themselves as so far called to judge other men as to conclude, all certainly damned for ever, that are not so well skilled in that Mystery, as not to believe every word there written. One of the articles of the Creed is this, 'The Holy Ghost is of the Father and the Son.' In this article the Greek Church hath differed from the Latin, and held that the Holy Ghost proceeds from the Father only. And it is by consequence implied that the Greek Church must be held undoubtedly Damned, which was an uncharitable Censure in which they durst not Concur."

Third. With regard to the scruples felt in taking the oath of Canonical Obedience, Calamy mentions too many for me to transcribe the passage. There were weighty objections felt to some of the canons. "One Capital reason," he says, "was because they found the Episcopal Government managed by Chancellors' Courts . . . where Lay-men exercise the Church Keyes by decretive Excommunications and Absolutions. They found too that the word 'Ordinary' meant not only the Bishop of the Diocese, but the Judges in their Courts."

Fourth. The abjuring of the Solemn League and Covenant was felt by many who had never signed the Covenant to be an injury to the consciences of those who had. It was teaching the people to commit perjury. This portion of the Act dropped in [illegible].

Fifth. Besides the oath of Allegiance and Supremacy all in Holy Orders were by the Act of Uniformity obliged to subscribe another Political Declaration—that it is not lawful on any pretence whatsoever to take Arms against the King.

"Though the Silenced Ministers were as free as any for the Oath of Allegiance and ready to give the Government any assurance that could reasonably be desired of a peaceable Subjection yet they were not for making and subscribing this Declaration for fear of contributing to the Betraying the Liberties of their Country. For being sensible, that it was very possible for the Law, and the King's Commission to be contrary to each other, they esteemed it the duty of Englishmen as free people to adhere rather to the Former than the Latter, but could not discern how the so doing could be reconciled with this Declaration. . . . This continued till our late Revolution, and then (as it was high Time) was superseded.

"For such reasons as these, the Ministers who were ejected, durst not comply with the Act of Uniformity, and fall in with the National Establishment. Hereupon they have been generally aspersed and blacken'd with all imaginable Freedom. But this must be acknowledged after all; that if they erred in this matter, it was for fear of erring; and therefore they deserved Respect rather than Reproach, because they acted like Men of Integrity, according to the light they had."

The Act of Uniformity did not stand alone. Other Acts were passed without delay in the endeavour to suppress Nonconformity. Calamy tells of the suffering caused by them.

"On June 30, 1664, the 'Conventicle Act' passed the House of Commons and soon after was made a law, viz., 'That every one above 16 years of age, present at any meeting under pretence of an exercise of religion, in other manner than is the practice of the Church of England, where there are five persons more than the household, shall for the first offence, by a justice of peace be recorded and sent to gaol three months, till he pay 5£, and for the second offence six months, till he pay 10£, and the third time being convicted by a jury, shall be banished to some of the American plantations, excepting New England and Virginia.' It was a great hardship attending this Act, that it gave power to the Justices to record a man an offender without a jury: and if he did it without a cause there was no remedy, seeing every justice was made a judge. Before, the danger & sufferings lay on the ministers only, but now the people also were included. . . .

"In 1665 the Parliament which sat at Oxford was busy in making an Act to render their [the Nonconformist Ministers] case incomparably harder than it was before, by putting upon them a certain oath, which if they refused, they must not come (unless upon the road) within five miles of any city or corporation, any place that sent burgesses to parliament, any place where they had been ministers or had preached after the Act of oblivion. The main promoters of this Act among the clergy were Archbishop Sheldon & Bishop Ward. Though some vehemently opposed it, the Lord Chancellor Hyde & his party carried it. The oath was this: 'I, A. B., do swear, that it is not lawful upon any pretence whatsoever, to take arms against the king: and that I do abhor the traitorous position of taking arms by his authority against his person, or against those that are commissioned by him, in pursuance of such commission; and that I will not at any time endeavour any alteration of the government, either in church or state.' When this Act came out those ministers who had any maintenance of their own found out some places of residence in obscure villages, or market towns that were not corporations. Some who had nothing, left their wives and children, and hid themselves, sometimes coming to them privately by night. But the majority, resolved to preach the more freely in cities and corporations, till they should be sent to prison. Their difficulties were truly great; for the country was so impoverished, that those who were willing to relieve them had generally but little ability. And yet God mercifully provided for them; so that scarcely any of them perished for want, or were exposed to sordid beggary: but some few were tempted against their former judgments to conform."

The above is quoted from "The Nonconformists' Memorial," originally written by Edmund Calamy, D.D. Abridged by Sam. Palmer, 1802, p. 55. Calamy, writing elsewhere on the same subject, says:—

"Our Fathers (among other things) had a most horrid Law against them (call'd the Act against Conventicles, that passed in 1664, and was renew'd and made yet more severe, in 1670) by which Magna Charta was torn in Pieces, and the worst and most infamous of Mankind were as it were hir'd to accuse them: Multitudes of Perjuries were committed; Convictions made without a Jury, and without any hearing of the Persons accused; Penalties inflicted; Goods rifled; Estates seized and embezzled; Houses broken up; Families disturbed, often at most unseasonable Hours of the Night, without any Cause or Shadow of Cause, if only a malicious Villain would pretend to suspect a Meeting there.

"Our Fathers were hard put to it. We may well wonder how they and their Families subsisted, when they were dispersed and scattered by the Oxford Act. Reproaches, Fines, & Jails, were their common Lot. They met with cruel Mockings, and were most scornfully reviled, as Schismaticks, Fanaticks and Rebels; and the Body of the Nation was exasperated against them: But thanks be to our Good God, it is now [1727] otherwise as to us. . . . In the main we are engaged in the same cause with them. We stand upon their shoulders. . . . They had indeed some advantages above & beyond us who succeed them. Many of them had Episcopal Ordination (which made them the more acceptable to the Episcopal Party) and all of them (very few excepted) were in possession of the Public Churches, before the storm overtook them. . . . They generally had their Education in our two Celebrated Universities with very valuable Helps through the whole Course of it; while most of us

have been bred more privately,
could be furnished with in those
were driven. . . .

"The main Principles of Non
Time that they were before; and
that Day to this that they
all true Church Power must be
That where a Right to comm
Obedience is a Duty is wanting
necessary to an Entrance into the
getting safe to Heaven: That as lo
continued, a farther Reformation
order to the more general &
Christianity; And that every
hereafter, must judge for himself
Principles of the Old *Puritans.*
Fathers; and they are also ours.
being well supported."

The above is taken from the D
Continuation of the Account of the
Fellows of Colleges and Schooln
after the Restoration in 1660, by or
Locke, who was thirty years o
was passed, and who knew several
them as follows:—

"Bartholomew Day 1662
by throwing out a very great num
orthodox divines, who could not co
that Act. And it is worth your knowled
in carrying on this church-affair, nd
required, that if you compare the time
time allowed for the clergy to subscribe
thereby established, you shall plainly find
distributed so as one man in forty could
they did so perfectly assent and c ent

[The reference given for this qu tation
Des Maizeaux, Col. p. 62 Fol. 2nd d. p. 2
quality.]

The historian J. R. Green, in his "Sho
People," says much the same:—

"The change wrought by St. artholom
distinctly religious change, & it change
& completeness stood utterly alone. The rec
driven out were the most learned d the mo
The bulk of the great livi ghout the
hands. They stood at the of the London

clergy stood in general repute at the head of their class throughout England. They occupied the higher posts at the two Universities. No English divine, save Jeremy Taylor, rivalled Howe as a preacher. No parson was so renowned a controversialist, or so indefatigable a parish priest, as Baxter. Behind these men stood a fifth of the whole body of the clergy, men whose zeal and labour had diffused throughout the country a greater appearance of piety & religion than it had ever displayed before.

"But the expulsion of these men was far more to the Church of England than the loss of their individual services. It was the definite expulsion of a great party which from the time of the Reformation had played the most active and popular part in the life of the Church. . . . With the expulsion of the Puritan clergy, all change, all efforts after reform, all national developement, suddenly stopped. From that time to this [1902] the Episcopal Church has been unable to meet the varying spiritual needs of its adherents by any modification of its government or its worship. . . . But if the issues of St. Bartholomew's day have been harmful to the spiritual life of the English Church they have been in the highest degree advantageous to the cause of religious liberty. At the Restoration religious freedom seemed again to have been lost. . . . A common suffering soon blended the Nonconformists into one. Persecution broke down before the numbers, the wealth, and the political weight of the new sectarians. . . . The impossibility of crushing such a body as this wrested from English statesmen the first legal recognition of freedom of worship in the Toleration Act. . . . The sight of learned and pious clergymen driven from their homes & their flocks, of religious meetings broken up by the constables, of preachers set side by side with thieves and outcasts in the dock, of gaols crammed with honest enthusiasts whose piety was their only crime, pleaded more eloquently for toleration than all the reasoning in the world."

INDENTURE OF ROBERT SCOTT

May 19, 1703.

This Indenture made the Nineteenth day of May in the year of our Lord God One Thousand Seaven Hundred and Three Between Robert Scott Son of John Scott of Ilton in the County of Somerset, Yeoman of thone part And Robert Everett of Milborne Wake in the said County of Somerset Lining Weaver of thother part. Witnesseth that the said Robert Scott voluntarily & of his free Will and Choice as alsoe by & with the Consent and good likeing of the said John Scott his Father Hath and by these presents doth put place & bind himselfe Apprentice to and with the said Robert Everett and with him to dwell, Serve and abide as an Apprentice in and to the Trade Art

Mistery or occupation of a Linning Weaver from the day of this date hereof for and during the full and whole Terme of Seaven Years from thence next ensuing fully to be compleate & ended. During all which said Terme hee the said Robert Scott doth hereby Covenant & promise to and with the said Robert Everett That he will be to him Carefull diligent and attendant his Secrets Close keep his lawfull Comands and honest services everywhere shall gladly doe obey & performe Hurt unto him he shall not do consent or procure to be done but to his power the same shall let & hinder Taverns Alehouses or such like places he shall not haunt or frequent except about necessary business for his said Master. Cards or any other unlawfull Game or Games he shall not play The Goods of his said Master he shall not give lend Imbezle Wast or Consume but shall be accountable and Answerable for such part or Soe much thereof as shall be remitted or come to his Care Charge Trust or Custody He shall not Marry or contract himselfe to any Woman during the said Terme Nor depart or absent himselfe out of the service of his said Master without his Lycense or a reasonable Excuse but during all the s^{d} Terme as an honest true diligent & faithfull Apprentice Shall & Will demeane & behave himselfe And the said Robert Everett for and in Consideration of the Sume of Twelve pounds of Lawfull English Money unto him in hand well and truely paid by the said John Scott for the binding of the s^{d} Robert Scott Apprentice unto him the said Robert Everett The receipt whereof the said Robert Everett doth hereby acknowledge Doth Covenant and promise to and with the said Robert Scott That hee will Teach and Instruct or Cause him to be taught and instructed in the Trade Mistery or occupation of a Lining Weaver after the best manner he can or is able And alsoe shall and Will give find and provide for and allow unto the said Robert Scott Sufficient fitt and Convenient Meat Drink Apparel Lodging Washing Houseroom and all things needful for him as well in Sickness as in health during the said Terme And at the end of it shall give unto him Two decent and handsome Suites of Apparell fit and Convenient for his Wearing In Witnesse whereof the parties to these presents theire hands and Seals Interchangably have Sett the day and Year first above written.

ROBEART SCOTT.

Sealed and delivered in the presence of
ISA. HORNE.
THO. HOELDINOTT.

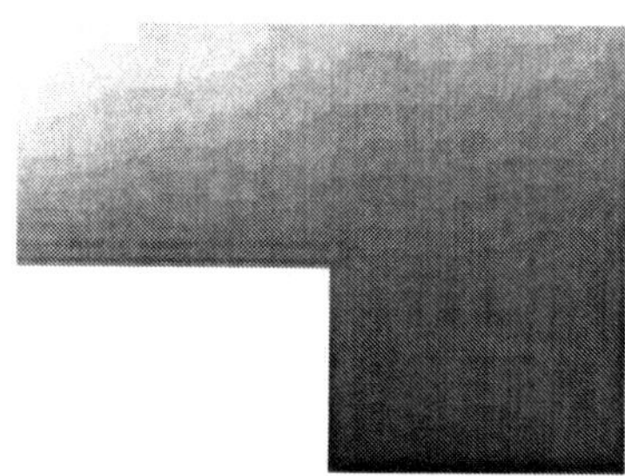

EXTRACTS FROM TWO SERMONS BY JOHN SPRINT.

No. I. The Bride-Woman's Counsellor.[1] A Sermon preach'd at a Wedding, May 11, 1699, at Sherbon in Dorsetshire.

"But she that is married careth for the Things of the World, how she may please her Husband."—1 Cor. vii. 34.

The Word *careth*, in the Original signifieth more than ordinary Care, and implies a dividing of the Mind into divers Thoughts, casting this Way and that Way, and every Way, how to give the best Content. . . .

It is a Duty incumbent on all married Women to be extraordinary careful to content and please their Husbands. From which doctrine I shall take Occasion faithfully to present the Duty of married Women to their Husbands. And why so? may the Women say, why could not you have pitched upon Ver. 33 and have taken occasion from thence to have told married Men their Duty to their Wives? . . .

(1) Because the Woman's Duty is harder & more difficult than that of the Man. . . . For Women will acknowledge that Men can learn to command & rule fast enough, which, as Husbands, they ought to do; but 'tis very rare to find that Women learn as fast to submit & obey, which, as Wives, they ought to do. Women have need of Line upon Line, Precept upon Precept, here a little and there a little, and all little enough to make them perfect in their Lesson.

(2) Because Women are of Weaker Capacities to learn than Men, and therefore, when they have a hard & difficult Lesson to learn, and but weak Abilities to learn it, they had need of more Help and Assistance offered them. . . .

(3) Because that (according to the Observation I have made) most of those Distractions and Disturbances which have attended a married Life . . . are owing to the Indiscretion & Folly, if not to the Obstinacy & stubbornness of disobedient Wives; and I shall not scruple to affirm that the number of those bad Husbands which their Wives have made so, is greater, by far, than the Number of those whom their Wives have found so when they were first married. . .

"Neither was the Man created for the Woman but the Woman for the Man" (1 Cor. xi. 9). The great End of her Creation (next the Glory of God) was, that she might be serviceable and helpful unto Man; and therefore you find, when the wise Creator was about to make the Woman, he assigns this very reason for it. "And the Lord

[1] Extracted from a volume entitled [illegible] a Collection of Ingenious and Delightful [illegible]. London: Printed and sold by J. Watson, over-against [illegible] in the Strand [illegible]. Price One Shilling and Six-pence.

God said, it is not good that Man should be alone, I will make an Help meet for him" (Gen. ii. 18). Now, if the Woman owes her Being to the Comfort and Profit of Man, 'tis highly reasonable that she should be careful and diligent to content and please him; otherwise she doth wickedly pervert the End of her Creation. . . .

Man in his Innocency had nothing of Morosity and Sowreness in his Nature, but had all that Affability and Sweetness of Temper as rendered him highly endeared to his Yoke-fellow. He was then so kind and good-humoured that he required nothing at her hands, but what she could perform with Delight and Ease; all his Commands were so full of Charms, that the Woman must first have offered Violence to her Inclinations, before that she could have been able to have resisted them.

He rul'd, and she obey'd; yet she
Did, in obeying, rule as well as he.

Until that fatal Hour came, when the Woman seduced her Husband from his Innocency; and then the Nature of Man was sadly changed, his Temper grew harsh and severe; and Humours became troublesome and tedious, so that the Pleasing of him is now become a Business that requires a great deal of Art and Skill, of Diligence and Industry; and she that is married divides her Mind into divers Thoughts, casts about every Way, and useth Variety of Methods to please her Husband: and this I believe is experienc'd Truth with most Women; which if it be, you may thank your Mother *Eve* for it, who, when she had gotten a good natured and loving Husband, that was easy to be pleased, could not then be contented, but must try Practises with him, till she had spoil'd him; which proved fatal not only to her, but to her Daughters also; who, if they will have Husbands, and have them good too, must take a great deal of care & pains to make them so.

Upon the doing or neglecting of this, the Happiness or Misery of a married Life doth depend. A good Wife, says one, should be like a Mirrour which hath no Image of its own, but receives its Stamp and Image from the Face that looks into it; so should a good Wife endeavour to frame her outward Deportment and her inward Affections, according to her Husband's. . . . She cherisheth a high Esteem of him in her mind, when she thinks on him as one whom God hath appointed and ordained to be her Superior and Head. . . . When that high Esteem is expressed or declared either in Words or Actions, giving those Titles which may bespeak the Dignity and Excellence of his Person; so Sarah called her Husband Lord, and is commended for it, as being a fit pattern for other women to imitate (1 Peter iii. 6). 'Tis a Custom more common than comely, for Women to call their Husbands by their Christian names, as *our John* & *our Thomas*, &c. as if they esteemed them at no higher a Rate than their very servants that wait upon them ; nay, it may be they will call him by reproachful names, such as Fool, Sloven, Clown, Sot, &c. &c. . . .

Love, Honour, and Obey, & carry it accordingly, in your Practices, towards your Husbands, and I am persuaded that you'll find as great a Scarcity of bad Husbands *then*, as there is of good Wives *now*. . . .

The sermon ends with two short paragraphs addressed to men, bidding them, if they marry, to marry "*in the Lord*," & when married to love their wives, as Christ loved the Church. It closes with these words, "But I must forbear Enlargement, lest that, by overlading the Memories of the Women, I should cause them to forget their Duty, which has been set before them."

No. II. GREAT BRITAIN'S WONDER, A GOOD KING AND GOOD MINISTERS: Set forth in a Sermon preach'd at Milburn-Port in Somersetshire, Jan. 20, 1714-15. Being the Day of Public Thanksgiving for King George's Peaceable and Happy Accession to the Throne. By John Sprint. 1715.

"Behold a King shall Reign in Righteousness, and Princes shall Rule in Judgment."—ISA. xxxii. 1.

A King which reigns in Righteousness is a very great Wonder. This I gather from the word (Behold) with which this Prophecy is ushered in, which is a Note of Attention and Admiration, and is often used in Scripture to denote, that what is spoken after it is very surprizing & justly challenges Admiration. One compares it to the sounding of a Trumpet before some notable Proclamation ; another to a Hand in the Margin pointing to some remarkable Matter. . . . And so here in my text, "Behold, a King shall reign in Righteousness;" whereby is shewn, that it is no common or ordinary Thing, which may be passed over in an unregarded manner, but is worthy of a strict Observation, as being that which is wonderfully strange and very admirable. And that it is so will evidently appear, if you consider,

(1) The woful Degeneracy of Human Nature, as 'tis corrupted and deprav'd by the Fall of our first Parents. Every Mother's Child that is born into the World, whether Prince or Peasant, is a *degenerate Plant*. The greatest Monarchs, as well as the meanest Subjects are *by Nature Children of Wrath*. . . . The wonder-working Power of Divine Grace in making Kings and Queens, that are born with a Spirit of Tyranny. Oppression and Injustice, to become Nursing-Fathers and Nursing-Mothers to their Subjects is very astonishing.

(2) This will be yet further evident, if you consider that Kings above all Persons in the World, are liable to have their natural

Corruptions elicited, and drawn forth into Action. The Thrones they sit on are plac'd in the midst of dreadful Snares, and are surrounded with a numberless Variety of strong and powerful Temptations. . . .

(3) Consider what State and Condition the Kingdoms of the World are in, and you will have just reason to wonder, that any of them hath a King reigning over them in Righteousness. Do not all the Kingdoms of the World wallow in Wickedness? . . . Then let us stand and Pause, & with Admiration view the great Blessing we are assembled with Joy and Thankfulness to commemorate, which is the peaceable Accession of our good and gracious King George to the Throne of these Kingdoms of Great Britain and Ireland. Are we not a sinful People, laden with Iniquity? . . . We, that have been so cold & careless, in reference to our Holy Religion; we that have had so many among us, who by their doctrines of *Passive-Obedience* and *Non-Resistance*, would fain have induced us tamely to surrender our Liberties and Properties, which our Fore-Fathers have handed down to us, with the Expence of so much Blood and Treasure: How justly might a provoked God have given us into the Clutches of a Popish Pretender, and made us and our Posterity perpetual Slaves to Popery and Tyranny! And this certainly had been no more than what we have duly deserved. But, O astonishing Goodness! . . . behold we have a King, King George, who Reigns in Righteousness. . . .

We may from the Text observe, that to compleat a Kingdom's Happiness, 'tis requisite not only to have a good King, but the King also must have a good Ministry. . . . They must both know their Place, and fill it up. *The King must Reign;* and yet without any Diminution to his just Prerogative, *The Princes must rule in a lower Sphere;* and all for the Publick Good. But when an ill Ministry is employ'd, tho' the King be never so good, the State will be sure to suffer Damage by it. . . . The Mischiefs which the late Ministry have done to this Kingdom, and the Benefit we at present receive, and hope for the future more plentifully to receive by the Change our good and gracious King George has made of them, are too great to be pass'd over in Silence upon this occasion: A brief, but very comprehensive Account of which we have given in that noble Address presented to his Majesty by those brave Britons, the Lord Mayor and the rest of his Majesty's Commissioners of the Lieutenancy for the City of London: an Address worthy to be written in Letters of Gold and to be fixed in a Frame set with Diamonds. . . . What Pity it is that so great and good, so wise and just a Monarch as His Majesty King George is, should be so unhappily deprived of the Benefit that might acrew to his Government by the Services of some of his most faithful Subjects, I mean the *Protestant Dissenters*, who have ventured their All for the promoting his Majesty's Interest, and have been exposed to the extreamest Hardships for not complying with those Measures the late Ministry had taken to obstruct the Protestant Succession. That they, though many of them are Men of Sense and Substance, Men of Sobriety and Integrity, that heartily love and honour His Majesty King George, and all the Royal Progeny, must now stand with their Hands ty'd behind them, and not be permitted to serve his Majesty in the Government: That they who bear so large a Share of the Burden of the Government, must yet be excluded from all Places of Profit and Trust, merely because they are Dissenters; whilst Men of less Estates and less Sense, that are abominably Lewd & Vicious, that give too much Cause of Suspicion of their being ill affected to the Government, by drinking the Pretender's Health, and pleading for Hereditary Right, bawling out *the Doctor and the Church*, in opposition to the Acclamations of *Long live King George*, can yet qualify themselves to be employ'd in the Government, and have the privilege of eating the King's Bread, tho' they lift up their Heel against him. O Pity! Pity! Pity!

We may hence learn, how greatly it concerns us at this Juncture to look well to our Choice of those who are to be our Representatives in the ensuing Parliament. . . . Men of Parts & Courage, that dare look the most potent Enemies of the Government in the Face. . . . Men truly religious, who will fear to offend God by doing Injustice, but not fear to offend Men by doing Right. . . . Honest upright Men, whose Love to Truth will make them sift it out by hearing both Sides patiently, with impartial Attention and unbyass'd Affection. . . . Not greedy of money, but abhorring Bribes and all base Ways of Gain. . . . And if the Inhabitants of this Kingdom will carefully endeavour at this Time to chuse such to represent them in the ensuing Parliament, my Heart within me even leaps for Joy, to think what the happy Consequences will be. . . . When his Majesty King George shall be assisted by such a Parliament to reign in Righteousness . . . then the Inhabitants of this Land shall *find Gladness; and Sorrow and Sighing shall flee away;* which God of his infinite Mercy grant, for Jesus Christ, his Sake. Amen.

THE "COVENANT OF THE CHURCH" AT MILBORNE PORT

"We whose names are hereto subscribed believe that there is but one God the Father of all, by Whom are all things, and we by him, Whose power is great, Whose authority is over all. We believe that the Father, Son, and Holy Spirit are three Persons, and the only one living and true God. That he has a right to all persons things and services. That this our God has created all things for his own glory in which we are no less concerned. We believe that he is to be worshipped with pure and spiritual worship which he has nowhere revealed but in his word, which we profess to be, and take to us, for a rule of faith and practice; and that all that is necessary to be known believed and done is contained therein. We believe that it is the duty of all to know worship and fear him; that he has not left it indifferent whether any will be subject to him, and obey his word, or not. And in his infinite wisdom and goodness that he has appointed suitable means for the advancing his glory and the bringing in and building up his people. That as it is the duty of all to love and serve God, and to give themselves up to him to be ruled and saved by him, so it is our duty particularly, and that each one for ourselves, to give up ourselves to God, to be his, to be for him, and for none other. We believe that Christ has appointed particular societies or Churches on earth for his peculiar glory and the good and salvation of his people whom he has called by his grace out of the world that they might have communion with their Lord and God and fellowship with each other, that they might shew forth his praise, walk in all his ordinances, and keep all his commandments which are not to be done out of such communities and which he has given special privileges and promises to and wherein his presence peculiarly dwells.

"That to every particular church Christ has given the power of binding and loosing, and carrying on the rule and government amongst themselves. We therefore from a sense of duty, and desirous of Christ's glory and our own salvation do now solemnly profess the Lord to be our God, and willingly and unreservedly give ourselves up to Him and to each other according to his will as his church and people to obey Him who is our Head, and to walk in all his commandments & ordinances, to observe all the institutions of his word, particularly the word preached, sacraments, prayers and thanksgiving. We profess love to our Lord Jesus Christ and to each other, and desire to build up each other in our most holy faith, to watch over one another and to submit to one another in the Lord.

"These things we declare in the name and strength of Christ."

"1744, *April 22nd*."

It will be seen that the points chiefly insisted on above are the sufficiency of Scripture as a rule of faith and practice, and that the government of each congregation is to be held from Christ and him only.

The Milborne Port congregation now assumed the name of an Independent or Congregational Church, and so remains to the present day.

Looking, as the Dissenters did, to the Scriptures only as their authority in matters of belief, some of them began, as time passed on, to find that the ordinary orthodox doctrines were not supported by Scripture, and were therefore no longer tenable. My grandfather and others passed first into Arianism and then into Unitarianism.

CPSIA information can be obtained at www.ICGtesting.com
Printed in the USA
LVOW10s2340260116

472427LV00015B/164/P

9 781163 634677